Matthew and the
Roman Military

Matthew and the Roman Military

How the Gospel Portrays and Negotiates Imperial Power

John E. Christianson

LEXINGTON BOOKS/FORTRESS ACADEMIC
Lanham • Boulder • New York • London

Published by Lexington Books/Fortress Academic
Lexington Books is an imprint of The Rowman & Littlefield Publishing Group, Inc.
4501 Forbes Boulevard, Suite 200, Lanham, Maryland 20706
www.rowman.com

86-90 Paul Street, London EC2A 4NE, United Kingdom

Copyright © 2022 by The Rowman & Littlefield Publishing Group, Inc.

All rights reserved. No part of this book may be reproduced in any form or by any electronic or mechanical means, including information storage and retrieval systems, without written permission from the publisher, except by a reviewer who may quote passages in a review.

British Library Cataloguing in Publication Information Available

Library of Congress Cataloging-in-Publication Data Available

ISBN 9781978712218 (cloth) | ISBN 9781978712232 (paperback) | ISBN 9781978712225 (electronic)

Contents

Figures and Table   vii

Acknowledgments   ix

Introduction   1

1   The Impact of the Roman Military on Local Populations in Syria   13

2   Coping with the Danger from Roman Rulers: Herod and Antipas (Matthew 2:1–23; 14:1-12)   63

3   Coping with the Abuse of Imperial Power: Negotiating Ἀγγαρήιον as Active Non-Violent Resistance (Matthew 5:41)   99

4   Responding to Direct Imperial Requests: Jesus, the Centurion, and His Slave (Matthew 8:5–13)   125

5   Imagining the Destruction of Eagles: Divine Retribution on the Roman Empire (Matthew 24:27-31)   153

6   Enduring Imperial Power over Life and Death: Jesus in the Hands of the Roman Military (Matthew 26:1–28:20)   173

Conclusion   215

Bibliography   219

Index   235

Biblical References   239

About the Author   243

Figures and Table

FIGURES

Figure 0.1	Inner relief from the Arch of Titus in Rome, showing spoils and captives from Jerusalem	2
Figure 3.1	A sestertius of Nerva (67 CE)	106
Figure 4.1	A bronze as minted in Rome (73 CE)	141
Figure 5.1	A tetradrachm of Vespasian (69 CE)	161
Figure 6.1	A tetradrachm of Vespasian (69–70 CE)	178

TABLE

Table 6.1	Matthew 26–28	175

Acknowledgments

This book represents the intersection of two lifelong interests: study of the New Testament and of the Roman army. I would like to thank Professors Shelly Matthews, Francisco Lozada, and especially Warren Carter for challenging my reading and expanding my views of biblical interpretation. It is thanks to Dr. Carter's advice that this work came into focus and is as strong as it is.

Several other New Testament colleagues have also been helpful in shaping my thinking and providing encouragement and feedback. These include David Lull and Mark Given who saw the first forays into this topic and encouraged its development and Christopher Zeichmann and Jill Engelhardt who each read the entire manuscript and provided timely and specific suggestions. The library staff at Texas Christian University, Grinnell College, and Wartburg Theological Seminary also enabled my work through personal assistance and access to their collections. Likewise, Neil Elliott and Gayla Freeman, my editors at Lexington Books/Fortress Academic, provided patient support through the editing process.

The people of several churches have supported me while this project has continued. These include Grace Episcopal Church (Carthage, MO), First United Methodist Church (Jasper, MO), Living Faith and Toledo United Methodist Churches (Tama Co., IA), and St. Paul's United Methodist Church (Williamsburg, IA). I thank them for bearing with me.

There are also many friends and family who have been with me along the way. These include epicurean and exegete Steve Wilson (*requiescat in pace*), road trip companions Dan Schwerin and Dave Wiedenkeller, and my brother Dan Christianson. I am especially appreciative to my parents, Paul and Sandra Christianson; and in-laws, Karen Bair and the late Tracy Bair: *dormit en pace*.

Finally, this book is dedicated to daughters Anna and Megan, and my wife Wendy. I could not have done it without you.

Introduction

Pouring into the alleys, sword in hand, they massacred indiscriminately all whom they met, and burnt the houses with all who had taken refuge within.... running everyone through who fell in their way, they choked the alleys with corpses and deluged the whole city with blood . . . Towards evening they ceased slaughtering, but when night fell the fire gained the mastery, and the dawn . . . broke upon Jerusalem in flames – a city which had suffered such calamities during the siege.
Josephus, *Jewish War* 6.404–408[1]

Suddenly, one of those with Jesus put his hand on his sword, drew it, and struck the slave of the high priest, cutting off his ear. Then Jesus said to him, "Put your sword back into its place; for all who take the sword will perish by the sword. Do you think that I cannot appeal to my Father, and he will at once send me more than twelve legions of angels? But how then would the scriptures be fulfilled, which say it must happen in this way?" At that hour Jesus said to the crowds, "Have you come out with swords and clubs to arrest me as though I were a insurrectionist? Day after day I sat in the temple teaching, and you did not arrest me. But all this has taken place, so that the scriptures of the prophets may be fulfilled." Then all the disciples deserted him and fled.
Matthew 26:51–56[2]

MATTHEW'S NEGOTIATION WITH ROMAN MILITARY POWER

The violence of the Jewish-Roman War from 66–70 CE had far-reaching effects on the land and people of Judea, which saw its major city, Jerusalem, and its central cultic site, the Temple to YHWH, destroyed and occupied by the Roman military. The war also had an effect on the lands and people of greater Syria, which served as a staging area for Roman soldiers and source of supplies before entrance into the war,[3] and saw increasing tensions between its Jewish and Greek residents, who competed—sometimes violently—among themselves to solidify group identity and secure their place in the Roman Empire.[4] After the fall of Jerusalem in 70 CE, major military victory parades were held to honor the victorious (and now ruling) generals of the Flavian family. These public spectacles, featuring captives and spoils from Jerusalem, were held in Jerusalem, Caesarea, Berytus, Antioch, the capital of Syria, and Rome (See figure 0.1).[5]

Figure 0.1 **The Arch of Titus (Rome) was built to honor the Emperor Titus as conquering general in the Jewish-Roman War of 66–70 CE.** The inner relief shows spoils and captives from Jerusalem, presenting a scene from the multi-day triumph in Rome, which honored Vespasian and his sons Titus and Domitian. According to Josephus (Josephus, JW 7.132-133, trans. Thackery, LCL), it was "impossible to adequately describe the multitude of those spectacles and their magnificence . . . whether in works of art or diversity of riches or natural rarities . . . by their collective display on that day displayed the majesty of the Roman Empire." *(Source: Matt Thomas, used with permission.)*

It should come as no surprise, then, that the gospel of Matthew, written in the years following these cataclysmic events, and perhaps in Antioch, negotiates the reality of Roman military power throughout its narrative.

Beyond the scope and horror of violence conducted by Roman military forces during the siege and destruction of Jerusalem in 70 CE (illustrated by the quote from Josephus, above), the threat and use of military violence was frequently employed in constructing and maintaining the empire.[6] During Roman conquest, pacification, and rule of lands far from their capital city, it is possible to catalog the assertion of imperial military power and its effects on local populations, including late first century CE Syria.[7] Reading with an understanding of this context, it is possible to see how Matthew's gospel reflects an awareness of the potential of Roman military violence and the ways that it could be threatened and unleashed on those who opposed Roman imperial rule. Matthew's depiction of life in relation to the Roman Empire suggests ways to negotiate daily realities of living near and interacting with Roman military personnel, including the threat and use of violence. This presentation is ambivalent and often guarded—using opaque and coded language to produce what James Scott calls a hidden transcript of resistance.[8] The purpose of such a text is not merely to record factual events and data, but to construct a narrative world which increases the capacity of Matthew's audience to survive, and perhaps thrive, while living under the dominion of imperial Roman rule.

Matthew begins with a warning about Rome's use of violence to maintain power (2:1–18) and concludes with a vision that mimics imperial ideology in which Rome is overthrown by the eschatological Son of Man (24:29–30; 26:64; 28:18–20). Matthew's Jesus is arrested by the agents of Roman allies (elite Jerusalem leaders), setting off a chain of events in which he is sentenced to death and crucified by the Roman governor and soldiers as one who has challenged their power.[9] Matthew's narrative proclaims, however, that this victory is transitory—as Jesus asserts in 26:51–56 (the second quotation above) and God's angel demonstrates in 28:2–4, where Pilate's soldiers are immobilized "like dead men" as a prelude to the eschatological redemption of God's people and judgment against the nations who have oppressed them. Until that time, Matthew's narrative suggests a variety of strategies by which its audience may negotiate the reality and dangers of Roman military power—including avoidance, submission, benign cooperation, ambivalent accommodation, non-violent resistance, and envisioning its ultimate and violent overthrow by heavenly power.

APPROACHES TO MATTHEW'S GOSPEL

Matthean scholarship has engaged in important discussions as to possible locations for the provenance of Matthew.[10] Proposals have centered on questions of location, composition of the Matthean community, and conflicted relationship to a synagogue,[11] with a general consensus that points toward Antioch, the capital of Roman Syria, as a likely place for the writing and use of the gospel.[12] References by Ignatius show that the gospel was read there early in the second century and the majority of scholars date the text to the last quarter of the first century CE.[13] I am in agreement with arguments for an Antiochene provenance, which at the very least serve as parameters for the argument made here: that the presence and activity of the Roman military in Syria and surrounding regions in the years following the Jewish-Roman War in 66–70 CE are important factors for understanding the gospel.[14]

Much of this same scholarship has also tended, unfortunately, to characterize Matthew's gospel as primarily a religious or theological text and relegated its relationship with the Roman Empire to the background—rather than foregrounding the Empire as the narrative context of Matthew's account and the historical context of the Matthean community.[15] As such this scholarship tends to neglect or underplay the daily realities of Roman military presence in the city and region and how this power had to be negotiated by those who encountered it regularly.

In recent years, a growing number of scholars adopting an empire-critical approach have done important work in foregrounding the pervasive influence of imperial power across Roman society. As Warren Carter writes, this approach investigates the daily strategies by which people negotiated the Roman imperial system, including "how the [New Testament] texts represent and engage the vision of human existence and societal organization enacted by Rome, how the writers of the texts conceive of life in the empire for those committed to the purposes/empire of God manifested in Jesus, and how... [they] validate, cooperate with, imitate, reinscribe, contest, compete with, counter, or attack (and combinations thereof) the ways in which life and society are organized under Roman rule."[16] In the case of the lands from which Matthew originates, empire-critical scholars are acutely aware of events during 66–70 CE, including the destruction of Jerusalem and the social and political repercussions in the war's aftermath for Jewish people in Syria and throughout the Empire.[17] I do not disagree with their conclusions. However, even among those who take an empire-critical approach, the specific topic of the Roman military and Matthew's negotiation with it has been undervalued or ignored. Many write incisively about the Roman military's warfare and threat of violence. Yet none specifically addresses the place and role of the military in the Roman imperial system—neither as an entity that threatens and delivers violence at specific times and places, nor as a vehicle for ongoing expressions of imperial power, nor Matthew's negotiation with it.[18]

A MILITARY-FOCUSED EMPIRE-CRITICAL APPROACH TO MATTHEW

This work, then, seeks to fill the aforementioned gaps in Biblical scholarship in several ways. It begins, as do other empire-critical readings, with the observation that Matthew—no less than other texts written in similar times and places—is a product of the Roman Empire, a social system which actively propagated itself, creating networks of power with political, economic, military, and ideological components.[19] This does not mean that the gospel narrative has identical aims as intentionally imperialist propaganda, such as Josephus's account of the Jewish-Roman War, Virgil's *Aeneid*[20] or monuments such as the Arch of Titus (figure 0.1), the statue of Augustus at Prima Porta,[21] the *Ara Pacis* (altar of Augustan peace) in Rome,[22] and Trajan's column that celebrate victory over foreign nations.[23] Nevertheless, Matthew's historical context indicates that the text participates in and is engaged with the structures of empire—including those which uphold its political, economic, military, and ideological power.

For Matthew, engagement with the military facets of the Roman imperial system occurs in a variety of ways. As will be shown in subsequent chapters, in different places in the text and with assorted techniques, Matthew counsels such strategies as avoidance, submission/cooperation, non-violent resistance, endurance, and eschatological expectation of the Empire's overthrow. These multivalent approaches are typical of New Testament (and other) texts produced within the Roman imperial context. As Carter points out, "multiple forms of engagements and interactions [indicate] that such engagements between Jesus-followers and the empire were not monolithic. New Testament texts are neither wholly opposed to the imperial world nor wholly in support of it. Rather, they negotiate it with diverse, simultaneous interactions."[24]

While Matthew shares strategies of engagement with other similar texts, it is the gospel's own particular approach that is the focus here—especially the ways in which the narrative constructs and negotiates with Roman military power. Following this Introduction, Chapter 1 provides an account of the social context of Matthew's gospel, arguing that the Roman military (legionary, auxiliary, and allied) was a pervasive expression of imperial power and influence in the lands of greater Syria, the land from which the gospel most likely originates. This power was expressed in at least four main ways, insofar as soldiers (1) carried out social control through the threat and use of violence through such activities such as policing, taxation enforcement, anti-banditry actions, and warfare; (2) impacted the shape of regional economics through taxation, demands on food and grain and other supply, and construction of roads and bridges; (3) impacted social relationships, including marriage and the treatment of women and slaves; and (4) acted as bearers of Roman imperial ideology through material presence (dress, coinage, iconography, army standards) and corporate actions, such as vows of allegiance to the emperor; religious ritual; parades of Jewish captives 71 CE; and the execution of bandits/revolutionaries.

With this context in mind, subsequent chapters provide an empire-critical reading of a number of Matthean texts. Chapter 2 examines the presentation of Herod and Antipas as agents of Roman power (2:1–18; 14:1–12). Chapter 3 situates Jesus's advocacy for non-violent resistance in relation to ἀγγαρήιον/*angaria*, the requisition of goods and labor by Roman army personnel and government officials (5:38–42). Chapter 4 argues that Jesus's ambivalent response to the centurion at Capernaum (8:5–13) is likely due to Matthean contextual concerns. Chapter 5 engages a vision of eschatological retribution on Roman forces represented by imperial eagles (24:27–31). Finally, Chapter 6 addresses the gospel's presentation of the role of soldiers under the command of Roman allies (chief priests and elders) and the Roman governor in the arrest, torture, crucifixion, of Jesus—culminating in their terror and immobilization at his death and resurrection (26:1–28:20).

The contention of these chapters is that Matthew's construction of the Roman military points toward an effort to negotiate the overarching presence of the Empire in Syria and the surrounding region. Matthew 2:1–18 and 14:1–12, for instance, present Herod and Antipas as agents of Roman power who are able to send soldiers to kill civilians and execute prisoners without fear of repercussion. In these texts the gospel presents Roman military power (including the royal troops of client rulers) as dangerous and arbitrary in the hands of imperial elites. This power is something to be wary of and avoided when possible (Matt 2:13–15, 19–23). In Matthew 5:38–42, Jesus's teaching addresses the Roman practice of ἀγγαρήιον/*angaria* by encouraging some members of the Matthean readership to non-violent resistance. Yet in Matthew 8:5–13, Jesus's response to the centurion at Capernaum seems to be much more accommodationist. Jesus praises the soldier's faith while leaving unchallenged the hierarchies of power that the centurion is embedded in, and appears willing to replicate them. Matthew's Jesus thereby acquiesces to, deflects, and even replicates and upholds the system of Roman military power and its threat of violence. In contrast to this, in Matthew 24:27–31, Jesus replicates imperial military power in a vision of eschatological retribution in which Roman eagles fall, thereby symbolizing the destruction of Roman military power at the return of the all-conquering eschatological Son of Man. Likewise, Matthew 26–27 describes in detail the arrest, sentencing, and execution by crucifixion of Jesus at the hands of soldiers under the command of elite Roman allies and the Roman governor. This is an example of the fullest expression of Roman military power's capacity to wield violence and death. This "ultimate" arbitration of power, however, is challenged directly and overturned in Matthew 28, where Jesus is resurrected (28:1–10, 16–17); the soldiers guarding the tomb are paralyzed with fear (ὡς νεκροί, "like dead men") and bribed to lie about what happened (28:4, 11–15); and the disciples are sent into the world with "all authority" until the end of the age (28:18–20).

This chapter does not attempt an overarching history of Roman military action in Syria or the East, nor does it offer any new account of the political machinations that so often accompany wars, treaties, boundaries, and ruling power. These have been treated elsewhere and will be referred to as relevant.[25] Likewise it does not attempt to catalog every instance of Matthew's engagement with the power and ideology of the Roman Empire. These are multitudinous and would result in a larger work than is possible here. Instead, the focus will remain on instances where Matthew is engaged specifically with military power and personnel. The choice of texts illustrates the gospel's multifaceted construction of this power (benign, threatening, death-dealing) and the ways in which Jesus's followers are instructed to negotiate it (acquiescence, non-violent resistance, future eschatological revenge, and promise of divine justice). This focus on Matthew's construction and negotiation with Roman military power thus examines one hitherto neglected dimension of the gospel's complex and multivalent negotiation with Roman power.

NOTES

1. Thackeray, LCL.
2. New Revised Standard Version, used throughout except where noted; λῃστής is translated here as "insurrectionist" rather than the NRSV "bandit."
3. Josephus, *JW* 5.521.
4. Josephus, *JW* 2.266; 284–292; *Ant.* 20.173; Philo, *Gaius* 200–203.
5. Josephus, *JW* 7.37, 39, 100–101, 105–107.
6. Examples include the famous victory of Julius Caesar at Alesia, at which he besieged and defeated a Gallic confederation led by Vercingetorix (Julius Caesar, *Gallic War*, 7.69–90), and Pompey's victories in the East, in which he defeated Mithridates, added a new province (Syria) and several client states (Armenia, Judea) to the Roman orbit, and fixed the Euphrates River as the eastern Roman boundary with the Parthians (Plutarch, *Pompey* 33). For a more detailed examination of Roman siege techniques, see Adam Ziolkowski, "*Urbs direpta*, or how the Romans sacked cities," in *War and Society in the Roman World*, John Rich and Graham Shipley, eds., 69–91 (New York: Routledge, 1993). Stephen L. Dyson, although focused on the western empire, provides thoughtful analysis of the tensions inherent to the Roman imperial system in "Native Revolt Patterns in the Roman Empire," *ANRW* 2.3, 138–175.

7. On the far western edge of the Empire, similar events unfolded in the early 60s CE, when the Iceni tribe in Britain revolted after heavy-handed Roman rule (Tacitus, *Ann.* 14.31, 37); this was repeated in the 70s among other tribes in Britain under successive Roman governors (*Agricola* 14ff), and is the occasion of Calgacus's well-known critique of the Roman empire (*Agricola* 30, [Hutton, LCL]): "Robbers of the world, now that earth fails their all-devastating hands, they probe even the sea . . . East nor West has glutted them . . . To plunder, butcher, steal, these things they misname empire: they make a desolation and call it peace."

8. James C. Scott, *Domination and the Arts of Resistance: Hidden Transcripts* (New Haven, CT: Yale University Press, 1990), 2, 4. A key concept for Scott, 45, 50, is the performance of social acts that become part of the fabric of society through habit, repetition, and enforcement by the powerful, which he identifies as *public transcripts* expressed as the "dramaturgy of power . . . [which takes effort, and] can be sustained only by continuous efforts at reinforcement, maintenance, and adjustment." Because these societal norms are designed to benefit the elite, efforts to enforce them often generate social friction between rulers and ruled, and resistance sustained by *hidden transcripts* to the imposed hierarchies is both predictable and expected.

9. This is seen in the *titulus* on Jesus's cross: "The King of the Jews" (27:37) and his association with λῃστής, -αι (26:55; 27:38).

10. John P. Meier, in Part One of Raymond E. Brown and John P. Meier, *Antioch and Rome: New Testament Cradles of Catholic Christianity* (New York, Paulist Press, 1982), 18–27, provides a nice summary of prior work. See also Graham Stanton, "The Origin and Purpose of Matthew's Gospel: Matthean Scholarship from 1945–1980," *ANRW* 2.23.3 (1985): 1890–1951; David Sim, "Matthew: The Current State of Research," *Mark and Matthew I*, eds. Eve-Marie Becker and Anders Runesson, Wissenschaftliche Untersuchungen Zum Neuen Testament 271 (Tübingen: Mohr Siebeck, 2011); Ulrich Luz, *Matthew 1–7* (Minneapolis, MN: Fortress, 2007), 56–59; and Jack Dean Kingsbury, *Matthew as Story* (Minneapolis, MN: Fortress, 1988), 147–160.

11. J.A. Overman, *Matthew's Gospel and Formative Judaism* (Minneapolis: Fortress, 1990); A. Saldarini, *Matthew's Christian-Jewish Community* (1994); D. Sim, *The Gospel of Matthew and Christian Judaism* (London: A&C Black, 1998); and Anders Runesson, "Rethinking Early Jewish–Christian Relations: Matthean Community History as Pharisaic Intragroup Conflict," *JBL* 127.1 (2008): 95–132, argue for the so called *intra-muros* position: Matthean Christ-followers are to be found within the bounds first century CE Judaism, and their disagreements with synagogue authorities (represented by Scribes and Pharisees) is an intra-group conflict. D. Hagner, "The *sitz im leben* of the Gospel of Matthew," (1996) and G. Stanton, *Gospel for a New People* (Louisville: Westminster John Knox, 1992) take the opposite position, arguing that separation from the synagogue has already taken place (*extra-muros*). Additionally, while leaning towards the *intra-muros* position, Matthias Konradt, *Israel, Church and the Gentiles in the Gospel of Matthew* (Baylor/Mohr Siebeck, 2014), 365, calls into question the adequacy of the *extra-/intra-muros*

model, arguing for a more general conclusion: "Judaism constitutes the primary context for the life of the Matthean community, and more specifically, the historical situation in which the Matthean Jesus story is anchored is substantially characterized by the conflict between believers in Christ and the predominantly Pharisaic synagogue."

12. The majority of current scholars follow, with slight adjustments, B.H. Streeter, *The Four Gospels* (London: MacMillan, 1930), 500–507, who argues for Antioch based on: (1) widespread acceptance in the 2nd century implying the backing of an important and established church; (2) an interest in Peter, associated elsewhere with Antioch; (3) the large Jewish population of the city; (4) the most explicit connection with Hebrew Scripture; (5) the least influenced by "the spirit of Paul" than any other book in the New Testament; (6) the value of a *stater* equaling two *didrachmae* (Matt 17:24–27) in Antioch and Damascus alone; and (7) evidence in Ignatius (see below).

13. Streeter, *Four Gospels,* 505 notes the fifteen references in Ignatius' seven letters that have linguistic connection to Matthew: nine of these are also found in Mark and Luke, but six are particular to Matthew, especially Jesus' baptism by John so that "all righteousness might be fulfilled" (Smyrn 1.1 πληρωθῇ πᾶσα δικαιοσύνη // Matt 3:15 πληρῶσαι πᾶσαν δικαιοσύνην); and Jesus' work as the embodiment of Isaiah "he bore our diseases" (Polyc 1.2–3 πάντων τὰς νόσους βάσταζε // Matt 8:17 τὰς νόσους ἐβάστασεν). A more recent summary of the Ignatian evidence is found in David Sim, "Matthew and Ignatius of Antioch," in *Matthew and His Christian Contemporaries,* ed. David Sim and Boris Repschinski, The Library of New Testament Studies 333 (London: Bloomsbury T&T Clark, 2008), 139–154. On the dating of the gospel, see Luz, *Matthew,* 58–59; Brown and Meier, *Antioch and Rome,* 27, 45ff.; Warren Carter, *Matthew and the Margins: A Sociopolitical and Religious Reading* (Maryknoll, NY: Orbis, 2000) 16–17.

14. Christopher Zeichmann, *Essential Essays for the Study of the Military in First-Century Palestine: Soldiers and the New Testament Context* (Eugene, OR: Pickwick, 2019), xi, argues for increased awareness of the importance of the Roman military as a presence in New Testament studies: "Though Christianity's place within the Roman Empire has been a major topic of scholarly interest for the past two decades, there is strikingly little engagement with the Roman military." Zeichmann's own work, *The Roman Army and the New Testament* (New York: Lexington/Fortress Academic, 2019), joins others such as D.B. Saddington, "Roman Military and Administrative Personnel in the New Testament," *ANRW* 2.26.3 (1996): 2409–2435; T.R. Hobbs, "Soldiers in the Gospels: a Neglected Agent" in *Social Scientific Models for Interpreting the Bible: Essays by the Context Group in Honor of Bruce J. Malina,* 328–348, ed. Bruce J. Malina and John J. Pilch (Leiden and Boston: Brill, 2001); and Michael P. Speidel, "The Roman Army Under the Procurators: The Italian and Augustan Cohort in the Acts of the Apostles," *Ancient Society,* 13/14 (1982/3): 233–240 as a partial remedy to this absence. I agree with Zeichmann's contention and aim, although this work is framed in and proceeds from a different perspective than his.

15. Oft-cited examples include Ulrich Luz, *Theology of the Gospel of Matthew* (Cambridge: Cambridge University Press, 1995); R.T. France, *Matthew: Evangelist and Teacher* (Exeter: Paternoster Press, 1995); or William D. Davies and Dale Allison, *A Critical and Exegetical Commentary on the Gospel according to Saint Matthew*, 3 vols. (Bloomsbury T&T Clark, 2004).

16. Warren Carter, "Empire Studies and Biblical Interpretation," in *The Oxford Encyclopedia of Biblical Interpretation*, ed. Steven L. McKenzie (Oxford University Press, http://www.oxfordreference.com, 2014).

17. cf. *In the Shadow of Empire,* Richard Horsley, ed. (Louisville: Westminster John Knox, 2008); *The Gospel of Matthew in its Roman Imperial Context*, ed. John Riches and David Sim, The Library of New Testament Studies (London: Bloomsbury T&T Clark, 2005); Robert Mowery, "Subtle Differences: The Matthean 'Son of God' References," *Novum Testamentum* 32.3 (1990): 193–200; Maziel Barreto Dani, "This Land is 'Our' Land: Recolonization in Matthew's Gospel" (PhD diss., Brite Divinity School, Texas Christian University, 2019).

18. K.C. Hanson and Douglas Oakman, *Palestine in the Time of Jesus: Social Structures and Social Conflicts* (Minneapolis: Fortress, 1998), 167–187, for instance, define an ample number of terms (23 by my count) relating to the Roman military (e.g. Aquila, Auxiliary troops, Centurion, Ethnarch, Fall of Jerusalem, Legion, Soldier, and Veteran), and include two charts of military organization (figures G.1 and G.2)—but these are found in the glossary, rather than comprising their own section or chapter of the text.

19. Michael Mann, *The Sources of Power: Volume 1, A History of Power from the Beginning to AD 1760,* 2nd ed. (Cambridge, UK: Cambridge University Press, 2012), 1–2.

20. Virgil, *Aeneid* 1.278–279 (Fairclough, LCL), writes how Jupiter, father of the gods, has ordained the Romans to conquer nations: "For these I set no bounds in space or time; but have given empire without end" (*his ego nec metas rerum nec tempora pono; imperium sine fine dedi*); and (*Aeneid* 1.289–291) how Jupiter also tells Venus (progenitrix of the Caesars) of the emperor Augustus: "in days to come shall you . . . welcome [him] to heaven, laden with Eastern spoils . . . then wars shall cease and savage ages soften" (*hunc to olim caelo, spoliis Orientis onustum . . . aspera tum postis mitescent saecula bellis*). Later, Virgil 6.851-53 (Goold, LCL) also writes of Roman destiny: *tu regere imperio populos, Romane, memento (hae tibi erunt artes), pacique imponere morem, parcere subiectis et debellare superbos* ("Remember, Roman, it is for you to rule the nations with your power (that will be your skill) to crown peace with law, to spare the conquered, and subdue the proud"), A.S. Kline (2002) translation, http://www.poetryintranslation.com/PITBR/Latin/VirgilAeneidVI.htm#anchor_Toc2242942.

21. Karl Gallinsky, *Augustan Culture: An Interpretive Introduction* (Princeton, NJ: Princeton University Press, 1996), 155–164; Jane Clark Reeder, "The Statue of Augustus from Prima Porta, the Underground Complex, and the Omen of the *Gallina Alba*," *American Journal of Philology* 118.1 (1997): 89–118.

22. Gallinsky, *Augustan Culture*, 141–155; Paul Zanker, *The Power of Images in the Age of Augustus*, trans. Alan Shapiro. (Ann Arbor, MI: University of Michigan Press, 1990), 172–183.

23. Jonathan Coulston, "Trajan's Column," in *The Oxford Classical Dictionary*, 4th ed., ed. Simon Hornblower and Antony Spawforth (Oxford University Press, 2012); Martin Beckmann, "Trajan's Column and Mars Ultor," *JRS* 106 (2016):124–146; Penelope Davies, "The Politics of Perpetuation: Trajan's Column and the Art of Commemoration," *AJA* 101.1 (1997): 41–65.

24. Carter, "Empire Studies and Biblical Interpretation."

25. See Fergus Millar, *The Roman Near East: 31 BC – AD 337* (Cambridge, MA: Harvard University Press, 1993), 27–99; Benjamin Isaac, *The Limits of Empire: The Roman Army in the East,* rev. ed. (Oxford: Clarendon, 1990), 14–53; *The Roman Army in the East,* JRA Supplementary Series 18, ed. David L. Kennedy (Ann Arbor, MI: Journal of Roman Archaeology, 1996); Kevin Butcher, *Roman Syria and the Near East* (Los Angeles: J. Paul Getty Museum, 2003), 19–44; and Edward N. Luttwak, *The Grand Strategy of the Roman Empire: From the First Century A.D. to the Third* (Baltimore, MD: Johns Hopkins University Press, 1976).

Chapter 1

The Impact of the Roman Military on Local Populations in Syria

Children and kin . . . are swept away from us by conscription to be slaves in other lands; our wives and sisters, even when they escape a soldier's lust, are debauched by self-styled friends and guests: our goods and chattels go for tribute; our lands and harvests in requisitions of grain; life and limb themselves are worn out in making roads through marsh and forest to the accompaniment of gibes and blows.

Tacitus, *Agricola* 31[1]

On the road we encountered a tall man whose dress and manners marked him as a legionary. He inquired in a haughty and arrogant tone where my master [a gardener] was taking his empty donkey. But my master. . . , [who] did not know Latin, walked right past him without a word. The soldier, unable to restrain his natural insolence, took offence at the gardener's silence as if it were an insult and struck him with the vine-staff he was carrying, knocking him off my back. The gardener then humbly answered that he could not understand what the soldier said because he did not know the language. So the soldier responded in Greek. "Where," he asked, "are you taking that donkey of yours?" The gardener replied that he was taking him to the next city. "Well, I need his services," said the other. "He must carry our commanding officer's baggage from the nearby fort with all the other pack animals." He immediately laid hands on me, took hold of my lead rope, and started to drag me away.

Apuleius, *Metamorphoses* 9.39[2]

Chapter 1

INTRODUCTION

For readers of Matthew who are unfamiliar with the ways in which agents of the Roman Empire worked to expand its structures and networks of power, it may be easy to undervalue the ways in which the gospel writer negotiates Roman military power in the narrative. Before discussing in subsequent chapters the varying ways in which this occurs, it is important first to give an account of Matthew's likely historical situation in Syria during the late first century CE following the Jewish-Roman War in nearby Judea. While many histories, beginning in antiquity, take the Roman perspective to depict this context, the focus of this chapter is on the experiences of local populations. These, rather than those of elite actors and their retainers, more fully inform the narrative of Matthew and likely experiences of his audience.

During the Roman intervention, conquest, control, and rule of Syria and the surrounding region (including Judea), civilian residents experienced firsthand how the imposition of Roman rule was inextricably intertwined with the deployment of the Roman military. The ongoing presence of Roman military personnel was intended to promote compliance through the threat (both veiled and overt) and use of varying degrees of violence, to which locals could respond in a variety of ways. Civilian cooperation with imperial domination can be imagined on a spectrum of behavior. Cooperation might be willing, with some residents seeking to benefit (often at the expense of their neighbors) from proximity to growing networks of Roman imperial power. It might be outwardly compliant but—fed by an imbalance of power and demeaning and humiliating interactions between civilians and soldiers—disguise deep frustrations and resentment, which occasionally burst into violent reaction or outright rebellion. It also might entail combinations of behavior and attitudes, varying with circumstances and over time.

For local residents in a region like Syria, then, there was an ongoing need to negotiate growing networks of Roman imperial power, including (1) the threat and use of violence by military forces throughout the province and region; (2) the payment of taxes designed to uphold and support the military; (3) challenges to social relationships, in particular those between soldiers and local women; and (4) an increased presence and promotion of imperial ideology. The following sections address the ways in which local people were impacted by and responded to these expressions of imperial power, and thereby elaborate some of the experiences that Matthew's audience would have drawn on as they encountered military figures and imagery in the gospel in the aftermath of the Jewish-Roman War of 66–70 CE.

DEPLOYMENT AND PACIFICATION: THE THREAT AND USE OF VIOLENCE

While much has been written on the first Jewish-Roman War as a singular event,[3] when set in the context of Roman imperial rule, the few years of this war (66–70 CE; or –74 CE, until the fall of Masada) were not an aberration. They instead represent one major episode in several centuries of local encounters with a growing imperial presence that left an indelible imprint on the region. Throughout this time, civilian residents were forced to cope with the specter of violence—both threatened and actual—that came from the assertion of Roman military power and the ongoing presence of Roman legionary, auxiliary, and allied royal forces.

Direct Roman intervention in Syria began with the eastern campaigns of armies under Pompey. While engaging the armies of Armenia to the north, Pompey sent a force south to Antioch, deposed the last of the Seleucid rulers and annexed the territory, creating a new province of Syria in 64 BCE.[4] Soon after, the Romans inserted themselves into the Hasmonean dynastic politics, seeking treaties and alliances that would be to their own advantage, and finally allying with the faction of Hyrcanus and his supporter Antipater, father of Herod (Josephus, *JW* 1.127–51). From this point onward, Judaean rulers were backed by, aligned with, and increasingly integrated into the Roman imperial system. This integration took the form of clients (Herod and his children) and their retainers beholden to the Roman state and, later, direct administration by Roman governors.[5] Following the Jewish-Roman war, the territory was reorganized into the new Roman province of Judaea, and the Tenth Legion (*Legio X Fretensis*) stationed at Jerusalem.[6] All of these events had effects in Syria proper, as will be seen below.

Because the specter of outright war in much of greater Syria faded after 72 CE, it is tempting to view the period during which Matthew was likely written (post-70 CE through the end of the first century) as an interval of "peace" in the region analogous to that of the United States following the Second World War, in which demobilization, reduced deployment, and changes in the focus of economic production occurred. This comparison, however, does not accurately take account of the continuing presence and role of Roman military forces in Syria during this time or of the deeply imprinted history and legacy of local experience with Roman military forces.[7] Instead, it is correct to picture Roman emperors, governors, and military commanders as continuing to press forward in the performance of empire—but now adopting different methods and strategies by which to exercise their military power. In Syria (as elsewhere), local residents continued to encounter Roman forces since the latter were not simply passive occupiers confined to military bases or a benign intrusion limited to a change in government titles or the language used in official documents. Rather, Roman aristocratic governors directed their soldiers to actively engage in ruling the populace so as to suppress any resistance to their authority and to participate in remaking the region's economy and infrastructure in order to incorporate it more firmly into the imperial system.

This tightening of provincial rule occurred simultaneously with ongoing goals for further Roman eastward expansion. Although the Romans worked throughout the period under consideration to maintain a tenuous peace with Parthia, their relationship was marked by military incursions and skirmishes on both sides, but increasingly by the Romans.[8] Within the province, local people post-70 CE could not escape the Roman military presence in their territory. The methods and strategies of military activity in Syria during this period were what Michael Mann calls *pacification*, which he argues is the second phase of imperial development after the conquest of a region. Mann observes that: "with increasing internal pacification, the legions were now required around the frontiers of the empire . . . [and] preservation of the legionary economy required major and unrelenting expenditure of money and manpower. There could be no end to Rome's militarism, even though its strategies might change."[9] These strategies of pacification were not haphazard but grew out of the desire for imperial dominance over local populations, and entailed two simultaneous approaches.

First, local populations encountered Roman forces as they pursued a double mission: the deployment of forces on provincial and regional levels was designed to guard and control conquered territory from both external enemies (primarily the Parthians) and internal threats to Roman order (such as bandits or rebellious subjects in Judea). Deployment by Roman governors and generals did not simply entail the placement of troops at strategic bases, but also included work by soldiers to expand imperial capacity for communication and logistics/transportation. This increased capacity did promote a certain kind of economic and agricultural development—but one which came at a great cost to local populations, especially small scale rural farmers who survived at just above the subsistence level from year to year.[10] These residents of Syrian towns and villages bore an inordinate share of the tax burden, collected in grain and other crops, labor, and coin (described below), because they possessed the fewest resources to mitigate such demands from the provincial government. This systemic exploitation was not due to accident, but design. Along with other facets of the empire, the economic system was intended to function for the benefit of elite members of Roman society and to secure their continued rule over residents of the provinces. Local populations paid the price for supplying aristocratic retainers such as the military, whose needs always took precedence over the needs of farmers who grew grain and produce.[11] The economic aspects of military presence are discussed more fully in the next section; for now, it will suffice to note that economically the military presence more often exploited and depleted local populations than benefitted them. Any benefits to local residents should be understood as a byproduct, and of secondary importance to the Romans.

The second way in which local populations encountered the deployment of soldiers was on communal and interpersonal levels, insofar as any resistance to the social changes brought about by increasing Roman control was met by the strength of the Roman military, as its soldiers actively enforced Roman laws and policy and forced cooperation of the local population. Enforcement might include the collection of taxes, and guarding of highways, trade routes, and population centers through constant presence and regular patrols. A partial duty roster (*P.Gen.Lat.* 1) from late first-century CE Egypt illustrates these tasks: soldiers were assigned to guard duty in camp and in the nearby town (at an arena and local temple) or to assist various officers; others had no specific duty (but were assumedly ready to be called on in the event of an incident or emergency); more than half were on extended duty away from the century.[12] While some local residents likely welcomed such rule and sought to benefit from it, others would have resented the enforcement of Roman rule, and this imbalance of power, as Scott argues, would provide conditions for a wide array of creative acts of resistance.[13]

For Jews and Jewish Jesus-followers in Antioch and its environs—regardless of their position on the rebellion and war—the presence and actions of the Roman government must have stirred feelings of deep ambivalence about their status and place in Roman society. On the one hand, they were long-time residents whose status and security as a protected minority group was recognized and affirmed by imperial decree. In 71 CE this protection was affirmed by Titus when Greek residents of Antioch sought to expel them following the War in Judaea.[14] On the other hand they were beholden to an imperial power that sometimes viewed and treated them with suspicion, and claimed ultimate authority for itself over their land and persons in contradiction to the scriptural commandments about the authority of God. Besides having to address questions about their loyalty in the years leading up to, during, and in the immediate aftermath of the war, Antiochene Jews (including Jesus-followers) were forced to confront the scope of Roman power during the rule of Vespasian and his sons after 69 CE. Just a few years after the war in Judea concluded in 70 CE, the new emperor appointed Marcus Ulpius Traianus (father of the future emperor) as governor of Syria from 73/74 to 77/78.[15] Traianus was an experienced general, having distinguished himself during the recent war as commander of the Tenth Legion, operating east of the Jordan River and commanding that portion of the army during the siege and destruction of Jerusalem, when it was encamped on the Mount of Olives across the Kidron Valley from Temple.[16] During the early period of Vespasian's rule, Traianus was tasked with continuing to consolidate the Roman hold on greater Syria, and did this by implementing a variety of pacification strategies throughout the region by supplying, reallocating, and supporting military forces to the north in Cappadocia and to the south in war-scarred Judea.[17] One such action was to take Herodian military units that formerly served alongside Roman ones and incorporate them more fully into the Roman army as auxiliary cohorts.[18] The *ala Sebastenorum* and *cohors I Sebastenorum* had been recruited from and garrisoned in Judea under Herod and his sons; after 70 CE until 93 and 91 CE, respectively, military *diplomata* indicate that they were transferred to new bases in Syria.[19] Their presence indicates that some of the same units and soldiers who had been involved in the siege and destruction of Jerusalem were later present in Syria during the time in which Matthew was likely written.

As will be seen below, the demands for provisions for the army were a heavy burden on local subsistence farmers, who found the removal of their crops through taxation difficult to bear.[20] Besides annual tax assessments, additional supplies were demanded when the army prepared for campaigns and went to war.[21] Josephus (*JW* 5.520) notes that during the siege of Jerusalem Roman troops had "abundant supplies of corn [grain] and other necessaries from Syria and the adjoining provinces."[22] This requirement to furnish provisions would have also been true for multiple campaigns by Syrian-based legions throughout the first and second centuries. The constant pressure created by the demands of Roman provincial authorities to supply the army could lead to feelings of resentment, acts of resistance, and at times outright rebellion. Josephus captures some of the people's anger in his account of King Agrippa's unsuccessful attempt to dissuade his people from rebelling, arguing that other subject people provide grain for tax and tribute to Rome without complaining.[23] Likewise, Tacitus (quoted above) gives voice to provincial resentment in a speech by Calgacus, a British chieftain resisting Roman rule: "our goods and chattels go for tribute; our lands and harvests in requisitions of grain . . . Britain pays a daily price for her own enslavement, and feeds the slavers."[24] Thus, we may surmise that wherever Roman forces were deployed across Syria the local population was often frustrated, ambivalent, resentful, and fearfully compliant, while occasionally their resistance hardened to the point of armed rebellion. Looking beyond the aura of imperial glory projected by Roman propaganda, life in the provinces was for many: "empty forts, settlements of veterans, and feeble and quarrelling towns, made up of ill-affected subjects and unjust rulers."[25]

Given the significant numbers of imperial troops deployed across the province of Syria, local populations experienced ongoing interactions with Roman military personnel. During Traianus's governorship three legions and twenty cohorts of auxiliaries and cavalry *alae*—comprising about 30,000 soldiers—were deployed throughout Syria in urban areas and at other strategic points for the purpose of securing Roman control over both territory and population. Additional legions and auxiliaries were moved from Syria (and elsewhere) to nearby Cappadocia and Judea.[26] Major legionary bases in Syria were located at Zeugma (an important crossing of the Euphrates north east of Antioch) and Raphanaea (south of Antioch on the eastern side of the coastal mountains), which were likely the bases for two Syrian legions.[27] A third legion was stationed at Samosata, an important crossing on the upper Euphrates; the former capital of Commagene, the city was given a new official name—"Flavia Samosata"—and governed from the Roman provincial capital at Antioch.[28] Additional large legionary bases were located at Beroea (modern Aleppo) and Apamea.[29]

It is important to note that Roman military units were not deployed only at legionary strength, nor did they simply operate in the vicinity of major bases. Throughout the Empire, legions were frequently divided into smaller units (vexillations) that, along with auxiliary cohorts, were stationed more or less permanently in various locations across each province where they were located. At present there is "meager" evidence in Syria, but the archaeological record seems to show a similar diffuse deployment across the region. These sites include outposts such as Dura Europos, perhaps the most richly preserved site in Roman Syria; a fort at Hauarra (Humayma, Jordan) built to house 500 soldiers, where a granary is preserved (both are described below); and the bases of auxiliary cohorts such as the *ala Sebastenorum* and *cohors I Sebastenorum*, referred to above.[30] As with large legion-sized bases, the dispersal of forces to smaller locations was intentional and strategic: the objective was to impose greater imperial control over the territory and civilian population. Likewise, far-flung dispositions of soldiers were not isolated from one another, but in constant communication with the provincial government in Antioch and with each other. They participated in a province-wide trade and supply network for food (especially grain, olive oil, and wine), fodder for animals, and other non-perishables (such as timber, stone, leather, and metals). Thus, even if one of the larger military bases was not in the immediate neighborhood, the civilian population of Syria would have been aware of the constant movement of soldiers and supplies moving on highways, roads, and rivers throughout the province. Thus, the constant Roman military presence and activity in and around larger forts and smaller installations, the capital in Antioch, and other cities, towns, and villages increased the likelihood of interactions between soldiers and civilians.

In addition to the strategic deployment of legions and auxiliaries at provincial and regional levels, the daily practices of the Roman military illustrate the second aspect of pacification: the fine-grained imposition of Roman rule over the province on communal and interpersonal levels. On a daily basis, Roman military forces were called to muster each morning by their officers, who took a roll call of their men; read the *admissa* (commander's orders for the day) and any letters from the governor or emperor, along with announcements of upcoming events; gave the watchword (*signum*); and assigned soldiers to various work in and outside the camp.[31] This daily work assignment brought soldiers into regular contact with residents of the province. Designated tasks included guard duty at camp and at various outposts; policing duties in the countryside, in towns and cities, and at markets; judicial duties such as guarding and escorting prisoners, and enacting executions; and logistical duties including procuring food and supplies, cooking, and manufacture of needed goods.[32] These daily practices were in keeping with the primary mandate from each emperor to his provincial governors: to keep the province "pacified and quiet" (*pacata atque quieta*).[33]

The response of provincial residents to this mandate can be inferred by reading against the grain of the public transcript. While governors and soldiers acted and made proclamations to maintain order, control, and compliance with Roman rule, the response of those living under such rule was much more ambivalent. Interactions between soldiers and civilians were occasions for the display of authority and dominance on the part of soldiers, which they might enact in a variety of ways—from calm request and routine procedures to threats and use of forceful violence. While imperial subjects were expected to submit to these displays of authority, their compliance might be more or less willing. Some residents may have welcomed and benefitted from the growth of Roman imperial networks, seeing opportunities for economic or social advancement through cooperation. Others, as Scott suggests, may have acquiesced to Roman dominance while masking feelings of dissent, with interactions creating the conditions for resistance in a variety of subtle and subversive ways such as evasion, concealment, dissimulation, lying, pilfering, or banditry—as well as outright rebellion.[34]

While Scott lists a variety of public acts of resistance (gestures of defiance, assertion of status, demonstrations, revolt), provincial residents intent on resistance had every reason to be cautious of openly provoking the soldiers stationed among them. This was because of the soldiers' constant training. A daily weapons drill for recruits entailed practice against a tall post with weighted wooden sword and heavy wicker shield; experienced soldiers squared off in the *armatura*, using actual weapons against a training partner.[35] The character of Roman training is recorded by Josephus, seemingly to reinforce the impression of imperial invincibility (*JW* 3.73–74): "they never have a truce from training, never wait for emergencies to arise . . . each soldier daily throws all his energy into his drill, as though he were in action. . . . It would not be wrong to describe their maneuvers as bloodless combats and their combats as sanguinary maneuvers."[36] Thus, although an individual or group of civilians might surprise or overpower a single soldier or small patrol (as bandits did to a grain escort outside of Emmaus),[37] soldiers would have the advantage in almost all cases because their training, weapons and armor, and concentrated numbers prepared them to exert violence to maintain control. Unhappy provincial residents, then, would need to disguise or repress overt or explicit expressions of dissent.

As noted above, the posting of soldiers among local populations throughout the province of Syria was a useful strategy for regular contact with and direct control of imperial subjects. Evidence for this strategy is found at Dura Europos, located in the middle Euphrates River valley downriver from the major legionary base at Zeugma; the town and surrounding area was incorporated into the province of Syria and held by the Romans from 165 to 256 CE.[38] There is also evidence for the stationing of other "small detachments [that] were strung along the Euphrates in this period."[39] The disposition of troops throughout this territory was not subtle, but intended as all Roman deployments were to expand influence and increase control of an area. Archaeological finds at Dura reveal "clear evidence for the close integration of the army into the life of the town,"[40] with the military displacing previous local occupants and taking over a quarter of the space within the walls after capturing it. This military sector took control of civilian houses, remodeling them to serve as barracks, and building new facilities (such as baths, a praetorium, a Mithraeum, and an amphitheater) to serve the needs of the soldiers stationed there.[41] It is unknown where the previous occupants were displaced (in Dura or elsewhere? in similar dwellings or worse ones?); how the transfer of property from civilian owners and occupants to the military took place; or whether property owners were compensated at full value in the exchange. What is clear, however, is that the arrival of Roman soldiers could not be ignored by the newly conquered residents of Dura. Likewise, the ongoing assertion of military power could not be avoided or disregarded. Epigraphic evidence from Dura shows how soldiers, in particular, the auxiliary unit *cohors XX Palmyrenorum*, were on duty throughout the city: at gates and guard towers, patrolling streets and crossroads, and at city granaries.[42] Additional documents show soldiers interacting with civilians by buying and selling property and agricultural land, making legal contracts, and participating in financial transactions (loans).[43] This evidence points toward some interactions between civilians and soldiers that may have had a degree of benefit (financial or otherwise) for the residents of Dura; at the same time it is important to keep in mind other, more ephemeral, daily interactions informed by the imbalance of power between members of the two groups—all of which took place with the implicit threat of violence that came with the conquest of the town and imposition of Roman rule.

In Antioch, Jewish citizens saw this implicit threat blossom into full-blown civic strife in the months following the Jewish-Roman War. It was during this period that Josephus (*JW* 7.41–62) records how Jews—still suspected of treason and blamed for the recent war—suffered violence at the hands of mobs backed by soldiers: an unknown number were killed in the theater and the streets, and falsely blamed for planning and starting a fire that burned part of the city (*JW* 7.55–62). Buildings engulfed by the fire included the office of debt records, the destruction of which was the goal of the arsonists, "who under the pressure of debts, imagined that if they burnt the marketplace and the public records they would be rid of all demands" (7.61–62). Josephus, no friend to non-elite civic disorder, calls them ἀλιτήριοι ("scoundrels"), and they may well have been simply criminal; but the act may also represent the depths of resentment and frustration caused by the economic pressure of Roman rule, and the risks some provincial citizens—whether Jews or Greeks—might take to resist it.

The fear and apprehension raised by the threat of civic violence were not limited to Antioch. Further south, pre-war residents of Jerusalem lived under the watchful eyes of soldiers from Herodian royal forces (organized later as Roman auxiliaries) and Syrian-based legions and auxiliary cohorts. Prior to the war, there was a permanent stationing of soldiers in the Fortress Antonia attached to the Temple complex. These troops were regularly stationed at the Temple on peacekeeping duty and conducted policing actions throughout the city. While some residents may have appreciated the presence of such soldiers, many would have chaffed at their presence. Daily interactions created opportunities for anger and frustration due to the inability of civilian residents to adequately respond to the unjust use of force and the ease at which it could break out, escalating quickly and unpredictably. Josephus (*JW* 2.293–308) describes one incident in which the procurator Florus ordered Roman soldiers to disperse a crowd of non-violent complainants: they killed indiscriminately; looted the market and nearby houses; and arrested and crucified members of the upper class. In another incident, the procurator Pontius Pilate commanded disguised soldiers to disperse a crowd with clubs (ξύλα); many were killed by the blows and ensuing stampede to escape (*JW* 2.175–177).

For the Jewish worshippers in Jerusalem during religious holidays, many of whom may have traveled from nearby areas such as Antioch,[44] anxiety over potential actions of peacekeeping forces would have been an ever-present concern. Josephus (*Ant.* 20.106–112; *JW* 2.223–227) notes how soldiers from the Fortress Antonia were stationed along the roof of the portico during Passover as a show of force, with reinforcements readily available if needed. The presence of these soldiers from primarily non-Jewish units such as the *cohors I Sebastienorum* (recruited from Samaria) or other legionary and auxiliary units (from elsewhere in the empire) could produce friction and resentment, as on one occasion when a soldier provoked trouble by exposing himself to those below gathered to worship. The crowd, understandably, was offended and responded by calling for punishment and throwing rocks at the soldiers. The situation escalated when Ventidius Cumanus, the Roman governor, called for reinforcements—the deployment of which provoked a stampede in which thousands were killed in the crush at the narrow exits.[45]

On such occasions the soldiers, for their part, were also at a heightened state of alert because of large crowds which gathered, and in which protestors against the imperial order might find a large audience to inflame.[46] This sense of threat is implicit for readers of Matthew 26–27, where Jesus is arrested at Passover by a crowd of disguised soldiers (see chapter 6) from the chief priests armed "with swords and clubs" (μετὰ μαχαιρῶν καὶ ξύλων, 26:47, 55). He is accused of disturbing the peace and turned over to the Roman governor and his soldiers for torture and execution (Matt 27:1–2, 11–44).[47]

ECONOMIC IMPACTS OF ROMAN MILITARY DEPLOYMENT

Beyond widespread deployment across the region for the purpose of pacification and maintenance of imperial rule, the presence of the Roman military on the population of Syria had economic effects as well. Of the many ways in which local residents had to negotiate the presence of Roman military operations on the economy, there were three that had a significant effect on a large segment of the population: (1) taxation of agricultural production; (2) requisition of transport and labor; and (3) construction and maintenance of roads and infrastructure.

The work of several scholars helps to set the following discussion in context. To begin with, Gerhard Lenski argues that ancient agrarian empires—including that of Rome—subscribed to a *proprietary theory of state*, in which a ruler had extensive privileges over the property of the realm. These privileges were used primarily for the personal advantage of the ruler and elite allies, rather than for the good of the state or the whole population. Advantage was exercised "through the collection of taxes, tribute money, rents, and services," supplemented by "booty obtained through foreign conquest," and enforced by retainers such as soldiers, tax collectors, and scribes.[48] In addition, Steven Friesen has proposed a Poverty Scale with seven gradations that seeks to describe the economic status of different segments of the Roman population.[49] Friesen's three uppermost groups—*imperial, regional,* and *municipal elites*—comprised 2.8% of the population; three mid-range groups comprised two-thirds of total: *moderate surplus* (around 7%), *stable near subsistence* (around 22%), *at subsistence* (40%); the lowest group was *below subsistence*, comprising 28%. Furthermore, Bruce Longenecker interacts with Lenski and the joint work of Friesen and Walter Scheidel,[50] arguing that in Roman urban areas the *imperial, provincial,* and *municipal elite* comprised 3% of the population; those with a *moderate surplus* comprised 15%; those *stable and above subsistence* level comprised 27%; those *at subsistence* 30%; and those *below subsistence* 25% of the total.[51] The reason for these inequalities, Longenecker writes, is rooted in "the acquisitive character of power in advanced agrarian societies . . . with the elite being well-placed to use their power to acquire the resources of others."[52] These figures (for Lenski: 93–94%; for Friesen and Longenecker: 97%) point directly to the non-elite civilian residents of a province like Syria, where they show that those struggling at or below subsistence included the vast majority of the population. It is these sorts of people who were most at risk when subjected to imperialist economic practices enacted by elites and enforced by the military to maintain Roman rule.

Food Supply

The first way in which local residents encountered the economic impact of Roman rule involved the production, distribution, and consumption of food. Perhaps one-third of all food produced annually in the province of Syria was collected as taxes, and Peter Temin suggests that the "army may have consumed up to three-quarters of the tax revenue" amassed each year.[53] Greg Woolf summarizes what has been argued above, with an eye toward the agriculture dimension of the Roman economic practices:

> Empires are political systems based on the actual or threatened use of force to extract surpluses from . . . [their] subjects. Imperial elites spend these revenues on the infrastructure necessary to maintain power, and retain a profit . . . distributed to groups that are privileged by virtue of their place within the imperial hierarchy. Pre-industrial empires [such as Rome] . . . extracted surplus from economies that were primarily agrarian. . . . Economically, however, empires were first and foremost tributary structures, and most of the limited energy at their disposal was devoted to ensuring adequate supplies of cash, labour and agricultural produce from the areas under their control.[54]

Although much of the literary and archaeological data for the Roman Empire comes from urban areas, it should be emphasized that the majority of the population was rural, living in small towns, villages, and farms—with perhaps 80% of the total population involved in agricultural production that accounted for up to 60% of the empire's wealth.[55]

Although land tax rates for local farmers in Syria and throughout the empire appear quite low—only 1% of valued property[56]—this rate masks the reality that all taxes favored wealthy large-scale landowners over against small farmers, as well as the impact of other levied taxes, and the dynamics of tenancy contracts on both private and state-owned land during this period in Roman history. Pollard categorizes the taxes collected on residents in Syria by the Roman government during the early empire into three types: (1) regular direct taxes, including the *tributum capitis* (head tax for each adult man aged 15–65 and woman aged 12–65) and the *tributum soli* (land tax);[57] (2) regular indirect taxes, including *portoria* (harbor fees; import customs collected at border crossings such as Zeugma, which could run as high as 25%); and (3) irregular dispositions, such as the *aureum coronarium* (gold for the crown), or other levies "including free or cheap food supplies for the army under such names as *annona*, *copiae*, and *indictiones*."[58] In addition to imperial taxes, provincial residents could also be taxed by local municipalities,[59] including road construction and maintenance taxes, which are discussed below.

For adherents to Judaism, including Jesus-followers in Matthew's community, there were additional tax burdens. Following the Roman victory in 70 CE, the Roman government took over a two-drachma (δύο δραχμαί or δίδραχμα) tax, calling it the *fiscus Iudaicus*, that formerly went to the Jerusalem Temple.[60] In the 80s to mid-90s, Domitian seems to have pressed for expanded and forced collection of this tax, creating conditions which L.A. Thompson characterizes as "a witch-hunt for so-called Jewish tax-evaders and a spate of prosecutions of alleged evaders."[61] Appian alludes to the tax burden on all Jewish residents of the empire when he notes that they were assessed a higher *tributum capitis* (the *fiscus Iudaicus* or perhaps another tax) as a collective punishment and deterrent against further rebellion.[62]

In addition to the tax burdens placed upon them by Roman and local authorities, small-scale farmers faced other economic perils as well. Many of these small farmers were not landowners, but tenants who rented lands for farming and assumed many of the financial risks associated with it. Dennis Kehoe describes the *locatio-conductio* ("lease-hire") contract under which tenants provided all moveable property such as tools, livestock, and perhaps slaves, while landowners provided fixed assets such as farmland, buildings, wine- and olive-presses, and in-ground amphora for storage.[63] The tenant's property was pledged as collateral against the rents due at harvest, which placed the tenant at risk of financial disaster should the crops fail due to drought, flooding, disease, or pestilence—or should crop prices be too low to cover the expenses stipulated in the contract. Besides the burden of taxation, financial ruin from crop failure or price drops was a perennial risk, and although there was legislation that allowed for *remissio mercedis* (remission of rent), this was limited to major disasters, such as earthquake, war, or extreme drought.[64] Thus the majority of risk fell upon the shoulders of the small tenant farmer. Figures on farm rent rates are not available for much of the empire; in North Africa, however, there are records of tenant farmers (*coloni*) working imperial estates who paid one-third of their harvest as rent each year.[65]

The dynamics of Roman taxation and tenancy in relation to food supply are captured by Michael Given, who begins his comparative study on the effects of colonial rule with a scene from nineteenth- or early twentieth-century Cyprus.[66] It is worth quoting in full here for its similarities to the situation of the Roman provincial small farmer:

> Harvest time. Out in the wheat fields beyond the village the women and men wield their iron sickles, grasping a handful of stalks with their left hand, pulling the curving blade sharply across them with their right. Behind them more women and the older children gather up the swathes and tie them rapidly with a few twisted lengths of straw, and the sheaves are bundled and strapped onto both sides of a donkey. Almost hidden underneath the family's livelihood, the little line of donkeys is led down the path towards the village.
>
> Each threshing floor is heaped up with the family's income for the year. This is not stalks and ears, or an abstract number of kilos or litres. This is bread, porridge, gruel, lumps of cracked wheat and yoghurt dried and stored for making soup in winter. They spread out their harvest across the threshing floor with pitchforks, and bring on the threshing sledge. . . . With a prayer to the appropriate deity . . . a winnowing wind springs up. With a regular rhythm they shovel the threshed harvest into the air, and let the straw, chaff and grain fall into different fractions on the threshing floor. . . . Everywhere is the wonderfully rich smell of fresh grain and straw. . . . This is not a symbol of life, or a substitute for money, or a representation of family wealth, pride and prestige. It *is* that life and wealth, in its ultimate tangible, edible form.
>
> And then two strangers come into the village. They come straight to the cluster of threshing floors on the village edge, and begin their work. They are officials; that is immediately clear from the way they dress, and the way they look at the villagers. . . . The family and some friends and neighbours stand in a nervous semi-circle, watching every movement as the [official measuring] bin is filled and emptied, filled and emptied. Are they under-filling the bin, these two men, to pretend that there are more measures of grain than there really are? Are they counting the number of bins properly? Will they really take away a third of the harvest as they say, or could the family lose as much as half of its year's sustenance?
>
> . . . The officials finish measuring, and this is the time for negotiation, protest, argument, pleading. But a third or more of the family's crop is loaded onto government donkeys and taken away to some distant store, never to be seen again. In return, the family receives a piece of paper. . . . They look at it uncertainly, and watch the government donkeys carrying away their food.[67]

Given goes on to argue that the effects of colonial rule are experienced by the colonized in just such a tangible way each time taxes are collected. The taxation system is not designed for their benefit or prosperity, but to establish and maintain the ruling power. When it comes to food production surpluses, appropriation (through plunder or taxation) allows elite members of a society to control distribution and redistribution, enabling them to support governmental agents (like the military), acquire status goods, and increase their hold on power: "the actual foodstuffs and the mechanisms of their movement and storage are crucial to the relationship between different social groups."[68] Given highlights a key concept that is relevant to the effects of Roman taxes in provincial Syria and elsewhere: that taxes are paid *in-kind*, which is non-monetary (i.e., not paid in coins) but based on an assessment of economic value. Given writes: "when taxes in kind are extracted they must be stored centrally in a state granary or tithe barn, before being redistributed, sold or used for paying members of the state bureaucracy."[69] In Roman provinces, these state officials included the governor and his small staff, but the majority was reserved for the military forces stationed within the province.

Evidence points toward an elaborate and well-organized system of in-kind taxation that procured from local farmers both food and fodder for the army. Paul Erdkamp argues that through the collection of taxes in-kind, "the Roman authorities in the provinces controlled huge amounts of corn [grain], which were used in three ways: to contribute to the supply of the populace of the capital city, to sustain the Roman armies and fleets, and occasionally to alleviate temporary shortages in various provincial cities."[70] In the late Republic, along with monetary pay, the Roman Senate provided food for their armies that came from stockpiles collected by annual taxation of the provinces. This food was allocated annually to each province in which military forces were stationed, and each provincial governor seems to have been responsible for maintaining the food supply for the soldiers in his territory.[71] Under the emperors, the Republican system continued to function under the direction of the *praefectus annonae*, an official appointed for this purpose. Some of this taxed grain was brought to and stockpiled in Rome, where there were at least 290 governmental storehouses (*horrea*) in the first century CE which held grain, oil, wine, and other foodstuffs.[72] Other collections remained in the provinces themselves, a reminder to the provincials of the power of the empire to extract and deprive.[73]

Examples of *horrea* found across the empire seem to have been built to exacting specifications, with thick walls or on raised platforms designed to keep temperature and moisture content low so as to prevent loss from spoilage and vermin. Due to effort and expense in building granaries, as well as to prevent theft and unauthorized usage, facilities were centralized, secured, and guarded.[74] Roth notes that inside the *horrea* grain was likely stored in sacks, which served the dual purpose of encouraging air flow (to prevent spoilage) and making distribution easier: "since each Roman soldier received 850 grams of grain per day, two sacks could easily have carried the 70 kg. (150 lbs.) necessary for an 80-man century."[75] One of the few examples of such a storehouse from greater Syria is found at Hauarra (Humayma), where a fort built to house 500 soldiers contained within its walls a *horrea* with stone walls 1.1–1.2 meters (3.5–4 Roman feet) thick.[76] The ruins of this rectangular building are 22.5 meters wide by 15 meters long (approximately 75 by 85 Roman feet), and are divided into three rooms 7.5 meters wide by 15 meters long (25 by 50 Roman feet); the walls of these storerooms are plastered for moisture reduction, with floors paved in terracotta or local sandstone.[77] On the south side of the *horrea* is a 5 foot wide doorway leading directly to a courtyard paved also with sandstone; this open space (presumably for delivery and distribution) extends from the *horrea* to the main east-west road (*principium*) that runs through the fort.[78] Kelsey Koon calculates that this granary could store a "yearly supply of grain for roughly 480 men," although if there were any number of horses, grain stores would necessarily be used more quickly.[79] Koon argues that the food supplies of this remote outpost could be produced by the arable land surrounding the fort, including the possibility that "the garrison was renting out land under its jurisdiction to civilian tenant farmers in return for a portion of their agricultural produce."[80] While the presence of the garrison would have offered local farmers protection from possible bandits, the integration of 500 soldiers into the small community of 450 civilians must have posed significant disruption, increasing risk of food shortages, while also dealing with the risks of cultivation in the desert environment.[81]

To gain a sense of the volume of foodstuffs local farmers were required to produce for the army (either by taxes in-kind or through markets), Peter Kehne's calculations are helpful. He notes that the Roman army supplied each soldier with 880 grams of unground wheat per day to make *puls* (porridge), *panis militaris* ("military bread"), or *buccelatum* (hardtack, a biscuit made of wheat flour, water, and sometimes salt). In addition, each soldier received approximately 620 grams of other kinds of food, including "pulses or vegetables, fruits, nuts, small quantities of cheese, . . . meat, especially smoked or air-dried like bacon (*laridum*), or fish, about a half-pint of sour wine or vinegar (*acetum*), some olive oil, and salt."[82] Based on his estimate of 1,500 calories supplied and a total of 34,500 soldiers and non-combatant personnel, Kehne estimates that the annual food supply needed in Syria was: "8,176 tons of wheat for the men, i.e. 22.4 tons per day, and (excluding pack animals) at 2,505 tons of barley for the horses, i.e. circa 6.9 tons per day."[83] The need for this large amount of food was met primarily through the in-kind taxation of local residents in the province.

As in other facets of the imperial system, the collection of in-kind taxes left local populations open to abuse from soldiers and extortion from unscrupulous governors and their agents. Isaac notes that, "generally speaking, it is hard to distinguish between excessive taxation and plain robbery by soldiers."[84] He points to rabbinic discussion in the Talmud and to Luke 3:12–14, where John the Baptist instructs tax collectors and soldiers not to over-collect or coerce money from people, "the implication, of course, is that such behavior was the norm with such people."[85] Isaac also highlights the account of Libanius (*Oration* 47), which describes a third-century problem around Antioch: soldiers and civilian peasants in the villages where they were stationed formed an extortion racket over neighboring villages, forcing them to pay or be subject to harm of life and property.[86] In the first century CE, provincial governors could also engage in such unscrupulous (but legal) behavior. Erdkamp notes that several ancient authors make mention of a problem caused by the high cost of overland transport for heavy and bulky grains, which penalized more remote communities by increasing their costs dramatically.[87] For this reason, an allowance designed to eliminate the high cost of transportation was made for communities located at a great distance from the capital: they could pay in-coin rather than in-kind. However, like the ἀγγαρήιον/*angaria* (discussed below), the allowance could be abused. Erdkamp notes that each governor was allowed to set the price for this alternative tax in-coin, and he could therefore demand a much higher rate than the in-kind tax would have originally cost.[88] This abuse of power was one of several serious complaints that led to unrest and armed rebellion in Britain in 60/61 CE, just a few years before the rebellion in Judaea in 66–70 CE. Erdkamp refers to Tacitus's praise of his father-in-law Agricola (*Agricola* 19) as an apparent outlier to the common practice. Agricola, who was appointed governor of Britain after the rebellion in 60/61 CE, eliminated the abusive practices of previous governors, while making the collection practice more efficient and effective in its collection:

> Demands for grain and tribute he made less burdensome by equalizing the burdens: he abolished all the profit-making dodges which were more intolerable than the tribute itself. As a matter of fact, the natives used to be compelled to go through the farce of dancing attendance at locked granaries, buying grain to be returned and so redeeming their obligations at a price: side roads or distant districts were named in the governor's proclamations, so that the tribes with winter quarters [for soldiers] close at hand delivered at a distance and across country, and ultimately a task easy for everyone became a means of profit to a few.[89]

For all of these reasons threats to the well-being of small tenant farmers in Syria were great. While greater integration into imperial economic networks may have increased some opportunities for marketing produce, goods, and services, it also imposed additional risks and burdens. Besides the annual risks associated with farming (crop failure, among others), the vast majority of the population engaged in agricultural production bore the burden of supplying at a minimum approximately one-third of their grain and foodstuffs to the provincial governmental stockpile, and of finding the coinage for census and other taxes. Besides this, they bore the brunt of extra demands from soldiers, governors, and tax collectors, who might assess additional taxes, requisition, or simply steal what they wanted.

Requisitioned Transport (Ἀγγαρήιον/*Angaria*)

A second way in which the imbalance of power led to economic abuse of local populations by Roman military personnel is seen in the practice of *angaria* (Greek: ἀγγαρήιον). Matthew's Jesus addresses the practice in Matthew 5:41 by giving advice about going a second mile (See chapter 3). *Angaria* was a system, supposedly limited in nature, by which transportation was requisitioned from civilians for military and government business. Stephen Mitchell notes that "under the empire the burden of providing . . . transport fell largely on the subject communities of Italy and the provinces, and the complaints of these communities against unauthorized seizure of men [for labor], animals, wagons, hospitality in billets and other facilities for state transport form a recurrent theme in Roman history."[90]

Examples of the abuse from *angaria* come from documents found throughout the empire.[91] One such document from the reign of Domitian (81–96 CE) shows how the system was commonly misused.[92] It comes from a public inscription put up in the city of Epiphania (Hama), north of Emesa and southeast of Apamea in Syria:

> From instructions of Imperator [Dom]itianus Caesar, son of Augustus, Augustus. To Claudius Athenodorus, procurator: Among items of special importance that required great attention by my father, the god Vespasianus, I know that he gave great care to the cities' privileges. With his mind fixed on them he ordered that neither by the rending of beasts of burden nor by the distress of lodging should the provinces be burdened, but, nevertheless, by conscious decision or not, deliberate neglect has set in and this order has not been observed, for there remains up to the present an old and vigorous custom which, little by little, will progress into law if it is not obstructed by force from gaining strength. I instruct you to see to it that nobody commandeers a beast of burden unless he has a permit from me. For it is most unjust that, either by the favor or prestige of certain people, requisitions should take place which nobody by myself can grant. Therefore, let there be nothing which will break my instructions and spoil

my intent, which is most advantageous to the cities, for to help the weakened provinces is just, provinces which with difficulty have enough for the necessities of life. Let no force be used against them contrary to my wish, and let nobody commandeer a guide unless he has a permit from me, for, when farmers are torn away from their homes, the fields will remain without their attention.[93]

What is noteworthy in this inscription are the apparently common practices that it seeks to limit—practices that inflict inconvenience and financial stress on common people. The practices of *angaria* described include commandeering beasts of burden to haul or pull a load (assumedly accompanied by their owner or handler) and local residents to serve as guides across a section of territory. The statement in this inscription ("farmers are torn away from their homes, the fields will remain without their attention") coupled with a positive statement by Suetonius (*Domitian* 7, 14) on Domitian's agricultural production policy has led some scholars to propose that his concern was to protect the citizens of the provinces.[94] This appearance of concern, however, does not capture the intent of Domitian's decree—which mandates that rights for transportation are to be reserved for those holding imperial *diplomata*.[95] Thus the emperor's concern was not to lessen the burden on the local population in Syria, but to assert his own power and control over the imperial system of requisitioned transport. In any case, Mitchell concludes that the large number of decrees about the *angaria* point to the ineffectiveness of imperial decrees to curtail its misuse:

> [There are] a long series of imperial documents, beginning in the reign of Tiberius and culminating in a group of rescripts from the emperors of the fourth and early fifth centuries collected in book VIII of the Theodosian Code. Almost without exception these documents record abuses of the system or attempts to rectify them. . . . Officials and soldiers were always the first source of trouble.[96]

The potential for local populations to experience abuse through the misuse of *angaria* is also illustrated by the Roman satirist Apuleius. In his satire, *Metamorphoses* (quoted at the start of this chapter), Apuleius describes the requisitioning (i.e., theft) of a donkey from a farmer by a centurion from the nearby legionary base (9.39). While leading his donkey along the road, the farmer is approached by a centurion who demands that he give up his animal. When the farmer refuses, the centurion beats him with his vine-staff (*vitis*)— the symbol of his authority as well as the literal means by which he can enforce the demands of empire. Apuleius describes the farmer's immediate, but ultimately futile, resistance to the public transcript of military authority and civilian obedience: he retaliates, escalating the violence by fighting back and getting the better of the soldier (even stealing his sword). The centurion, however, follows him into town and calls upon some fellow soldiers who are stationed there to assist him (9.40–41). These soldiers, in cooperation with local magistrates, search from building to building to find where the farmer has gone into hiding and haul him away to prison and execution (9.41). The next day, the centurion leaves with the donkey (10.1–2).

This story, while fictional, is written with verisimilitude. It resonates with the pressure experienced by common people, living under the burden of taxation and *angaria*, and threatened with violence to ensure their compliance. The feelings of resentment that spill out of Apuleius's farmer are not far-fetched but give voice to a common experience of indignity and humiliation. Pollard judges that "the casual military brutality toward civilians depicted by Apuleius . . . probably was not literary hyperbole but a typical experience for many inhabitants of the empire," and gives an appropriate reminder that "ultimately the Roman army was the occupying force of an imperial power, and a primary function of the army was the control of conquered territory."[97] It is for this reason that when Matthew's Jesus teaches about ἀγγαρήιον in Matthew 5:41 he assumes that the practice is burdensome and cannot be refused—but still finds a way to turn the tables for those who are oppressed by the practice. This text, as well as the prior examples, is discussed more fully in chapter 3. For now, it is sufficient to note how local populations struggled with this assertion of military power.

Road Construction

The third way in which provincial citizens were forced to participate in strengthening control by the Roman military over their own territory was through the construction and maintenance of Roman highways and roads. While it is true that civilians could make use of such roads for transportation and trade, the primary purpose of the transportation network was the movement of soldiers, supplies, and military communication; any "economic benefits that may have resulted from their existence were only a by-product."[98] As in the creation of other forms of imperial control, the goal of Roman road-building, in short, was for the agents of Roman power to more effectively rule the province and empire.[99] To this end, Roman emperors viewed the construction and maintenance of major roads as a priority—as both an administrative necessity (for the movement of troops and supplies) and an opportunity for displaying the propaganda of imperial rule. Beginning in 20 CE, Augustus and his successors took the title of *curator viarum* ("curator of roads") and designated a special milestone—the *miliarium aureum* ("golden milestone"), which stood in the center of the Forum in Rome—as the symbolic center and starting-point of all Roman roads.[100] In the provinces, the authority for road construction and maintenance fell under the direct control of the imperially appointed governor, with assessment for road-related taxes made by his agents, working in close cooperation with the military.[101]

In Syria Roman soldiers were heavily involved in a number of major projects that changed the landscape of the province. One of the earliest examples of this involvement is an inscription from 56 CE identifying a Roman-built road from Antioch to Ptolemais, which had recently been settled with veterans and refounded as a *colonia*.[102] During the governorship of Traianus (mid-70s CE), detachments from four different legions and twenty auxiliary cohorts dug a canal outside Antioch that diverted and improved navigation on the Orontes from the seacoast, allowing for more efficient transfer of supplies. An inscription that records this work is now in the Antioch Museum.[103] Soldiers were also involved in a major road building project in 75 CE that connected Palmyra in the south (beyond the borders of Syria) to the Euphrates and the Roman road and trading network running up its western bank.[104] Milestones are found throughout southern Syria indicating the work of soldiers to improve roads for military use.[105] There was also work to develop cities in the Roman orbit: Palmyra and Gerasa both had improvements made to their city centers in a coordinated effort to increase and sustain Roman influence.[106] Based on this evidence, some scholars have emphasized the role of soldiers in the construction of paved roads or improvement of existing roads for military use: "labor was usually furnished by the army, whose ranks provided an abundance of capable men skilled in the various requisite specialties. Moreover, using soldiers to build roads was a way to keep them profitably busy in times of peace."[107] While this is undoubtedly true, it provides an incomplete picture of how roads were constructed and maintained in the province. This is because—just as has been observed above in relation to food production and transportation of army supplies—road building also involved labor owed the government, and performed by convicts, slaves, and non-elite civilians.[108]

In the provinces, costs for road construction and maintenance were levied on two groups of people: property owners and local communities served by particular roads. The reason for this assessment was primarily financial, so that the costs of imperial governance were borne by the people of the province. Theodor Kissel notes that the "construction of a public road, including all the traditional features such as bridges, *praetoria, mansiones, mutationes,* and milestones . . . was a costly undertaking [of up to 500,000 sestertii per mile] which would have left the Roman state bankrupt, if it had had to finance it on its own. For this reason . . . Rome satisfied her increasing financial needs by passing on the expenses to the local communities."[109] In this way the administration of road construction and maintenance were similar to the way in which the government assessed and collected taxes on land and agricultural produce, and requisitioned transportation services. Just as the provincial government assessed the land for taxation, it also declared the duty to build or maintain public roads to be a "*munus publicum* that weighed on the property"[110] of landowners. As in the case of land tax, the wealthy were better able to afford such assessments than small-scale property owners. For the wealthy, fulfilling this public service could be accomplished by financing the portion of the road that ran through their lands, hiring laborers, or providing their own slaves to do the work. For less well-off landowners with less to spare all around, extra capital and labor for road building requirements were more difficult to provide—and any time spent on road work was time and labor taken away from work in their own fields to pay other taxes and keep their families fed.

Besides individual property owners, the public responsibility for a road could also be applied collectively—to the residents of communities large and small. Collective costs were assessed against those "whose territory was traversed by a *via publica*"[111] and in proportion to the property assessment tax that the community was required to pay. As with individual landowners, larger towns and cities would have an easier time raising funds for the additional tax. Larger communities could appeal to the euergertism of wealthy donors, draw upon their own capital resources, or exact additional taxes from residents. Smaller communities, however, were less likely to have wealthy citizens and excess capital—and the additional tax would have to be levied in labor, or from those who could least afford it—putting them, like the small farmer, at higher risk of financial distress or ruin.

In Syria, a well-preserved monument dated to 166 CE illustrates the collective responsibility for road work. Located in the Beqaa valley on the east-west road from Damascus to the coast, "one of the most important transversal highways in Syria,"[112] the monument's inscription commemorates road repairs after a landslide. The repairs were paid for by the residents of Abila Lysaniae, a nearby city—which had financial resources not only to complete the repairs, but also to commemorate the work in stone. Another inscription dated to 73 CE at the town of Aini (on the Euphrates north of Rumkale) reveals the negotiation that local populations made to Roman rule: soldiers from the III Gallica and IIII Scythia legions built a hydraulic installation there that was paid for by the local community.[113] This installation lifted water from the river to provide water for the soldiers and animals stationed there, and perhaps for local residents to use as well.

In addition to those who lived along a major route, the burden of road maintenance could also be enforced upon communities located beyond the immediate vicinity, especially for major projects such as bridges. Kissel notes that the "large-scale repair work on roads and bridges attested by many inscriptions was . . . imposed on a wider range of contributors or on a community as a whole . . . in order to share the burden of compulsory service."[114] Again, from the Roman government's perspective, this was not primarily a matter of sharing costs for the purpose of regional economic development to benefit private individuals, but instead represents an approach by which it could increase control of a region through extra taxes and labor. Unfortunately, there is a dearth of knowledge concerning the costs to local landowners and communities, the numbers of civilians required to participate in road building and maintenance projects, and with what frequency or duration such persons were required to provide labor.[115] A simple answer ("they worked until the road or bridge was completed") is complicated by many factors of geography and terrain. But the sheer number of projects—and miles of road improvements completed—attests to the scale of the work by both civilians and soldiers.[116] In all cases, it is difficult to gain a sense of the impact such work had on the common people: Was it a minor inconvenience or something more? How much did the labor impact their livelihoods as farmers or craftspeople? Did they appreciate the convenience represented by new roads? Were they filled with resentment over the ability for Roman soldiers to increasingly intrude on their lives? Or was it some combination of several of these? Perhaps the speech of the British chieftain Calgacus (Tacitus, *Agricola* 31) that is quoted at the start of this chapter provides a sense of the frustration that was produced by Roman demands to build and improve roads for their military: "Children and kin . . . are swept away from us by conscription to be slaves in other lands . . . our goods and chattels go for tribute; our lands and harvests in requisitions of grain; life and limb themselves are worn out in making roads through marsh and forest to the accompaniment of gibes and blows."[117]

SOCIAL RELATIONSHIPS: LOCAL WOMEN AND SOLDIERS

In addition to ongoing imposition of control over territory and the economy, exercised through the deployment of soldiers throughout the province, taxation, and road building, the people of Roman Syria also had to negotiate a third facet of imperial rule: social relationships, specifically the relationships that local women might have with soldiers. These relationships might include: "marriage" (which was technically illegal for soldiers) or long-term domestic partnership; slave and owner; or freedwoman "wife" of a soldier (when he had owned and freed her). It might also include the women forced into prostitution (most were slaves) as well as victims of rape and sexual assault. Although a significant number of relationships between soldiers and provincial women may have evidenced a degree of partnership and mutual affection, the realities of imperial rule and the culture of hegemonic masculinity (defined by R.W. Connell as the social construction which normalizes and reinforces the dominance of elite males)[118] created another arena in which residents had to negotiate the implicit imbalance of power between Roman soldiers and civilian populations.

The first and most positive way in which this negotiation occurred is seen in the way that some, and perhaps many, relationships between civilian woman and soldiers benefitted both the woman and the soldier by offering a measure of personal and financial security, increased status, familial relationships (including children), and the possibility of mutual respect and affection. The potential for positive relationships to exist (at least in the perception of elite Roman senators) on a widespread basis is shown by Tacitus (*Hist* 2.80) who refers to the outrage provoked in Antioch over a rumor that legionaries there would be redeployed from Syria to Germany: "For the provincials were accustomed to live with the soldiers, and enjoyed associations with them; in fact, many civilians were bound to the soldiers by ties of friendship and of marriage [*contubernio*], and the soldiers from their long service had come to love their old familiar camps as their very hearths and homes."[119] Positive aspects of civilian-soldier relationships are also attested for non-citizen Auxiliary soldiers whose *diplomata* (diplomas granted upon discharge) from the time of Claudius record a change in Roman law which granted citizenship upon completion of 25 years of service to both the soldier and to his children; the soldier's wife was named as *conubio*, a legal status that recognized her marriage to the soldier, but did not grant her citizenship.[120] The potential for situations of ambiguity and contradictory social positioning was perhaps less likely among the wives of men serving among the Auxiliary cohorts, due to similar legal status as non-citizens (for the duration of the soldier's service). In cases where citizen legionaries sought recognition for non-citizen or freedwomen "wives," their legal rights and claims for children and inheritance were often denied by Roman courts and government, as will be seen below.

In her thorough treatment of the evidence for "marriage" relationships among legionary soldiers (for whom Roman citizenship was required), Sara Elise Phang points to another aspect of the negotiation required for social relationships: the general trend of "quasi-marital relationships (stable, long-term) with relative social equals."[121] Phang delineates several scenarios in which local women formed familial relationships with legionaries, either by choice or by coercion, and provides evidence for long-term unions that were technically illegal, but often tolerated by emperors and unit commanders. The majority of such relationships for which there is evidence includes enslaved or freedwomen and citizen legionaries, and these "unions . . . appear to have been a significant phenomenon."[122] Due to the differing legal status of the legionary soldier as freeborn citizen and the woman's as slave or freedwoman (former slave), such relationships had some social stigma attached to them.[123] Nevertheless, evidence for such relationships during the first century appears in several places throughout the empire, in some places comprising 25–40% of relationships recorded in funeral inscriptions.[124]

Phang argues that "soldiers' relationships with slave women or with their own freedwomen were probably an adaptation to the exigencies of military service: possibly these soldiers could not find freeborn women whose families would agree to the drawbacks of 'marriage' with a soldier."[125] The solution was thus to purchase a slave with the intent of forming a marriage-like partnership with her. At all times, due to the prevalence of slavery in Roman society, but especially following successful military campaigns, soldiers would have access to a ready source of enslaved women. Josephus (*JW* 6.8–9) notes how after the fall of Jerusalem in 70 CE, the people captured there were sent to labor in Egyptian mines, held for spectacles, and sold into slavery—"for a trifling sum per head, owing to the glut on the market and the dearth of purchasers."[126] It is not known where soldiers purchased female slaves they intended to form a partnership with: perhaps from a wealthy local household with many slaves, from auctions in a recently conquered territory or city, a slave market, or on an individual basis from a local family or another soldier.[127] It is also impossible to know if such women were purchased by the soldier with the intention of forming a "marriage" relationship (did he know her?) or if this aspect of their relationship came later, after she had lived with and served him for some period of time.

The social interactions negotiated by enslaved women purchased by soldiers were especially complicated. On the one hand, there are positive examples evidenced by gravestones, wills, and papyri which proclaim mutual affection, close family bonds, and children whom the soldier viewed as worthy of inheritance.[128] One such example is seen in a gravestone from Satala which commemorates Flaviae Valentinae, who died at age 25; she was the wife (*uxor*) of Flavius Silvanus who may have been a soldier with the Legio XV Apollinaris.[129] Another is found in the will of the soldier Lucius Titius who sought to give his slave Pamphila to a comrade Sempronius on the condition that he free her, while also making her heir to his estate.[130] On the other hand, it would be incorrect to assume modern values (egalitarian roles, sexual consent) in such relationships, given their social context of Roman hegemonic patriarchy. Phang is correct to point out the inherent risks for the woman in a soldier-slave relationship. The soldier chose such a relationship "for his own convenience, especially if he found it difficult to 'marry' a free (especially freeborn) woman. Needless to say, the *ancilla* [enslaved woman] had no choice in the relationship."[131] A soldier might have had a financial incentive to treat his slave well—but "the relationship was potentially exploitative and brutal: a slave was a non-person, with no legal rights."[132] Roman slave owners had access to their slaves sexually, could beat their slaves with impunity, and could sell them and/or their children at any time and for any reason.[133]

While such experiences would surely have marked the experience of some women and children in relationships with soldiers—and lurked in the background due to cultural assumptions and practices as a possibility for each one—Phang concludes with a moderate assessment: "the soldier's personal slave woman was, as a domestic servant, probably better off than most slaves (agricultural laborers). She was also better off than slave prostitutes (most prostitutes were slaves), unless of course the soldier decided to prostitute his personal slave woman. She was likely to be manumitted, at latest [upon his death] in the soldier's testament."[134] At times, the woman was given her freedom for the purpose of marriage, but this, too, reveals her ambiguous social and legal position: "her status was not equivalent to that of freeborn women, since she was obliged to 'marry' her *patronus* the soldier and could not leave him without his consent."[135] The children of such relationships were also in a legally nebulous zone: a legionary citizen father could claim his children, but because their mother was not freeborn, provincial authorities would usually not recognize their citizenship. The children of non-citizen auxiliary soldiers did not face such hurdles, as stated above; their legal status was tied to their father's term of service, with Roman citizenship granted after 25 years. Thus, the status of women in "marriage" relationships with soldiers in the Roman Empire was ambiguous and required ongoing negotiation: there were both benefits and risks for those who—willingly or unwillingly—participated in it.

Besides these quasi-familial relationships, there is also evidence that some women, especially enslaved women, were forced into prostitution for the (supposed) benefit of soldiers. For such women, threatened and actual physical coercion and limited economic choices narrowed the range of options within which they could exhibit agency or choose the nature of their social interactions. Accurate figures about these *meretrices* (*meretrix*: "a woman who earns") are impossible to know, but David Potter suggests that a rate of 1:48 (woman to soldiers) found in eighteenth-century British India is plausible.[136] In Syria this would equate to 625 women to 30,000 soldiers, but this seems like a gross underestimate. In the second century BCE, Livy (*Periochae* 57) records that, upon arrival to his new command in Numantia, the Republican general Scipio Aemilianus threw 2,000 prostitutes out of the camp.[137] These numbers were extreme (perhaps an exaggeration), and for this reason noteworthy by Roman historians to illustrate the trope of military laxity and Aemilianus's ability to command and instill self-control in his soldiers. Although he suggests the 1:48 ratio as a rough approximation, Potter's suggestion does not take into account the conditions of many poor and marginalized women who might work as *tabernariae* (waitresses) or performers/actors whose duties also included prostitution,[138] daughters who were forced (sometimes temporarily) by parents to perform acts for the financial survival of the family, or freeborn women who made the choice for the same reason of economic necessity.[139] Neither does it address Roman slavery, consisting of up to 30% of the population in some areas, in which slaves (women, boys, and men) were forced to accede to the sexual demands of their owners.[140] All of these people shared one or more traits (gender, poverty, social status) that intersected to increase their risk of exposure to prostitution; all lived at the margins of Roman society.

The marginality and low social status of free or freed (ex-slave) female prostitutes in the Roman Empire was codified under Augustus's marriage and adultery laws, with the result that prostitutes "were forbidden to marry freeborn Roman citizens [including legionary soldiers], though they were allowed (and one might even say tacitly encouraged, at least to some extent) to marry freedmen."[141] At the same time, "by exempting them from liability for adultery and criminal fornication, [prostitutes were granted] . . . recognition as an approved extramarital sexual outlet for men," although this identification served as "a key role in safeguarding the chastity of respectable women [by providing] . . . a highly negative example."[142]

In 40 CE, acts of prostitution were further codified by Emperor Caligula who instituted a tax at the rate of one sexual encounter per day.[143] Thomas McGinn writes that "Caligula's purpose, at minimum, was to raise as much money for the state as possible, a goal realized in such abundance that, where possible, responsibility for collection of the tax was transferred from civilian tax collectors to the military, evidently for reasons of security."[144] Caligula's tax also ensured the continued marginalization of prostituted women; as Rebecca Flemming notes: "it effectively exploits the situation in which prostitution is entirely licit, but its personnel are legally and socially compromised; not disallowed but disadvantaged . . . persons who could not defend themselves from imperial depredations, and who were unlikely to find any champions amongst the honorable and powerful."[145]

Thus, throughout the Roman Empire, female prostitutes were forced to work in brothels located in many establishments; often in a back or upstairs room in a tavern, inn, or near bath complexes.[146] Such establishments were usually controlled or owned by *lenes* (pimps), who located them in major cities such as Antioch or Samosata, or among the *lixae* (camp followers) that accreted in the ad hoc communities (called *canabae* or *vici*) that appeared outside the walls wherever the army set up bases,[147] and extensive graffiti attests to the presence of soldiers at such establishments throughout the empire. Rebecca Flemming's description of brothels (as portrayed in Roman literature) provides a sense of the suffocating nature of such places:

> The slave *lupanar* [brothel] appears as an enclosed world, with the women confined to the premises, their basic needs provided for by the *leno* who rules his domain in a cruel and coercive manner, driven by greed and depravity. He

sets the prices, displayed along with the woman's name on the *tituli* set over the entrances to the small *cellae* in which they worked, and he takes the money.[148]

As one might expect, these conditions were dreadful; McGinn notes that: "many prostitutes lived and worked in an atmosphere redolent not only of poverty, but of disorder and criminality . . . [especially] crimes against property, such as theft . . . [in which they] might be victims as well as perpetrators."[149]

The trade to supply soldiers with women for prostitution extended beyond cities and forts with settlements, reaching even the most remote places where soldiers were stationed. Among desert outposts in eastern Egypt, the Roman camp at Didymoi and surrounding outposts were supplied by a businessman named Philokles. He traded in grain, fruits and vegetables, meat and fish—and women, whose bodies were sold on a monthly basis to the soldiers stationed in these outposts. Yanne Broux notes that "the average price for a month was 60 drachmas, to which was added a fee (*quintana*) of 12 drachmas, which is the money meant for the conductor [who accompanied her] . . . The soldiers who wanted to make use of this service all chipped in together to meet the price."[150] The practice of transporting women for this purpose is verified by a toll list found elsewhere in Egypt, which catalogs a series of tariffs to be collected at the army-staffed toll station: "Red Sea captain—8 drachma; guard—5 dr.; sailor—5 dr.; craftsman—8 dr.; women for prostitution (γυναικῶν πρὸς ἑταιρισὸν)—108 dr.; soldiers' women (γυναικῶν στρατιωτιῶν)—20 dr."[151] The significantly higher toll charged for women who would be engaged in prostitution makes sense when compared to the rates charged by Philokles: 108 drachma represents 15% of his 720 drachma per year profit. It goes without saying that he and other *lenes*, rather than the women, kept the profits.[152] In greater Syria, there is evidence that in a least one location the army bypassed suppliers such as Philokles and was directly involved in supplying women for its soldiers. At Dura Europos two officers were appointed to supervise traveling performers and slave prostitutes as entertainment for soldiers based there; it is likely that all of these performers and prostitutes were owned by the army.[153]

Like the women who formed familial relationships with soldiers, women forced into prostitution for soldiers and other men occupied a tenuous and marginal space in Roman society. Flemming notes that "becoming a *meretrix* is, as the word suggests, primarily understood as an economic act, but one that belongs far less to the prostituted woman herself than to those around her; to those who profit from her initial and recurrent sale."[154] The evidence for the prostitution of women leads to the conclusion that it was sustained by the intersection of slave labor and the ability of elite males to shape cultural attitudes making women sexual objects for the pleasure of men; however, as Flemming points out, the "attitudes amongst those lower down the social order and thus most likely seriously to consider prostitution amongst their restricted economic options . . . are unknown."[155] Also unknown is what members of the Matthean community may have thought about or experienced in relation to the prostitution of slaves and other women—although Matthew's Jesus speaks of "prostitutes" (αἱ πόρναι) who believed (πιστεύω) John the Baptist "going into the kingdom of God" before the chief priests and elders (21:31–32), and this familiarity may indicate the presence of such people in Matthew's audience and an openness to them in Matthew's community.

Another aspect of the threats faced by marginalized women (and men) in Roman society is the experience of what is today called rape and sexual assault. The Latin terms that address these traumatic experiences are *stuprum* (illicit or improper sexual relations between a Roman male and an unmarried woman or freeborn boy) and *raptus* (enslavement and rape of conquered people during wartime, and in the case of non-citizen provincials, perhaps during peacetime as well).[156] While such incidents undoubtedly occurred in Roman society just as they do in others, calculating their frequency is next to impossible. Neither the Roman government nor Roman writers nor Matthew's gospel were interested in such topics: indeed, the attitudes they promulgated encouraged and reinforced the marginalization of victims, as will be seen below. Certainly Roman soldiers were not the only Roman men who engaged in rape or sexual assault; neither is it true that every soldier committed such acts. Yet all soldiers were implicated in the practice of *raptus*, regardless of individual self-restraint. Still, it will be important to remember that, as Phang notes, "the extent to which Roman soldiers raped or sexually harassed women (and boys) . . . is even more indeterminable than the prevalence of prostitution."[157]

Unlike modern prohibitions against rape which are understood as a violation of the victim's personal rights to bodily integrity and sexual choice, prohibitions against sexual assault in Roman culture were based on status. In short, those of higher status had more protections and recourse to legal remedy than those of lower status—including the poor, provincial non-citizens, slaves, and prostitutes. Roman law did not consider mutual consent to be a mitigating factor, but instead, as Phang notes: "in regular *stuprum* of a Roman citizen woman or a boy, the active partner (*stuprator*) could be punished, since he had corrupted the chastity of the woman or violated the sexual integrity of the boy."[158] In these cases, the family of the violated could seek legal remedy in the courts. In the case of slaves, a different set of criteria applied: that of *iniuria* (outrage, injury), wherein the owner of a harassed or violated slave could prosecute for violation of his property.[159]

On certain occasions, *stuprum* of provincial women was a proximate cause for revolt. Tacitus (*Ann.* 14.31) reports that upon the death of the

Roman-allied Iceni king Prasutagus, "his daughters were sexually violated" (*filae stupor violate sunt*), his wife and recent widow Boudicca whipped, and the territory and people ransacked and despoiled by centurions and veterans from a recently settled colony, "as though they had been spoils of war" (*velut capta vastarentur*). These acts provoked such anger among the Iceni and surrounding tribes that the entire province of Britain rose in revolt.

The other aspect of sexual violation has more direct connections to the acts of soldiers during warfare. Ancient historians, according to Ziolkowski, assumed that *raptus* (verb: *rapere*) occurred in the course of military conquest; they use the term *diripio* to describe soldiers' sacking of cities, which included looting, arson, killing, enslavement, and sexual violence once the walls were breached and the defenders defeated.[160] He writes: "the fact that sexual violence was inherently contained in the semantic field of *diripio* is of utmost importance for discerning the decisive connotation of the term in the context of sacking cities, i.e. the ravagers' freedom of action."[161] The terror of *diripio* is described by Josephus (*JW* 6.403–408, 414–434) in the Roman sack of Jerusalem: when the city was captured, it was looted and burned, thousands were killed and enslaved, and soldiers caught up in the heat of battle had free reign to do what they would to the inhabitants. In the immediate aftermath of the war these events would have created an indelible impression in those who lived through it and survived—associating Roman soldiers with sexual violation, slavery, and death. In the years that followed, such impressions would have been solidified into the communal memory of all who heard tell of it, including Jewish followers of Jesus in nearby places such as Matthew's community in Antioch and the surrounding region.

While there were occasions when soldiers were seemingly allowed free reign to conduct savage acts, there were also limitations on such behavior from commanding officers and social values. Phang argues that "it is unlikely that the Roman commanders or emperors directly ordered or condoned [rape and sexual assault] as a policy of terror, especially when it was likely to arouse a revolt."[162] For this reason, "most soldiers were probably restrained by their superiors; at least, they confined sexual molestation to 'safe' women—especially prostitutes and those with the reputation of prostitutes (entertainers, waitresses)."[163] While in many cases the values of Roman hegemonic masculinity were a contributing factor in the actions of men in relation to women, in some cases it might serve as a reason for self-restraint. Polybius (*Hist.* 21.38) recounts the story of a Roman centurion who raped a captured woman named Chiomara, the wife of a Galatian chieftain, and then arranged her ransom for a sum of gold.[164] When Chiomara was brought to the exchange, she showed manly courage by exacting retribution on the centurion—ordering her tribesman to kill him, and then bringing his head to her husband. For Polybius and his Roman audience, the events served as warning for men not to lose self-control, giving in to hedonism and greed. For Chiomara and unnumbered women like her, when *raptus* was unavoidable, it could only be responded to after the fact—and occasionally with a measure of justice.

Finally, it is difficult to know the social conditions for women in a territory when the conquest of a territory was complete and pacification under imperial rule began. It is possible that Roman soldiers changed their behavior; but the personal experiences and communal memory of invasion and *diripio*, as well as the ongoing threat of sexual violence, would have remained. For this reason, Phang concludes that "to what extent provinces remained on a wartime footing, the Roman army an army of occupation, soldiers and civilians alienated from and hostile to one another; in these regions soldiers' rape and sexual harassment of civilians seem more likely than in provinces where soldiers and civilians were friendly."[165]

This section has thus far described a number of possible associations between local women and male soldiers that center around social relationships and sexual activity. This leads to the question of whether such heterosexual relationships were the only outlet for Roman soldiers, and how local populations of men, male slaves, and young boys negotiated such practices. Phang argues that, just as in the rest of Roman society, "imperial Roman soldiers were permitted to have homosexual relations with male slaves and prostitutes. . . . Whether soldiers were permitted to have sexual relations with each other, or whether this was punished, is far more obscure; it seems such practices were punished in the mid-Republic, but evidence from the Principate is lacking."[166]

In contrast to modern discussions of sexual identity as the guiding factor in choice of sexual partners, cultural and behavioral norms in Roman society centered on the values of *virtus* (manliness, valor) and *imperium* (rule over self and others) through which masculine control and dominion could be expressed in a variety of ways.[167] Thus an elite Roman male (and those who sought to mimic him) could seek sexual partners that included women (as described above), male slaves, or male prostitutes, so long as the Roman male was not the passive partner.[168] How prevalent such relationships were is almost impossible to measure, due to a lack of literary and archaeological evidence—although there were a large percentage of male slaves owned by soldiers who were present in a variety of capacities in and around the military camp.[169] As to relationships between soldiers themselves, Phang again points to a lack of evidence: there are scattered references to such relationships from Republican Rome, but few if any from the imperial period.[170] Republican soldiers could be punished for such actions if caught, but discipline of imperial soldiers seems lacking, although such soldiers likely would have encountered social "opprobrium."[171] Phang concludes that "the issue may have become less relevant as the . . . Principate's soldiers, in stationary camps, had more access to women, to male slaves, and to prostitutes of either sex; sexual relations between soldiers may only have come up if a soldier was very young or effeminate in appearance."[172]

Besides these social relationships, which took place on an interpersonal level, there were also ways that the elite made use of male slave prostitution to advance their own interests while reinforcing the relationships of power in imperial society. A.B. Bosworth suggests that Vespasian, based on a comment in Suetonius (*Vespasian* 4.3) that identifies the future emperor as a *mulio*, was a trader in eunuch slaves.[173] Vespasian's nickname derived from "the slave dealer's business [which] was in part to produce human mules, males who were sterile."[174] These trafficked boys, "if they were doctored after the onset of puberty" by surgeons working for the slave traders, would retain their ability for sexual vigor for a time.[175] These eunuchs were apparently popular with elite men and women as sexual partners, and expensive; the emperor Nero "may even have popularized . . . [and] inspired members of the upper classes . . . to follow his example, in which case the demand for quality eunuchs might have increased sharply—at a time when Vespasian was active in the trade."[176] Thus Vespasian, in the years following his governorship in Africa (62 CE) and just before receiving from Nero overall command of the campaign in Judea (67 CE), was improving his financial situation in the most sordid yet lucrative manner available: the purchase, castration, and sale of enslaved boys for the sexual use of Roman aristocrats. This may appear to be a minor point in the history of Roman rule during the last half of the first century CE. More than a footnote, however, the possibility of Vespasian's personal involvement in the creation and sale of eunuch slaves for the sexual pleasure of elite Roman society serves to underscore that the networks of social power in the empire were designed to function for the benefit of the ruling elite, rather than the common people.

The discussion in this section concludes with a general observation: that the experience of marginality experienced by women in various kinds of relationships with soldiers—from *conubium* ("wife"/marriage) to *ancilla* (slave) to *meretrix* (prostitute)—would have been especially relevant to members of Matthew's community, whose members also appear to have experienced social and economic marginalization. Matthew's Jesus addresses such people in the Sermon on the Mount (5:1–12ff.), calling them blessed (μακάριος) and including them in God's empire, although the gospel is also ambivalent—and silent on several dimensions of the interactions of women and soldiers described above. When we remember the number of Jewish women enslaved following the war with Rome, and the deep connection Matthew's community had with the Jewish population of Judea and the surrounding area, the experience of marginalization becomes especially relevant. This is not to suggest that Matthew's audience and the "wives," female and male slaves, and prostitutes of Roman legionary and auxiliary soldiers in Syria are the same. Nevertheless, there may well have been some overlap, as all women (and marginalized men) would have had to negotiate the ambiguous and sometimes fraught experiences that accompanied provincial interactions with soldiers.

IDEOLOGY OF EMPIRE

The fourth, and final, aspect of imperial power addressed in this chapter moves beyond the practical (deployment of soldiers authorized to use violence, collecting taxes, building roads) and interpersonal (marriages, daily interactions) means by which the Roman military and its soldiers implemented and maintained control over greater Syria, and the ways that provincial residents had to contend with them. Just as important were the ideas, thinking, and justifications the Romans gave for creating, expanding, and maintaining their empire—what we may call imperial ideology. Mann argues that ideological power is one of the four networks of social power; like other networks, it is an "institutional means of attaining human goals," valued for its efficacy to achieve social purposes by those who deploy it.[177] For the Romans, the use of ideological tools was not only a way of thinking and expressing values, but also a set of techniques by which empire was created and maintained.[178] This ideology of empire was promulgated through the use of words, symbolic imagery, and space in a variety of media, including architecture, coinage, sculpture, and literature. It aimed to fill the space inhabited by provincial residents—and residents had to negotiate its inexorable growth and dissemination on an ongoing basis.

The Roman ideology of empire comes into focus clearly in the reign of Augustus when the first emperor had emerged victorious from the civil wars that ended the Roman Republic and began to promote his rule as a golden age of peace, liberty, concord, and prosperity. Examples of this ideological messaging appear in Rome, for instance, where Augustus built the *Ara Pacis* (Altar of Peace) on the edge of the field of Mars, the traditional mustering grounds for Roman armies outside the city walls. The monument was carved with reliefs of the imperial family, offering sacrifices of thanksgiving, tying imperial rule to the favor of the gods, and linking peace and prosperity for the Roman people to the emperor, his family, and his rule.[179] When Augustus died, he had an account of his reign memorialized in the *Res Gestae Divi Augusti* (*Acts of the Divine Augustus*); these were recorded on bronze tables in his mausoleum, with copies made for distribution and public display throughout the empire.[180] Another tool that assisted in the dissemination of imperial ideology was the *Aeneid*, an epic poem written by Augustus's friend and court poet Virgil about the founding of Rome. In *Aeneid* 1.279 Virgil offers words from the mouth of Jupiter that proclaim divine sanction for and the inevitability of Rome's empire: "For these I set no bounds in space or time; but have given empire without end."[181] As a written work, copies of the *Aeneid* could be—and were—distributed across the empire, becoming part of the educational curriculum among elite members of society.[182] The message of peace, prosperity, and imperial rule by divine sanction was continued and elaborated upon by subsequent emperors until the time of Nero, when the Julio-Claudian line ended under the dark accusations of tyranny and the emperor's forced suicide.[183]

After the tumult and insecurity of the civil war that brought Vespasian to the throne in 69 CE, imperial ideology was employed by the new emperor in a very specific way: to declare his right to rule through military power, to legitimize his reign in relation to those of his predecessors, and to solidify the position of the Flavian family. As with Augustus and previous emperors, the ideology of Flavian rule was expressed in a variety of media, including public monuments, literature, and coinage. The first of Vespasian's architectural monuments was the *Templum Pacis* (Temple/Precinct of Peace), built in Rome from 71 to 75 CE, and consciously connected to the *Ara Pacis* and all that it represented.[184] The Templum was a square outdoor green space (134 by 137 meters) enclosed by a portico and wall, with rectangular rooms along the southeast side. It featured an altar, famous Greek sculptures, and a series of decorative fountains or large gardens (only concrete foundations remain).[185] In his own work, *The Jewish War* (itself an ideological tool by which the empire was propagated), Josephus (*JW* 7.159–162) records that the "vessels of gold" (χρυσᾶ κατασκευάσματα) from the Jerusalem Temple were displayed in the *Templum Pacis*, following Vespasian's triumphal parade of these sacred treasures through the city in 71 CE.[186] The Templum was dedicated to the goddess *Pax*, whose statue likely stood in the centermost room and whose blessing was invoked after the military victories of Vespasian's legions.[187]

A second monument begun under Vespasian in 70 CE and completed after his death by Titus in 80 CE was the Flavian Amphitheater, known today as the Colosseum. This large double theater (189 by 156 meters in footprint, and 48 meters high) contained representations of Roman power and glory: statues of gods, heroes, and golden shields adorned the facility.[188] The construction was financed by the looting of Judea and Jerusalem, including the Temple, as one version of the (reconstructed) dedicatory inscription reads:

Imperator Caesar Vespasian Augustus
ordered the New Amphitheater to be built . . .
[paid for] by the proceeds of war spoils.[189]

For centuries the Amphitheater served as a landmark that shaped the urban fabric of Rome and it continues to communicate as it was designed to: as a testament to imperial power, glory, and longevity.

A third monument that employed this same imperial ideology is the Arch of Titus, completed after his death by Domitian in 82 CE, and designed to communicate again the Flavian family's glory, honor, and right to rule based on military victory in Judea.[190] It is here that the famous images of Roman soldiers carrying off the golden lampstands (menorah), trumpets, and other treasures from the Temple were sculpted (see fig. 0.1); these are images of the Triumphal parade celebrated in 71 CE and described so vividly by Josephus (*JW* 7.116–157).[191] At the top of the Arch there is a carved relief of the recently deceased Titus looking over the shoulders of a flying Roman eagle; this represents his apotheosis—the act of transformation in which a human joins the divine pantheon.[192]

Besides the building of monuments and literature that promoted dynastic history, the Flavian administration used the medium of coinage to similar ideological purpose and effect. In a similar vein as Mann's overlapping networks of social power (here, economic and ideological), Carlos Noreña views Roman coins as "commodities in which two different regimes of value, the economic and the symbolic converged and reinforced one another."[193] Before and during the time in which Matthew was likely written, the Flavian emperors minted coins in Antioch and elsewhere that circulated throughout the east. Jane Cody classifies these coins into four types: (1) *provincial capta* ("captured province"); (2) *supplicatio* ("supplication"); (3) *adoratio* ("adoration"), and (4) *provincia restituta* ("restored province").[194] The *capta* type, in particular, projects images of Roman control, in which "the provincial is represented as utterly defeated and the conqueror all powerful."[195] One such coin minted in Caesarea in 70–81 CE features the head of Titus on the obverse; the reverse is inscribed with a palm tree (representing Judea) and a woman, seated and bound—a caption identifies her as *Judaea Capta* ("Judea Captive"), a representation of the Jewish people.[196] Davina Lopez points out the gendered representation of the conquered Jewish people in the *capta* coins in which a female personification of the land is often pictured as subdued by the emperor dressed as a Roman general: these are the "basic imperial power relations: dominant and subordinate, active and passive . . . using gendered bodies both to show the differences between the conquerors and conquered and to communicate social superiority and inferiority . . . Allusions to penetration and domination emphasize and reinforce his prowess."[197] As with other forms of ideological messaging that sought to tie the Flavians with prior elements of Augustan rule, Cody notes that "after the Augustan period, the barbarian *capta* type disappears from Roman coinage . . . [but] reappears in the very first year of Vespasian's rule (69–70 CE), and recurs in numerous variations throughout his reign and the reigns of his two sons."[198] Thus imperial coinage —paid to soldiers, circulated in markets among provincial traders, artisans and farmers, returned in taxes by villages, towns, and individuals—fulfilled its purpose of strengthening Roman economic transactions while also promoting the ideology of empire and its rulers among their provincial subjects.

Besides these specific examples of ideological communication, there were other ways in which Roman military personnel transmitted the ideology of empire during encounters with provincial residents. The forms of this communication were varied, and included verbal and non-verbal, symbolic elements. Some of the ways described above in which civilians were forced to negotiate Roman military power also have an ideological component: soldiers stationed in cities and towns; construction of military bases; paved roads with mile markers; toll booths and tax collection; Roman coins; and victory parades celebrating the triumph of Roman forces in Judea (including the execution of Jewish captives) all contain—beyond daily interaction and interpersonal verbal communication—non-verbal messages that project authority and control. Other instances of such messaging included visual representations of dominance in Roman soldiers' uniforms and equipment (e.g., red tunics; the soldiers' *cingulum* or belt; decorated helmets, armor, shields; standards with imperial iconography);[199] use of Latin language in official documents; the Roman calendar, including month names, holidays, and religious observances (including birthdays of the imperial family); celebration of the imperial cult;[200] and the settlement of veterans colonies.[201]

All of these examples illustrate Mann's contention, and the argument of this section: that ideological power organizes human experience by providing meaning, offering norms of behavior and belief, and promoting ritual practices that serve the ends of those promulgating them.[202] In this case, elite Roman power holders (emperors) and their allies and agents (the Senate, local elites, soldiers, poets, architects and builders, mint workers) used a variety of techniques and media to deploy messages that constructed and maintained the ideology of empire, supporting and reinforcing their power and rule.

CONCLUSION

This chapter has argued that the people of Syria negotiated various expressions of Roman military power, including (1) the threat and use of violence by Roman military forces; (2) the collection of taxes, including grain and agricultural products, labor for road building, and coin; (3) the challenge of social relationships, especially those between soldiers and local women; and (4) the pressure to accept and accede to the messages of imperial ideology. All of these experiences together provide a context in which to read

Matthew's gospel, and an understanding of the constant, daily negotiation that Matthew's audience would have had to make to live in the Roman province of Syria. This evidence sets the stage for the following chapters which argue that a variety of Matthean texts engage some of these common experiences of provincial residents interacting with the power of the Roman empire and its military forces. In particular scenes, the Gospel constructs and negotiates Roman military power, offering strategies for personal survival and a vision for a community of Jesus-followers to persevere, possibly thrive, and eventually arise victorious over those forces that threaten them in Roman imperial society.

NOTES

1. Hutton and Ogilvie, LCL.
2. Apuleius, *Metamorphoses* 9.39. Hanson, LCL. The *miles e legione* ("soldier from the legion") is a centurion, as indicated by his *vitis* (vine-staff), a mark of rank.
3. Besides the original account by Josephus, *The Jewish War*, see Steve Mason, *A History of the Jewish War A.D. 66–74* (Cambridge, UK: Cambridge University Press, 2016).
4. For a thorough account of this history, see Fergus Millar, *The Roman Near East: 31 BC–AD 337* (Cambridge, MA: Harvard University Press, 1993), 27–78. On the complicated nature of research on the Roman military in this region, see David Kennedy, "The Roman Army in the East," in *The Roman Army in the East,* ed. David Kennedy, JRA Supplementary Series 18 (1996), 9–24.
5. Josephus, *JW* 1.282–285, recounts how Herod, while previously involved in the administration and military affairs of the Hasmonean king Hyrcanus, made his direct claim and ascent to the throne of Judea with the support of powerful allies Antony and Julius Caesar, who secured the approval of political and military assistance for Herod by the Roman Senate.
6. Josephus, *JW* 7.17, 163, 252.
7. This period corresponds to the rule of the Flavian emperors: Vespasian (Titus Flavius Vespasianus) ruled 69–79 CE, followed by his two sons in succession: Titus (79–81 CE) and Domitian (81–96 CE).
8. Isaac, *Limits*, 52–53, notes scholarly debates on the nature of Roman frontier policy, including the defensive vs. offensive nature of troop deployment during this period, and concludes that "Rome had long-standing ambitions to acquire parts of the Persian empire and frequently made attempts to realize them.... A survey of Rome's Persian wars shows that Rome usually was the attacker, and the distribution of the troops from the Flavian period onward indicates that the Roman army in the East... was prepared for further advance.... The periods of major warfare were: 65–36 BC; AD 52–63; 112–117; 163–165; 194–217."
9. Mann, *Sources of Power,* 277–278.

10. Steven Friesen, "Poverty in Pauline Studies" Beyond the So-called New Consensus," *JSNT* 26.3 (2004): 341–347, creates a model that helps to picture categories of economic status in the Roman Empire; the three levels at the bottom of his scale (PS 5–7) hover around subsistence (moderate surplus to below subsistence). The people found in these states include, 343, "the overwhelming majority of the population under Roman imperialism . . . [who could] survive for some time at the low end of this scale, but . . . [whose lives, if forced to live] below the subsistence level are usually shortened by chronic malnutrition and disease." Friesen, 345, also provides this sobering contrast of the difference between common people and the Roman elite: "the highest known annual salary was for senators who 'served' as proconsul of Africa or Asia. They received 1,000,000 sesterces for their year in office. This proconsular salary for one year would have supported a farm family of four in those provinces for over 800 years."

11. Mann, *Sources of Power*, 279–280.

12. Richard Alston, Soldier and Society in *Roman Egypt* (New York: Routledge, 1995), 97.

13. Scott, *Domination*, 45, "Relations of domination are…relations of resistance…. Inasmuch as [domination] involves the use of power to extract work, production, services, taxes against the will of the dominated, it generates considerable friction and can be sustained only by continuous efforts at reinforcement, maintenance, and adjustment . . . symbolization of domination by demonstrations and enactments of power."

14. Josephus, *JW* 7.103–111.

15. G.W. Bowersock, "Syria Under Vespasian," *JRS* 63 (1973): 133.

16. Bowersock, "Syria Under Vespasian," 133. Josephus, *JW* 5.67.

17. Josephus, *JW* 7.219–243 describes how in 72 CE Traianus' predecessor, Caesennius Paetus, unexpectedly brought overwhelming Roman military force against the allied ruler of Commagene to force the transition of political power to direct Roman rule. Paetus commanded Legio VI Ferrata and cohorts of auxiliary infantry and cavalry, and was joined by two local kings, Aristobolus of Chalcis and Sohaemus of Emesa and their armies for the short campaign against the Commagene royal forces. Besides the political pretext given for this invasion (which Josephus is slightly suspicious of), Millar, *Roman Near East*, 81–83, notes that Commagene was "an extensive, very fertile area, which could support a large population," and which would provide additional tribute and tax revenue to the Romans. To support this war—even though it was over quickly—the local population in Syria would have had to cope with the disruption of thousands of troops, cavalry horses, and draft animals moving through their towns and communities to assemble for the war, as well as provide supplies for the mobilization (see below). The costs of military action in Commagene were higher. While Josephus focuses on the outcomes for the Commagene royal family, there were undoubtedly many soldiers killed and wounded, and Millar, 82, 460–462, points to scattered evidence for the displacement of the civilian population—with refugees fleeing their homes and crossing the border into Parthia.

18. Zeichmann, *Roman Army*, 3–5.

19. Christopher Zeichmann, personal correspondence. Josephus (*JW* 2.52) notes that some three thousand soldiers from these units were stationed at the Fortress Antonia in Jerusalem, and at the death of Herod in 4 BCE assisted legionary soldiers from Syria in quelling popular uprisings throughout Judea. Later, Josephus (*JW* 2.236) mentions that the deployment of the cavalry unit *ala Sebastenorum* from Caesarea at the directive of the Roman governor Cumanus.

20. Jonathan Roth, *The Logistics of the Roman Army at War (264 BC – AD 235)* (Leiden, Boston: Brill, 2012), 143.

21. Roth, *Logistics,* 237.

22. Thackeray, LCL, 163–165.

23. Josephus, *JW* 2.383.

24. *Agricola* 31, Hutton and Ogilvie, LCL, 83.

25. Tacitus, *Agricola* 32. These provincial complaints about the burden of Roman rule provides a context in which to understand the appeal of Jesus' invitation in Matthew 11:29–30: "Take my yoke upon you, and learn from me; for I am gentle and humble in heart, and you will find rest for your souls. For my yoke is easy, and my burden is light." Although many commentators interpret this verse as pertaining to Torah observance, Warren Carter, *Matthew and the Margins: A Sociopolitical and Religious Reading* (Maryknoll, NY: Orbis, 2000), 259–261, argues that Jesus here addresses, "those who are burdened by life under Roman imperial control and its unjust political and socioeconomic structures. They are afflicted by . . . hard labor, by payment of taxes, tolls, and debts to the political, economic, and religious elite, and by control of social superiors.... Jesus' 'yoke,' . . . [in contrast] is kind and good, in displaying God's mercy, justice, and compassion and in liberating those who wearily toil and are burdened by Rome's exploitative and cruel yoke."

26. Two legions moved to Cappadocia: XII Fulminata, which participated in the Roman-Jewish War, and (most likely) the newly raised XVI Flavia. After the destruction of Jerusalem, X Fretensis remained there to enforce the peace. The III Gallica, IIII Scythia, and VI Ferrata were assigned to Syria under the direct command of Traianus. Information on the Roman military in Syria is inferred from a number of inscriptions, primarily one first translated by Denis van Berchem, "Une inscription flavienne du Musée d'Antioche," *Museum Helveticum* 40.3 (1983): 186–187, who notes that "Notre inscription désigne comme gouverneur de la province le légat M. Ulpius Trajan" as well as mentioning the presence of soldiers from four legions (III, IIII, VI, XVI) and twenty auxiliary cohorts. See also Josephus, *JW* 7.1, 17–18 and Tacitus, *Ann.* 4.5. For further discussion see Nigel Pollard, *Soldiers, Cities, and Civilians in Roman Syria* (Ann Arbor: University of Michigan Press, 2000), 23; and Isaac, *Limits,* 33–53.

27. Pollard, *Soldiers,* 24. In the second century, there is evidence for IIII Scythia in Zeugma and III Gallica at Raphanaea, which may represent a continuation of earlier deployments. D. L. Kennedy, "Legio VI Ferrata: The Annexation and Early Garrison of Arabia," *Harvard Studies in Classical Philology* 84 (1980): 283, locates VI Ferrata at Samosata, IIII Scythia at Cyrrhus, and III Gallica at Raphanaea in 98 CE.

28. Wheeler, "Laxity" 256; Bowersock, "Syria Under Vespasian," 135, believes that the XVI Flavian legion is stationed here; others (noted above) argue for III Gallica.

29. Isaac, *Limits*, 39. This is not the same Beroea mentioned in Acts 17:10–13; 20:4, which is near Thessalonica in northern Greece.

30. Although Pollard, *Soldiers*, 24, argues that "it is not clear whether legions were routinely broken up into dispersed vexillations at this period as they were throughout the second century A.D.," and goes on to note that most evidence at present is from urban areas, Zeichmann, *New Testament*, figure 2.1, provides evidence of many smaller outposts and stations in nearby Palestine, and this sort of deployment is evident elsewhere throughout the Empire. In Syria proper, archaeological work has been limited and difficult; therefore, confirmation of additional vexillation sites awaits further research.

31. R.W. Davies, "The Daily Life of the Roman Soldier," *ANRW* 2 (1975): 314. Josephus, *JW* 3.86, also notes that soldiers in the legion ate morning and evening meals together and at set times each day.

32. Davies, "Daily Life," 319–323. More will be said about logistical duties in the following section on the economic impact of the military. Christopher Fuhrman, *Policing the Roman Empire: Soldiers, Administration, and Public Order* (New York: Oxford University Press, 2012), 6, describes how policing by the military took a variety of forms, including: (1) guard duty (guarding/escorting officials, patrols, night watches to prevent theft and arson); (2) mitigating disturbances (by a show of force, punishment of individuals); (3) involvement in judicial processes, "especially their use of physical compulsion or the threat thereof: arresting suspects, serving summonses, searching for people who have gone missing"—including fugitive slaves; and (4) political assassination.

33. Ulpian, *Dig.* 1.118; quoted in Christopher Fuhrman, *Policing*, 4 n.4

34. Scott, *Domination*, 198.

35. G.R. Watson, *Roman Soldier*, 55–61.

36. LCL, Thackery, 27.

37. Josephus, *Ant.*, 17.278: the centurion Arius and forty soldiers were killed and the grain was stolen.

38. Pollard, *Soldiers*, 46. During the reign of Septimus Severus (c.200 CE) the province was divided into three parts; at this time Dura became part of Syria Coele, with its capital at Antioch.

39. Millar, *Roman Near East*, 131.

40. Millar, *Roman Near East*, 133.

41. Millar, *Roman Near East*, 132–133. See also Pollard, *Soldiers*, 44–50.

42. Pollard, *Soldiers*, 46–47.

43. Millar, *Roman Near East*, 131.

44. Acts 2:7–11 provides a glimpse of the diverse origins of pilgrims and worshippers; Acts 11:19–30 gives Luke's perspective on the relationships between Jewish Jesus-followers in Jerusalem and Antioch prior to 66 CE.

45. Josephus, *Ant.* 20.106–112; *JW* 2.223–227. Cumanus was procurator in 49 CE (*Ant.* 20.103–104, Feldman, LCL, 57n.).

46. Josephus, *Ant.* 20.106.

47. In Acts 21:27-39, Paul is arrested by soldiers for provoking a riot in the Temple complex; the tribune confuses him for another who has broken the peace.

48. Lenski, *Power and Privilege*, 214, 217.

49. Steven Friesen, "Poverty in Pauline Studies: Beyond the So-called New Consensus," *JSNT* 26.3 (2004): 323-361.

50. Walter Scheidel and Steven Friesen, "The Size of the Economy and the Distribution of Income in the Roman Empire," *JRS* 99 (2009): 61-91.

51. Longenecker, Bruce Longenecker, *Remember the Poor: Paul, Poverty, and the Greco-Roman World* (Grand Rapids, MI: Eerdmans, 2010), 44, 53.

52. Bruce Longenecker, *Remember the Poor*, 27.

53. Peter Temin, *The Roman Market Economy* (Princeton, NJ: Princeton University Press, 2013), 146.

54. Greg Woolf, "Imperialism, empire, and the integration of the Roman economy," *World Archaeology* 23.3, *Archaeology of Empires* (Routledge, 1992), 283.

55. Simon Elliot, *Empire State: How the Roman Military Built an Empire* (Oxford, UK: Oxbow Books, 2017), 121.

56. Appian, *Syrian War* 50, LCL 3: "The Syrians and Cilicians also are subject to an annual tax of one hundredth of the assessed value of the property of each man."

57. Pollard, *Soldiers*, 173, notes Ulpian's description (*Dig.* 50.13) of the *tributum capitis*: also called a poll tax, it was collected in cash (coin), and was based on census figures collected by the provincial government. A census that brought portions of Judea under more direct Roman control was taken by the Syrian governor P. Sulpicius Quirinius, most likely in 6 CE when Herod's son Archelaus was deposed. The census is referred to in Luke 2:1-7 as the reason for Joseph and Mary's journey to Bethlehem, at which time Jesus is born. For discussion on the census and Luke's chronology, see D. S. Potter, "Quirinius," *ABD* 5, 588-589.

58. Pollard, *Soldiers*, 173-177. On the *aureum coronarium*, which was initially a tribute displayed at a victorious general's triumph, and later came to be a tax collected at the accession of every new emperor, see Cicero, *In Pisonem* 37; Dio Cassius, *History* 51.

59. Temin, *Market Economy*, 148.

60. Josephus, *JW* 7.218; Suetonius, *Dom.* 12. The tax was rooted in biblical law (Exod 30:12-16), and is the topic of Jesus' discussion with Peter about paying taxes in Matthew 17:24-27. See Warren Carter, "Paying the Tax to Rome as Subversive Praxis: Matthew 17:24-27" *JSNT* 76, 3-31 (1999): 28-29, who writes, "Rome imposes the tax to assert its supremacy and to subjugate, humiliate and punish. The story of the fish, though, shows the tax to be subject to God's power and sovereignty. From the tradition of the kings of the earth [in Hebrew scripture] and from the Gospel's point of view, the audience knows that God's sovereignty is supreme. Paying the tax, then, is no longer for disciples of Jesus an action defined by Rome... [but] invokes, for those with eyes to see, God's sovereignty. That is to say, paying the tax becomes a subversive not a subjugating act, a defiant act which relativizes and undermines what the tax is supposed to reinforce: Rome's absolute power and control of its subject's reality."

61. L.A. Thompson, "Domitian and the Jewish Tax," *Historia: Zeitschrift für Alte Geschichte* 31.3 (1982): 329, argues that, "whatever the original liability, it is clear that an innovation of some kind was introduced by Domitian in the collection of this tax. Suetonius [*Dom.* 12] saw this innovation as 'an extremely harsh exaction' of the tax: *Iudaicus fiscus acerbissime actus est*. Three further facts are evident. First, that the rigorous administration of the *fiscus Iudaicus* under Domitian involved a witch-hunt for so-called Jewish tax-evaders and a spate of prosecutions of alleged evaders. Second, that Domitian's successor, Nerva, considered it important not only to put a quick end to this witch-hunting and the associated injustices, but also to advertise his corrective action through the medium of the imperial coinage; hence the legend *fisci Iudaici calumnia sublata* ('To commemorate the suppression of wrongful accusations in regard to the Jewish tax') on some coins minted at Rome early in Nerva's reign. Third, that the last years of Domitian's reign were also marked by accusations against Roman *honestiores* on charges of having 'drifted into Jewish ways,' and that a good number of the accused were on that account severely punished under the law of *maiestas*. [Dio 67.14]." For further discussion see Martin Goodman, "Nerva, the Fiscus Judaicus and Jewish Identity," *JRS* 79 (1989): 40–44; Sara Mandell, "Who Paid the Temple Tax When the Jews Were under Roman Rule?" *Harvard Theological Review* 77.2 (1984): 223–232.

62. Appian, *Syrian War* 50, LCL 3: καὶ διὰ ταῦτ' ἐστὶν Ἰουδαίοις ἅπασιν ὁ φόρος τῶν σωμάτων βαρύτερος τῆς ἄλλης περιοικίας ("On account of these rebellions the poll-tax imposed upon all Jews is heavier than that imposed upon the surrounding peoples").

63. Dennis Kehoe, "Contract Labor," in *The Cambridge Companion to the Roman Economy*, ed. Walter Scheidel (Cambridge, UK: University of Cambridge Press, 2012), 116.

64. Kehoe, "Contact Labor," 117–118.

65. Kehoe, "Contact Labor," 119.

66. Michael Given, *The Archaeology of the Colonized* (New York: Routledge, 2004).

67. Given, *Archaeology*, 1–2.

68. Given, *Archaeology*, 36.

69. Given, *Archaeology*, 36.

70. Paul Erdkamp, "The Corn Supply of the Roman Armies During the Principate (27 BC–235 AD)," in *The Roman Army and the Economy*, ed. Paul Erdkamp (Amsterdam: J.C. Gieben, 2002), 59. The use of "corn" and "corn supply" by many modern scholars and translators sounds unusual to American speakers of English. The usage comes from the British meaning of the term, wherein "corn" refers to any type of grain. For the Romans, wheat and barley were the most common grains grown and eaten. It should not be understood as maize, which was unknown in the Mediterranean basin at that time.

71. Erdkamp, "Corn Supply," 50–52.

72. David Kaufman, "Horrea Romana: Roman Storehouses," *The Classical Weekly* 23.7 (1929): 50.

73. Simon Elliot, *Empire State*, 130. Elinor Husselman, "The Granaries of Karanis," *Transactions and Proceedings of the American Philological Association*

83 (1952): 56–73, describes granaries found in the town of Karanis, Egypt along with the barracks and headquarters for the Roman soldiers stationed there, next to the largest granary in the town. Husselman, 69, also discusses a large three-story complex (C123) identified as a *horrea*; documents connected with this *horrea* suggest private ownership—first by a family leasing state-owned cropland, and second by the family of Gaius Julius Apollonarius, identified by the titles στρατιώτ(ης) λε(γεώνος) γ Κυρ(ηναικῆς) and φρουμεντάριος Ρώμης, and thus connected with the Roman government's grain collection for both locally-based troops and Rome itself.

74. Roth, *Logistics*, 185.

75. Roth, *Logistics*, 186. Roth's estimate of the grain allotment is slightly less than Kehne's 880 grams per day. Sacks of grain should also be pictured in the memorable story from Acts 27:1–44, where Paul's ship is foundering: the captain and crew, in consultation with the centurion, "lightened the ship by throwing the [sacks of] wheat (ὁ σῖτος) into the sea" (27:38).

76. J.P. Oleson, M.B. Reeves, G.S. Baker, E. de Bruijn, Y. Gerber, M. Nikolic, A.N. Sherwoodet, *Preliminary Report on Excavations at Al-Humayma, Ancient Hawara, 2004 and 2005* (Amman, Jordan: Department of Antiquities of Jordan, 2008), 325.

77. Oleson, et al, "Excavations," 325.

78. Oleson, et al, "Excavations," 326.

79. Kelsey Koon, "Granaries and the Grain Supply of Roman Frontier Forts: Case Studies in Local Grain Production from Haurra (Jordan), Vindolanda (Britain), and Vindonissa (Switzerland)," MA Thesis, University of Victoria (ProQuest, 2012), 69.

80. Koon, "Granaries," 89.

81. John Oleson, "Landscape and Cityscape in the Hisma: The Resources of Ancient Al-Humayma" in *Studies in the History and Archaeology of Jordan VI* (London: Routledge, 1997), 178; quoted in Koon, "Granaries," 80.

82. Peter Kehne, "War- and Peacetime Logistics: Supplying Imperial Armies in East and West," in *A Companion to the Roman Army*, ed. Paul Erdkamp (Blackwell, 2007), 324. Kehne, 325, also notes that these basic food supplies were paid for via a payroll deduction; other foods could be purchased at the soldier's own expense "in canteens, in hot food stalls (*popinae*) in the *canabae* [settlements/towns near a base], or from the many sutlers (*lixae*) usually following the troops."

83. Kehne, "Logistics," 325. This is based on three legions, 19 auxiliary cohorts, 8 *alae* of cavalry, 2,500 mariners, and military servants/slaves.

84. Isaac, *Limits*, 283.

85. Isaac, *Limits*, 283.

86. Isaac, *Limits*, 273.

87. Erdkamp, "Corn Supply," 58–59.

88. Erdkamp, "Corn Supply," 59.

89. LCL, Hutton and Ogilvie, 65.

90. Stephen Mitchell, "Requisitioned Transport in the Roman Empire: A New Inscription from Pisidia," *JRS* 66 (1976): 106.

91. See Mitchell, "Requisitioned Transport," 111–112, 114, for one important inscription from Sagalassus in central Pisidia (then in the province of Galatia) that will be discussed in chapter 3. Naphatali Lewis, "Domitian's Order on Requisitioned Transport and Lodgings," *Revue international des droits de l'antiquite* 15 (1968): 135–142; Lewis, 140, discusses an edict by Germanicus, linking it to the Capito inscription, in which a *diplomata* is required for use of the *angaria*: "μηδέν λαμβάνειν εἰ μή τινες ἐμὰ διπλώματα ἔξοσιν." See also Kolb, 97.

92. IGLS V, no. 1998.

93. IGLS V, no. 1998, transl. R.K. Sherk, quoted in Fergus Millar, *Roman Near East,* 85–86.

94. Barbara Levick, "Domitian and the Provinces," *Latomus* 41.1 (Jan–Mar 1982), 50–53.

95. Levick, "Domitian and the Provinces," 52–53, 73.

96. Mitchell, "Requisitioned Transport," 106, 114.

97. Pollard, *Soldiers,* 85.

98. Theodor Kissel, "Road-Building as Munus Publicum," *The Roman Army and the Economy,* ed. Paul Erdkamp (Amsterdam: J.C. Gieben, 2002), 129; Roth, *Logistics,* 215.

99. Romolo Staccioli, *The Roads of the Romans* (Los Angeles: Getty Trust Publications, 2004), 83, writes: "every one of these [empire-spanning] roads reflected the very history of Rome's conquests . . . the entire road system was . . . the result of tremendous effort . . . [and] indispensable to the control, administration, and defense of an empire spanning three continents."

100. Plutarch *Galba* 24.4; Cassius Dio 54.8.4; Tacitus, *History* 1.27. See also Amanda Claridge, *Rome: An Oxford Archaeological Guide* (New York: Oxford University Press, 2010), 85–86; Strong, "Public Buildings," 104; Staccioli, *Roads,* 83.

101. Kissel, "Road Building," 144; Roth, *Logistics,* 215.

102. Millar, *Roman Near East,* 65.

103. Van Berchem, "Une inscription flavienne," 189: "Le danger parthe provisoirement écarté, Trajan était libre d'affecter à d'autres tâches les troupes dont il disposait. . . . l'inscription . . . que de nous renseigner sur la composition de l'armée de Syrie dans les premières années du règne de Vespasien. Car on peut admettre que toutes les unités nommées dans ce document appartenaient alors à la garnison permanente de la province."

104. Bowersock, "Syria Under Vespasian," 136; Isaac, *Limits,* 34–35.

105. Isaac, *Limits,* 35: Caesarea–Scythopolis (by Traianus before his governorship in 69 CE); near the crossroads of the Apamea–Palmyra and Calcis–Emesa roads (75–76 CE).

106. Bowersock, "Syria Under Vespasian," 136–138. Gerasa, a city of the Decapolis and part of Roman Syria since 63 CE, is the site of an exorcism by Jesus in Mk 5:1–20 // Lk 8:26–37. A group of demons named "Legion" (Λεγιὼν) begs Jesus not to destroy them; he casts them out and they enter into a herd of swine, which rush into the sea and drown. In Matthew 8:28–34, a version of this story is told in which Jesus also allows the demons to enter the herd and drown, but the episode takes place

in Gadara (the textual authorities do not agree: some say Gergasa or Gerasa); there are two demon possessed men, and they do not call themselves "legion."

107. Staccioli, *Roads of the Romans*, 59–60. Tacitus, *Ann.* 1.20, Moore and Jackson, LCL, records an incident in which vexillations of soldiers have been sent "for the repair of roads and bridges, and other service" (*missi ob itinera et pontes et alios usus*), but quickly abandon it when they catch wind of a mutiny, in which they become willing participants. Roth, *Logistics,* 216–217, points out that even in so-called peacetime, road construction was often a prelude to military campaigns: "roads were intended primarily for wagon travel, in order to facilitate supply . . . There is epigraphical evidence for Vespasian building and repairing roads in Syria, Cappadocia and Asia Minor during the mid-70s [CE]. This may well have been connected to Vespasian's experience with supply problems during the Jewish War. Due to the ongoing warfare on the Empire's eastern frontier, this region had a particularly thick network of military roads."

108. Kissel, "Road Building," 155–156.
109. Kissel, "Road Building," 130.
110. Kissel, "Road Building," 136.
111. Kissel, "Road Building," 136.
112. Kissel, "Road Building," 138.
113. Isaac, *Limits,* 36. Alfred Michael Hirt, *Imperial Mines and Quarries in the Roman World: Organizational Aspects 27 BC – AD 235* (Oxford, UK: Oxford University Press, 2010), 177.
114. Kissel, "Road Building," 142.
115. Kissel, "Road Building," 132–133.
116. Roth, *Logistics,* 215, estimates 56,000 miles of Roman roads throughout the empire by the time of Diocletian in the mid-2nd century CE. Kissel, "Road Building," 127, tallies 100,000 km (62,000 miles).
117. Hutton and Ogilvie, LCL
118. R.W. Connell, *Masculinities* (Berkeley: University of California Press, 1995), 76–77.
119. Moore, LCL, 289–290.
120. Isaac Haynes, *Blood of the Provinces: The Roman Auxilia and the Making of Provincial Society from Augustus to Severus* (London: Oxford University Press, 2013), 57.
121. Sara Elise Phang, *The Marriage of Roman Soldiers (13 B.C – A.D. 235): Law and Family in the Imperial Army* (Boston: Leiden, 2001), 230.
122. Phang, *Marriage,* 231.
123. Phang, *Marriage,* 235, 236.
124. Phang, *Marriage,* 193, 232–233. In other places the percentage is quite low (under 10%); there is great variety depending on place and time.
125. Phang, *Marriage,* 235. Drawbacks might include familial insecurity due to possible redeployment, social stigma, and resistance due to association with those involved in policing, tax collection, and enforcement of Roman rule.
126. Thackeray, LCL, 289.

127. Matthew's narrative includes reference to such large households with multiple slaves on several occasions, using enslaved people as characters to illustrate relationships and behavior in the Kingdom of Heaven and at the eschaton (18:21–35; 24:45–51; 25:14–30), and in depicting the arrest and accusations against Jesus and his movement by members of the high priest's household (δοῦλος, 26:51; παιδίσκη, 26:69–75).

128. Phang, *Marriage,* 232–235, 237–238.

129. D. H. French and J. R. Summerly, "Four Latin Inscriptions from Satala," *Anatolian Studies* 37 (1987): 21.

130. Phang, *Marriage,* 234, refers to the 2nd century CE jurist Paul (Julius Paulus Prudentissimus), who rules (*Resp.* 11) that Pamphila may be manumitted, but may not inherit from Titius. It is evident that Titius held Pamphila in high esteem and tried to provide for her upon his death. It may be inferred that she was his partner/wife.

131. Phang, *Marriage,* 239.

132. Phang, *Marriage,* 239.

133. Jennifer Glancy, *Slavery in Early Christianity* (Minneapolis: Fortress, 2006) 12, 21–24.

134. Phang, *Marriage,* 243–244.

135. Phang, *Marriage,* 242.

136. David Potter, "Introduction," in *Life, Death, and Entertainment in the Roman Empire,* ed. David Potter and David Mattingly (Ann Arbor, MI: University of Michigan Press, 1999), 13.

137. *Duo milia scortorum a castris eiecit.* Quoted in Phang, *Marriage,* 246–247, who also refers to Appian, *Spanish Wars* 85; Froninus, *Stratagems* 4.1; and Valerius Maximus 2.7: "for it is well know that that greatest number of hucksters and camp followers was present, with two thousand prostitutes" (*nam constat tum maximum inde institorum et lixanrum numerum cum duobus milibus scortorum abisse*).

138. Phang, *Marriage,* 247, 249.

139. Rebecca Flemming, "Quae Corpore Quaestum Facit: The Sexual Economy of Female Prostitution in the Roman Empire," *JRS* 89 (1999): 42.

140. Glancy, *Slavery,* 12–14. John Madden, "Slavery in the Roman Empire Numbers and Origins," *Classics Ireland* 3 (Dublin: Classical Association of Ireland, 1996), 110–114, summarizes various scholarly estimates, with percentages highest in Rome and Italy (for which there is also the most data), and perhaps slightly less in the provinces.

141. Thomas McGinn, "Roman Prostitutes and Marginalization," in *Social Relations in the Roman World,* ed. Michael Peachin (Oxford, Oxford University Press, 2011), 654.

142. McGinn, "Marginalization," 654.

143. McGinn, "Marginalization," 647.

144. McGinn, "Marginalization," 647.

145. Flemming, "Sexual Economy," 54. The term *lupanar* derives from *lupa* (she-wolf), one of many slang terms for a prostituted woman in Roman society.

146. McGinn, "Marginalization," 649; Phang, *Marriage,* 247.

147. Phang, *Marriage*, 247; David Potter, "Introduction," in *Life, Death, and Entertainment in the Roman Empire*, ed. David Potter and David Mattingly (Ann Arbor, MI: University of Michigan Press, 1999), 13.
148. Flemming, "Sexual Economy," 43.
149. McGinn, "Marginalization," 654.
150. Yanne Broux, "Trade Networks among the Army Camps of the Eastern Desert of Roman Egypt," in *Sinews of Empire*, ed. Håkon Fiane Teigen, Eivind Heldaas Seland (Oxford, UK: Oxbow Books, 2017), 7–9.
151. Phang, *Marriage*, 245.
152. McGinn, "Marginalization," 649, points out that *lenes* were not necessarily solo-operators, but could be part of a network: "the sale of sex in the Roman world was a cash-rich enterprise . . . with relatively large profits.... Members of the upper classes had good reason to avoid identification as pimps, because of the social censure and civic disabilities this entailed, but such evasion was fairly easy to accomplish through the use of slaves and others as middlemen."
153. Phang, *Marriage*, 248–249; McGinn, "Marginalization," 649; Pollard, *Syria*, 53–54, 188, "the entertainers' guild center/brothel at Dura seems to have been army administered, rather than a purely local civilian enterprise. At least a proportion of the prostitutes and entertainers there were slaves, and given the evidence for army involvement . . . it is likely that they were army-owned slaves, comparable to army-owned gladiators, individuals of similarly low status."
154. Flemming, "Sexual Economy," 42.
155. Flemming, "Sexual Economy," 42, 50.
156. Phang, *Marriage*, 252, 254–255.
157. Phang, *Marriage*, 253.
158. Phang, *Marriage*, 257.
159. Phang, *Marriage*, 257.
160. Ziolkowski, "Urbs Direpta," 72–74.
161. Ziolkowski, "Urbs Direpta," 73.
162. Phang, *Marriage*, 258.
163. Phang, *Marriage*, 259.
164. Polybius, *Hist.* 21.38. The incident takes place during the Roman war in Galatia (189 BCE). See also Plutarch, *The Virtuous Deeds of Women* 22; and Livy, *Hist.* 38.24.
165. Phang, *Marriage*, 256.
166. Phang, *Marriage*, 263–264.
167. Craig Williams, *Roman Homosexuality* (New York: Oxford University Press, 1999), 127, 133.
168. Phang, *Marriage*, 264.
169. Phang, *Marriage*, 265, 271–274.
170. Phang, *Marriage*, 288, "The problem is very obscure; except for Suet. Dom 10, scandals such as those in Valerius Maximus 6.1.10–12 are not reported. What evidence there is suggests the army's disapproval of effeminacy, but this is not linked directly to sexual practices."
171. Phang, *Marriage*, 292, 294.

172. Phang, *Marriage*, 294.

173. A.B. Bosworth, "Vespasian and the Slave Trade," *Classical Quarterly* 52.1 (2002): 350.

174. Bosworth, "Slave Trade," 352.

175. Bosworth, "Slave Trade," 352.

176. Bosworth, "Slave Trade," 352. In the years following 62 CE, when Vespasian returned from his governorship in Africa.

177. Mann, *Sources of Power*, 2.

178. Mann, *Sources of Power*, 20–23.

179. Galinsky, *Augustan Culture*, 141–155; Zanker, *Power of Images*, 172–183.

180. Augustus, *Res Gestae Divi Augusti* (Shipley, LCL).

181. Fairclough, LCL: *his ego nec metas rerum nec tempora pono; imperium sine fine dedi.*

182. Bruce Longenecker, "Peace, Prosperity, and Propaganda: Advertisement and Reality in the Early Roman Empire," in *Introduction to Empire in the New Testament*, ed. Adam Winn (Atlanta: SBL Press, 2016), 21–22. Augustine, *Confessions* 1.20–21 reflects on its use in his own education as a young man; its use appears standard by the 3rd century when he writes.

183. Dio Cassius, *Hist.* 63; Suetonius, *Nero* 57; Tacitus, *Hist.* 1.4.

184. Rashna Taraporewalla, "The Templum Pacis: Construction of Memory Under Vespasian," *Acta Classica* 53 (2010): 145. See also Jodi Magness, "Some Observations on the Flavian Victory Monuments of Rome," *KOINE: Mediterranean Studies in Honor of R. Ross Holloway*, ed. Derek Counts and Anthony Tuck (Oxbow Books, 2009), 38–39.

185. Carlos Noreña, "Medium and Message in Vespasian's Templum Pacis," *Memoirs of the American Academy in Rome* 48 (2003): 26.

186. Josephus takes great pains to praise the conduct of Vespasian and Titus through the Jewish War; they are his literary patrons and sponsors.

187. Noreña, "Medium and Message," 29–31, argues convincingly that a *Pax* coin type was issued empire-wide on two occasions: in 69–70 CE following the Civil War and in 75 CE upon dedication of the Templum Pacis, and that this effort was conscious, centrally planned, and authorized for the purpose of promoting Flavian rule. He concludes, 34–35, that "the Ara Pacis was a monument not to domestic concord but to imperialism and the military pacification of the Roman world.... [specifically] of foreign peoples . . . under the guidance of the new Flavian dynasty."

188. Noreña, "Medium and Message," 36; Claridge, *Rome*, 312–319; Kathleen Coleman, "Entertaining Rome," in *Ancient Rome: The Archaeology of the Eternal City*, ed. Jon Coulston and Hazel Dodge (Oxford, UK: Oxbow Books, 2011), 229–235.

189. Geza Alföldy, "Eine Bauinschrift aus dem Colosseum," *Zeitschrift für Papyrologie und Epigraphik* 109, 195–226 (1995): 210: *I[mp(erator)] Caes(ar) Vespasi[anus Aug(ustus)] amphitheatru[m novum (?)] [ex] manubis (vac.) [fieri iussit (?)]*; translation quoted in Noreña, "Medium and Message," 36.

190. Claridge, *Rome*, 121–123.

191. The Triumph followed previous parades conducted by Titus in Syria in 71 CE (Josephus, *JW* 7.96–97, described above); in Berytus, Antioch, and elsewhere the celebration of the Roman victory in Judea featured the execution of Jewish captives. This spectacle (θεωρία, *JW* 7.96) was another form of ideological messaging, meant to communicate the fate of all who might rebel against Roman power.

192. Naomi Norman, "Imperial Triumph and Apotheosis: The Arch of Titus in Rome," in *KOINE: Mediterranean Studies in Honor of R. Ross Holloway*, ed. Derek Counts and Anthony Tuck (Oxbow Books, 2009), 41–53.

193. Carlos Noreña, "Coins and Communication," in *The Oxford Handbook of Social Relations in the Roman World*, ed. Michael Peachin (New York: Oxford University Press, 2011), 248–249.

194. Jane Cody, "Conquerors and Conquered on Flavian Coins," in *Flavian Rome: Culture, Image, Text*, ed. A.J. Boyle and W.J. Dominik (Leiden: Brill, 2003): 103–124.

195. Cody, "Flavian Coins," 105.

196. Gabriela Bijovsky, "The Coins from Khirbat Burnaṭ (Southwest)," *'Atiqot* 69 (2012): 153. See also Martin Goodman, "Coinage and Identity: The Jewish Evidence," in *Coinage and Identity in the Roman Provinces*, ed. Christopher Howgego, Volker Heuchert, and Andrew Burnett (Oxford, UK: Oxford University Press, 2005), 166.

197. Davina Lopez, *Apostle to the Conquered: Reimagining Paul's Mission* (Minneapolis, MN: Fortress, 2008), 35–38.

198. Cody, "Flavian Coins," 106–107.

199. For discussion and illustration of Roman military equipment, see M.C. Bishop and J.C.N. Coulston, *Roman Military Equipment: From the Punic Wars to the Fall of Rome* (Oxford, UK: Oxbow Books, 2006), 73–128; Pat Southern, *The Roman Army: A Social and Institutional History* (Santa Barbara, CA: ABC-Clio, 2006), 150–158.

200. Isaac Haynes, "The Romanisation of Religion in the 'Auxilia' of the Roman Imperial Army from Augustus to Septimus Severus," *Britannia* 24 (1993): 141–157; Eric Birley, "The Religion of the Roman Army: 1895–1977," *ANRW* 2 (1978): 1506–1541; J. Helgeland, "Roman Army Religion," *ANRW* 2 (1978): 1470–1505; Oliver Stoll, "The Religions of the Armies," in *A Companion to the Roman Army*, ed. Paul Erdkamp (Blackwell, 2007), 451–476.

201. For a general treatment of the topic, see: Eric Birley, "Veterans of the Roman Army in Britain and Elsewhere," *Ancient Society* 13/14 (1982/83): 265–276; Gabriele Wesch-Klein, "Recruits and Veterans," in *A Companion to the Roman Army*, ed. Paul Erdkamp (Blackwell, 2007), 435–450. For discussion prior to and following the period under consideration, see: Will Broadhead, "Colonization, Land Distribution, and Veteran Settlement," in *A Companion to the Roman Army*, ed. Paul Erdkamp (Blackwell, 2007): 148–163; Edward Dąbrowa, "Military Colonisation in the Near East and Mesopotamia under the Severi," *Acta Classica* 55 (2012): 31–42.

202. Mann, *Sources of Power*, 22–24.

Chapter 2

Coping with the Danger from Roman Rulers

Herod and Antipas (Matthew 2:1–23; 14:1–12)

> Caesar . . . convened the Senate . . . presented Herod and dwelt on the services rendered by his father and his own goodwill towards the Roman people. . . . These words stirred the Senate, and when Antony came forward and said that with a view to the war with Parthia it was expedient that Herod should be king, the proposal carried unanimously. The meeting was dissolved and Antony and Caesar left the senate-house with Herod between them, preceded by the consuls and the other magistrates, as they went to offer sacrifice and to lay up the decree in the Capitol. On this, the first day of his reign, Herod was given a banquet by Antony.
>
> Josephus, JW 1.283–285[1]

INTRODUCTION

The following chapters move from a discussion of some of what we know about imperial structures and expressions of Roman military power in the region of Syria to specific texts in the gospel of Matthew. There are a number of scenes throughout the gospel in which Matthew portrays Jesus and his followers as having to negotiate the military power of the Roman Empire. The objective of these chapters is to offer a perspective that has been neglected by other commentators, namely, the ways in which Matthew constructs and negotiates Roman military power.

This chapter focuses on two scenes, Matthew 2:1–23 and 14:1–12, which construct Roman military power as a threat to Jesus and the people around him and offer one way to negotiate such power: by avoidance, if possible, until such time as God's eschatological purposes are fulfilled. Matthew introduces the threat of military violence in the persons of two rulers: Herod and his son Herod Antipas, who hold the power of life and death over their subjects. Each ruler orders soldiers to carry out violence against their citizens (the children of Bethlehem and John the Baptist), and both stories foreshadow and set the stage for a final encounter between Jesus and the Roman authorities in the closing chapters of the gospel.

THE DANGER FROM HEROD (MATT 2:1–23)

Directing, Avoiding, and Suffering Roman Power

From the moment of Jesus's birth, Matthew establishes the threat of Roman military power and the need to negotiate it. This danger lurks throughout the entire scene, and hangs like a menacing cloud over the gospel narrative as a whole. At what might otherwise be a time of joyful celebration, the machinations of Herod, Rome's client king, force Jesus's parents to flee with him and leave other families bereft as Herod commands soldiers into action against his own citizens (2:1–23). Upon learning of a possible threat to his rule in the birth of a rival "king of the Jews" (2:2), Herod immediately begins to act against any nascent kings who might be revealed by heavenly signs or the words of the prophets. When his would-be informants (the Magi) do not produce the necessary intelligence for a discreet elimination of the infant Jesus (2:7–8, 12), Herod takes a more heavy-handed approach.[2] In a simple phrase of understated horror, Matthew writes that Herod "sent and killed" (ἀποστείλας ἀνεῖλεν) all the male children of Bethlehem (2:16). This action is described with two verbs that place full responsibility for the killing on Herod: ἀποστείλας is a nominative, masculine, singular, aorist active participle and ἀνεῖλεν is an aorist, active, indicative, third person singular verb. Matthew does not state directly, but elliptically, that Herod's soldiers are the ones who carry out his order of indiscriminate killing in Bethlehem. At the same time, Joseph and Mary are not defenseless in this threatening scene: they have divine protection revealed through a dream warning that they must escape from Judaea to safety in Egypt (2:13), and another dream of guidance in which God tells them it is time to return (2:22).

It is not only Joseph and Mary who must negotiate Roman power; each character in the scene—including Herod—does so in a variety of ways. As will be shown below, Herod is a full participant in the Roman imperial system: his power derives from the backing of the Roman military, and he is willing to use violence to maintain his political power. Those who fall into Herod's orbit have varying responses. In Matthew's account, the leaders and people of Jerusalem are "frightened" or "troubled" (ταράσσω) by a heavenly sign that might signal a change in the ruling regime. The verb ταράσσω can have a sense of political unrest, especially in the passive voice which Matthew uses in 2:3 (ἐταράχθη).[3] This may not be evident in many English translations, but underscores the imperial context which Matthew's characters inhabit. The leaders of Jerusalem foster an opposition to Jesus among the crowd that gathers around him that grows throughout the gospel (23:29–39), culminating with a plot to arrest and kill him (26:3–4) and public calls to the Roman governor for him to be crucified (27:12–26).[4]

In contrast to this opposition, the Magi travel to Bethlehem to worship Jesus as the newly born "king of the Jews" (2:2, 10–11). After asking a foolish question (2:2) that causes distress in Jerusalem (2:3) and precipitates the events that follow, the Magi wisely avoid entanglement in Herod's plot, despite his best attempts to ensnare them (2:7–8), when they heed a dream warning (from God) to leave Bethlehem by a safer road (2:12). Joseph also receives a warning from a divine messenger, prompting him and Mary to take the infant Jesus and flee to Egypt, where they escape the effects of Herod's order, an atrocity called rightly in Christian tradition "the slaughter of the innocent" (2:13–15).[5]

Finally, the people of Bethlehem, whose young sons are killed by Herod's soldiers, are unable to avoid the indiscriminate use of military power and suffer for it. The effects of this killing on the mothers and fathers of Bethlehem are expressed in Matthew's quotation from Jeremiah 31:15: "A voice was heard . . . wailing and loud lamentation, Rachel weeping for her children . . . because they are no more" (2:19). Yet Matthew also does not address two important moral and theological questions. The first question is why Herod is able to act with seeming impunity. The scene in 2:1–23 offers no direct criticism of Herod, who is clearly culpable for the killing. Even close to a century after Herod's death, Matthew's characterization of the king is what points to his moral failing—rather than a more direct critique of his behavior or policies taken by some biblical prophets with whom Matthew is clearly familiar.[6] One reason for this may lie in Matthew's own context: he has need for circumspection and a certain degree of opaqueness when negotiating the power of rulers in his own day. Another reason also appears to be Matthew's intention to craft a story in which God's Messiah is both protected by divine favor and fulfills Matthew's reading of scripture (cf. 2:5–6, 15, 18), which seeks to draw connections to the birth and rescue of Moses from the hand of Pharaoh (Exod 1:22ff.).[7] This intention also answers the second question which Matthew does not address directly at this stage of the narrative: one of theodicy. Matthew's portrayal of God's involvement on behalf of Jesus implies that similar action could have been taken toward the children of Bethlehem. And God's lack of action regarding the murdered innocent raises the question of divine culpability or inability to act. Matthew does not dwell on these questions here, but rather depicts a situation in which God's intervention is limited and focused on Jesus. Readers must wait for Matthew's answer to these questions in later chapters, where Jesus is depicted as the resurrected and eschatological Son of Man who will one day return to enact justice and punish the wicked (Matt 25:31–46, 64; 27:50–54; 28:1–10, 18–20).[8]

Sadly, when Matthew's readers encounter the results of Herod's orders in this scene, they are left with a feeling of dread. Even the innocent often cannot avoid the effects of military violence—which emperors, governors, and kings can order at any time through their soldiers—as a means of achieving political ends. At the same time, the narrative also reveals a slender ray of hope: God's Messiah has been born, and God's protection allows him to avoid the power of empire, finding safety until the time is right for his public work to begin, even though that work will upset the elites who will conspire to kill him.

As will be seen below and in subsequent chapters, Matthew's portrayal of various characters serves to build and emphasize recurring themes throughout the gospel. Through this characterization Matthew's narrative suggests a variety of strategies by which readers may cope with the power and threat of the Roman Empire. The following sections describe more fully the ways in which Matthew depicts the power of Herod and Antipas, who as Roman agents are supported by, enmeshed in, and aligned with Roman networks of power, especially the power of the Roman military as the basis of their rule over the Jewish people. This chapter also shows the implications for people who must contend with these rulers and seek to avoid the danger of their self-benefitting use of military power. Finally, it addresses a tendency among Matthean scholars to read the gospel scene as a historical report with primarily religious or theological concerns, relegating any commentary on the imperial context of Herod's reign to the background or to silence.

Approaches to Matthew's Representation of Herod

It is not the intention of this or subsequent chapters to disparage the comments of previous scholars, many of which are insightful. Rather, the purpose is to demonstrate how attention to the presence of imperial military power illuminates Matthew's negotiation with the context and the concerns of his audience. For this reason, a full examination of other works will not be included in subsequent chapters but referred to as relevant. A brief discussion here, however, will illustrate previous approaches to Matthew's text and highlight the focus and contribution of this work to ongoing conversations about the gospel.

While most Matthean scholars readily acknowledge Herod's connection to elite Roman power brokers such as Marcus Antonius (for whom Herod renamed the fortress adjacent to the Temple) and Octavius Caesar (later

Augustus, the first Roman emperor), much Matthean scholarship—focused on Matthew's theological and Christological claims and the relationship between the Matthean community, a synagogue, and nascent rabbinic Judaism—has tended to downplay or relegate to the background Herod's political obligations as a client ruler in the Roman imperial system and his reliance on Roman military power as the basis for his reign. This is especially true when providing commentary on Matthew 2:1–23, a scene in which Matthew depicts Herod ordering the killing of young male children in Bethlehem.

The focus on theology/Christology is seen across a wide survey of recent work. Raymond Brown, for instance, frames his discussion with questions of Christology, noting the connection between the events in 2:1–18 and Matthew's messianic genealogy and birth of Jesus in 1:1–25.[9] Similarly, W.D. Davies and Dale Allison argue that Matthew's purpose is to contrast the misrule of Herod with the divinely favored rule of the Davidic Messiah.[10] Graham Stanton focuses on the hostility between Jesus and the Jewish leaders (at Matt 2:1–6; 9:34; 21:9 and 15), including Herod as one such power broker who opposes Jesus throughout the gospel.[11] Stanton is typical in framing the conflict in theological terms: "they perceive the Davidic Messiah to be a threat. Matthew hints (but does not explain fully) that their understanding of Messiahship is faulty."[12] This focus on the religious or theological purpose of Matthew, seemingly divorced from its imperial context and the realities of Roman military power, is perhaps a byproduct of twentieth-century scholarship in which religious concerns were framed as a special category of inquiry, set apart from other fields such as politics or history. Such approaches may acknowledge and show an awareness of Herod's ruthlessness as a political operator but tend to read his orders against the children of Bethlehem as motivated by theological issues and connected to his psychology, based on Matthew's and Josephus's descriptions of his fear and paranoia.[13] They do not, as a general rule, address the structural factors and personnel of the imperial context in which Matthew's work was written. Nor do they address the ways in which Matthew contributes to his context by presenting a scene in which elite power brokers order soldiers to kill infants in order to maintain the imperial system and their position within it.

A second tendency among Matthean scholars has been to seek answers to the question of community identity or ethnicity, which in 2:1–23 leads to perspectives on the purpose and identity of the Magi. Ulrich Luz characterizes the history of interpretation of the passage as one that has lifted up both Christological and soteriological motifs, and in which the Magi are viewed as representative of later followers of Jesus: "For the [early] church, the presupposition for this story was God's turning to the Gentiles, the experiences of (its own?) preservation from the blows of (Jewish?)

enemies, the knowledge of Jesus' victory over worldly powers."[14] This was true from the time of Origen and Augustine, insofar as the "salvation-history interpretation [that] focused on the Gentile mission . . . [saw] in the magi the . . . *primitiae gentium*" and "figures with whom the Christian readers can identify."[15] Stanton picks up the thread of ethnicity as important to readership among a Gentile audience: through Matthew's characterization of the Magi, implied readers are "encouraged to identify with the wise men who come to worship Jesus, but end up 'fleeing' from the machinations of Herod."[16] Davies and Allison, also, describe the "sharp contrast between the Jewish elite (represented by Herod and all of Jerusalem and the chief priests and scribes) on the one hand and the gentile world (represented by the magi) on the other—a contrast which fits Matthew's interest in universal mission and his disappointment in the Jewish people, especially their leaders."[17] The question of ethnicity, shaped in theological terms, has opened a discussion concerning the life experiences of the Matthean community, but in a limited fashion. It is more concerned about the degree of inclusion of Gentile readers among the community of Jesus-followers and their relationship with synagogues and nascent rabbinic Judaism, and provides little argument about the efforts of either group to find and maintain a place in Roman imperial society.

In contrast to the approaches favored among scholars just mentioned, there are others who attend to the implications of the imperial context and content of the scene. J. Andrew Overman notes that Matthew 2:1–18 "initiates the conflict between Jesus and the local client political system that ultimately does him in. . . . By announcing the birth in this fashion in 2:1 ('during the period of Herod the King'), Matthew makes plain the larger political picture into which the birth scene must be placed."[18] Beyond these specific observations, Overman also writes of Matthew's imperial context:

> The conflict presaged in the birth and early history of Jesus continued in the life and setting of Matthew's church. Indeed, the tension and crisis between Matthew's community and local leaders was really a continuation of the conflict initiated at Jesus' birth. Two generations after the death of Jesus the relations between local political leaders, as well as the ubiquitous international force of the Roman Empire, remained a salient issue for the Matthean community. . . . Matthew connected the imperial political reality of Judea and Galilee in the first century with both the start and conclusion of his story. Matthew believed local leaders had successfully enlisted the power of Rome to inhibit or destroy the movement gathered around Jesus. Roman power and the realities that it posited locally serve as bookends to this Gospel and cast a shadow over the entire book. Most commentaries on Matthew make virtually no mention of this important factor. Matthew's story about Jesus and the author's own community are

sandwiched between these explicit and potent narratives—the birth and death of Jesus—which emphasize the contours of the day-to-day political realities of Matthew and his church. . . . The entire Gospel is played out within this abiding reality of Roman political power and local division and contention around those political realities.[19]

This argument is welcome; however, where Overman emphasizes the political aspects of Roman power (through local leaders, such as Herod) that Matthew's community must contend with, this and subsequent chapters argue that the ways in which Matthew constructs and negotiates the military power by which Rome expanded and maintained its political rule are integral to the gospel's narrative.

Chapter 1 showed that the framework of empire sustained by military power provides the context in which the Matthean community lived and in which the gospel was read and received. In this situation, Matthew's portrayal of Jesus and his followers shows them to be at odds with those such as Herod, the chief priests, and scribes (2:4) who benefit from the system and are in favor of maintaining it. As Warren Carter writes: "Jesus and the . . . [societal] leaders occupy very different places in the imperial world. . . . [They] are part of its power structure. They represent its interests. They like things the way they are. Jesus has a very different set of values and social vision. . . . They understand his attempts to change it as an attack on their power, wealth, and status."[20] With regard to Matthew's community and assumed audience, Carter writes elsewhere that:

> There is a basic contrast between the urban elite, the powerful center which resists God's purposes, and those marginal to that center (the magi, the town of Bethlehem) who encounter God's purposes. The magi model important dimensions of discipleship: their marginality, their discovery of God's purposes, worship, faithfulness, and obedience to God's purposes in the face of Herod's actions. The world of empire is a dangerous place for those who seek God's purposes and respond positively to God's initiatives. . . . It is to such an existence that the gospel calls its audience.[21]

Thus, while much scholarship has neglected the realities of Roman imperial power in its interpretation of Matthew's gospel, there is growing support for the approach advocated here—one which acknowledges and foregrounds the presence of Roman military power, the effects such power had on the general population, and the ways in which Matthew and his readers negotiated such realities.[22]

Negotiating the Military Violence of Herod's Reign

Herod, Leaders in Jerusalem, and the Magi

In Matthew 2:1–23, the gospel writer portrays Herod, secure in his capital city, and with many resources at his disposal, confronted with news of a new and rival "king of the Jews" (2:1). The scene that Matthew creates is one in which Herod, as a client king and loyal ally of the Romans, uses military force as the final move in a series of escalating actions designed to protect his own position in Roman networks of power. The appearance of a new king presents questions of legitimacy for Herod (who had been officially sanctioned as King of the Jews by the Roman Senate): either he has been unknowingly supplanted, or the newborn child is a pretender, whose claims must be diffused and eliminated. Besides Herod, who fully participates in the perpetuation of the empire, there are several other groups of people in Matthew's narrative who must also negotiate its military power. This section addresses the variety of ways in which these characters respond to the threat of military violence in the scene.

When the Magi arrive in Jerusalem, they come with news that a heavenly sign has revealed a newborn "king of the Jews" (βασιλεὺς τῶν Ἰουδαίων, 2:2). They come to Jerusalem to confirm this birth, and to honor the newborn king, whose star they "observed . . . at its rising" (εἴδομεν . . . τὸν ἀστέρα ἐν τῇ ἀνατολῇ, 2:2). There is one problem, however: the child is not Herod's son, and when the king learns of the Magi's inquiry (2:3) he reacts quickly to learn more about it. (Readers of the gospel, in contrast, are already aware of the child's identity, having read Matthew's genealogy in 1:1–17 and the account of Jesus's birth in 1:18–25.) Many commentators make note of Herod's response, of which Matthew writes: "When King Herod heard this, he was frightened (ταράσσω), and all Jerusalem with him" (2:3).[23] But why is he troubled? And what disturbance and unrest is the king afraid of? Matthew does not say explicitly, but the way in which the narrative portrays Herod as fearful, conspiratorial, and violent highlights Matthew's negative presentation in this scene of imperially sanctioned military power—and offers the gospel's audience a narrative in which God, through Jesus, will address the problems that such power brings.

The first way in which Matthew's portrayal addresses the experiences of living in Roman-integrated territory (whether administered by governors or client rulers) assumes knowledge of the way in which the imperial system treated the rulers of its client states, and how such rulers were expected to act to remain in power. As a young man, Herod himself was supported by the patronage of powerful Romans, including Marcus Antonius and Octavius Caesar (Augustus), who sponsored his promotion before the Roman Senate and his ratification as king of the Jews.[24] The confirmation of Roman support for Herod was accompanied by military forces, which the Roman Senate authorized to back Herod's campaign in 39–37 BCE to claim the throne.[25] Roman support of client rulers could continue indefinitely so long as a client was successful in solicitation of patronage; Herod was effective at this, and held in good esteem by a series of Roman power-brokers throughout his long reign.[26] Roman support could also be removed, if a client was ineffective or if the Romans decided for their own purposes to administer a client's territory directly. Examples of this include the removal of Herod's son Archelaus in 6 CE[27] and the annexation of Commagene in 72 CE cited in chapter 1.[28] In this environment, a ruler like Herod would always be vigilant to maintain good relations with his patrons so as to ensure that they would not choose another ruler to replace him.[29]

Herod was also vigilant about plots among members of the royal family, where various sons, wives, ex-wives, and courtiers were constantly jockeying for position, influence, and inheritance (cf. Josephus, *JW* 1.445–513). Herod executed several family members, including his wife's grandfather and brother (Josephus, *JW* 1.433–434, 437); wife Mariamne (*JW* 1.444); and sons Alexander, Aristobulus (*JW* 1.550–551), and Antipater (*JW* 1.664).[30] These acts are often cited as examples of Herod's unstable mental condition, but should instead be viewed as the ruthless application of imperial values and as Herod's negotiation of Roman patronage.[31] When Rome granted Herod the right and authority to rule, he determined to exercise it against all challengers.

Just how much, if any, of these details a Matthean audience might know is unclear. But it is reasonable to claim that Matthew's portrayal of Herod as plotting against the newborn Jesus as a potential threat to his rule and using his soldiers to ruthlessly suppress such a potential challenger would ring true to the gospel's audience. While Matthew's audience did not have personal experience living under the rule of Herod, his descendants ruled in Judea during the time in which the gospel was likely written. Moreover, the accounts of Josephus indicate that the character of Herod's rule and his nature of his deeds *could* be known—including the ways in which he established and maintained his position as a loyal friend of Rome backed by military power. Awareness of such historical events would only enhance an audience's engagement with Matthew's scene.

The second way in which Matthew portrays the nature of imperially sanctioned power is in Herod's view of the infant Jesus. The Magi identify Jesus (2:2) as one "who has been born king of the Jews" and they declare they have come to "pay him homage" (προσκυνέω).[32] Matthew's audience would likely recognize immediately the challenge of the Magi's statements: the newborn child has not been sanctioned as a ruler by Roman patrons. From Herod's perspective, therefore, the child must be a pretender and a threat to his Roman-backed kingship and rule.

Historically, there were many such instances during Herod's reign in which the king and his soldiers dealt harshly with those who contested or would not submit to the Roman power embodied by his rule. Prior to his reign as king, Herod's first act when appointed governor of Galilee was (with the help of his soldiers) to capture and kill a bandit-chief (ἀρχιληστής) named Ezekias, along with many other bandits (Josephus, *JW* 1.204).[33] Later, during the campaign to secure his rule, Herod's opponents fought against him in Galilee: conducting asymmetrical warfare, they retreated to caves and marshes in the wilderness in which they could find a safe place for their families while continuing to oppose and harass Herod's forces in a variety of ways (Josephus, *JW* 1.304, 309–314). To defeat this resistance, Herod "killed a large number of the rebels, besieged and destroyed all their fortresses, and imposed on the towns, as a penalty for their defection, a fine of a hundred talents" (Josephus, *JW* 1.316 [Thackeray, LCL]). Following this fighting, Herod commanded his soldiers in action north of Jerusalem, where they "ravaged the enemy's territory, subdued five small towns, slew two thousand of their inhabitants, [and] set fire to their houses" (Josephus, *JW* 1.334 [Thackeray, LCL]). At the end of Herod's reign, a group of Jews whom Josephus calls "insurrectionists" (δημοτική τις ἐπανάστασις) climbed a gate of the Jerusalem Temple to tear down golden statues of Roman eagles. Herod's soldiers arrested them quickly, and Josephus (*JW* 1.648–655) describes the result of Herod's furious anger (ὑπερβολὴν ὀργῆς): the two religious teachers who called for the action and the 40 young men who perpetuated the deed were burned to death; others were simply "turned over to his executioners."

In light of these accounts, Matthew's portrayal of Herod as a king who is concerned about a child whom others claim as king would be credible to the gospel's audience. Matthew's characterization of Herod's ruthlessness is both typical for him and for any ruler in the Roman imperial system: he must view any claimant as a potential source of instability and insurrection, and deal with such people swiftly and harshly so as to maintain his power and position, as well as the stability of the imperial system as a whole.

Matthew's scene exposes Herod's strategies in securing his own position in the imperial system. After learning about the birth of a rival king, Herod's first action is to call upon his allies for support, advice, and counsel. Matthew characterizes Herod and "all Jerusalem with him" as filled with fear at the Magi's news (2:3); but, working together, Herod musters leaders of the people—chief priests and scribes—to help him maintain the stability of the kingdom (2:4).[34] Beyond Matthew's brief portrayal, the historical Herod had an extensive network of relationships with the chief priests and scribes in his kingdom. Peter Richardson points out how closely linked the ruling priests were to Herod, who had replaced the Hasmonean high priestly families with those of his own choosing: "he created his own ruling elite . . . members of his extended family took on that role; it appears that there were transfers in land ownership and social dislocation that were likely the result of shifts in wealth and power... In short, a transformation of the upper layers of society was underway."[35] These elite leaders were more than simple functionaries of the administration; they comprised a retainer class that was invested in maintaining the imperial system and their own self-benefitting position within it.[36]

Thus, although Matthew's audience (living, perhaps, in Antioch rather than Jerusalem and after the destruction of the Temple) would not have been directly impacted by the actions of Herod's Temple leaders, Matthew's portrayal would likely reflect their own experiences in which elite members of society collaborated and conspired to maintain their positions and power. Matthew's characterization of priests and scribes working alongside the king would not be surprising—nor would their informing the king about scriptural traditions regarding a ruler (ἡγούμενος) who will come from Bethlehem (according to Micah 5:2), nor would the king's use of such information against such a potential threat.[37]

Matthew next depicts Herod, armed with new information, seeking to ensnare the Magi in his intrigues and machinations. Matthew 2:7 describes how the king "secretly called" (λάθρᾳ καλέσας) the astrologers together to learn more about the child's birth: "the exact time when the star had appeared" reveals the birth date—a fact that will soon involve the residents of Bethlehem in a dreadful way. As with dependence on Roman military forces, Matthew's portrayal of Herod's secret gathering of information and back room plotting for the purposes of control would be a widely known practice and typical behavior for rulers in the Roman Empire.

In the later Empire, Roman emperors and governors employed a special category of soldier called *frumentarii*, who served as collectors of information, spies, and informants among local populations.[38] This practice was not new, however, predating the second century (although organized differently),[39] and it was also used by at least one of Rome's client kings. Josephus (*Ant*. 15.366–69 [Marcus and Wikgren, LCL]) reports on Herod's practices of ensuring loyalty and compliance with his reign:

[The people] were always being provoked and disturbed. Herod, however, gave the most careful attention to this situation, taking away any opportunities they might have (for agitation) and instructing them to apply themselves at all times to their work. No meeting of citizens was permitted, nor were walking together or being together permitted, and all their movements were observed. Those who were caught were punished severely, and many were taken, either openly or secretly, to the fortress of Hyrcania and there put to death. Both in the city and on the open roads there were men who spied upon those who met together. And they say that even Herod himself did not neglect to play a part in this, but would often put on the dress of a private citizen and mingle with the crowds by night, and so get an idea of how they felt about his rule. Those who obstinately refused to go along with his (new) practices he persecuted in all kinds of ways. As for the rest of the populace, he demanded that they submit to taking an oath of loyalty, and he compelled them to make a sworn declaration that they would maintain a friendly attitude to his rule. Now most of the people yielded to his demand out of complaisance or fear, but those who showed some spirit and objected to compulsion he got rid of by every possible means.[40]

Josephus (*JW* 1.526) reports elsewhere that on one occasion, after learning of a plot by his sons against him, "the king . . . burst into ungovernable fury [εἰς ἀνήκεστον ὀργὴν ἐξαγριοῦται]," and had two soldiers implicated in the plot tortured for information.[41] On another occasion, Herod learned of a plot against him, and had the slaves of the accused tortured to find out the truth (Josephus, *JW* 1.586). Again, it is not necessary that Matthew's audience knows the details of Herod's reign. Yet with cultural knowledge of the ways of rulers and their own experiences of living under Roman rule, Matthew's audience would understand the depiction of the Magi's initial compliance with Herod's request to be both prudent and expected.

Matthew first shows the Magi acting carefully in order to negotiate an audience with a potentially dangerous ruler, who is both conspiratorial and ruthless in the application of power to maintain his administration; this situation would be familiar to anyone living in the imperial environment. Later, however, Matthew's narrative offers a surprise, when the Magi—warned in a dream by God—momentarily subvert Herod's plans by returning home on another road (2:12). Although the Magi at first agree to comply with Herod's duplicitous intentions (2:8), the divinely sent dream enables them to realize it would be wise not to trust the king. Thus, after finding the child Jesus and acknowledging him as king of the Jews, kneeling in deference and worship (προσκυνέω), and giving gifts of gold, frankincense, and myrrh (2:11),[42] they do not return to Herod. Leaving by another road, they successfully "trick" (2:16) the king and subvert the threat of his power while participating in God's purposes to send "a ruler who is to shepherd my people Israel" (Matt 2:6). These acts (outward compliance, openness to divine guidance, worship of Jesus), then, serve as ways in which Matthew's audience may also participate in God's purposes to resist and subvert imperial power.

Joseph and Mary

Along with the Magi, the Matthean narrative portrays Joseph and Mary as able to negotiate the threat created by Herod's command of violence, and thus save Jesus—for the time being—from suffering at the hands of Roman-aligned military power. The means by which this negotiation occurs is a divine messenger, sent to Joseph in a dream, who warns of Herod's plan: "Herod is about to search for the child, to destroy him" (2:13).[43] This phrase represents another instance in Matthew 2:1–23 in which the gospel writer emphasizes the threat that Herod represents to God's King, and the opposition that he (and others) embodies to the intentions of God. Following the dream warning, Joseph and Mary take Jesus and leave Bethlehem immediately. Jesus has avoided imperial violence, but its lurking threat—and the need to negotiate it—will be present throughout the gospel narrative.

In comparison to Joseph and the Magi's actions, Matthew's portrayal of Mary's agency in these events is minimal, especially when read in comparison to other female characters such as Herodias and her daughter (Matt 14:1–12), who will be discussed in subsequent chapters. In dealing with the threat of Herod, Mary's singular role is that of Jesus's mother. On the first occasion in which she is mentioned (2:11), Matthew identifies her with the phrase "the child with Mary his mother" (τὸ παιδίον μετὰ Μαρίας τῆς μητρὸς αὐτοῦ); the three subsequent occasions (2:14, 20, 21) are similar: "the child and his mother" (τὸ παιδίον καὶ τὴν μητέρα αὐτοῦ). In all cases, the male characters around Mary are active, making decisions, and finding ways to negotiate Herod's power. Mary, in contrast, is passive—present in the very conventional role of being the mother of an infant king but nothing more. Thus Elaine Wainwright is correct in observing that: "the Matthean rereading [of Exodus] situates the birth of the liberator, Jesus, completely in the context of male power struggles."[44] In contrast to her portrayal in Luke as a faithful servant of God,[45] Matthew's Mary has no response when the Magi arrive "at the house" to give gifts and bow before Jesus in homage (2:11), or when accompanying Joseph to Egypt and back (2:14, 21). The trivialization and lack of agency in Mary's role at this point in the narrative is underscored by the angel's divine guidance to Joseph about "the child and his [nameless] mother" (2:20); even God, in Matthew's view, treats Mary as an accessory to acts of resistance when negotiating imperial power. In this scene she will accompany Joseph and care for her child (which is not unimportant), but little else.[46]

As noted above, the family's flight to Egypt evokes connections between the lives of Jesus and Moses. Like Pharaoh in Exodus 1–2, Herod is a king who issues a royal decree to oppress the innocent by state-sanctioned murder carried out by military forces under his command. Like Moses, the child Jesus is saved from death by those who work covertly to thwart the king,[47] and by family members who act in the face of danger to preserve his life. As will be shown below, there is a connection between the Hebrew people, whose sons are killed by Pharaoh's soldiers, and the residents of Bethlehem, whose identity as righteous sufferers has scriptural antecedents.⁴⁸ The parallels between Jesus and Moses may go far in explaining the framework and certain narrative features of the gospel narrative. Yet at the same time the episode reveals a number of ways in which Jesus—like all those who live within the Roman imperial system—is exposed to the dangers posed by the abuse of military power.

It is important to note that Mary and Joseph's flight from Bethlehem with Jesus would not take them outside the sphere of Roman military influence. Prior to the beginning of Herod's reign and throughout the New Testament period, Egypt was a Roman province, with legions and auxiliary forces stationed throughout the territory.⁴⁹ There were forts at key locations, including Pelusium in the eastern delta, which guarded the road and the border where any travelers from Judaea would likely enter.⁵⁰ Like other border crossings in the Empire such as Zeugma or Dura Europos in Syria, Matthew's audience would understand that anyone like Mary and Joseph who traveled to and within Roman Egypt would have encountered soldiers guarding roads and towns, and collecting tolls. Those passing through Koptos in southern Egypt, for example, included sailors, guards, traders (some with camels), soldiers' women (γυναικῶν στρατιωτῶν), and prostitutes (γυναικῶν πρὸς ἑταιριςμ ὸν).⁵¹ These tolls were assessed at varying rates, depending on a traveler's profession.⁵² Matthew's audience would also picture a variety of people on the roads and stopping at such Roman toll stations. In this situation, Joseph and Mary would be understood to have blended in with other travelers, crossing the border in anonymity. Matthew gives no indication that Herod knows they have escaped, and so Jesus remains safely in Egypt "until the death of Herod" (2:15, 19), after which time the family returns. By a combination of divine intervention and human agency, they have successfully avoided the threat of Herod and his soldiers. Sadly, the same cannot be said of the children in Bethlehem.

The Children of Bethlehem

The children "living in and around Bethlehem" (Matt 2:16), and under two years of age, are guilty of nothing more than being born in the wrong place at the wrong time. They are innocent and vulnerable; their parents, unaware of Herod's plot and orders, are unprepared and unable to avoid or flee the soldiers sent by the king. Many commentators have focused on the question of historical evidence for or against the killing of these boys, but this is not the focus here.⁵³ Instead, as with the other characters in Matthew's scene, the focus is on the ways by which the atrocity of the children's deaths highlights and reveals the systems of the imperially sanctioned, military violence the gospel is negotiating. The children's inability to escape would resonate with the experiences of Matthew's readers, who had experience (either personal or in collective memory) of the killing and trauma of the recent Jewish-Roman War; the siege of Jerusalem and destruction of the city and Temple; anti-Jewish sentiment in Antioch following the war; and general experiences of threat and casual violence from soldiers at work in Syria.[54] Because of these experiences, the deaths of the children of Bethlehem would evoke great pathos among Matthew's audience, highlighting their own experiences as suffering people and their own hopes for deliverance. Matthew underscores this situation with a quotation from Jeremiah 31:15, taken from a passage that describes the experiences of the Jewish people following the Babylonian destruction of Jerusalem and Exile, including a divine promise of restoration. Thus, as powerful as Herod and his military are, the text's evocation of Babylonian power indicates that imperial power is not permanent but is subject to God's purposes and power.

Ways to Survive Roman Imperial Power

Each of the characters in Matthew 2:1–23 illustrates difference facets of the gospel writer's negotiation of Roman military power. Herod, as Rome's client king, is fully invested in the perpetuation of Empire; he uses the soldiers under his command for this purpose, ordering them to extinguish and exterminate all possible threats to his rule and the Roman order. The elite chief priests and scribes, who share in Herod's rule of Judaea,[55] are not directly involved in military operations—but support Herod's regime as allied leaders and benefit from his Roman-backed rule in a variety of ways. Although they have knowledge of scripture, this does not mean they are in alignment with Matthew's claims about God's purposes: none goes in search of Jesus, to find or worship him. The difference between the elite chief priests and scribes and Jesus becomes increasingly clear throughout the gospel narrative.[56] The Magi, perhaps naïvely, stumble into Herod's machinations and secret gathering of information; with God's help, however, they are able to express a hidden transcript of resistance, worshipping the infant king and subverting Herod's plan to kill him. In the end, the Magi "from the east" return home safely—beyond the reach of Herod and Roman military power. Joseph and Mary, again with God's intervention, are able to sidestep Herod's plot and avoid immediate trouble by fleeing. They remain within the networks of Roman power, however, which is fitting insofar as it is within the Empire that Jesus will undertake his work to reveal the Empire of God. Sadly, the children of Bethlehem are not able to avoid the atrocities of violence; they and their families suffer greatly at the hands of Herod's soldiers. In this they mirror something of the experiences of Matthew's community and audience, residents of the empire living in the aftermath of the Jewish-Roman War, the destruction of Jerusalem, and the hostile sentiment that lingered in Antioch and elsewhere in the years that followed.

THE DANGER FROM ANTIPAS (MATT 14:1–12)

The Risk of Challenging Imperial Agents

A second scene that portrays the necessity of negotiating imperial military violence is found halfway through the gospel, at Matthew 14:1–12. This account, presented as a flashback that stands out as an interruption of the narrative flow, and anticipated by the brief and unelaborated reference to John the Baptist's arrest at 4:12, tells of John's execution in prison by the soldiers of Herod Antipas.[57] The scene is directly related to Matthew 2:1–23 insofar as it involves another ruler who carries out an act of violence against God's purposes and people.[58] Matthew 14:1–12 highlights the role and responsibility of Ἡρῴδης ὁ τετραάρχης ("Herod the tetrarch," 14:1) for John's death.[59] So as not to confuse Herod Antipas with his father, I will identify him as Antipas hereafter for the sake of clarity. After his father's death in 4 BCE, Antipas ruled a portion of his father's kingdom; like his father, Antipas was also an imperial client, backed by Roman military power and willing to use it to maintain control and dominance over his subjects.[60] Matthew's scene also depicts several other characters, all of whom must negotiate state sanctioned violence that Antipas threatens and then orders his soldiers to carry out in order to silence John the Baptist and his followers.

In language that foreshadows plotting against Jesus by the chief priests and elite leaders in Jerusalem (26:3–4; 26:59), Matthew recounts that Antipas "wanted to put John to death," but did not want to risk angering his subjects, who "regarded him [John] as a prophet" (14:5).[61] After arresting John (Matt 4:12) and keeping him in prison for some amount of time (11:2–6), Antipas finds a way to fulfill his desire. At his own birthday celebration Antipas makes a public vow to give his stepdaughter a gift—whatever she might wish—and she, after consulting with her mother, asks for John's head.[62] As in the earlier episode in Jerusalem (2:16), Antipas does not carry out the execution himself. Instead, like his father Herod against the children of Bethlehem, Antipas "sent and had John beheaded" (πέμψας ἀπεκεφάλισεν, 14:10). Matthew again does not state explicitly, but readers can easily infer that Antipas's soldiers carry out the killing.[63] As in 2:16–18 where innocent children are murdered, here the righteous prophet John is executed by order of the ruler—while Jesus again withdraws to a safe place (14:13) before continuing his work of proclaiming and revealing the Kingdom (Empire) of God.[64]

Negotiating Antipas' Power and Threat of Violence

The Royal Family: Antipas, Herodias, and her Daughter

Matthew 14:1–12 presents a scene in which Antipas and his royal court gather for a palace banquet during which the fate of a popular prophetic figure is decided—not based on God's justice, but on palace intrigues and elite considerations of status, oaths, and honor. Matthew's portrayal of Antipas is one of a ruler who is negotiating a variety of considerations in the process of making his decision to condemn John to death; Antipas's actions reveal his willingness to use military violence to maintain his position within the imperial system, thus upholding and perpetuating the Empire. Matthew's scene also shows the dangers for those who—like John, Jesus, their disciples, and the crowd who follow them—must find ways to negotiate the dangers of military power deployed to pacify and control the citizens of a territory.

Matthew's scene begins with Antipas hearing "reports about Jesus" (14:1), whom he associates with John the Baptist, who "has been raised from the dead" (14:2). The gospel writer's initial characterization of Antipas creates parallels to the earlier scene in Matt 2:1–3, where Herod hears from the Magi about a king announced by divine portents (the star). Just as Herod calls his chief priests and scribes to ask about the Messiah (2:4), Antipas talks to his "servants" about what the news of Jesus's work could mean for them. The exact status of these servants is not specified, insofar as Matthew uses the word παῖς (which contains the semantic range of child, slave, servant, personal attendant, or courtier); they are nonetheless Antipas's people, hearing personal and confidential discussions of the ruler, and serving as a sounding board for his plotting.[65] While Antipas's statement to his servants about Jesus does not rise to the level of Herod's "fear" (2:3), his concern to maintain order is clear, and leads directly to his subsequent decision to execute John. Like his father and the leaders of Jerusalem, Antipas also resists and refuses to acknowledge God's sovereignty—choosing instead to kill the prophet who sought to correct him according to Biblical commandments (14:4).[66] Antipas's concern about Jesus is also noteworthy because it connects the story to later events in the narrative. Just as Herod and the chief priests and scribes ascertain where the Messiah will be born, Antipas correctly and ironically identifies the "powers at work" in Jesus (14:2): ἠγέρθη ("he has been raised") is an aorist indicative passive third person singular verb that is also used to describe God's act in relation to Jesus in Matthew 27:64 and 28:6–7. Like John, Jesus will be killed by imperially sanctioned violence; however, with ironic foreshadowing, here it is Antipas rather than God's angel (28:6–7) who points toward Jesus's resurrection.[67] Through attitude, outlook, and actions, then, Matthew characterizes Antipas in a similar way as Herod.

Readers are to associate the two rulers—father and son—and this is all the more compelling considering how Matthew identifies both as "Herod."

The second element of Matthew's characterization of Antipas reveals more clearly the ways in which his familial and social connections are expressions of imperial negotiation. In 14:3, 6–8 readers learn of Herodias, who is married to Antipas, but who was formerly married to his brother Philip; Herodias has an unnamed daughter, who is the step-daughter of Antipas.[68] These three members of the royal family are the main actors in the decision to execute John, who Matthew says was opposed to the marriage based on Levitical law (Lev 18:16; 20:21), and had been rebuking Antipas because of it. Commentators are divided as to who among the royal family is ultimately responsible for John's death, noting differences between Mark, who portrays Herodias's agency and motivation (Mark 6:17: she has a "grudge" against John) in relation to that of Antipas, and Matthew, who eliminates her role to focus narrative attention on Antipas.[69] So Corley observes that "In Matthew, it is Herod [Antipas] who resents John's objection . . . and wants John dead . . . the women, now present for the meal, are exonerated in the process."[70] It should be noted that not all interpreters agree that Mark holds Herodias responsible. Glancy, for example, argues that Mark holds Antipas responsible:

> At whose volition does the girl dance? Mark offers no clue; he says simply that she entered and danced. Is this her initiative? Her mother's? Mark does not suggest that either female initiated the action, nor that they anticipated Herod's extravagant promise . . . What makes best sense of the narrative, and what would be most plausible to a first century reader? What effect will it have on our interpretation if we posit that Herod [Antipas] invited the girl to dance? A man who has already married a woman who is both his niece and his sister-in-law may well ogle that woman's daughter.... Herod [Antipas] the king, not Herodias, not the child, retains power in the scene.[71]

Regardless of which contention about responsibility one favors, it is safe to say that (for various reasons and in various ways) all members of the royal family use the prerogatives of their imperial power to contribute to John's death. When read in the context of imperial networks, Antipas, Herodias, and her daughter all make use of their ability to break social norms, to act with little regard for the citizenry, and to wield the power of life and death in pursuit of their goals as members of the ruling family. Not only do Antipas and Herodias marry against social convention and biblical tradition (Matt 14:4), but, according to one centuries-old vein of interpretation, Herodias' daughter transgresses social and sexual norms by dancing scandalously and seductively "in the midst" (ἐν τῷ μέσῳ) of the party guests (14:6).[72]

More recently, feminist scholars have criticized one aspect of interpretations that elaborate on the nature of the daughter's dance, noting that a focus on sexual transgression is only one possible rendering of the text. Matthew 14:6 states that "she danced" (ὠρχήσατο) and that Antipas "was pleased" (ἤρεσεν)—which may imply sexual arousal (Esth 2:4, 9 LXX), but also simple happiness or satisfaction (cf. Rom 15:1–3; Gal 1:10).[73] Further, Florence Morgan Gillman notes that the κοράσιον (a diminutive form of κορέ) in Matthew 14:11 (based on Mark 6:22, 28) is not a "little girl," but may refer to a "young girl at or near marriageable age" perhaps around 12 years old—and also "denotes the pupil of an eye or the 'apple' of an eye."[74] These options provide a field for discussion about Antipas's motivation: is he a "proud parent" or drunkenly incestuous? Gillman also points to Janice Capel Anderson's discussion of gender in relation to interpretation of the scene, which is worth quoting from its source:

> How does one understand the girl and her dance? How does one understand Herod and his guests' pleasure? The guests named are all elite males. Do we have a king and his guests charmed by the innocent dance of his young daughter, the apple of his eye, or do we have a king and his guests aroused—incestuously in the king's case—and hypnotized by an erotic dance, a young nubile body offering an apple like Eve? Readers have answered the questions in both ways. The daughter and her dance are not described. They are mirrors in which Herod [Antipas], Herodias, and interpreters are reflected.[75]

Despite this critique of interpretations that exaggerate the supposedly scandalous and sexually transgressive nature of the daughter's role and Antipas and his guests' response to it, Gillman maintains that Herodias is able to act with "brutal malevolence" and "as a perpetrator of evil," with her daughter "as a willing accomplice."[76] Matthew's Herodias, Gillman argues, takes the role of a "political wife-interventionist" who seeks to influence the outcome of public events.[77] In contrast to Pilate's wife, who seeks to free Jesus (Matt 27:19), Herodias, with the assistance of her daughter, intervenes in such a way as to cause the death of John.[78] Gillman and others' argument about the ability of some elite women in patriarchal societies to exercise a degree of autonomy and wield power in ways traditionally reserved for men highlights an important aspect of Matthew's scene and should not be ignored. As wife and step-daughter of the ruler, Herodias and her daughter have a position of privilege from which they can influence the outcome of events for their own benefit and that of the royal family. Although they may be constrained by the gender roles of imperial society, they use their proximity to Antipas to negotiate this system in such a way that their own interests, and the interests of Antipas, are maintained—by silencing a critic of their family and its prerogatives.

Thus, although Antipas initially "feared the crowd" (14:5) he ultimately finds a way—with the assistance of his wife and step-daughter—to accomplish the family's desire: the death of John the Baptist, which was intended to ensure the stability and security of his rule. As much as Herodias prompts her daughter to ask for John's head (14:8), it is Antipas who has John arrested (14:3), who wants to put him to death (14:5), who "orders" (κελεύω) John's execution (14:9), and who sends soldiers to accomplish the beheading (14:10).

Antipas's Retainers and Patrons

In addition to his wife and stepdaughter, Antipas is connected with other members of elite Judaean society whom he invites to attend his birthday celebration (14:6, 10). It is these select persons whom Antipas, according to Matthew, cannot disappoint after he makes an extravagant public oath to his step-daughter (14:7). These guests represent members of the ruling class and retainers as in Lenski's model and must be considered as more than mere functionaries.[79] Due to their position and influence in society, it is worth Antipas's time and effort to cultivate a positive relationship with his guests by inviting them to his birthday feast. It is also true that the party guests have already gained status and honor from their association with the tetrarch—and attendance at such a party reinforces the mutual interdependence between Antipas and his guests. Thus, just as with Herod and the chief priests and scribes of Jerusalem, proximity to the ruler serves to uphold and maintain the imperial system. While it may be true that the three members of the royal family are using Antipas's oath in the presence of his guests as a convenient public transcript to mask their plotting, it is also true that the guests are complicit in their ruler's scheme.[80] They do not object to Antipas's oath or order to send for John's head; they do not remind him that he, as a sanctioned Roman ruler, cannot dispose of his kingdom; they do not (unlike Joseph of Arimathea who appeals to Pilate for Jesus's body) even assist John's disciples with his burial.[81] Matthew implies that Antipas will use his guests' witness to the oath to give himself cover for what he knows will be an unpopular decision, and he is counting on their description of the event to counteract, absorb, and dissipate the anticipated anger among the general population for whom the death of a popular prophetic leader will cause unrest and outrage.

Another aspect of the imperial network revealed by the relationship between Antipas and his guests is the tetrarch's own relationship with Roman authorities. While it is true that the party guests are bound to their ruler and support his regime directly, they also participate in the Roman imperial system through Antipas's status as a Roman client. Just as his father Herod before him, Antipas was a ruler who depended on Roman patronage, which granted him power, position, and influence—including the authority to imprison John and command soldiers to kill him there.[82]

Antipas's status, like that of his father or any Roman client ruler, was not guaranteed but required constant attention and the ability to negotiate well—for the sake of maintaining his own position, that of his supporters, and the stability of the territory he ruled. Antipas came to power after his father Herod's death in 4 BCE when the emperor Augustus read and approved the king's will, dividing the kingdom of Judaea into several parts, and appointing Herod's sons as rulers.[83] Antipas and his brother Phillip were each declared tetrarch ("ruler of one-fourth") of territories belonging to their father, with Antipas appointed to rule over Galilee and Peraea, lands that yielded "revenue of two hundred talents" annually.[84] Their brother Archelaus was declared ethnarch ("ruler of a people") over a larger portion—almost half their father's kingdom—and ruled from Jerusalem, as noted in Matthew 2:22.[85] In 6 CE, Archelaus was deposed by Augustus and sent into exile for excessive cruelty; Judaea became a province under the direct rule of Roman governors.[86] Antipas, however, remained in good standing with Augustus, and continued to rule his own territory. When Augustus died and Tiberius came to power in Rome in 14 CE, Antipas was successful in securing continued Roman patronage; he continued to reign until the death of Tiberius in 37 CE.[87] At this time Antipas was deposed due to plotting and intrigue by his nephew Agrippa, son of Aristobulus, who had been nurturing a client-patron relationship with the new emperor Gaius (Caligula) for many years.[88] While the gospel's audience need not know all the details of Antipas's situation, they would understand his alignment with and location in the imperial system. Thus, the maintenance of a successful relationship with Roman emperors was important not only for client rulers such as Antipas, but also for their clients and retainers—and for the people of their territories, whose lives and livelihoods were subject to rulers who sought to rule vigorously and were encouraged to put down any perceived unrest, rebellion, or revolt with ruthless force—including the execution of a popular prophetic figure who dared to criticize his ruler's family.

John and Jesus

Besides Antipas and other elite members of Judaean society who are the focus of much of Matthew 14:1–12, there are others who must negotiate the tetrarch's use of state sanctioned violence. These include John, who as a prisoner has few options and must bear the cost of the ruler's death sentence; John's disciples, who have some freedom of movement to visit him, retrieve and bury his body, and report to Jesus; and the crowd who had followed John, who were now (in Antipas's mind) devoted to Jesus—and the cause for some concern. In Matthew 14:2 the tetrarch equates John and Jesus—yet he does not act against Jesus; like the infants in Bethlehem (2:16), John cannot escape the power of state sanctioned violence, but Jesus—once again—escapes.

Matthew 14:3–4 (as a narrative flashback) recounts how John had been arrested and imprisoned by Antipas for confronting him about his marriage to Herodias. This confrontation was not a one-time event but an ongoing act of public resistance, as Matthew indicates with the use of ἔλεγεν, an imperfect active third person singular verb. Indications of John's provocation appear earlier in the gospel, such as at Matt 3:1–12, where John appears in the wilderness, dressed in rough clothing, and begins to preach that all must prepare for the return of the Lord. Many people respond to John's message[89]—and these are the crowd that Antipas is later concerned about, who believe John to be a prophet (14:5). Matthew elaborates his portrayal of John in 11:7–15 where Jesus speaks of John as one opposed to Antipas. In gendered language designed to insult, Jesus proclaims that John's rough, manly clothing stands in contrast to the dress of Antipas's family and party guests, "who wear soft/effeminate robes" (μαλακοῖς ἱματίοις ἠμφιεσμένον) and live in royal palaces (11:8). Jesus knows these palace-dwellers are also dangerous, however, because they command military forces and use these soldiers to suppress dissent: "from the days of John the Baptist until now the kingdom of heaven has suffered violence, and the violent take it by force" (11:12).

Matthew thus portrays both John and Jesus as preachers who are critical of the ruling powers, and whose words are attractive to the crowd that Antipas is concerned about.[90] For the non-elite people who flock to John and Jesus, their provocative words and community-oriented actions (calls for repentance, feeding, healing) comprise a hidden transcript—a counter-narrative that helps common people stand up to the powerful and cope with the stress of life in the imperial system. It is risky work, however, as the narrative strands concerning both John and Jesus bear out.

John's Disciples

Another group of people whom Matthew shows negotiating the powers of empire are the disciples of John. In 14:12, after John's death, his disciples (οἱ μαθηταὶ αὐτο) are able to retrieve his body and bury it; they then report to Jesus what has happened. Perhaps surprisingly (if readers recall the events of 2:1–18), although John has been arrested in 11:2–3 and 14:1–12, his disciples have not been rounded up by Antipas's soldiers.[91] The portrayal of their freedom of movement represents one facet of negotiation with the military power of Antipas. The actions of the disciples reveal their ability and willingness to directly interact with Antipas's soldiers in such a way that the ruler and his troops do not view them as a threat. If John was held in Machaerus, we may picture John's disciples coming and going to and from, and perhaps living in, the town overlooked by the palace-fortress.[92] These disciples would know that the tetrarch, elite city leaders, and soldiers guarding the prophet are all in varying degrees opposed to John's message and social movement. This awareness perhaps would cause nervousness and fear (and the temptation to lie about their commitments and affiliation as Peter does in Matt 26:57–58, 69–75); yet for the sake of their teacher, John's disciple would have to overcome such feelings to visit him with food and fresh supplies. To gain access, the disciples would have to adopt an attitude of respectful deference to the soldiers who are guarding him over some period of time. Finally, when informed of their teacher's death, despite their grief, the disciples would also have to also muster courage and show deference to ask for his body, so that they may offer him a proper burial.[93] Thus, of all the characters in Matthew's scene, it is the disciples of John who have the most direct contact with the military forces commanded by Antipas, and show how such interactions may be conducted successfully—even while their teacher suffers a terrible fate at the hands of these same soldiers.

The Crowds Who Support John and Jesus

The final group which must negotiate imperial power is the crowd (ὁ ὄχλος) whom Antipas considers when plotting how to execute John (14:5). The appearance of the crowd around John and Jesus has been mentioned above. Although they are offstage as the scene begins in 14:1–12 (returning in 14:13), the crowd is on Antipas's mind: they are the subjects whom he rules, with some power to cause him concern—but not enough, in the end, to keep John alive and protect him from the ruler's desire for his death. We may picture the crowds as composed of common people: non-elite, agrarian farmers and craftspeople that comprise the vast majority (over 90%) of the population. It may also include those further to the margins of society: πόρναι (female prostitutes and courtesans) who follow both John and Jesus.[94] The crowd hails from "Jerusalem and all Judea . . . and all the region along the Jordan" (Matt 3:5) and stand in need of the food and healing that Jesus provides (14:13–21, 34–36). The people of the crowd are both the audience for and supporters of John's and Jesus's message, who respond positively to their critiques of elite morals and practices. When Jesus speaks of John's arrest in Matt 11:7–15, he addresses the crowd that knows John and his message of resistance which it approves of and applauds him because his words express their own hidden transcript of dissent and resentment. When Jesus says that the kingdom of heaven is suffering because "the violent take it by force" (11:12), he is speaking not only of John's arrest, but also of the murdered children of Bethlehem, and of the experience of living under the threat of military violence.[95] These are the people to whom Matthew (4:16) applies the words of Isaiah 9:1–2: "the people who sat in darkness have seen a great light, and for those who sat in the region and shadow of death light has dawned." For this reason, although they do not appear in the foreground of the scene in 14:1–12, the crowds are an important group to remember—representing John's and Jesus's supporters, and Matthew's audience as well.

CONCLUSION

This chapter has argued that two scenes in Matthew's gospel, 2:1–23 and 14:1–12 portray facets of imperial rule and the ways in which people must negotiate its threat of violence. Some of Matthew's characters participate in the imperial system by seeking to uphold it and their own position in its networks. They are willing to plot, scheme, and ultimately command military forces to commit acts of violence on their subjects—including infants who are deemed guilty by association and a prophet who represents popular criticism of the ruler—in order to secure imperial order and their place in its networks of social power. The characters who seek to uphold the imperial system include Herod and Antipas (rulers hand-selected by the Roman emperor); Herodias and her daughter (members of the royal family); and elite retainers such as the chief priests and scribes of Jerusalem, members of the tetrarch's court, and soldiers who serve them.

Other characters represent the vast majority of people who are governed by rulers in the Roman system. The infants of Bethlehem do nothing more than exist at the "wrong" time and place—and suffer death because of it. John the Baptizer risks his own death by actively resisting imperial domination by speaking out against abuses of power by Antipas and his elite allies. The disciples of John and the crowds that follow him support his efforts because of their own ongoing suffering at the hands of imperial agents. The same is true of Jesus and those who follow him.

In these parallel scenes, Matthew's depiction of imperially sanctioned violence would have seemed familiar for all in his audience who also had to negotiate the realities of living in the Roman Empire. Matthew's message to such people is that sometimes the violence of imperial control cannot be avoided, and that some unfortunates such as the infants of Bethlehem and John will be killed by it. Such actions fuel anger and resentment against the ruling elite, provoking additional resistance. Matthew also shows that there are ways to survive and endure such dangers, sometimes with divine intervention and assistance: the Magi; Joseph, Mary, and the infant Jesus; John's disciples; and a mature Jesus during his public work are all able to employ strategies of avoidance that deflect the attention of Roman-aligned military power.

These are a few of several ways in which Matthew's characters negotiate the Roman Empire's military power in the gospel narrative. Others will be addressed in the following chapters; we turn next to Jesus's practical advice for those who encounter Roman soldiers on the road.

NOTES

1. Thackeray, LCL.

2. In contrast to information that *is* provided by Judas to the chief priests, which leads to Jesus' death (Matt 26:14–16, 47–50).

3. See "ταράσσω," Henry Liddell and George Scott, *A Greek-English Lexicon*, 9th ed. (New York: Oxford University Press, 1968), 1757–1758: "2. *trouble* the mind, *agitate, disturb*.... 3. of an army, etc. *throw into disorder*, Hdt. [Herodotus] 4.125, 9.51 ... 5. Freq. of political agitation ... Pass., *to be in a state of disorder or anarchy*. Th[ucydides] 2.85 ... D[emosthenes] 2.14."

4. Ulrich Luz, *Matthew 1–7*, Hermeneia (Minneapolis, MN: Fortress Press, 2007), 113, notes another dimension of Matthew's portrayal: "Everyone who was at all familiar with the historical situation must have been surprised at the Matthean sketch: apart from the members of the ruling class who were supporters of the king, Herod was so unpopular with the people of Jerusalem that news of the birth of a royal child—or especially a messianic child—would have caused great rejoicing. Matthew is not concerned about such things." Luz, like many others, is concerned with the question of historical probability, and seeks to compare Matthew with Mark and Josephus to determine his reliability.

5. Cyprian, *Epistles* 55.6, writing in the 3rd century, is the first to call the children "the innocent."

6. cf. Jeremiah 32:1–5.

7. Daniel Harrington, *The Gospel of Matthew,* Sacra Pagina (Collegeville, MN: The Liturgical Press, 1991), 46–50.

8. A discussion on the question of theodicy raised by Matthew's construction of this scene might also center on the ways in which Matthew has already identified Jesus: Messiah (1:1, 18; 2:4–5), Emmanuel (1:24), and King (2:2) who will shepherd the people (2:6)—and the implications of this when compared with the use of violence by Roman and Roman-allied rulers such as Herod, Herod Antipas, Pilate, and their soldiers.

9. Raymond Brown, *The Birth of the Messiah: A Commentary on the Infancy Narratives in the Gospels of Matthew and* Luke (New York: Doubleday, 1999), 29ff.

10. W.D. Davies and Dale Allison, *The Gospel According to Saint Matthew*, 3 vols. (Edinburgh, UK: T&T Clark, 1988), 1:227.

11. Graham Stanton, *A Gospel for a New People* (Louisville, KY: Westminster/John Knox, 1993), 184–185.

12. Stanton, *Gospel for a New People*, 182.

13. For instance, Craig Keener, *A Commentary on the Gospel of Matthew* (Grand Rapids, MI: Eerdmans, 1999), 102, who acknowledges that "Herod ... was widely known to have achieved rule by warfare and politics, not by birth" and, because he "had rewarded prophets who appeared to validate his reign ... one can understand

just what sort of threat the Magi's announcement represented to him." On Matt 2:1–23, Keener, 111, wonders about likelihood when imagining a scene in which "Herod could even have personally dispatched soldiers from his fortress-palace called the Herodium (on which see Jos. *JW* 1.419–420) . . . this fortress was four miles southeast of Bethlehem and visible from there. The event is thus neither historically documented nor historically implausible." At the same time, Keener, 110, stops short of a full discussion of Herod's place in and connections to imperial networks, preferring to characterize Herod's actions as "paranoid brutality" in line with descriptions found in Josephus of political assassinations of family members carried out under Herod's orders (*JW* 1.437, 550–551, 1.664–665; *Ant.* 16.394; 17.187). Keener, 103, 107, is correct to note Matthew's literary intention to connect Jesus to the story of Moses in Exodus 2, but in arguing that Matthew seeks to address the "spiritual complacency" of Jewish leaders when faced with the birth of Jesus the Messiah, neglects ways in which other characters negotiate Herod's use of violence to maintain power. Harrington, *Gospel of Matthew*, 46–50, takes a similar approach as Keener.

14. Luz, *Matthew 1-7*, 108.

15. Luz, *Matthew 1-7*, 108–109, and 108. n.56, which refers to Origen, frag. 29 (GCS Origines 12.27) and Augustine, *Sermons*, 200.1 and 202.1.

16. Stanton, *Gospel for a New People*, 202. Stanton, 201–203, connects the flight from danger (ἀναχωρέω) in Matt 2:12, 13, 14, and 22 (as well as 4:12; 14:13; 15:21) to persecution in an eschatological context of Matt. 10:17–18 and 24:15–20.

17. Davies and Allison, *Matthew*, 1:229–230. Saldarini, *Christian-Jewish Community*, 65, whose focus is on the boundaries and identity of the Matthean community, also describes the antagonism of Herod and his sons towards Jesus and his followers. He does not, however, address Matthew 2:1–18 directly: "Herod (2:1ff) and his son Archelaus (2:22) are hostile to Jesus. In the passion narrative, the chief priests, scribes, and elders oversee Jesus' arrest and execution (26:14–15, 47–69; 27:1–10), turn the people against him (27:20–25), mock him themselves (27:41–43), secure a guard for the tomb (27:62–66), and begin a rumor that the resurrection is a hoax (28:11–15). John the Baptist attacks the Pharisees and Sadducees, who are presumably from Jerusalem (3:5), and tells them to repent (3:7–10)."

18. J. Andrew Overman, *Church and Community in Crisis: The Gospel According to Matthew* (Valley Forge, PA: Trinity Press International, 1996), 40–41.

19. Overman, *Church and Community in Crisis*, 46–47.

20. Warren Carter, *Matthew and Empire: Initial Explorations* (Valley Forge, PA: Trinity Press International, 2001), 35.

21. Warren Carter, *Matthew and the Margins: A Sociopolitical and Religious Reading* (Maryknoll, NY: Orbis Books, 2000), 82.

22. Adam Kolman Marshak, *The Many Faces of Herod the Great* (Grand Rapids, MI: Eerdmans, 2015), in a recent account of Herod's life, does not address the scene in Matt 2:1–23, thereby indicating a judgment that the scene is not historical, but provides a treatment of Herod's rise and rule that emphasizes the king's skill at securing Roman patronage—first through Marcus Antonius, and later through the emperor Augustus.

23. The verbs ταράσσω and φοβέω are used throughout Matthew to indicate the response of characters to competing claims of power and authority between Jesus, the agent of God's Empire, and that of Rome. For further discussion, see Chapter 6.

24. Josephus, *JW* 1.283–285, cited at the beginning of this chapter.

25. Josephus, *JW* 1.290–294, 301–302, 346.

26. Josephus, *JW* 1.387–390 describes how Herod appeared before Octavius (Augustus); as a friend of Antony, Herod's position was tenuous following the battle Actium: "The king ... went to Rhodes, where Caesar was sojourning, presented himself without a diadem, a commoner in dress and demeanor, but with the proud spirit of a king. His speech was direct ... 'Caesar,' he said, 'I was made king by Antony, and I acknowledge that I have in all things devoted my services to him ... I am come to you resting my hope of safety upon my integrity, and presuming that the subject of inquiry will be not whose friend, but how loyal a friend I have been.'"

27. Josephus, *JW* 2.111 (Thackeray, LCL): "Archelaus ... treated not only the Jews but even the Samaritans with great brutality. Both parties sent deputations to Caesar to denounce him, and in the ninth year of his rule he was banished to Vienna, a town in Gaul, and his property confiscated to the imperial treasury." The result of Archelaus' removal was the creation of the Roman province of Judaea, governed by a procurator appointed by the emperor, "with full powers, including the infliction of capital punishment" (*JW* 2.117). Josephus (*JW* 2.212) also tells of a dream which Archelaus calls upon Chaldeans (akin to Magi) to interpret: like Pharaoh's dream of cows and grain in Genesis 41, Archelaus will fall upon hard times.

28. Josephus, *JW* 7.219–243. See also Tacitus, *Ann.* 14.31ff, where shameful Roman treatment of the Iceni royal family following the death of the client king Prasutagas in 60/61 CE was coupled with the removal of lands and status from Iceni nobles. These actions provoked a widespread revolt across Britannia, led by the widowed queen Boudicca, which resulted in thousands of deaths among the Romans at Londinium, the new veteran settlement at Camulodunum, and elsewhere (*Ann.* 14.31–33), and the eventual defeat and destruction of Iceni armed forces, followed by a famine throughout the province (*Ann.* 14.34–38).

29. Josephus, *JW* 2.14, 20–25, 93–100 notes how the sons of Herod were ratified as rulers only after approval by the emperor Augustus: a lengthy series of hearings were held to determine how the inheritance of the kingdom would be divided.

30. See also Josephus, *Ant.* 16.395; 17.187.

31. Richard Horsley, *The Liberation of Christmas: The Infancy Narratives in Social Context* (Eugene, OR: Wipf and Stock, 2006), 40, 44, argues that the Jewish people suffered under Herod's rule because of the ways in which he exercised and maintained his power; after providing a cogent summary of Herod's rise to power ("king by the grace of Rome, ... he conquered the Jews with the help of Roman legions"), he rightly points to the economic burden that Herod's rule placed upon the common people: "Herod's extraordinary expenditures for the massive building projects, the homages to Caesar, and the many impressive benefactions for foreign cities and imperial figures placed a heavy burden on the Jewish peasantry. But they also compounded what were already inordinately large demands for tithes, tribute, and taxes.... [to support] court, army, multiple palaces, impregnable fortresses,

building projects in Jerusalem such as the Temple . . . Herod was in fact bleeding his country and people to death." This situation continued well after the time of Herod —into Matthew's own time, in which the economic burdens of living under Roman rule were borne heavily by those in Syria during the late first century CE. Leaning on Josephus (*Ant.* 15.242, 291, 332–325, 366–369; *JW* 1.265, 419–421), Horsley, *Christmas* 46–47, goes on to describe the regime that Herod created as a "police state, complete with loyalty oaths, surveillance, informers, secret police, imprisonment, torture, and brutal retaliation against any serious dissent." He notes, *Christmas* 46, that "many treatments of Herod's tyranny focus on his utterly paranoid behavior, particularly his treatment of his sons, toward the end of his long reign.... Focusing on such enormities arising from his increasingly ugly mood toward the end of his life, however, should not be allowed to divert attention from the intensely repressive and brutal regime he instituted from the outset." Herod's reign was thus marked by practices of repression, occasions of popular resistance, repression, and reprisals – what Horsley, *Christmas* 48, calls a "spiral of resistance" that often took on language of messianic expectation among groups who would "acclaim one of their number as 'king' [who would embody the struggle to] reclaim their liberty." Horsley, *Christmas*, 49, concludes that it is this environment of "Herodian exploitation and tyranny" which Matthew evokes when writing the scene of 2:1–23.

32. Matthew indicates to his audience that worship (προσκυνέω) is the appropriate response to Jesus; see also 2:11 (the Magi present gifts to Jesus in Bethlehem); 14:33 (disciples in a boat); and 28:9, 17 (women and other disciples who meet the resurrected Jesus).

33. In Matt 26:55; 27:38, 44 Jesus is also associated with λῃστής (banditry, insurrectionism).

34. At the end of the Gospel, Matthew shows these leaders taking their own initiative to deal with the perceived threat of Jesus: they accuse him of being a false Messiah and take him to Pilate the Roman governor, who executes him as a pretender "king of the Jews" (26:3–5, 57–68; 27:11–14, 37–43).

35. Peter Richardson, *Herod: King of the Jews and Friend of the Romans* (Minneapolis, MN: Fortress, 1996), 242.

36. Lenski, *Power and Privilege*, 245–246, 284.

37. The sharing of information with the king also serves Matthew's own exegetical purposes, which are bolstered by a quotation from "the prophet" (Micah 5:2) supporting the view that the Messiah will come from Bethlehem.

38. Webster, *Roman Imperial Army*, 274, "Originally this officer was responsible for the collection of corn [grain] in the provinces. His travels among the provincials gave him opportunities of exchanging and collecting gossip which he no doubt reported to his commander on reaching base. This useful role was developed and Hadrian turned them into agents, but the name remained unchanged." See also William G. Sinnigen, "The Origins of the 'Frumentarii,'" *Memoirs of the American Academy in Rome* 27 (1962): 211–224; J.C. Mann, "The Organization of Frumentarii," *Zeitschrift für Papyrologie und Epigraphik* 74 (1988): 149–150.

39. N.B. Rankov, "Frumentarii, the Castra Peregrina and the Provincial Officia," *Zeitschrift für Papyrologie und Epigraphik* 80 (1990): 176–182, provides an

overview of both the later and earlier work of such agents: "the *frumentarii* were attached to a *numerus frumentariorum* based in Rome, complete with its own organization and officers.... [which] allowed them to be employed by the emperor for his own purposes. The *Life of Hadrian* tells the story of a *frumentarius* sent to eavesdrop on a prominent senator, and the *frumentarii* appear as imperial spies in the *Lives* of Macrinus and Claudius and as assassins in the service of the emperor in the *Lives* of Commodus, Iulianus and Niger as well as in a passage of Herodian describing an attempt by Septimius Severus to eliminate Clodius Albinus. It is clear that by the early third century they had acquired a thoroughly unsavory reputation which evidently led to the disbanding of the corps and its replacement by the *agentes in rebus*.... Their principal function was to carry dispatches between [Rome and the provincial governors, but duties included] spying, or even murder. No doubt, they told their governor what was going in Rome, and they certainly told the emperor what was happening in the provinces." Rankov, 176–177, also notes the gravestone of a *frumentarius* from Legio VI Ferrata who was stationed in Syria Palaestina.

40. Horsley, *Christmas*, 46, quotes this same passage to illustrate his point. See n.31 above.

41. Josephus emphasizes that this plot against Alexander and Aristobulus was fabricated by their half-brother Antipater for his own gain.

42. See n.32 above.

43. Matthew's verb here is ἀπόλλυμι, also used at 9:17; 10:28; 12:14 (the Pharisees conspire to destroy Jesus); and 22:7 (in Jesus' parable a king is "enraged," sends soldiers to destroy "murderers" of royal servants, and burns the city in recompense). Matthew uses a related verb, καταλύω, on two other occasions, when Jesus (26:61) and his accusers (27:40) speak of destroying/throwing down the Temple.

44. Elaine Wainwright, *Shall We Look for Another? A Feminist Rereading of the Matthean Jesus* (Maryknoll, NY: Orbis, 1998), 61.

45. In Luke's portrayal, Mary is visited by an angel who addresses her directly and by name, declaring that God is with her, and she responds as a faithful "servant of the Lord" (1:26–38). She goes on to visit her cousin Elizabeth and proclaim a hymn of praise (1:39–56); give birth to Jesus in Bethlehem (2:1–7); receive shepherd visitors, treasuring and pondering their words "in her heart" (2:16–19); hear words of blessing from a righteous and devout elder at the Temple (2:33–35); and speak to a young Jesus when he has been lost in Jerusalem (2:48–51).

46. Later, Matthew depicts Mary as the mother of other children (13:55), and as one who is present courageously at Jesus' crucifixion, tomb, and resurrection (27:56, 61; 28:1–10). See chapter 6.

47. The Magi's act of disobedience parallels that of the Hebrew midwives, who "feared God" rather than Pharaoh (Exod 1:15–22).

48. Matt 2:17–18 quotes Jeremiah 31:15 ("A voice was heard in Ramah, wailing and loud lamentation, Rachel weeping for her children; she refused to be consoled, for they are no more"), perhaps because these lines capture the parents' pathos and grief that is missing in Exodus 2, as well as making connection to a return from Exile (Jer 31:1–40) that Matthew has previously highlighted in 1:17.

49. Richard Alston, *Soldier and Society in Roman Egypt* (New York: Routledge, 1995), 23–38, describes the two legions (based in Nikopolis, outside Alexandria) and numerous auxiliary and cavalry units stationed throughout Egypt during this period.

50. Alston, *Roman Egypt*, 18, 33–35. See also Ronald Zitterkopf and Steven Sidebotham, "Stations and Towers on the Quseir-Nile Road," *The Journal of Egyptian Archaeology* 75 (1989): 155–189.

51. Phang, *Marriage*, 245. Alston, *Roman Egypt*, 36, notes that Koptos was one of several "main centers of military activity" in Roman Egypt. See chapter 1 for more on Koptos, in relation to relationships between women and soldiers.

52. Phang, *Marriage*, 245. A person like Joseph the τέκτων ("carpenter," Matt 13:55) would perhaps have been charged the rate of a "craftsman" at Koptos: 8 *drachma* (if this narrative was a historical report).

53. cf. Davies and Allison, *Matthew*, 1:265; Keener, *Matthew*, 110–111.

54. Matthew 24:15–22 is another expression of this experience: "So when you see the desolating sacrilege standing in the holy place, as was spoken of by the prophet Daniel (let the reader understand), then those in Judea must flee to the mountains; the one on the housetop must not go down to take what is in the house; the one in the field must not turn back to get a coat. Woe to those who are pregnant and to those who are nursing infants in those days! Pray that your flight may not be in winter or on a sabbath. For at that time there will be great suffering, such as has not been from the beginning of the world until now, no, and never will be. And if those days had not been cut short, no one would be saved; but for the sake of the elect those days will be cut short."

55. Josephus, *Ant.* 20.251.

56. cf. Matt 4:6 (the devil also has knowledge of scripture and tries to divert Jesus from his purpose); 9:3–6, 11–13; 12:6–8 (the chief priests are far from God).

57. Carter, *Matthew and the Margins*, 301, notes how Matthew 14:1–12 fits into a larger narrative section (11:2–16:20) in which Jesus manifests God's empire, "which critiques imperial structures and reverses human misery and want (hunger, sickness) with plenty and wholeness.... The politically powerful resist God's empire; unbelief is expressed in hostility and violence; God's empire requires faithfulness even to death." In regard to John' critique of the marriage between Antipas and Herodias (14:3–4), Carter, *Margins*, 303–304 goes on to note that such relationships among the privileged were never simply personal, but always had political dimensions: "ruling elites used intermarriage to build alliances, expand territory, and increase power," and thus Antipas' desire to eliminate John is aimed at silencing a critic of the ruling family—all of whom (Antipas, Herodias, and her daughter) seem to be in favor of, and complicit in, John's execution.

58. Overman, *Matthew and Formative Judaism*, 23, frames his discussion of the conflict in Matthew as one that is primarily religious in nature: "the accusation that they [Jewish leadership] persecute the righteous and have shed innocent blood . . . reflects the social location of these sectarian communities.... [which] claim an association with the prophets of old, who were . . . unjustly persecuted by unjust leaders." Luz, *Matthew 8-20*, 307, also calls attention to the Biblical "tradition of murdered prophets that Matthew frequently uses (5:12; 17:12; 21:33–41; 22:3–6; 23:29–36)."

While both point to Matthew's negotiation with the threat of violence, neither address the system of military power of Antipas and his Roman allies as a factor in the death of John the Baptist in Matthew 14.

59. Jennifer Glancy, "Unveiling Masculinity: The Construction of Gender in Mark 6:17–29," *Biblical Interpretation* 2 (1994): 38: "the frame of the story indicates that Herod [Antipas] takes responsibility for the execution; the story itself functions as Herod's flashback to these earlier events." Although she is discussing Mark, Glancy's comments on gender and the framing of the narrative are applicable to Matthew as well. Kathleen Corley, *Private Women, Public Meals: Social Conflict in the Synoptic Tradition* (Peabody, MA: Hendrickson, 1993), 158, writes similarly that: "Matthew's redaction [of Mark] places the blame for the incident firmly upon Herod [Antipas] and allows for the presence of Herodias at the meal." Likewise, Overman, *Church and Community in Crisis*, 215, calls upon Josephus' account (*Ant.* 18.118) that "Herod [Antipas] became alarmed (δείσας, from δείδω)" to imagine how John's preaching could lead to "*stasis* . . . a disturbance . . . or outright revolt," and identifies Antipas' act as a "preemptive strike against the Baptist and his growing movement."

60. Richard Horsley, *Bandits, Prophets, and Messiahs: Popular Messianic Movements in the Time of Jesus* (Minneapolis, MN: Winston Press, 1985), 245, makes a historical analysis of events portrayed by Matthew, noting the variety of peasant movements present throughout Galilee during the time of John and Jesus: "the fundamental conflict in Jewish Palestine was between the Jewish ruling groups and the Romans on the one side and the Jewish peasantry on the other." The large-scale revolts in 4 BCE and 66 CE, Horsley, *Bandits*, 253, argues, were one manifestation of response to the military power used by the Romans and their elite Jewish allies to maintain their rule: "Action by the ruling groups was almost always violent, manifest in the very conditions which gave rise to the various kinds of movements. The Romans conquered and continued their control by violent means, including intimidation by terror. Herod maintained security by means of repressive violence. The high priests preyed violently upon and tortured their own people." See also Horsley, *Galilee: History, Politics, People* (Valley Forge, PA: Trinity Press International, 1995), 256–275, for a brief account of the popular unrest, protests, and banditry in Galilee that resulted from the social and economic stress of subsistence farming under autocratic rule. This is the environment in which Jesus was raised and the conditions which his work sought to address; it also serves as a context in which to read the accusations of false kingship levelled against him in Matt 27:37–38 by those in control of and benefitting from the system.

61. In contrast to Mark, who assigns blame for John's death to Herodias, Antipas' wife, who "had a grudge (ἐνέχω) against him" (6:19).

62. Several scholars approach the scene with a question about historicity, including Davies and Allison, *Matthew*, 2:465, who note "problematic" aspects of Matthew's narrative, including differences between the accounts of John's death in the Synoptics and Josephus; historical improbabilities ("how could Herod [Antipas], who was under the Roman thumb, have promised half his 'kingdom'?"); influences of motifs and themes from Hebrew scripture; and "parallels to the passion narrative . . . which implies a manipulation of the facts for theological ends." Ulrich Luz, *Matthew 8–20*,

Hermeneia (Minneapolis, MN: Fortress, 2001), 305, notes (with reference to Mark and Josephus) that "Matthew is a narrator who is by no means uninformed, but on the level of the reported story he has little interest in clarity and coherence." Keener, *Matthew*, 397–398, also points to scholars who view the scene as more (Theissen) or less (Meier) historically probable, before concluding that "from a purely historical standpoint, we can be certain that Antipas had John executed for preaching that he took as undermining his honor."

63. Mark's version (6:17, 27) is more direct: "For Herod himself had sent men (Αὐτὸς γὰρ ὁ Ἡρῴδης ἀποστείλας ἐκράτησεν) who arrested John, bound him, and put him in prison . . . the king sent a soldier of the guard (ἀποστείλας ὁ βασιλεὺς σπεκουλάτορα) with orders to bring John's head. He went and beheaded him in the prison." BDAG, 936–937: σπεκουλάτωρ is a Latin loanword denoting a particular type of soldier; the *speculator* was a various times a spy, scout, courier or executioner. This is reflected in the KJV, NAS and NIV. Fuhrman, *Policing the Empire*, 193, notes that from the time of Augustus, the *speculator* could serve as a bodyguard for the emperor or governors, as well as executioner.

64. For John as a righteous prophet, see Matt 11:7–11; 17:10–13; 21:26, 32. On Jesus withdrawing in the face of dangerous opponents, see Matt 2:13–14, 22–23; and 4:12–17.

65. BDAG, 3rd ed., 750–751. The cognates παῖς and παιδίον are used throughout Matthew: the centurion's slave or boy (8:6); children in the marketplace (11:16); recipients of food (along with men and women) in the wilderness (15:38); a child possessed with an evil spirit (17:18); children brought to Jesus (18:1–5; 19:13–14); children praising Jesus in the Temple (21:15); two slave girls in the High Priest's household (26:69, 71); and Jesus himself (Matt 2:8–14; 12:18).

66. There is a clear connection here to another king and queen, Ahab and Jezebel, who seek to kill the prophet Elijah (1 Kings 18–19). Later, Jesus makes this association explicit: "if you are willing to accept it, he [John] is Elijah who is to come" (Matt 11:14).

67. In Matt 27:62–64, the chief priest and Pharisees express concern to Pilate (Jesus' disciples will say that he has been raised) that is similar, but not identical to Antipas' concern.

68. Mark 6:22 identifies Herodias' daughter as having the same name: Herodias. Josephus, *Ant.* 8.5 identifies her as Salome.

69. See Florence Morgan Gillman, *Herodias: At Home in That Fox's Den* (Collegeville, MN: Liturgical Press, 1989); Janice Capel Anderson, "The Dancing Daughter," in *Mark and Method: New Approaches in Biblical Studies* (Minneapolis, MN: Fortress, 2008), 111–143; Ross Kraemer, "Implicating Herodias and Her Daughter in the Death of John the Baptizer: A (Christian) Theological Strategy?" *JBL* 125.2 (2006): 321–349; Alice Bach, "Calling the Shots: Directing Salome's Dance of Death," *Semeia* 74 (1996): 103–124.

70. Corley, *Public Meals*, 159.

71. Glancy, "Unveiling Masculinity," 40–41.

72. cf. Luz, *Matthew 8–20*, 307: "the daughter of Herodias dances in front of the invited men . . . as a still unmarried girl . . . a princess plays a role in this men's

banquet that courtesans ordinarily played." Luz, *Matthew 8–20*, 308–309, also provides an excursus on traditions that developed around this daughter, who is often called Salome (following Josephus) in later interpretations of this scene. Despite the centuries of interpretation focusing on the sexual transgression of the scene, Luz, *Matthew 8–20*, 307, prefers to focus on Antipas' oath, which runs counter to Jesus' teaching in Matt 5:33–37, and "leads to a crime." See also Adela Yarbro Collins, *Mark: A Commentary* (Minneapolis, MN: Augsburg Fortress, 2007), 303–314, who concurs with the traditional view when reading Mark 6:14–30 in parallel to Matthew 14:1–12. Yarbro Collins, 309–310, also notes the dynamics of power and gender relations in ancient texts, referring to such stories as Xerxes granting a favor to his daughter-in-law Artaÿnte, with whom he has had an affair (Herodotus, *Hist.* 9.109); Esther seeking a favor from her husband Ahasuerus (Xerxes), who promises her anything, "even to the half of my kingdom" (Esther 2:7; 5:1–6); and Agrippa (the brother of Herodias) seeking a favor from Caligula at a feast (Josephus, *Ant.* 8.289–301).

73. See Gillman, *Herodias*, 55 n.6, 85; Capel Anderson, "Dancing Daughter," 129.

74. Gillman, *Herodias*, 56–57.

75. Janice Capel Anderson, "Dancing Daughter," 129. Gillman, 57, quotes an earlier edition.

76. Gillman, *Herodias*, 68–69. Gillman, 69, also argues that Matthew, in comparison to Mark, truncates the portrayal of the two women: "Herodias is stylized as a murderess and Salome as a seductress, two typical androcentric depictions of the evil female," and thus reduces them to conventional roles in patriarchal society. See also Kraemer, "Implicating Herodias and Her Daughter," 324. Again, for a contrasting view, see Glancy, "Unveiling Masculinity," 38–42, who argues for Antipas' culpability in "active voyeurism" and objectification of his step-daughter, but the one around whom the entire scene is framed: "the women in the scene have no power that Herod [Antipas] has not given them."

77. Gillman, *Herodias*, 69–70.

78. Gillman, *Herodias*, 69–70.

79. Lenski, *Power and Privilege*, 246: they comprise 6–7% of the population and assist in supporting and securing the ruler's regime.

80. John has broken the public transcript of assent to Herod's rule by criticizing him and his marriage. This act of resistance, according to Scott, *Domination*, 2, is "a declaration that breaches the etiquette of power relations, that breaks an apparently calm surface of silence and consent, carries the force of a symbolic declaration of war," to which Antipas responds accordingly.

81. Matt 27:57–60.

82. See Josephus, *JW* 1.283–285 (quoted at the beginning of this chapter), for another example of banqueting as a means by which elite actors and power brokers affirmed their mutual interdependence.

83. Josephus, *JW* 2.93–100; *Ant.* 17.317–323. Josephus, *JW* 2.100, also notes how Herod's will included a generous bequest of one thousand talents to the emperor; Augustus, in a show of munificence, "distributed among the family Herod's legacy to himself ... reserving only some trifling works of art which he kept in honor of the deceased."

84. Josephus, *JW* 2.95.

85. Archelaus' rule is also threatening to Jesus and his family: Joseph refuses to settle in the region, choosing instead, "after being warned in a dream," to settle in Nazareth of Galilee. Matthew's account in 2:22–23 appears to be guided by exegetical concerns (to provide scriptural precedent for Jesus' residence in Nazareth), rather incisive political awareness: the reason given for Joseph's decision (to avoid living under Herod's heir) appears moot, as both Judaea and Galilee were ruled by sons of the late king.

86. This situation is reflected in Jesus' trial, sentencing, and execution under the governor Pontius Pilate (Matt 27:1–66), and continued into the second century CE. Josephus (*Ant.* 17.355 18.1–6) reports that the removal of Archelaus resulted in a Roman census, conducted for purposes of taxation under the authority of the Quirinius, the governor of Syria, and Coponius, the newly appointed *praefectus* of Judaea. There is much discussion of this in relation to the dating of Jesus' birth and the accounts of Matthew and Luke; see Edward Dąbrowa, "The Date of the Census of Quirinius and the Chronology of the Governors of the Province of Syria," *Zeitschrift für Papyrologie und Epigraphik* 178 (2011): 137–142; Mark Smith, "Of Jesus and Quirinius," *CBQ* 62.2 (2000): 278–293.

87. Josephus, *JW* 2.167–168.

88. Josephus (*JW* 2.1) reports that after Antipas' brother Philip died, Agrippa was granted rule of his territory along with the title of βασιλεύς ("king"); at the urging of his wife Herodias, Antipas presented himself in Rome to petition for the same title and the increased status that accompanied it. Josephus (*Ant.* 18.251) also reports that Agrippa, in a scheme of his own, accused Antipas of plotting rebellion with the Parthians and used as evidence the stockpile of arms and armor in the royal treasuries: "equipment sufficient for 70,000 heavy-armed infantry" (μυριάσιν ἑπτὰ ὁπλιτῶν ἀρκέσουσα κατασκευὴ ἐν ταῖς Ἡρώδου ὁπλοθήκαις ἀποκειμέν). Unable to deny the truth of this, Antipas was unable to influence the new emperor, who removed him from power and sent him into exile in Spain (*JW* 2.181–183; *Ant.* 18.240–255).

89. Matt 3:5: "the people of Jerusalem and all Judea . . . and all the region along the Jordan."

90. In Matt 14:12–14, the crowds follow Jesus into the wilderness just as they once followed John.

91. The parallel here instead foreshadows Jesus' arrest in Gethsemane (Matt 26:31–32), where soldiers arrest him alone; Matthew emphasizes divine involvement in this event by citing scriptural precedent from Zech 13:7: "I will strike the shepherd, and the sheep of the flock will be scattered."

92. Josephus (*Ant.* 18.116–119) records that John's death occurred at Machaerus, one of the fortress-palaces built by Herod the Great. Elsewhere, Josephus (*JW* 7.171–177) describes the stronghold's construction by Herod, who: "enclosed an extensive area with ramparts and towers and founded a city there, from which an ascent led up to the ridge itself.... he built a wall, erecting towers at the corners, each sixty cubits high. In the center of the enclosure he built a palace with magnificently spacious and beautiful apartments . . . numerous cisterns . . . to receive the rainwater and furnish an abundant supply . . . [and] stocked it with abundance of weapons

and engines and studied to make every preparation to enable its inmates to defy the longest siege." Josephus (*JW* 7.164–167) also notes how "the site that is fortified is itself a rocky eminence . . . entrenched on all sides within ravines . . . not easy to traverse and impossible to bank up." Archaeologist Győző Vörös, "Machaerus: The Golgotha of Saint John the Baptist," *Revue Biblique*, 119. 2 (Leuven, BE: Peeters Publishers, 2012), 250, 252, notes that "Machaerus had been a member of a military fortress-network aimed at the defense of Jerusalem from the east during the first centuries BC and AD," along with the fortresses at Masada, Herodion, Hyrcania, Cypros, Doq, and Alexandreion. Outside the citadel of Machaerus a city was built, and it was here, Vörös argues, "where the prison of John the Baptist had to be situated." From or within this lower city, John's disciples could approach and visit their teacher with some degree of access.

93. There are obvious parallels to Joseph asking for the body of Jesus in Matt 27:57–60.

94. Corley, *Private Women*, 152–153, notes that Matthew is the only gospel in which Jesus declares that πόρναι will "enter the kingdom of God" (Matt 21:31–32) and argues for a connection to Matt 11:16–19, where παῖδες sit in the marketplace "bemoaning the lack of response to their flute playing and mourning . . . the image of hired slaves or servants who were often sent to the marketplace by their masters to seek additional employment." In relation to Matt 14:12, Corley, 159, argues that "after John's death, the disciples of John were incorporated into Jesus' group. Among these would no doubt be the 'tax collectors and prostitutes' who are said to have 'believed John' in Matthew 21:31–32," and, 153, that "Matthew's incorporation of such sectarian slander terminology reflects the situation of the Matthean community, that of a Jewish-Christian sect in controversy with other Jews."

95. Matthew's audience would also be aware of Jesus' allusions and references to his own suffering and death elsewhere in the gospel (cf. 12:40–42).

Chapter 3

Coping with the Abuse of Imperial Power

Negotiating Ἀγγαρήιον as Active Non-Violent Resistance (Matthew 5:41)

> I instruct you to see to it that nobody commandeers a beast of burden unless he has a permit from me. For it is most unjust that, either by the favor or prestige of certain people, requisitions should take place which nobody but myself can grant. . . . Let no force be used against them contrary to my wish and let nobody commandeer a guide unless he has a permit from me, for, when farmers are torn away from their homes, the fields will remain without their attention.
>
> Emperor Domitian (81–96 CE)[1]

INTRODUCTION

While chapter 2 argues that Matthew's two scenes involving Herod (2:1–23) and Herod Antipas (14:1–12) depict various strategies for negotiating Roman power in the form of imperially sanctioned rulers who wield military authority and maintain their rule through the threat and use of violence against their subjects, this chapter focuses on how these subjects negotiated the implementation (and abuse) by Roman personnel of an imperial policy. This practice, which the Roman government called ἀγγαρήιον or *angaria*, was part of an imperial system in which civilians provided service to the state in the form of requisitioned transportation and other forms of labor. The policy was at best inconvenient for those forced to comply, and often abused by those with access to the prerogatives the system afforded.

From the perspective of imperial subjects, ἀγγαρήιον/*angaria* represented an ongoing imposition of imperial control enacted by military personnel that regularly impacted their daily lives, energies, and possessions. Matthew's

Jesus addresses the practice at 5:41 when he teaches: "If anyone forces you (ἀγγαρεύω) to go one mile, go also the second mile." This chapter argues that Jesus's instruction outlines a self-protective practice of active non-violent resistance to ἀγγαρήιον/*angaria* which has the potential to express dissent while preserving lives, elevating dignity, and embodying the Empire of God, which stand in discrete and asymmetrical opposition to the Empire of Rome until such time as God brings it to eschatological fulfillment.

While other scholars have rightly noted the historical context of Matthew 5:41 in relation to Roman military practices, this chapter emphasizes a number of aspects of negotiating imperial power which have not been addressed heretofore. These aspects include dimensions of gender at work in the practice, and concerns of Roman administrators to curb egregious abuses of the practice that stoked resentment and anger among subjugated provincials. First, this chapter sets the teaching of the Matthean Jesus on ἀγγαρήιον/*angaria* in relation to the possible cultural knowledge of the gospel's audience, noting its development and providing examples from throughout the Empire, including Syria. Next, it notes the contributions of other scholars to interpretations of Matthew 5:41—in particular Walter Wink who emphasizes the role of non-violent action as a means of self-preservation and resistance. Finally, it argues that Matthew's reference to a widespread Roman military practice points toward practices of imperial negotiation among Jesus's followers that have the potential to express dissent while preserving their lives, elevating their dignity, and embodying the Empire of God.

JESUS' RESPONSE TO EVERYDAY VIOLENCE (MATT 5:41)

Numerous scholars have noted the placement of Mathew 5:41 in a series of "antitheses" or "supertheses" in Matthew 5:21–48.[2] These short statements contain commentary on Torah with a formula that first quotes scripture (thesis), then offers Jesus's teaching (antithesis/superthesis) on how to fulfill it: "you have heard *x*, but/and I say to you *y*."[3] The collection of statements is designed to illustrate Matthew's contention that Jesus has come to fulfill the commandments of Torah and prophets and to teach his followers to do the same, so that they "will be called great in the empire of heaven" (5:19).[4] Jesus's speech takes a well-known saying and intensifies it—a rhetorical technique designed to spur the thinking and behavior of Jesus's followers so that their "righteousness exceeds that of the scribes and Pharisees" (5:20), and that they may be perfect (τέλειος), "as your heavenly Father is perfect" (5:48).

Within the larger section of Matthew 5:21–48, the thesis and superthesis found in 5:38–42 address the question of reciprocal violence as a form of justice with reference to Exodus 21:24, Leviticus 24:20, and Deuteronomy 19:21. Jesus begins by saying: "You have heard that it was said, 'An eye for an eye and a tooth for a tooth.' And I say to you, Do not resist violently (μὴ ἀντιστῆναι) an evildoer" (5:38–39a). He follows this proposal with four illustrations. These include:

(1) if struck (ῥαπίζω), turn the other cheek (5:39b);
(2) if sued (κρίνω) for a tunic, give your cloak also (5:40);
(3) if forced (ἀγγαρεύω) to go one mile, go a second mile also (5:41);
(4) if someone begs (αἰτέω) and seeks to borrow (δανίζω), do not refuse to loan to them (5:42).

It is noteworthy that the first, second, and fourth examples can be imagined as interpersonal or intercommunal situations or problems, as will be seen in the arguments of several scholars below.[5] To make sense of the third example, however, it must be understood in its Roman imperial context. Beginning with the insightful work of Walter Wink, this chapter argues that Jesus's teaching on going a second mile is formulated specifically to address the practices of Roman military requisitioning of animal and human labor (ἀγγαρήιον/*angaria*).[6] This approach frames the Matthean Jesus's teaching as both practical advice on avoiding physical harm and violence and as a practice of active non-violent resistance that pierces the public transcript of imperial domination and counters it.

Although a cursory reading of Jesus's command in 5:39a ("Do not violently resist an evildoer") may lead to the impression that Jesus is talking solely about interpersonal conflict, there are many instances where the verb, ἀνθίστημι, is used in a military context—where the common translation "stand against" serves as a euphemism for individuals and armies fighting and doing battle with each other.[7] The verb therefore often denotes violence as a key means of expressing opposition. Josephus uses the word to denote military violence on several occasions: Agrippa points out to his subjects that their forefathers "failed to fight against" (οὐκ ἀντέσχον) a small portion of Roman military power (*JW* 2.357); outside Jerusalem, the Roman general Titus fights alone against a force of Jewish defenders who rush up the hill toward him (δὲ καθ' αὐτὸν ἀνατρέχουσιν ἀνθίσταται, *JW* 5.89); in the battle for Jotapa, Josephus (with authorial hubris) claims that the Jewish defenders would not have been able to fight against (ἀνθίστασθαι) the enemy if he had deserted (*JW* 3.196).[8] In the Bible, the Israelites are warned that the results of idolatry will be an inability to fight against their enemies (ἀνθίστημι, LXX Lev 26:37; Josh 7:13; 23:9); the followers of Jesus are counseled to participate in heavenly warfare by making a stand (a battle line) against evil and resisting (Eph 6:13; Jas 4:7; and 1 Pet 5:9).⁹ In 3 Macc 6:19 the verb is also used when angels appear from heaven to fight against the enemy army (ἀντέστησαν καὶ τὴν δύναμιν τῶν ὑπεναντίων) of King Ptolemy Philopator to save the Jews.¹⁰ Beyond this, Wink points out that there are similar cognates of ἵστημι:

> The verbal stem . . . is compounded in a wide variety of terms devoting violent warfare, attack, revolt, rebellion, insurrection, and revolution:
>
> *aphistemi*: "Judas the Galilean rose up"—Acts 5:37
> *ephistemi*: "they attacked Jason's house"—Acts 17:5
> *epanistemi*: "children will rise up against parents"—Mark 13:12 // Matt. 10:21
> *katephistemi*: "the Jews made a united attack!"—Acts 18:12
> *exanistemi*: "rise up from the ambush and seize"—Josh 8:7
> *antikathistemi*: "resisted to the point of shedding blood"—Heb 12:4
> *sunephistemi*: "the crowd joined in attacking"—Acts 16:22¹¹

In Matthew 5:39a, ἀνθίστημι indicates a negative command: do not violently fight in opposition to powerful adversaries. This is good advice for untrained and unarmed provincials, but it does not imply that Jesus's hearers (including those in Matthew's audience) are to passively accept domination by soldiers who insist upon assistance, or to acquiesce to powers opposed to God's will. As in other situations throughout Matthew's gospel, the choice to not "resist" with physical violence is both tactical and strategic. Tactically, it would be unwise to disobey a party of well-trained and well-armed Roman soldiers while on the road; strategically, followers of Jesus are to wait for and trust in God's own timing for the defeat of Rome's empire, when the Son of Man will return in eschatological judgment to secure victory over the nations.¹² For these reasons, the necessity of negotiating abusive imperial practices such as the ἀγγαρήιον/*angaria* is both provisional and kerygmatic—important for the survival and well-being of the Matthean community until they complete their work at the end of the age (Matt 28:20). The scope of Roman *angaria* is wide and pervasive throughout its provinces, including Syria; and it is to a description of this practice that we now turn.

ἈΓΓΑΡΉΙΟΝ AS A MEANS OF IMPERIAL CONTROL

The Greek historian Herodotus provides the earliest documentation for the practice of ἀγγαρήιον, a system of horseback couriers in the Persian empire in which messages were passed from one rider to another, for as long as was necessary to complete the journey.[13] In the Roman period, a similar system called the *cursus publicus* was adopted and developed by Emperor Augustus. The Roman practice at first made use of a series of runners, but later was changed to individual messengers using multiple horses and conveyances. This provided greater security for private correspondence and allowed opportunity for the messenger to be questioned directly and provide additional observations to the recipient.[14] Within the *cursus publicus* (the overall system), the Romans seem to have understood the ἀγγαρήιον/*angaria* in reference to the requisition of animals, conveyances, and people for use in the system.[15]

Detailed evidence for the *cursus publicus* comes from an important inscription from Sagalassus in central Pisidia (then in the province of Galatia). Written in Latin and Greek, the inscription is an official edict to the townspeople from Sextus Sotidius Strabo Libuscidianus, the *legatus pro praetorae* of the emperor Tiberius (ruled 14–37 CE).[16] It addresses the ways in which the *cursus publicus* should be enacted by both provincial residents and Roman officials: (1) each town will provide a certain number of *vehiculi* (wagons or carts), mules or donkeys, and lodging for government officials; (2) the use of wagons/carts and animals will be paid for; and (3) only those authorized may use the system.[17] These authorized persons include the procurator (governor) of the province, senators, *equites*, centurions, and other soldiers, so long as they carry an official authorization (*diplomata*) or are traveling through the province on military business.[18] There are additional constraints at the end of the edict: "nothing [is] to be provided for those who transport grain or anything else of that sort either for their own use or to sell . . . [or] for anyone for their own personal baggage animals or their freedmen's or for their slaves' animals."[19] Sotidius concludes, however, that *mansio* (lodging/shelter) will be provided "without payment for all members of my own staff, for persons on military service from other provinces and for freedmen and slaves of the best of princes [the emperor] and for the animals of these persons, in such a way that these do not exact other services without payment from people who are unwilling."[20]

E.W. Black provides a detailed examination of the archaeological remains of *mansiones* in Britain from this same period.[21] These roadside facilities typically took the form of a boarding house with attached stables centered on a central courtyard: "In theory the existence of a particular building serving as a *mansio* exempted the inhabitants of a settlement from having soldiers or officials requisitioning accommodation in their homes. In practice it did not always work."[22] In rural Britain, the development of new Roman roads and "the decision to build a *mansio* were usually accompanied by the creation of a village or market settlement to service it."[23] This was not necessarily true in more fully developed areas of the eastern empire, but the requirements of a *mansio* were the same: "a pool of craftsmen and local suppliers for its efficient running. . . . [One list includes] mule-driver (*mulio*), wagon-driver (*carpentarius*), veterinary (*mulomedicus*), and groom (*hippocomus*) as personnel assigned to the *cursus publicus*."[24] In one case, a governor convinced a group of villagers to move to a new *mansio*-community by promising them a respite from taxes, military levies, and the *angaria*.[25] Black notes that the majority of the staff at the *mansio* itself was probably slaves.[26] These enslaved people, as emphasized below, did not have a choice as to their participation in the *cursus publicus*, and (as throughout the empire) were mixed in among the local population. The presence of slaves complicates and creates the need for a nuanced interpretation of Jesus's words in Matthew 5:41.

While it is true that the presence of the *cursus publicus* represented another aspect of imperial control of a region, it was not merely the increase of communication between Roman agents (governors, military commanders, soldiers at garrisons and outposts), the requisitioning of local animal and human labor, and construction of *mansiones* supported by slave labor that was the problem for local populations. It was also that the practice of *angaria* was rife with abuse. Stephen Mitchell notes that the inscription from Sagalassus cited above is but one in

> a long series of imperial documents, beginning in the reign of Tiberius and culminating in a group of rescripts from the emperors of the fourth and early fifth centuries collected in book VIII of the Theodosian Code. Almost without exception these documents record abuses of the system or attempts to rectify them. . . . Officials and soldiers were always the first source of trouble.[27]

A number of documents bear out this contention. Mitchell provides an "incomplete" list of 21 inscriptions and letters from a variety of persons, locales, and time periods that include: an edict of the emperor's son Germanicus in Egypt (19 CE); two from prefects L. Aemiliius Rectus and Cn. Vergilius Capito during the reigns of Gaius Caligula (37–41 CE) and Claudius (41–54 CE); one from C. Vergilius Capito in 48 CE; and one from M. Petronius Mamertinus during the reign of Hadrian (117–138 CE).[28] Elsewhere, although it is not mentioned by name, Tacitus records two events that imply the abuse of the *cursus publicus*. The first was by rebellious soldiers of Legion XXI detained in Gaul by the Helvetii, "who intercepted some letters which were being carried in the name of the army in Germany to the legions in Pannonia, and they kept the centurions and certain soldiers in custody" during the months following Nero's death (68 CE).[29] The second was by Coenus, a freedman of Nero, who lied about Otho's death in 69 CE: "He had invented this tale to secure . . . a renewed validity for Otho's passports [*diplomata*] which were being disregarded."[30]

In the province of Syria, another example of abuse of the *angaria* is found in a public inscription from Epiphania (Hama), a city located north of Emesa and southeast of Apamea. It dates to the reign of Domitian (81–96 CE) and shows that the emperor himself was aware of the effects systemic abuse could have on provincial populations. An excerpt of this inscription is quoted at the beginning of this chapter; the full text reads as follows:

> From instructions of Imperator [Dom]itianus Caesar, son of Augustus, Augustus. To Claudius Athenodorus, procurator: Among items of special importance that required great attention by my father, the god Vespasianus, I know that he gave great care to the cities' privileges. With his mind fixed on them he ordered that neither by the rending of beasts of burden nor by the distress of lodging should the provinces be burdened, but, nevertheless, by conscious decision or not, deliberate neglect has set in and this order has not been observed, for there remains up to the present an old and vigorous custom which, little by little, will progress into law if it is not obstructed by force from gaining strength. I instruct you to see to it that nobody commandeers a beast of burden unless he has a permit from me. For it is most unjust that, either by the favor or prestige of certain people, requisitions should take place which nobody but myself can grant. Therefore, let there be nothing which will break my instructions and spoil my intent, which is most advantageous to the cities, for to help the weakened provinces is just, provinces which with difficulty have enough for the necessities of life. Let no force be used against them contrary to my wish, and let nobody commandeer a guide unless he has a permit from me, for, when farmers are torn away from their homes, the fields will remain without their attention.[31]

This imperial decree notes that the commonly abused practice of commandeering beasts of burden (accompanied by their owner or handler) to haul or pull a load and local residents to serve as guides across a section of territory resulted in both an inconvenience and loss of income for local populations. Some scholars have proposed that the statement in this inscription ("farmers are torn away from their homes, the fields will remain without their attention") coupled with a positive statement by Suetonius (*Domitian* 7, 14) on Domitian's agricultural production policy indicates that the emperor's concern was to protect the citizens of the provinces.[32] This appearance of concern, however, does not capture the intent of Domitian's decree—which mandates that rights for transportation were to be reserved for those holding imperial *diplomata*.[33] Thus the emperor's concern was not primarily to lessen the burden on the local population in Syria, but to assert his own power and control over the imperial system of requisitioned transport as well as to ensure that provincial farmers were able to work their fields, harvest their crops, and pay their taxes to support the Roman government.

Imperial interest in the effects of the *angaria* is further illustrated (See Fig. 3.1) by coins from the reign of Nerva (97 CE) that commemorate a government act: "VEHICVLATIONE ITALIAE REMISSA" (the remission of the *vehiculatio* tax for certain Italian towns). While this remission was surely a welcome development for the people of those communities near the imperial center, the emperor's interest was again to assert and strengthen imperial patronage and prerogatives. Likewise, the celebration of tax relief on the coins reinforces the impression that the system in general was burdensome, unstable, and unpopular—yet another occasion in which the powerful could exact goods and services and have their way with those below.

The perception of *angaria* as a practice rife with abusive violence was present in cultural vernacular during in first century CE as well. In his famous work, *The Metamorphoses*, the Roman author Apuleius creates a scene in which his protagonist (a man who has been turned into a donkey) narrates the ways in which *angaria* could be imposed on provincial populations. Although the *Metamorphoses* is a fiction, contains exaggeration for humorous effect, and is intended perhaps for an elite Roman audience, the scene is written with verisimilitude, and points toward ways in which the *angaria* was understood to be practiced throughout the empire. The scene begins:

> On the road we encountered a tall man whose dress and manners marked him as a legionary [*miles e legione*]. He inquired in a haughty and arrogant tone where my master [a gardener] was taking his empty donkey. But my master [,

Figure 3.1 This example of a sestertius of Nerva (67 CE) shows the emperor on the obverse; the reverse commemorates the remission of animal requisitions for the cursus publicus among Italian towns. Pictured are two mules, grazing in opposite directions. Behind them are poles, harness, and wheels of an upturned cart. The coin reads: VEHICVLATIONE ITALIAE REMISSA, SC. *(Source: Image from Wildwinds Coins, admin. Dane Kurth, http://www.wildwinds.com/coins/sear5/s3055.html. Used with permission.)*

who] ... did not know Latin, walked right past him without a word. The soldier, unable to restrain his natural insolence, took offence at the gardener's silence as if it were an insult and struck him with the vine-staff [*vitus*] he was carrying, knocking him off my back. The gardener then humbly answered that he could not understand what the soldier said because he did not know the language. So the soldier responded in Greek. "Where," he asked, "Are you taking that donkey of yours?" The gardener replied that he was taking him to the next city. "Well, I need his services," said the other. "He must carry our commanding officer's baggage from the nearby fort with all the other pack animals." He immediately laid hands on me, took hold of my lead rope, and started to drag me away.[34]

The encounter continues with additional casual and arbitrary violence: his animal requisitioned, the gardener tries to plead and bargain with the centurion, who responds by beating him again with the vine-staff. They begin to fight, and the gardener knocks the soldier down and wounds him with a stone from the roadside. He then tries to escape by riding away toward town on the narrator/donkey (*Metamorphoses* 9.40). The centurion follows, enlisting the help of fellow soldiers stationed in the town, who search out the gardener's hiding place. After finding him, they "handed him over to the magistrates, and took him off to the public gaol, no doubt for execution" (*Metamorphoses* 9.41–2). The next day, the centurion "unfastened me from the stable without anyone stopping him and led me away. He loaded me with his own baggage from his barracks ... and took me out on the road." When they arrive at the legionary fort, the centurion is immediately assigned to travel elsewhere, so he sells the donkey for eleven *denarii* (*Metamorphoses* 10.13)—a nice profit from a stolen animal that cost him nothing.

Apuleius's narrative reveals widespread awareness about the abuse of the *angaria*. It points toward haughty attitudes that soldiers could take toward provincial subjects they were sent to pacify, and the violence they could use to enforce imperial claims and rule. The authority of the centurion (and all soldiers) over local populations was understood as a fact of life across the empire; yet even Apuleius, writing for an elite audience, is aware of some strategies employed by those who might resist. Using his ignorance of Latin as a pretext, the farmer first feigns a lack of understanding about the centurion's intent. When this doesn't work, he makes a personal appeal, begging the soldier for mercy. Frustrated at the loss of his animal, the farmer resorts to an outburst of violence, and then must flee and hide. The power of the empire, however, is far-reaching and unforgiving: the farmer pays for his misstep into unsanctioned violence with his life.

It is noteworthy that Jesus, too, employs what might be considered the requisitioning of local animals in Matthew 21:1–7. Here, on the outskirts of Jerusalem, Jesus sends two disciples to find him an animal to ride on his "triumphal entry"—an event the gospel writers portray with reference to Zechariah 9:9 and which has allusions to the victory parades of Roman generals. Perhaps because of the usual practice of *angaria*, Jesus anticipates resistance to his plan, and says to his disciples: "If anyone says anything to you, just say this, 'The Lord needs them.' And he will send them out (ἀποστέλλω) immediately" (Matt 21:3). Matthew leaves unstated the response of any possible bystanders; the disciples go and return with the animals without incident.[35]

By the late empire the definition of ἀγγαρήιον/*angaria* had expanded to include almost any compulsory and burdensome act. In the Eastern provinces, Benjamin Isaac notes how the Babylonian Talmud makes a distinction between "returning *angaria*" and "*angaria* which does not return": "there are cases where an animal is taken temporarily for work for the authorities and there are cases where it is lost for good."[36] Dan Sperber likewise quotes the Palestinian Talmud, which describes the return of animals requisitioned in the ἀγγαρήιον: "Some teach that it is like death, whilst others teach [that] he may say 'Here before thee is thine.' Those who teach that *angaria* is like death [refer] to a case where he (the hirer) could have come to terms [when an animal is requisitioned. Whereas] they that teach 'Here before thee is thine' [refer] to a case where he could not have come to terms (with the authorities, and . . . is in no way personally responsible)."[37] These statements are attributed to rabbis from the mid-second to third century CE, and (as has been seen above) seem to indicate that whatever the official practices had been or were currently, the ἀγγαρήιον was either being abused or had been expanded so much so that requisitioned animals were routinely not returned to their owners. This potential loss of expensive and necessary animals, coupled with the risks of farming (drought, crop failure) and high tax burdens described in the chapter 1 was another burden the Roman Empire placed on the shoulders of provincial farmers.

The expansion of ἀγγαρήιον was not limited to animals and labor, but in time became applicable to other goods. Isaac notes how, during the empire-wide monetary crisis of the second and third centuries CE, the army accepted *annona militaris*: taxation as payment-in-kind for supplies such as grain, bread, wine, and clothing.[38] At times, "those whose property was confiscated were . . . forced to transport the goods themselves [to the army base,] and that would have been called *angaria* or *prosecutio annonae*."[39] This is the case in another story told by Rabbi Aha, in which a group of mule drivers "heard there was *angaria* in town. They said: come, let us unload these goatskins in this tomb and let us flee." They were worried about the loss of their transported goods and the animals on which their livelihoods depended.[40]

On still other occasions, the ἀγγαρήιον took the form of outright forced labor, such as that of Rabbi Ze'ira, who was compelled to carry myrtle to a government station of the *cursus publicus*.⁴¹ The Tosefta Baba Mezia also addresses this situation, ruling that: "He who hires a laborer, and this laborer is conscripted . . . he (the hirer) has to pay him his wages for so much as he has done."⁴² Along similar lines, the gospel writers describe how Simon of Cyrene, a man "coming in from the country" is compelled by soldiers to carry Jesus's cross.⁴³ Both Matthew 27:32 and Mark 15:21 use the verb ἀγγαρεύω, while Luke 23:26 uses ἐπιλαμβάνομαι to name this practice in a first century CE context.⁴⁴ According to Walter Wink, this episode in the gospels was one instance in which "whoever was found on the street could be compelled into service," and is also the topic under discussion in Matthew 5:41.⁴⁵

The rabbinic examples cited here, while falling outside the dates of Matthew's gospel, indicate a trajectory of development that is in line with the evidence seen at Epiphania, Sagalassus, and throughout the Empire. The system of ἀγγαρήιον/*angaria* was designed to benefit agents of the Roman Empire; in practice these same agents (soldiers and government officials) often abused the system in ways that were detrimental to local populations. The rabbinic sources offer glimpses of a subaltern group discussing and negotiating with the policies and practices of Roman imperialism in the second and third centuries CE by seeking just compensation among community members who are harmed by the practice, at times employing deception, but also complying with imperial rules and practices. Matthew 5:41 indicates that similar negotiation was taking place among the followers of Jesus at the time of the writing of the gospel.

The above examples serve to highlight the argument that the gospel presents the Matthean Jesus's teaching as a way for non-elites in Roman provinces like Syria to negotiate with the overwhelming presence and power of the Roman military. The advice about the ἀγγαρήιον/*angaria* is aimed at a rural population—especially male farmers who may have been forced from their fields and daily labor to transport burdens for soldiers and government officials. This imperial practice had—at a minimum—a detrimental impact on agricultural households in terms of lost work hours and income. When the practice was abused (as it often was), the burden became more onerous, and the risks to workers in the fields included intimidation, coercion, physical violence, stolen animals, legal trouble, and even death if they offered direct resistance. Thus, Jesus's teaching provides practical advice for active, non-violent resistance that has the potential to preserve lives, elevate dignity, and express dissent by embodying the Empire of God. The next section points out, however, that Jesus's teaching must be qualified: it is based (along with Matthew's gospel in general) on androcentric assumptions. Jesus's command to "go a second mile" appears to be directed at free males who have some ability to advocate for themselves in the imperial system, in contrast to women and slaves, whose options are more limited.

JESUS' ἈΓΓΑΡΉΙΟΝ AS A MEANS OF NON-VIOLENT SOCIAL CHANGE

As has been observed previously, the ways in which most scholars interpret Matthean texts tend to seek answers to questions of textual criticism, theology/Christology,[46] and ethnicity.[47] This holds true for Matthew 5:41, in which many scholars correctly identify the connection between Jesus's teaching on ἀγγαρήιον and Roman *angaria*, but neglect to address the imperial context and its implications for Matthew's readers. Understandably, many link Jesus's teaching in 5:38–42 with that of 5:43–48 in which loving (ἀγαπάω) and praying (προσεύχομαι) for enemies are to be signs that his followers are "perfect" like their Father in heaven. Keener, for instance, writes of 5:41 that "Matthew presumably means submission to a Roman soldier's demands. . . . Yet 'going the *extra* mile' is not only a case of submitting to unjust demands but exceeding them—showing love to one's oppressor, although one's associates may wrongly view this love as collaboration with the enemy occupation. It is bending over backward to show that one loves and takes no offense."[48] Unfortunately, without attention to the imperial context, this approach to Jesus's teaching relegates it to the realm of personal piety; neglects imperial structures, practices, and personnel; reinforces a sense of powerlessness and vulnerability among Matthew's audience; and fails to note any possibility that Jesus is counseling non-violent resistance to injustices perpetrated on God's people.

In contrast to other approaches, Walter Wink argues that Jesus's teaching on ἀγγαρήιον provides a practice of non-violent social change.[49] He begins by pointing out a long-standing interpretive problem of Matthew 5:41: "Christians have, on the whole, simply ignored this teaching. It has seemed impractical, masochistic, suicidal—an invitation to bullies and spouse-batterers. . . . Some who have tried to follow Jesus' words have understood it to mean non-resistance: let the oppressor perpetrate evil unopposed. . . . Interpreted thus, the passage has become the basis for systematic training in cowardice, as Christians are taught to acquiesce in [the presence of] evil."[50] Wink notes that fundamental to this misinterpretation is the failure to appreciate that the command, μὴ ἀντιστῆναι (5:39) has the sense of violent and/or military action: "It means to resist *violently*, to revolt or rebel, to engage in an insurrection. Jesus is not encouraging submission to evil. . . . [Instead,] he cautions us against being made over into the very evil we oppose by adopting its methods and spirit."[51] Taking each statement of Matthew 5:38–42 in turn, Wink shows how turning the other cheek (5:38–9), giving the outer garment (5:40), and going the second mile (5:41) are each creative examples of an approach that "can be used by individuals or large movements to intervene on behalf of justice for our neighbors—nonviolently."[52] Historically, he argues that these actions were methods of resistance and non-cooperation, by which "the oppressed can recover the initiative and assert their human dignity in a situation that cannot for the time being be changed."[53]

Wink emphasizes that Jesus's directions in 5:41 are designed to help his hearers in situations where structural changes to oppressive practices are not possible: Jesus "is helping an oppressed people find a way to protest and neutralize an onerous practice [*angaria*] despised through the empire. . . . He is formulating a worldly spirituality in which the people at the bottom of society or under the thumb of imperial power recover their humanity."[54] When faced with the ἀγγαρήιον, Wink imagines the hearing and application of Jesus's directions with sly humor:

> Imagine the soldier's surprise when, at the next mile marker, he reluctantly reaches to assume his pack, and the civilian says, "Oh no, let me carry it another mile." Why would he want to do that? What is he up to? Normally, soldiers have to coerce people . . . but this Jew does so cheerfully, and *will not stop!* Is this provocation? Is he insulting the legionnaire's strength? Being kind? Trying to get him disciplined for seeming to violate the rules of impressment? Will this civilian file a complaint? Create trouble? From a situation of servile impressment, the oppressed have once more seized the initiative.[55]

More so than other scholars, Wink's analysis considers the daily reality facing local populations in places such as Galilee and Syria. Wink argues for a historical scenario based in early first century CE Galilee: "Jesus' saying does not reflect a situation of daily occupation by Romans, but rather the occasional relocation of the legions guarding the empire's eastern flank . . . [including] frequent dispatches of mail, troops, and supplies. Roman soldiers also accompanied caravans and acted as police in suppressing robbers."[56] It is not necessary to fully agree with Wink's contention that Matthew 5:41 reflects particular circumstances in the time of Jesus; rather, it is enough to acknowledge that the experience of negotiating *angaria* was an ongoing concern of local populations throughout the Roman Empire over centuries—including the late first century CE during which Matthew's gospel was written. The clarity of Wink's argument is nevertheless persuasive: that the audience of the Matthean Jesus was one "whose lifelong pattern has been to cringe before their masters" and his teaching was intended as "a way to liberate themselves from servile actions and a servile mentality."[57]

Wink's analysis and argument is similar to Scott's assertion that a key element in the hidden transcript of an oppressed group subjected to "insults and slights to human dignity" is the assertion of self-esteem, self-respect, and regaining of reputation.[58] The hidden transcript—a narrative of indignation hidden from elite power holders (that only occasionally bursts forth)—"represent[s] nothing more than the safe articulation of the assertion, aggression, and hostility that is thwarted by the onstage power of the dominant. Discretion in the face of power requires that a part of the 'self' that would reply or strike back must lie low."[59] It is this dynamic of powerlessness that Matthew's Jesus addresses in 5:41, providing a means by which the gospel's audience may engage the power of the Roman Empire, and find ways to safely and non-violently express dissent while preserving lives, elevating dignity, and embodying the Empire of God.

THE "SECOND MILE" AS A STRATEGY OF IMPERIAL NEGOTIATION

Now that Jesus' advice in Matthew 5:41 has been situated in relation to the burdensome and often-abused Roman practice of ἀγγαρήιον/*angaria* and I have drawn on Wink's argument about the same, this discussion turns to several difficulties concerning the possibilities for resistance among local populations in Roman provinces, and the identity of those who may have sought to put Jesus's directions about the ἀγγαρήιον into practice. The identity, status, and agency of such people are revealed through attention to the characteristics of non-elite groups who organized to resist imperial power in a variety of ways.

In order to evaluate the efficacy of Jesus's teaching on the ἀγγαρήιον for non-elite Roman provincials it is important to note from the outset that extant evidence about the system and problems arising from its abuse are products of imperial ideology. The edicts, inscriptions, letters, and celebratory coins discussed above were produced by elite Romans to increase control and perpetuate their rule while pacifying dissenting voices of local populations. This is also true of Apuleius's novel, which I read not as a social critique, but as entertainment that reinforces stereotypes and cultural norms through humorous exaggeration even as it might inscribe some common non-elite negotiations. Although non-elite provincial subjects do not speak directly in official edicts, their voices can be heard in a muted fashion as the interlocutors of abusive practices. Despite the fact that they are now (mostly) silenced dialogue partners, official responses indicate that local populations were active in raising concerns and complaints to relevant officials about their mistreatment at the hands of those more powerful. Occasionally, these provincial residents appear to have been effective in securing a positive (albeit temporary) change for themselves within the system. Besides reading official documents against the grain to listen for these subaltern voices, we can also hear them more clearly in rabbinic discussions from the late empire and in the words of Matthew's Jesus from the late first century CE. Both the rabbis and Matthew are suggesting ways for their hearers to find ways to survive and live despite the overbearing system of Roman imperial power and control represented in the ἀγγαρήιον/*angaria*.

It is possible to interpret the evidence for these practices in a straightforward manner—with an awareness that complaints about abuses of the ἀγγαρήιον represent both "the destructive power of colonialism" and attempts by the imperial subjects to "question colonial authority."[60] But the situation is more than a simple binary such as Wink sets up in his dichotomy of powerful/powerless and oppressor/oppressed. A more nuanced approach is called for—one that acknowledges the hybrid identity and multiple overlapping social categories in which Matthew's audience participated. Ania Loomba notes Bhabha's formulation of colonial discourse: cultural and ideological interchanges in which the colonizer and colonized act in mutual influence on each other—much to the chagrin of those in power. She writes:

> Homi Bhabha suggests [that] the colonial discourses cannot smoothly "work" . . . In the very processes of their delivery, they are diluted and hybridized, so that the fixed identities that colonialism seeks to impose upon both the masters and the slaves are in fact rendered unstable . . . both are caught in a complex reciprocity and colonial subjects can negotiate the cracks of dominant discourses in a variety of ways.[61]

This ability to work the "cracks" is much like Wink's discussion of the oppressed finding ways to resist their oppressive situation, finding ways to enact transformation bit by bit—without resorting to violent revolution—and to recover their stolen dignity. It is similar also to Scott's depiction of the public transcript, which, when enacted, produces resistance in the form of a hidden transcript that covertly undermines the ideology of the powerful: "Far from being a relief-valve taking the place of actual resistance, the discursive practices offstage sustain resistance . . . [especially when] these are the forms that political struggle takes when frontal assaults are precluded by the realities of power."[62] Thus, in Roman Syria interaction between governors, officials, soldiers, and subaltern provincial subjects was conditioned by their social location and membership in multiple, overlapping groups—of which slavery and gender are especially relevant to an analysis of Matthew 5:41.[63]

As has been noted above, at least some percentage of workers involved in the *cursus publicus* system was enslaved. This included those assigned to the *mansiones*, as well as any who might have been under the control of local owners, then sent as laborers to fulfill the requirements of local requisitions, or to deliver or care for requisitioned animals for a period of time. These enslaved people would not have had the choice whether to walk 1 or 2 or 20 miles. A slave's option for resisting the ἀγγαρήιον by walking a second mile as Matthew's Jesus suggests would be constrained by the duty to follow a master's instructions. If the slave decided to go further than the required distance, there would be a risk of being accused of disobedience, and then punishment for not working as the master intended. If the master also sought to undermine a soldier's authority by indicating that he/she and the slave would continue carrying baggage for a second mile, there would be little room for the slave's personal choice or advocacy for the Empire of God. In this scenario, a slave may have participated in resistance to Roman domination expressed in the *angaria* but would remain enmeshed in another expression of Roman power—slavery. Following Wink's reading, an enslaved person *could* choose to seek dignity and recognition of their humanity by adopting the spirit of Jesus's teaching, but it would have been extremely difficult to follow the specifics of 5:41 as an unfree person.[64] Additionally, a master would not be likely to encourage or permit such thinking and behavior, which could rebound on the master in unforeseen ways.

The same constraints would apply to teaching found in the surrounding verses. In the first case, a slave could not be sued for cloak or tunic (5:40), as whatever clothing he or she might own was the property of the master. Slaves were considered property ("living tools"),[65] and did not have the same rights as a free person in a court of law; items used by or in their possession were viewed as a part of their master's property, and their testimony would only be admissible after torture.[66] Slaves did not have access to courts or the justice system; instead the master would serve as judge and prosecutor, and had great discretion to impose his or her will—up to and including death.[67] In the second case, a slave could be struck (5:40) on the cheek and elsewhere without repercussion, and often were.[68] The expected attitude for a slave was deference and submission, and the idea of active—let alone armed—rebellion (ἀντιστῆναι) usually ended in death for those slaves involved.[69]

With this reality in mind, the "crack" in which an enslaved person might work to demand recognition and justice was much smaller than that of a free person. The overlapping categories of subaltern slave and free would make implementation of Jesus's advice more difficult: what was helpful for the latter group may not have been possible for the former. Although there are a number of occasions in Matthew in which slave characters are featured positively and have personal agency,[70] the ability of actual slaves to act was much more tenuous than the situations depicted at 5:38–42. This ambiguity and discontinuity is not surprising. Wink's identification of Jesus's teaching at 5:41 as advocacy for "oppressed" people is correct but must be complexified by acknowledging realities of social status and the limits of possible responses for those who were constrained by multiple adverse identities in Roman society.[71]

A second factor in which complex categories of non-elite identity reveals the limits of implementing Jesus's teaching is the role of gender in Roman society. If non-elite males were oppressed by elite Roman males (and perhaps females), so doubly were non-elite females. In traditional Mediterranean societies, whether Jewish, Greek, or Roman, this double bind was found (among other places) in expressions of honor and shame, in which the status of men was linked to the behavior of the women in their families. This cultural constraint is described by Zeba Crook, who summarizes Bruce Malina's well-known work on the matter: "there are gender double standards when it comes to honor and shame. There is behavior that is expected and appropriate of males and females respectively, and mixing them is inappropriate."[72] In this context, it seems likely that the advice of the Matthean Jesus about creatively overturning or even protesting the dynamics of power in Matthew 5:41 is more applicable and directed to males (such as Rabbi Ze'ira, or Simon of Cyrene in Matt 27:32) rather than females (free or enslaved). Although there is no direct evidence when it comes to the *angaria*, it seems likely that Roman soldiers, socialized to the norms and expectations of Roman masculinity, would be more likely to seek out males for the gendered role of "hard" work to carry heavy equipment and baggage. At the same time, non-elite males would have also sought to prevent a situation in which the females in their families and communities had to do such work, so that they could uphold their own expectations about proper gender roles and to preserve this aspect of their own and their family's honor.

Crook also points out that elite Roman notions of honor and shame were intertwined with ideas about sexuality in which patriarchal discourse associated women with shame. He notes that it is not realistic to imagine that all women (especially non-elite women) were sequestered in their homes to preserve their moral and sexual purity.[73] This is the second reason that provincial women might raise questions about the wisdom of applying Jesus's teaching about the second mile. More serious than the shame of breaking social norms about gendered labor roles was the risk of sexual violence for women at the hands of aggressive soldiers. Tacitus (*Ann.* 14.31ff) tells of an infamous incident among the Iceni of Britain where this kind of violence took place, and sexual assault was one aspect of enacting imperial control. Upon the death of Prasutagus, a Roman ally and client ruler, the king's lands and property were annexed and Iceni territory turned into a Roman province. To demonstrate the symbolic and literal fall of the royal family, Prasutagas' wife, Boudicca (who may have objected to the annexation on behalf of her daughters and people, although Tacitus does not say), was publicly whipped and their two daughters were raped [*stupro violatae*] by Roman soldiers.[74] These acts were likely intended to serve as an example to the Iceni—representing an unsubtle threat toward the women and daughters of the common people. Tacitus blames the perpetration of this atrocity along with the pillaging of wealth and property throughout the territory on centurions and veterans in newly founded colonies; he sidesteps the imperial decree and involvement of elite Roman officials (emperor, governor, generals) that caused these actions to be carried out.[75] In response to this expression of imperial domination, the Iceni were provoked to widespread anger and outrage, and—led by their Queen Boudicca—allied with other British tribes to take up arms in open revolt. This example, while serving Tacitus as a cautionary tale against greed and loss of virtuous control, also speaks to the way in which Roman soldiers could threaten non-compliant women of a subject territory with sexual violence, and sometimes act upon it.[76]

Throughout the first century CE, it is *possible* that a non-elite woman in Galilee or Syria could have been forced to fulfill the requirements of labor associated with the ἀγγαρήιον. But if such a woman had to walk for 1 mile down a Roman highway from her village, why would she choose to extend this potentially dangerous situation any longer than necessary? No matter if she was compelled alone or with a group of other local men and women, the fear of sexual assault from soldiers with bad intent would have increased as the miles did. And those following such advice would be naïve at best and foolishly risking danger at worst. Thus, Jesus's teaching to go a second mile down the road is androcentric; for female members of Matthew's audience it is unwarranted.

In another more plausible scenario that assumes more stereotypical gender roles of household responsibilities, a woman may have been forced to comply with the requests of soldiers in her home. On some occasions the requirements of *angaria* could permit soldiers to demand lodging, food, and shelter along the road. This practice, called *hospitium* (billeting), was also subject to abuse—as is evidenced in a letter from the governor of Syria Julius Saturnius to the villagers of Phaena in 185/86 CE: "If any soldier or private citizen billets with you against your will, inform me and you will receive satisfaction. For you owe no contribution to strangers nor can you be compelled, if you have a guest-room, to receive into your houses strangers. Display this in a conspicuous place in your chief-village, lest anyone offer the excuse of ignorance."[77] In this context, a local woman and her household could have been exploited by the uninvited "guests" for however long they chose to stay. This exploitation would have included space (including beds and blankets in short supply), light and heat (by hearth or oil lamps), and food and drink (use of scarce household resources: time and cost to cook for additional people, perhaps breaking into winter stores), and the indignity (as Scott describes) of being so treated without redress. The economic risks posed by *hospitium* are all the more clear when recalling the status of most of the populace, which Friesen and Longenecker identify as just above subsistence (22–27%) or at subsistence (30–40%) levels, little able to afford the use of precious resources for billeting soldiers, and placing them at risk of sliding below subsistence levels along with a 25–28% of the rest of the population.[78]

In this intimate setting, there was increased risk from soldiers who might want to abuse their authority, especially by means of sexual violence against female members of the household. Yet there were also opportunities for the woman and her family to practice creative forms of resistance: Were good blankets hidden away, and old thin ones provided instead? Was the food cooked properly? Were the stone flakes from the quern picked out of the flour after grinding before bread was baked? Was the water clean? Was the wine watered? Would there be backlash to any perceived disrespect or non-compliance? Creative application of Jesus's non-violent resistance could be undertaken; but, again, carrying a burden for a second mile was not one of them.

Alongside the situation of non-elite women, the presence of any enslaved woman complicates the picture of female roles and the usefulness of Jesus's directions in Matthew 5:41. Like a male slave, the female slave was responsible to her master or mistress—and would have been constrained from following Jesus's directions for the same reasons of obedience and punishment.[79] Additionally, an enslaved woman in the ancient world was always "vulnerable to sexual abuse,"[80] and imagining that she would place herself in a potentially more risky situation on the road is difficult to fathom as any sort of creative negotiation that restores dignity, resists Empire, or witnesses to the "good news" (Matt 4:23) about the Kingdom of Heaven.

CONCLUSION

For all the above arguments of social status and gender it is difficult to imagine how Jesus's specific directions at 5:41 could be enacted easily by slaves and women who needed to avoid trouble with their masters and prevent the violence of sexual assault. However, if these same slaves and women (with their multiple, overlapping identities) understood Jesus's teaching on the ἀγγαρήιον as Wink suggests—illustrative, subversive, open to creative interpretation, and offering new horizons for resistance—it may point toward other ways in which they could participate in the personal and communal restoration that were hallmarks of God's Empire appearing among them (Matt 4:17). Such a reading illuminates a scenario in which all the members of Matthew's audience and community could, when encountering demands by Roman soldiers for compliance to ἀγγαρήιον/*angaria*, express agency and dissent while preserving their lives and elevating dignity. The importance of such creative responses is evident in another Matthean scene, where Jesus himself meets a soldier on the road, which is the subject of chapter 4.

NOTES

1. *Inscriptions grecques et latines de la Syrie* (IGLS) V, no. 1998, transl. R.K. Sherk, ed. L. Jalabert, R. Mouterde et al.; quoted in Fergus Millar, *Roman Near East*, 85–86.

2. Davies and Allison, *Matthew*, 1:504–509; Luz, *Matthew 1-7*, 226–232; Carter, *Matthew and the Margins*, 143–144.

3. Although many scholars have used the term "antithesis" to describe Jesus' teaching here, the term "superthesis" may be more appropriate to avoid the implication of supercessionism. Jesus is not replacing the Torah but explaining to his hearers how they may intensify commitment to and fulfill it (Matt 5:17). The Greek particle δὲ, BDAG, 3rd ed., 213, may be used: "to connect one clause to another, either to express simple contrast or simple continuation . . . [as in] a series of closely related data or lines of narrative, *and, as for* . . . [or as] a marker with additive relation, with possible suggestion of contrast, *at the same time* . . . [or] heightened emphasis, *but also*."

4. Davies and Allison, *Matthew*, 1:481–482; Luz, *Matthew 1-7*, 210, notes that "Matthew 5:17–20 introduces the main part of the Sermon on the Mount. With the catchwords 'law' (νόμος) and 'prophets' (προφῆται), 5:17 and 7:12 form an inclusion. The main part consists of the sections 5:21–48 and 6:19–7:11, which are of exactly equal length, and the shorter central section 6:1–18."

5. See n.47 and n.48.

6. Walter Wink, *Engaging the Powers* (Minneapolis: Fortress Press, 1992), 197, n.546.

7. ἀνθίστημι, Liddle and Scott, *Greek-English Lexicon*, 9th ed. (Oxford, UK: Clarendon Press, 1977), 140, refers to a variety of occurrences all related to warfare: Thucydides, *Peloponnesian War* 1.54, 105; (setting up a victory trophy against an enemy); 4.115 (in battle); Herodotus, *Histories* 5.72; 6.117; 8.75 (resisting the enemy in battle).

8. Other references include: *JW* 1.107; 7.246; *Ant.* 12.308; *Ap.* 2.23.

9. Other NT occurrences include Luke 21:15 and Acts 6:10 (adversaries cannot resist words of wisdom given by the Spirit); Gal 2:11 (Paul opposes Cephas "to his face"); and Rom 13:2 (Paul counsels Christ-followers to obey Roman law and not to resist authority).

10. The angels appear after the prayer of the righteous priest Eleazar (3 Macc 6:1–16); there are parallels here to Matt 26:51–54, where (following a prayer) Jesus says he may call upon "twelve legions of angels" for assistance.

11. Walter Wink, "Beyond Just War and Pacifism: Jesus' Nonviolent Way," *Review and Expositor*, Jan. 1 (1992): 209, n.6.

12. cf. Matt 24:1–31; 26:51–54. See chapter 5.

13. Herodotus, *Histories* 8.98, transl. Andrea Purvis, *The Landmark Herodotus: The Histories*, ed. Robert Strassler (New York: Pantheon, 2007), 642: "there are as many horses and men posted at intervals as there are days required for the entire journey, so that one man and one horse are assigned to one day. And neither snow nor rain nor hear nor dark of night keeps them from completing their appointed course

as swiftly as possible. The first courier passes on the instructions to the second, the second to the third, and from there they are transmitted from one to another all the way through, just as the torchbearing relay is celebrated by the Hellenes in honor of Hephastios. The Persians call this horse-posting system the *angareion*."

14. Suetonius, *Augustus* 49.3: "*Et quo celerius ac sub manum adnuntiari cognosique posset, quid in provincial quaeque gereretur iuvenes primo modicus intervallis per militaris vias, dehine vehicula disposuit.*" Discussed by Anne Kolb, "Transport and Communication in the Roman State: The *Cursus Publicus*," in *Travel and Geography in the Roman Empire*, ed. Colin Adams and Ray Laurence (New York: Routledge, 2001), 95–96. Culturally, this development also fits neatly into the Roman practice of patronage and personal networks, which is well-discussed elsewhere.

15. Mitchell, "Requisitioned Transport," 112, notes that the term *cursus publicus* "which is regularly used by modern writers to describe the postal or transport system in the early empire, is not attested before the fourth century ... The earlier term was apparently *vehiculatio*." The modern convention is used throughout this chapter. In a similar vein, there are also occasions in which scholars equate the ἀγγαρήιον with the *cursus publicus* during the early Imperial period; this conflation is understandable, as the terms are so intimately related: the *cursus publicus* could not function without the ἀγγαρήιον/*angaria*; without the *cursus publicus* the ἀγγαρήιον/*angaria* would not have reason to exist. See Naphatali Lewis, "Domitian's Order on Requisitioned Transport and Lodgings," *Revue international des droits de l'antiquite* 15 (1968): 135, for one example.

16. Mitchell, "Requisitioned Transport," 113, notes that "the new inscription does not give the date of his governorship, but internal evidence suggests that it spanned the death of Augustus and the accession of Tiberius.... Sotidius ... explicitly states that he had received these instructions [*mandata*] in person, [and] we must conclude that he had been appointed by Augustus and continued his term of office under Tiberius, when the edict was issued.... A date of c.13–15 [CE] would fit well."

17. Mitchell, "Requisitioned Transport," 107–109. Kolb, "Transport," 96, also writes that, "Augustus intended that only vital official dispatches would be carried. The first system of runners was no more than a courier service. The second system, however, which remained in effect throughout the later period, could do more ... [The] *vehicula*—that is to say pack animals, boats, or most specifically wagons— could [also] carry ... other persons as well as a limited amount of baggage or other freight."

18. Mitchell, "Requisitioned Transport," 109, translates the inscription: "the right to use this service will not be granted to everyone, but to the procurator of the best of princes and his son ... to persons on military service, both to those who have a diploma, and to those who travel through from other provinces on military service ... to senators of the Roman people ... to a Roman knight whose services are being employed by the best of princes." When he was governor of Bithynia, Pliny, *Letters*, wrote to the emperor Trajan twice on the topic of *diplomata*: once for advice about those with expired dates (the emperor says do not use them; he always sends new ones well in advance) (10.45–46); and a second time asking forgiveness for bending the rules to accommodate his wife's travel to her grandfather's funeral (10.120–121).

19. Mitchell, "Requisitioned Transport," 109.
20. Mitchell, "Requisitioned Transport," 109.
21. E.W. Black, *Cursus Publicus: the Infrastructure of Government in Roman Britain* (Oxford, UK: Hadrian Books, 1995). In Chapter 2 he also provides a helpful general summary of the *cursus publicus*.
22. Black, *Cursus Publicus*, 9.
23. Black, *Cursus Publicus*, 10.
24. Black, *Cursus Publicus*, 10.
25. Black, *Cursus Publicus*, 10.
26. Black, *Cursus Publicus*, 10.
27. Mitchell, "Requisitioned Transport," 106, 114.
28. Mitchell, "Requisitioned Transport," 111–112, 114. See also Kolb, "Transport," 97. The Germanicus edict is discussed by Naphatali Lewis, "Domitian's Order on Requisitioned Transport and Lodgings," *Revue international des droits de l'antiquite* 15 (1968): 135–142, 140, who links it to the Capito inscription, in which a *diplomata* is required: "μηδέν λαμβάνειν εἰ μή τινες ἐμὰ διπλώματα ἔξοσιν."
29. Tacitus, *Histories* 1.67 (Moore, LCL). The abuse of the *cursus publicus* was, in fact, part of a larger problem of embezzlement of tax monies by the Legion; the Roman general Caecina responded to the arrest of his soldiers by going to war against the Helvetii: "he immediately shifted camp, devastated the fields, and ravaged a place that during the long peace . . . was much resorted to for its beauty and healthful waters. Messengers were sent to the auxiliaries in Raetia, directing them to attack in the rear the Helvetians who were facing the Roman legions."
30. Tacitus, *Histories* 2.54 (Moore, LCL).
31. IGLS V, no. 1998, transl. R.K. Sherk, quoted in Fergus Millar, *Roman Near East*, 85–86.
32. Barbara Levick, "Domitian and the Provinces," *Latomus* 41.1 (1982): 50–53, recounts this argument and refutes it.
33. Levick, "Domitian and the Provinces," 52–53, 73; Naphatali Lewis, "Requisitioned Transport," 135–142; Kolb, "Transport," 97.
34. Apuleius, *Metamorphoses* 9.39 (Hanson, LCL). The gardener's usual practice is to load the donkey with vegetables and lead him to town; after selling the vegetables to local vendors, he rides home again (9.32). The soldier is a centurion, as indicated by his *vitis* (vine-staff), a mark of rank.
35. Matthew's account differs from that of Mark, who explicitly mentions "some of the bystanders [who] said to them, 'What are you doing, untying the colt?'" (11:5) and are satisfied with the reason the disciples give: "they told them what Jesus had said; and they allowed them to take it." (11:6).
36. Isaac, *Limits of Empire*, 292.
37. Dan Sperber, "Angaria in Rabbinic Literature," *L'Antiquite Classique* 38 (1969): 165; some of Sperber's explanatory comments are edited from this quotation.
38. Isaac, *Limits of Empire*, 285–291. Isaac argues that taxation in-kind began in the 2nd and 3rd centuries CE; see chapter 1 of this work, which argues that this took place earlier, and was the case throughout the imperial period.
39. Isaac, *Limits of Empire*, 293.

40. Isaac, *Limits of Empire*, 293.
41. Isaac, *Limits of Empire*, 295.
42. Sperber, "Angaria," 165.
43. ἐρχόμενον ἀπ' ἀγροῦ (Mark 15:21 // Luke 23:26); Matthew redacts this phrase.
44. ἐπιλαμβάνομαι BDAG, 3rd ed., 374, includes the sense of take hold of, grasp, catch ("sometimes with violence"), take into custody, arrest.
45. Walter Wink, *Engaging the Powers*, 203.
46. Davies and Allison, *Matthew*, 1:538–540, 546–547 and Luz, *Matthew 1-7*, 270–272, for instance, employ historical criticism to identify redactional traces in Matthew 5:41 as a way to highlight the ways in which Matthew used source material, some of which was perhaps rooted in the words and ministry of the historical Jesus. From this perspective, Davies and Allison, *Matthew*, 1: 546, conclude that Jesus is speaking about personal ethics and promoting interpersonal kindness, and is concerned with: "rooting out the spirit of personal vengeance and self-pity from his followers." For Luz, *Matthew 1-7*, 274, the teachings of Matthew's Jesus are "not very convincing ... [and] give no thought to what may be their quite ambivalent consequences." Instead, Luz, *Matthew 1-7*, 274–275, argues that these teachings are meant to "protest symbolically against the standard use of force. Their evidence is not that the behavior they demand would be plausible but that they are a 'sigh of the oppressed'... against dehumanizing spirals of violence and of the hope for a different kind of personal behavior than what can be experienced in everyday life." He concludes that the manifestation of the kingdom of God is thus an eschatological hope that reveals God's love for all, rather than what is argued in this chapter: that Jesus' teaching is a means by which Matthew's audience can negotiate the everyday powers of Rome's empire until it can be brought to eschatological judgment, overthrown, and replaced by God's Empire in the coming age.
47. The discussion of ethnicity seeks to identify the locus of Matthew 5:41 in the conflict between the Matthean community and nascent rabbinic Judaism and the boundaries between them. Sim, *Christian Judaism*, 130, writes that the purpose of Matthew 5:21–48 is to provide a scene in which "Jesus the Messiah provides a new and definitive interpretation of the Mosaic code based upon the principle encapsulated in the love command.... [so that it] is affirmed ... and its demands intensified." Sim, 141, argues that this "code of conduct" is an "ideal lifestyle" which "determines and sharpens the boundaries between the evangelist's group and those who live outside it." Saldarini, *Christian-Jewish Community*, 162–163, concurs, setting the teaching in the context of Matthew's leadership of "a reform group in the Jewish community ... [in which] justice and mercy is the core of Jesus' message and of the Matthean way of life." Saldarini, 163–164, also glosses over Matthew 5:41, emphasizing those verses around it that may apply to his argument: the Matthean community is one in which "legal retaliation will not be necessary, and love of enemies will repair broken relationships.... Matthew thus envisions his little group of believers-in-Jesus influencing Jewish society to become an ideal community ruled by God, that is, the 'kingdom of heaven.'" Although he comes to a different conclusion about the ethnic composition of the Matthean community than Sim and Saldarini, J. Andrew Overman, *Matthew and Formative Judaism*, 94–95, shares their perspective that the Gospel's purpose

is "community-forming," and that Matthew 5–7 serves as a constitution which addresses concrete issues of community members getting along with one another. For Overman, *Matthew and Formative Judaism*, 96, the intent of Matthew 5:39–42 is to address the "*disposition* of the members toward one another . . . [and encourage] forgiveness and reconciliation . . . [including] those whom the members might hold to be enemies or outsiders, and not just fellow members of the community." Thus, while those concerned with ethnicity may acknowledge that members of the Matthean community might interact with others beyond their own sectarian group, the imperial context in which community members live is invisible and left unexamined—and Jesus' teaching on the ἀγγαρήιον is grouped with other general directions that are intended to direct intra-community relationships.

48. Keener, *Matthew*, 200.
49. Chapter 9 of *Engaging the Powers*, 175–193: "Beyond Just War and Pacifism: Jesus' Nonviolent Way."
50. Wink, *Engaging the Powers*, 198. See also Carter, *Matthew and the Margins*, 151–152.
51. Wink, *Engaging the Powers*, 199.
52. Wink, *Engaging the Powers*, 198.
53. Wink, *Engaging the Powers*, 204.
54. Wink, *Engaging the Powers*, 205.
55. Wink, *Engaging the Powers*, 204–205. See also Carter, *Matthew and the Margins*, 152–153, who is indebted to Wink at this point.
56. Wink, *Engaging the Powers*, 213, n.30.
57. Wink, *Engaging the Powers*, 205.
58. Scott, *Domination*, 7.
59. Scott, *Domination*, 114.
60. Loomba, *Postcolonialism*, 192.
61. Loomba, *Postcolonialism*, 193–194.
62. Scott, *Domination*, 191–192.
63. Loomba, *Postcolonialism*, 198–199, also cautions that "subaltern agency, either at the individual level or at the collective, cannot be idealized as pure opposition to the order it opposes; it both works within that order and displays its own contradictions . . . [The term 'subaltern' should be used] to draw distinctions *within* colonized peoples, between the elite and non-elite . . . positioned simultaneously within several different discourses of power and resistance."
64. The status of enslaved females is addressed below.
65. Aristotle, *Politics* 1.2.4.
66. J. Albert Harrill, *Slaves in the New Testament: Literary, Moral and Social Dimensions* (Minneapolis, MN: Fortress Press, 2006), 158–159.
67. Matt 18:23–34 illustrates a typical legal scenario, where a slave is judged by his master for financial indiscretions.
68. Harrill, *Slaves*, 39.
69. Appian, *Civil Wars* 1.14, 116–120 (White, LCL), describes the most famous example of Spartacus, who, after a three year rebellion, was defeated and killed in battle: "A large number of his men fled from the battlefield to the mountains... and

continued to fight until they all perished except 6,000, who were captured and crucified along the whole road from Capua to Rome."

70. cf. Matt 20:25–28; 24:45–51; 25:14–30, where these type of slaves appear in metaphorical construction.

71. Harrill, *Slaves,* 87, 148–149, complicates these identities still further by pointing out hierarchies of slaves in large households: high ranking slaves could be assigned their own slaves; agricultural overseers and household stewards were responsible for teaching and directing other slaves in daily work on behalf of their common masters. This, however, goes beyond the point being made here.

72. Zeba Crook, "Honor, Shame, and Social Status Revisited," *JBL* 128.3 (Fall, 2009), 593. See also Margaret MacDonald, *Early Christian Women and Pagan Opinion* (Cambridge, UK: Cambridge University Press, 1996), 28.

73. Crook, "Honor, Shame," 609: "Malina's abstract model is built on the anthropological tradition that claims that the public sphere belonged to men while women were limited to the private sphere. The problem, as others have indicated, is that social 'laws' and social practice do not always correlate. There appears to have been an ideal world and a lived world, and in the lived world women *did* participate in public life, *did* compete for honor, *could* have greater honor than their husbands, *did* act as benefactors, and *were* given crowns, statues, and seats of honor. The presence of women in areas *traditionally* demarcated as male . . . is too amply documented to be deemed countercultural or exceptional."

74. Tacitus, *Ann.* 14.31, 35. See chapter 2, n.28.

75. Tacitus, *Ann.* 14.31.

76. Tacitus, *Agr.* 30.4–31 (Hutton and Ogilvie, LCL), expresses a similar sentiment in the words of Calgacus, another tribal chieftain facing Roman legions: "*raptores orbis . . . coniuges sororesque etiam si hostilem libidinem effugerunt . . . polluuntur*" ("Robbers of the world ... East nor West has glutted them . . . To plunder, butcher, steal, these things they misname empire . . . Children and kin are by the law of nature each man's dearest possessions; they are swept away from us by conscription to be slaves in other lands: our wives and sisters, even when they escape a soldier's lust, are debauched by self-styled friends and guests"). See chapter 1.

77. *OGIS* 609, quoted in S.R. Llewelyn, *New Documents Illustrating Early Christianity,* vol. 7 (Marrickville, NSW: Southwood Press, 1994), 80.

78. See chapter 1.

79. In the household of her mistress, the lodging of unwanted guests would have created more work (cooking, serving) and also made her vulnerable to additional harassment.

80. Carolyn Osiek and Margaret MacDonald, *A Woman's Place* (Minneapolis, MN: Fortress Press, 2006), 103; Glancy, *Slavery,* 27–29, 50–53. The situation of female slaves forced into prostitution is addressed in Chapter 1: these women could be found on the road and in the presence of soldiers, but would not be subject to the *angaria,* as they travelled under the watchful eyes of their owner or *leno.* The sexual abuse they suffered was not the same as the risk described here, although the need for negotiating imperial systems of oppression was just as acute.

Chapter 4

Responding to Direct Imperial Requests

Jesus, the Centurion, and His Slave (Matthew 8:5–13)

They wish the centurions not to be so much bold and adventurous, as men with a faculty for command, steady, and of a profound rather than a showy spirit; not prone to engage wantonly or be unnecessarily forward in giving battle; but such as in the face of superior numbers and overwhelming pressure will die in defense of their post.
Polybius, Histories 6.24[1]

It is by obeying, not by questioning, the orders of commanders that military power is kept together. And that army is the most courageous in the moment of peril, which is the most orderly before the peril comes.
Tacitus, History 1.84[2]

INTRODUCTION

Throughout the gospel narrative, Matthew portrays different dimensions of Roman military power and provides different ways to negotiate it, offering advice for residents of the empire who are his audience and members of the Matthean community. Previous chapters have examined Matthew's strategies for negotiating the power represented by Roman-aligned client rulers Herod and Antipas and the practice of ἀγγαρήιον/*angaria*. Each of these facets of military power represents a different challenge to contend with, and it is for this reason that Matthew's strategies are varied—including avoidance when possible, reliance on divine intervention, and creative non-violent resistance. This chapter addresses another facet of Matthew's portrayal of Roman military power: a scene in which a Roman soldier approaches Jesus with a direct request to receive the benefits of divine power.

Matthew 8:5–13 shows Jesus, coming home to Capernaum, encountering a centurion who seeks him out to request healing for a slave who is suffering "in terrible distress" (8:6). Jesus agrees to accompany the centurion to his home but is surprised when the man declares he need not come: formally deferential, the soldier proclaims that he only needs Jesus to speak a word and it will be so. Jesus is amazed, praises the soldier's faith, and pronounces that he will be among those who "come from the east and west" and join "the kingdom of heaven" (8:10–11). The soldier's slave is healed, and Jesus continues on his way.

Located as the central event in a three part cycle of healing stories (8:1–17), this episode reveals yet another facet of Matthew's strategies of imperial negotiation.[3] For it is not just any soldier who makes a request of Jesus, but a centurion: the backbone of the Roman army—a highly trained, extremely competent, responsible officer who was granted authority to command potentially hundreds of men in battle and lead detachments of soldiers in a variety of situations. It is this type of soldier Polybius (*Hist.* 6.24) describes as serious and capable: "men with a faculty for command, steady, and of a profound rather than a showy spirit . . . [and brave enough] in the face of superior numbers and overwhelming pressure . . . [to] die in defense of their post."[4] Centurions appear throughout Roman literature, and are characterized not only as Polybius does—with valor, bravery, and leadership skills—but also as undisciplined, prone to excessive violence, greedy, mutinous, and bullying.[5] While the likely identity of such a centurion would be that of a Gentile officer serving in Herod Antipas's royal forces (allied with and organized according to the Roman model), his potential unit and posting are immaterial for the argument here.[6] Instead, the focus of this chapter is on Jesus's encounter with a representative of the vast network of Roman military power, and Matthew's negotiation with this power in constructing the scene.

Matthew's narrative is centered on Jesus's response to the centurion, who identifies himself clearly: "I am a man under authority, with soldiers under me" (8:9). Matthew indicates a host of connections to systems of hierarchy, authority, and command in the ways that the centurion approaches and interacts with Jesus.[7] In response to this direct and specific request, Matthew's Jesus does not confront, but is "amazed" and bestows praise upon the soldier (8:10–12). This cooperation imitates and reinscribes the imperial ideology of authority and power the centurion represents and wields by virtue of his office.

In contrast to some other commentators, I argue in this chapter that Matthew's characterization of the centurion is ambiguous, and it is possible to view this soldier in a variety of ways.[8] He may be honorable and just (approaching Jesus honestly and with sincerity); he may be pragmatic, efficient, and self-serving (using persuasion, rather than threat, as the most expedient way to encourage Jesus to act so his slave may return to work); he may be heavy-handed and abusive (toward his slave, the cause of whose paralysis is unstated); or he may embody attributes of all of three. In a similar way, Matthew's portrayal of Jesus's response is also ambiguous: his amazement at the centurion's request may be viewed as happy appreciation or stunned incredulity. Whatever way Jesus's response is read, he ultimately cooperates and does not directly confront this soldier of the empire with regard to either the role of military power in enforcing imperial mandates or the demeaning institution of slavery: the paralyzed slave is healed and Jesus and the centurion continue on their respective ways.

Through this interaction Matthew shows his audience how, when the empire approaches, there are strategies by which its agents may (must?) be dealt with cooperatively—while waiting for ultimate (eschatological) judgment on the empire as a whole. Thus, just as Jesus's followers are instructed to turn the other cheek and go a second mile (Matt 5:38–41), here Matthew shows another way in which to negotiate imperial power non-violently for the present time while awaiting the final divine intervention. Healing the centurion's slave reveals the power of God to an agent of Rome (the centurion), allows for the possibility that even such an agent may be included in God's Empire, partially assists (through healing, but not freeing) one who is afflicted by imperial systems, and withholds divine judgment of Rome and its agents until a future time.

WHEN THE EMPIRE APPROACHES (MATT 8:5–13)

After teaching on a mountain (Matt 5–7), Jesus returns to Capernaum in a journey composed of three episodes in which he heals three unnamed persons: a man with leprosy (8:1–4); a paralyzed man enslaved by a centurion (8:5–13); and Peter's mother-in-law who has a fever (8:14–15).[9] The portrayal of Jesus on this journey elaborates the way in which Matthew characterizes Jesus's work earlier in the gospel. In 4:23–24 Matthew's audience learns that Jesus is one who teaches, announces the good news of God's empire, and helps people by "curing every disease and every sickness among the people . . . [including] those who were afflicted with various diseases and pains, demoniacs, epileptics, and paralytics." Jesus's reputation grows because of this work, spreading "throughout all Syria" (4:24), with crowds following him as they once followed John the Baptist (3:5).

With this characterization in mind, Matthew's readers will not be surprised that Jesus is contacted twice on the way to Capernaum with requests for healing.[10] Each episode begins with the same verb, προσέρχομαι ("approached," 8:2, 5), indicating that although Jesus and his disciples are on the move, individuals are seeking him out because of his reputation as a healer. In both cases, those approaching Jesus are respectful in their language and demeanor, although because of their differing social status the men who are requesting help speak with him in very different ways. In the first case, a man with leprosy "came to him and knelt before him" (προσελθὼν προσεκύνει αὐτῷ, 8:2); his deference and humility toward Jesus are in proportion to his socially undesirable disease. Nevertheless, when the man asks to be made clean, Jesus helps him without delay, and sends him to a priest who can certify that the man is no longer ritually unclean and thus able to return to his rightful place in society (Lev 14:1–20).

In the second case, "a centurion came to him, appealing to him" (προσῆλθεν αὐτῷ ἑκατόνταρχος παρακαλῶν αὐτὸν, 8:5) to help a paralyzed man (παραλυτικός).[11] The centurion's language reveals both his social position and Matthew's awareness of the ideology of the empire. Matthew introduces the soldier (who speaks in the first person) as "a man under authority, with soldiers under me" (8:9a), characterizing him as one who is used to giving commands and having them obeyed (8:9b). For these reasons, the centurion assumes that Jesus—with his reputation throughout the region as a healer—possesses an analogous status, ability, and outlook that will be employed toward his slave's paralysis. Like the man with leprosy, the centurion's demeanor toward Jesus is deferential: he addresses Jesus politely as κύριος ("lord, master") and proclaims his own unworthiness (οὐκ εἰμὶ ἱκανὸς) that such a powerful man as Jesus would enter his house (8:8). Yet unlike the man with leprosy, the centurion does not bow before Jesus; he, too, is a κύριος who controls his own property and disposes of it: "I say . . . to my slave, 'Do this,' and the slave does it" (8:9).[12] Jesus's response to the centurion is perhaps therefore all the more surprising. When the centurion declares that Jesus needs only to "speak the word" (8:8) for the paralyzed slave to be healed, Jesus is amazed (θαυμάζω), and says "Truly I tell you, in no one in Israel have I found such faith. I tell you, many will come from east and west and will eat with Abraham and Isaac and Jacob in the kingdom of heaven, while the heirs of the kingdom will be thrown into the outer darkness, where there will be weeping and gnashing of teeth" (8:10–12). Matthew's depiction of the healing is done with an ellipsis, to provide narrative contrast to the healing of the man with leprosy as well as narrative emphasis to Jesus's prior statement about the centurion's faith and the kingdom of heaven by those who are included and those who are excluded. Following Jesus's declaration, Matthew's scene concludes simply: "And the slave was healed at that very hour" (8:13).[13]

As in other scenes in the gospel in which Matthew reveals androcentric and free person-oriented assumptions, in 8:5–13 there is minimal characterization of the centurion's slave. The paralyzed man, although mentioned several times, never in fact appears in the scene. Instead, he remains unseen and unnamed. He is referred to three times by the centurion (8:6, 8, 9); once by Jesus (8:7), and once in a narrative comment by Matthew that completes the scene (8:13).[14] Matthew's vocabulary is noteworthy, and differs from that of a parallel account in Luke 7:1–10: the centurion refers to the paralyzed man as ὁ παῖς μου (8:6, 8) and ὁ δοῦλος μου (8:9), both of which can be translated "my slave." However, παῖς may refer to a slave, servant, or child; and this may present the possibility of a more colloquial and insulting diminutive: "my 'boy' is . . . in terrible distress."[15] The immediate reason for this distress is the slave's paralysis; however, the cause of this paralysis is not given (in contrast to Matt 17:14–20, where Jesus heals a boy whose malady is clearly identified as epilepsy caused by a demonic spirit).[16] In light of the conditions under which slaves lived in the Empire, we might wonder about the cause of this slave's paralysis: Was he stricken with an illness or parasitic contagion? While following orders did he hurt himself lifting too heavy a load? Did he have an accident falling from a height, or something falling on him? Did the centurion beat him so hard on the back and legs so as to cause a spinal injury? Any of these scenarios may explain the paralyzed man's condition; Matthew, however, is not concerned about its causes.

Matthew's account is focused instead on the centurion's πίστις ("faith, trust") in Jesus to heal his slave and Jesus's response. As with the slave, Matthew's lack of detail about the centurion (other than his dialogue with Jesus) creates an ambiguity. Readers are left to wonder about the soldier's motivations and mindset: Is he truly and humanely concerned about the slave? Is he annoyed at the inconvenience of lost work? Is he dispassionate and businesslike, hoping Jesus can help to restore order to his household? Interpretations that characterize the centurion affirmatively do so based on Jesus's response in 8:10, reading θαυμάζω ("amaze, wonder, marvel, be astonished") in a positive manner[17] contrasted with the negative evaluation of many in Israel who "will be thrown into the outer darkness" (8:11–12).[18] This positive interpretation of the centurion's demeanor is complicated, however, by other occurrences of θαυμάζω at Matt 9:33; 15:31; 21:20; 22:22; 27:14, which display a range of responses that are in keeping with the verb's broader range of meaning: "to be extraordinarily impressed *or disturbed* by something . . . the context determines whether in a good or bad sense."[19] Matthew's description of Jesus's response is thus ambiguous as well. He may be happily appreciative with the soldier's affirmation of his authority and power to heal. He may also be shocked and incredulous that an agent of the empire has approached him directly: not to threaten or terrorize a civilian, arrest and execute a prophet, or abuse the *angaria*—but to ask for assistance. While the words of judgment in 8:11–12 make it likely that Matthew intends a contrast between Jesus's negative evaluation of the (unfaithful) "heirs of the kingdom" and the (faithful) centurion, the imperial context introduces factors that complicate Matthew's presentation and allow for ambiguity in Jesus's response to the soldier.

The other feature of this scene in which Matthew shows Jesus sidestepping a direct confrontation with imperial power is in Jesus's response to the master-slave relationship. As in the case of Jesus's command to "go a second mile" (discussed in chapter 3), Matthew again focuses on free rather than enslaved people. While Jesus's teaching in Matthew 5:41 shows a way for non-elite free males to negotiate the empire by pushing back against the requirements of the *angaria*, here it is a free, slave-owning male whose faith and trust in Jesus (8:10–12) provides an opportunity for imperial negotiation. When read in relation to ethical commitments to human dignity and personal autonomy, it is clear that Matthew's portrayal of Jesus's actions—although they alleviate physical malady—do nothing to address the injustice of slavery. After hearing the request, Jesus neither seeks to overturn this system nor transform the centurion's relationship with his slave: he does not confront the man as a slave owner, nor free the slave, nor even offer moral advice on how to be a good master.[20] Instead his healing returns the slave, now able-bodied, to the work of slavery and praises the master. When read in connection with the third healing episode—where Jesus heals Peter's mother-in-law from a fever "and she got up and began to serve him" (8:14–15)—the paralyzed man's healing implies that he will immediately return to his subservient role. Although Jesus's healing word may bring relief from "terrible distress" (8:5) it also reinscribes the slave's position of required obedience to the centurion's orders and commands to serve. Missing is any prophetic word against his enslavement. For these reasons, Matthew's Jesus demonstrates an unwillingness to directly confront two fundamental structures of the Roman Empire: military power and slavery.

There is one additional aspect of Matthew's presentation that emphasizes the imperial ideology of obedience to those of higher social status. In 8:14–15 Matthew describes how Peter's mother-in-law, after being healed by Jesus (8:15), "got up and began to serve him" (ἠγέρθη καὶ διηκόνει αὐτῷ).[21] This use of διακονέω ("serve") points toward a connection between women and slaves who must work in subservient roles based on gender and low status. Matthew, however, also uses διακονέω throughout the gospel (Matt 20:26, 28; 23:11; 27:55) to denote serving as God's agent, rendering help and assistance, taking care of others, and serving in an official capacity ("minister")—all of which are positive attributes applied to Jesus and those around him.[22] For this reason, Peter's mother-in-law (and those who work as she does) may be understood to have agency: their work is integral to Jesus's work and mission, and the growth and success of God's Kingdom. Although readers might hope that Jesus's healing creates a similar opportunity for the recently unparalyzed slave, this possibility for future improvements in his condition is beyond the scope of Matthew's presentation.

In 8:5–13, Matthew constructs a scene in which Roman military power is embodied by one individual, a centurion who represents hierarchies of command and obedience, and affirms both the network and ideology of power that uphold it. When this agent of the empire approaches, Matthew's Jesus shows little inclination for direct confrontation and criticism of the domination embodied in the imperial structures of military hierarchy and slavery. In fact, after hearing these values voiced aloud by the centurion, Matthew's Jesus simply reiterates his tenets and includes the soldier in the eschatological feast (8:10–12). The imagery for such a feast comes from such passages as Psalm 107 and Isaiah 25:1–10a, which indicates that those included by God may come from near or far and may include Jews and Gentiles. What Matthew's Jesus makes clear in such places as 8:11; 22:8–10; and 25:31–40, however, is that the elite who oppress, exploit, and do violence to the common people are excluded, subject to divine judgment, and suffer in "outer darkness, where there will be weeping and gnashing of teeth" (8:12; also 13:42, 50; 22:13–14; 24:51; 25:41–46).

In contrast to other strategies of negotiation—such as avoidance (Herod and Antipas), non-violent resistance (going a second mile), and calls for eschatological judgment to replace the Roman Empire with that of God's (24:1–51)[23]—Jesus's tactic here is a model of cooperation, inclusion, and welcome. For those who must negotiate the public transcript of compliance and conformity to imperial power, this mask of acquiescence may be a strategy of survival: what good could possibly come for Jesus, his disciples, or the slave if Jesus were to denounce or angrily confront the centurion? It may also reflect Matthew's openness to all who recognize Jesus's abilities as a divinely empowered healer: whether Jew or Gentile, this soldier—because he trusts Jesus's power—will be welcome in the eschatological feast where the centurion's submission to God's empire will be required. Thus, Matthew creates a scene in which ambiguity of response is appropriate when directly interacting with agents of the empire like the centurion.

JESUS' AMAZEMENT: WHEN IMPERIAL AGENTS MAKE A DIRECT REQUEST

The Roman soldier who interacts with Jesus in Matthew 8:5–13 is one of several agents representing Roman military power that Jesus and his followers must negotiate in the gospel narrative. In this case, an imperial agent (the centurion) approaches Jesus and then surprises him with a declaration of trust in his healing power, providing an occasion for Jesus to comment on the inclusion of people from far away—"from the east and from the west" (8:11)—in God's eschatological kingdom.[24] God's purposes thus even embrace agents of the Roman Empire.

This section demonstrates how the centurion's declaration and Jesus's amazed response represent another facet of Matthew's presentation of strategies for imperial negotiation. Here Matthew allows for the possibility that some of Rome's agents will acknowledge God's power and perhaps benefit from it, while at the same time the gospel leaves unchallenged other aspects of imperial ideology—in particular relationships of hierarchical power represented by the centurion and his slave. Matthew's depiction of the centurion calls upon an understanding of the soldier's role in the military organizational and command structure; reveals a soldier whose motivations defy easy explanation; and reveals the soldier's belief in divine power—the "faith" that Jesus praises. The resulting display of divine power has immediate but limited benefits (for the slave who is healed, but not freed) and long-term implications (for those welcomed at the eschatological banquet), hinting at what might happen when agents of Rome acknowledge God's presence and power.

The Centurion's Role

The first aspect of Matthew's portrayal is the centurion's self-characterization as "a man under authority, with soldiers under me" (Matt 8:9). This reference to the longstanding Roman military system is one which Matthew's audience, living in the Empire, would undoubtedly have known. By the late first century CE when Matthew wrote his gospel, the rank of centurion as an officer assigned to legionary and auxiliary units had been established in the Roman military system for several centuries.[25] In Greek and Latin Roman literature the centurion (Greek: ἑκατοντάρχης/ἑκατόνταρχος or κεντυρίων; Latin: *centurio, -onis*) is portrayed as fulfilling a variety of roles that were crucial to the functioning, expansion and maintenance of the Empire. Graham Webster locates the centurion within an organizational structure used from the time of Augustus onward: a legion was commanded by the *legatus legionis* (legionary commander, selected from former tribunes), 6 military tribunes (typically young men from aristocratic families, who served for a few years prior to entering the Senate), *praefectus castrorum* (responsible for the camp, food supply, and procurement of equipment), and 60 ranked centurions (the highest being the *primus pilus* or "first spear"), who were each in charge of a Century of 80 *milites*.[26] Over all these military personnel stood the emperor himself, "whose *imperium* gave him official power to raise an army, [and who] appointed his own generals to command the legions in his place."[27]

No less than aristocratic legates and tribunes, centurions were also part of the imperial bureaucracy: their service records "were maintained in Rome by the *ab epistulis* [a government administrator] and his staff, and their appointment, promotion, and transfer were all in the last resort subject to the Emperor's approval."[28] Centurions were awarded their rank from a variety of prior positions, including promotion directly from the Praetorian Guard or civilian professions; however, as Webster notes, "the most obvious [path] would seem to have been through direct promotion from the ranks.... usually possible after at least twelve years' service, although outstanding martial powers and a gift for leadership shown in the field could shorten the period."[29] Once selected for the centurionate, a soldier's career could include even further promotion—up to and including entry into the ranks of the Roman aristocracy.[30] One notable example of this was C. Velius Rufus, who held the rank of centurion when he was decorated by Titus for acts of valor during the capture of Jerusalem in 70 CE, and eventually rose to procuratorial governorships of Pannonia and Dalmatia, and Raetia, as well as the ambassadorship to Parthia.[31] Thus, as Michael Grant states, "A centurion could be a veteran quartermaster nearing the end of his active service, a middle-aged staff officer, or a young company commander with a successful career in front of him."[32]

During the Imperial period, Grant emphasizes the "great variety of tasks a centurion had to perform." On a daily basis, the centurion "had to keep track of all [the century's] arms and equipment, with two clerks to help him.... [He] posted guards, conducted inspections and checked that work had been done.... [And also handled] training the rank and file . . . [because] recruits had to be trained within the legions."[33] This training included marching, physical training (running, jumping, swimming, carrying heavy packs), weapon training, training in the field (including creating the ditch and palisade of a marching camp), and battle formations.[34]

Wherever soldiers were stationed in any number throughout a province such as Syria, there was likely to be a centurion assigned to command them. Ancient authors also describe centurions who announced the start of each watch (Tacitus, *Ann.* 15.30), delivered letters (Tacitus, *Hist.* 1.67), escorted dignitaries (Tacitus, *Ann.* 1.41), guarded prisoners (Josephus, *Ant.* 18.195; Tacitus, *Ann.* 13.9; Livy, *Hist.* 4.34), engaged in policing and crowd control (Josephus, *JW* 2.297; Tacitus, *Ann.* 1.77), and oversaw building projects (Suetonius, *Caligula* 21). Furthermore, for all these tasks, it was necessary for the centurion to read and write, and lack of literacy "is why the great majority of the troops remained in the ranks."[35]

Besides his usual command of infantry *milites* ("soldiers"), the centurion could also command marines on a naval ship (Caesar, *Gallic Wars* 3.14), auxiliary cohorts (Tacitus, *Agricola* 28), cavalry (Josephus, *JW* 2.297), scouting parties (Suetonius, *Tiberius* 60), or detachments on special political missions (Tacitus, *Ann.* 15.25; 15.5), including assassinations (Appian, *Civil Wars* 4.4; 3.104; Tacitus, *Ann.* 14.8; 15.58-59; Suetonius, *Nero* 49; *Domitian* 10). In many instances, an individual officer's career might include service in a number of these types of units, in several different legions, or on the staff of a provincial governor or *legatus legionis*.[36]

Although some of the above description is specific to the legionary centurion, it is important to point out that the Roman system of military organization was not only used by the Romans themselves, but was also adopted by many Roman allies, including Herod "the Great." Herod's armies were, according to Josephus (*JW* 1.290), composed of "not a few foreign and native forces" (δύναμιν οὐκ ὀλίγην ξένων τε καὶ ὁμοφύλων), including soldiers from his territory (Galileans, Samaritans, Idumeans), and from other regions in the Roman orbit (Thracians, Germans, and Gauls).[37] Marshak points out several ways in which Herod reformed this army along legionary lines, including the fact that (in keeping with his obligations to his Roman patrons), "Herod's armies periodically served in an auxiliary capacity alongside Roman legions."[38] Marshak allows that "there is no *irrefutable* evidence that Herod's army was organized and trained according to Roman military patterns . . . However, the presence of officers who were likely Romans, Herod's own experience with Roman armies, the royal armies' later seamless absorption into the procuratorial army, and most importantly the greater utility in organizing the army according to a Roman model, all suggest the use of a Roman template for the organization of the royal army."[39] This organization and structure continued after Herod's death under the rule of his sons, and is the basis by which some scholars such as Saddington identify the centurion depicted in Matthew's scene as belonging to Antipas' army.[40] The identification of the centurion as a Herodian soldier may be important in terms of describing the likely deployment of soldiers and units during specific historical periods. It does not, however, change in any substantive way my argument about Matthew's portrayal of the centurion participating in the larger Roman military system, nor characterization of him as an agent of the Empire.

Thus, each of these aspects of the centurion's role in the military hierarchy shows how deeply the centurion in Matthew's scene can be understood to be embedded in the imperial system. He was one of the "most responsible officers in the legion,"[41] whose work and prowess at warfare and military command expanded the Roman Empire and helped to maintain it through the conquest and pacification of additional territory, including new provinces and client kingdoms. These facts of imperial power would have been well-known to Matthew's audience, especially through the likely ongoing interactions that provincial subjects had with members of the Roman army. The imperial context in which Matthew and his audience lived was steeped in hierarchies of power and authority which are not directly challenged in 8:5–13. In fact, the display of divine power that Jesus undertakes is of only limited benefit to the slave, who is healed—but not freed—by Jesus's word. The most immediate outcome of the scene benefits the centurion, whose paralyzed "boy" may now return to work supporting the officer as he fulfills his mandate to enact and maintain imperial rule.

While it is true that Matthew's Jesus points to a future eschatological judgment for those who do not listen to and follow his call to discipleship, the centurion is not included in this judgment. In fact, the scene allows for the possibility that even one such as the centurion may be included in God's plan. He represents those who recognize and trust God's power. As far as dealing with agents of the Empire, Matthew's construction of this scene communicates that it is best to cooperate, even when it is difficult to tell whether the motivations of such agents are benign and virtuous or expedient and self-serving.

The Centurion's Motivation

The second aspect of Matthew's portrayal of the centurion has to do with his motivation in requesting help for his παῖς. Like the man with leprosy (Matt 8:2), the centurion "appeals" (προσέρχομαι) to Jesus in a courteous manner appropriate to one making a formal request. As one who has some social authority, the centurion is deferential and respectful, but not submissive, in that he does not kneel before/worship (προσκυνέω) Jesus as the man with leprosy does in 8:2.[42] He describes the problem he hopes Jesus can help him solve: "my slave is lying at home paralyzed, in terrible distress (δεινῶς βασανιζόμενος)" (Matt 8:6). In this the officer represents a different facet of imperial power than Matthew's readers have previously encountered: unlike other imperial agents (Herod and his soldiers; soldiers employing and abusing the *angaria*; and, soon, Antipas and his executioner), this one acknowledges Jesus's access to divine power and seeks out its benefits. But what is the centurion's motivation? It may be true that a parallel scene found in Luke 7:1–10 has colored some interpretations of Matthew 8:5–13. Here, Luke portrays a centurion's use of negotiation, persuasion, and euergertism in a local community to accomplish his goals. Some of these tactics are present in Matthew's account, but not all. Furthermore, a reading of ancient literature demonstrates that depiction of a centurion's behavior might encompass a wide range of behaviors indicating various motives. In this context, Matthew's portrayal is more ambiguous than has been assumed previously.

Although her work is focused on Luke–Acts rather than Mathew, Laurie Brink's categorization of ancient literary stereotypes of Roman soldiers is a helpful starting point in recognizing a range of possibilities within which the behavior and motivation of Matthew's centurion should be understood. Brink identifies soldiers' roles on the battlefield, policing in the provinces, and as veterans encompassing a wide array of characteristics: from brave and pious warriors who defend, care for and rescue civilians and fellow soldiers; to undisciplined cowards, greedy and mutinous; to bullies and brutish.[43] Given "the ancient understanding that one's moral character was fixed at birth and becomes evident in adulthood . . . it is not surprising that literary portrayals appear as personifications of virtues and vices," and that "presentation of the soldier's dominant attribute" is the guiding principle of characterization.[44]

Brink goes on to suggest that the centurion in Luke 7:1–10 is the concerned owner of a valued household slave and argues that this characterization would have surprised Luke's audience: "a military character exhibiting such concern [for a slave] is contrary to the common stereotype of the bully."[45] This claim is not persuasive, however, as her own work establishes there were a number of stereotypes that might influence an audience's expectations. While Luke relies on a series of representatives (Jewish elders; friends) sent to approach Jesus and vouching for the centurion's character,[46] Matthew's centurion approaches Jesus directly, seemingly alone, and with a singular request. Without the supporting elaboration of Luke 7:3–7, the motivations of Matthew's centurion are opaque, and therefore Brink's reading of the centurion's character (based on his "worthiness") is not applicable to my argument. Rather, her overall analysis of soldiers' motivations and actions in Roman literature reveal a wide variety of possibilities with which to understand Matthew's portrayal of the centurion.

Theodore Jennings and Tat-Siong Benny Liew propose another possibility about the centurion's motivation based on social relationships: that the centurion and slave in Matthew 8:5–13 might be lovers.[47] They argue that the possibility of a pederastic relationship explains both the "urgency of the centurion's plea (8:5–6) . . . [and his] reluctance to have Jesus come to his house (8:8)."[48] Jennings and Liew base their argument first on the semantic range of παῖς as child, slave, servant, personal attendant, or courtier (discussed above), with the additional observation that the noun "is often used to refer to the 'beloved,' or the passive member (usually though not necessarily an adolescent boy) of a same-sex relationship."[49] They assert that "this use of παῖς . . . is, at least discursively, well attested concerning Greco-Roman military in general and Roman centurions in particular."[50] In addition, Jennings and Liew point out that "such relations between a Roman soldier and a youth who was *not* a Roman citizen were both legally permissible and socially prevalent."[51] They cite two examples from Tacitus (*Hist.* 3.33; 4.14) that provide a context within which to understand the Matthean centurion and his παῖς,[52] and propose that the centurion's refusal to invite Jesus to his dwelling may be rooted in fear and jealousy: in asking Jesus to heal his slave, the centurion seeks to become Jesus's client—and that, as a patron with more power and status, Jesus will rival and potentially supplant the centurion to his "beloved" slave.[53] Like other commentators who neglect the networks of Roman military power, Jennings and Liew's proposal does not take into account the status of the centurion as a representative and embodiment of Roman military power. While Jesus may have a reputation as a healer "throughout Syria" (Matt 4:24), this would not overturn—from the centurion's perspective—the nature of imperial hierarchies in which soldiers command and non-elite civilians obey, as Jennings and Liew argue.[54] These imperial realities, as I argue below, appear to be significant in the construction of the Matthean Jesus as well: when the Empire, in the person of the centurion, approaches him on the road to Capernaum asking for help, he complies with the request for assistance.

Beyond the examples provided by Brink, Liew, and Jennings, there are many other examples before and after the period in which Matthew was likely written that illustrate the various ways in which Roman writers could describe not only soldiers, but centurions in particular. Polybius (*Histories* 6.24) sets the idealizing tone for many of these portrayals when he writes that Roman military leaders "wish the centurions not to be so much bold and adventurous, as men with a faculty for command, steady, and of a profound rather than a showy spirit; not prone to engage wantonly or be unnecessarily forward in giving battle; but such as in the face of superior numbers and overwhelming pressure will die in defense of their post."[55] There are multiple examples of such centurions found in Roman literature, including:

- Quintus Fulginus, *primus pilus* ("first spear," the highest ranking centurion in a legion) of the Fourteenth Legion, who was killed while leading a detachment forward *antesignanos* (ahead of the standards) to capture a hill outside Ilerda, Spain.[56]
- Cassius Scaeva, an officer of Julius Caesar who lost an eye, and whose shield was full of hundreds of arrow holes following a battle (testifying to his bravery).[57]
- Titus Pullo and Lucius Vorenus, two centurions of the Thirteenth Legion who were constantly competing with each other for glory; in battle, each saved the life of the other.[58]
- Clemens Julius, well-respected by the common soldiers in Pannonia; when mutiny erupted, he was spared from death and selected by mutineers as trustworthy to carry their messages and demands to the emperor's son.[59]

These soldiers exemplify the virtues of Roman masculinity: bravery, firmness, honor, and the ability to act in any number of adverse situations.

At the same time, there are further examples that illustrate more negative traits of unrestrained greed and unnecessary physical violence. Centurions could be involved in ransacking allied towns (Livy, *Hist.* 29.17); oppressive taxation (Tacitus, *Ann.* 4.72); rape and extortion of prisoners (Polybius, *Hist.* 21.38; Livy, *Hist.* 38.24);[60] and political assassination (Appian, *Civil Wars* 3.3; 4.4; Tacitus, *Ann.* 1.6; 14.8, 58-59; 15.49; 16.9, 15; Suetonius, *Nero* 49; *Caligula* 59). They could be cruel, as when the emperor Tiberius sent a centurion to beat his daughter-in-law Agrippina, resulting in her blindness (Suetonius, *Tiberius* 53); or when another centurion, Lucullus, received the nickname *Cedo Alteram* ("Bring another") because he routinely broke his vine staff while beating the soldiers under his command (Tacitus, *Ann.* 1.23).

Taken together, these examples further illustrate what has been argued in previous chapters: that Roman military personnel used various methods and techniques to encourage and enforce the compliance of local populations for the furtherance of Roman imperial rule. These methods might range from simple requests, to pressure, to intimidation and threat of violence, to direct physical action of various kinds. Matthew's centurion makes use of polite request and flattery to enlist Jesus's assistance; his motivation, however, when set in the context of Roman literature, remains opaque.

When read in the context of Roman literature and cultural practices, which offer a range of options, Matthew's lack of detail about the centurion leaves open a variety of possibilities. The defining characteristics of the centurion at 8:5–6, 9–10 are his description of his slave's condition, a statement about military hierarchies, and his trust in Jesus as one who can heal. Matthew's centurion makes use of polite request and flattery to enlist Jesus's assistance. None of this, however, clarifies his character, motivation, or intentions. For this reason, Matthew's readers are left with an ambiguous understanding of the soldier's motives and priorities. It should be noted that this ambiguity does not disqualify the centurion from receiving Jesus's help or praise.

The Centurion's Faith

The third aspect of Matthew's portrayal of the centurion is shown in Jesus's declaration that the soldier has πίστις ("trust, faith, belief," 8:10).[61] From Matthew's perspective, this trust in Jesus's ability to heal reveals an eschatological truth: that people from far away will one day be included in the heavenly banquet. Jesus's statement in 8:10–12 begins with his amazement—the centurion has, defying expectations, approached him to ask for the benefits of God's healing power. This approach and request prompts Jesus to speak words of praise for those like the centurion who seek him out and accept him and his work, and words of condemnation toward those—Israel's leaders—who do not.

Jesus's language here echoes Psalm 107:3, which refers to those redeemed by God "and gathered in from the lands, from the east and from the west, from the north and from the south."⁶² With regard to this reference, Davies and Allison note that "almost all ancient and modern exegetes assume that Gentiles are meant. This is, we think, far from self-evident."⁶³ Their reasons for this contention include the fact that Psalm 107 is "a passage about the return of Jewish exiles to the land . . . The phrase 'east and west,' is, in Jewish texts, frequently associated with the return of diaspora Jews to their land . . . in Ps 107; Isa 25–7; 49; and Ezek 37–39, the theme of the pilgrimage of the diaspora Jews is brought into connection with the messianic feast, so . . . the usual interpretation [of Matt 8:5–13] is not what comes to mind to one steeped in the [Hebrew scriptures]."⁶⁴ While Davies and Allison's argument about the focus of Psalm 107 is correct, it is also incomplete. The multiple possibilities of the centurion's ethnic identity within the imperial system,⁶⁵ as well as other Biblical text such as Isaiah 25:1–10a (see below) suggest that Matthew has a much broader referent whereby those who come from the East and the West and North and South represent and include both Jews and Gentiles among the "all people" who recognize Jesus's authority and are welcomed into the eschatological feast.

Jesus's acceptance of the centurion's request and accompanying invitation to the eschatological feast in 8:10–12 are not only reflections of Matthew's interaction with Hebrew scriptures; they may also be read as another way in which Matthew contests imperial claims of power. These claims are found in numerous places, including Virgil (*Aeneid* 1.278–79) who claims a divine purpose for the Roman people when Jupiter says: "For these I set no bounds in space or time; but have given empire without end."⁶⁶ Augustus (*Res Gestae* 13) also claims that "peace, secured by victory" is a sign of divine favor of his dominion and rule over "the whole domain of the Roman people on land and sea." Matthew's feast imagery contests these all-inclusive claims of imperial ideology by depicting a world in which all people (both Jews and Gentiles) who acknowledge God's power—rather than that of Rome—are invited, welcomed, fed, and find a place to live in peace. Psalm 107 shows people gathering from all lands into a new community; Isaiah 25:1–10a describes a holy mountain, on which "the LORD of hosts will make for all peoples a feast of rich food, a feast of well-aged wines, of rich food filled with marrow, of well-aged wines strained clear" (25:6); and Zechariah 8:22, proclaims an inclusive vision: "Many peoples and strong nations shall come to seek the LORD of hosts in Jerusalem, and to entreat the favor of the LORD."⁶⁷

In Matthew's narrative, people who acknowledge God's reign are represented by the centurion (8:10–13) as well as the Galilean leper (8:1–4); Judeans (21:14–16); Gentiles like the Magi (2:1–12); and crowds fed by Jesus upon a mountain (14:13–21; 15:29–39). While it is true that Matthew's language (while rooted in Biblical imagery) mimics imperial claims, it does not merely replace one worldly empire with another. Rather, the eschatological vision of 8:10–12 is connected to the work that Matthew's Jesus is already involved with that repairs and heals the damage inflicted by Roman power: feeding the hungry, healing the sick, praying for enemies, and non-violently resisting those who seek to oppress God's people. For this reason, the values and expression of God's empire stand in complicated relationship to that of Rome. Through the long Biblical tradition of portraying divine presence in imperial language ("kingly" rule; benign and beneficent), Matthew's Jesus does not proclaim a "Kingdom of Heaven" that is wholly different than that of Rome, but one that is better due to its inclusion of those on the margins of society (4:23–5:12).

Jesus's Condemnation of Those Who Do Not Acknowledge Him

The final way in which this scene negotiates imperial power is in the content of Jesus's statement about the heirs of Israel, who will be "thrown into the outer darkness" (8:11–12) because they are not receptive to his power. These words are not directed toward all Jewish people (many of whom follow Jesus and participate in his efforts to realize God's reign), but rather at elite leaders who cooperate with Roman imperial rulers by enacting policies that harm the common people. The "dire warnings" directed at "some of the Jewish leaders" are found not only here in 8:11–12, but through the gospel (cf. 10:32f.; 11:21–24; 23:1–39).[68] Jesus's act of healing and language about "weeping and gnashing of teeth" (8:12) may reflect competition between Matthew and other strands of Judaism in the late first century CE,[69] but it also reveals another way in which Matthew must negotiate imperial ideology that claims faith, mercy, and judgment are the domain of emperors and imperial power.

The concept of πίστις ("faith"), introduced above, is one which Matthew's Jesus commends as connected in some instances to healing (8:10, 13; 9:2, 22, 29; 15:28);[70] associates with trust in God (6:30) and fulfillment of the Torah (23:23); enables disciples to witness and partake of his divine power (8:26; 14:31; 16:8; 17:17, 20; 21:22–23); and serves as a measure of behavior for community members at the eschatological judgment (24:45). In a number of these occurrences (6:30; 8:26; 14:31; 17:20), Matthew uses the word ὀλιγόπιστος ("little faith") as an antithesis to πίστις; this criticism highlights what the Matthean Jesus expects of his followers and warns them clearly to maintain a good relationship with him. In 17:17 Jesus refers to the γενεὰ ἄπιστος καὶ διεστραμμένη ("faithless and perverse generation") who should place their trust in his work but do not;[71] to emphasize this critique, Jesus shows them *his* faithfulness by healing a possessed boy that his disciples have been unable to help.

In the ancient world, the concept of πίστις (Latin: *fides*) encompassed ideas of confidence, assurance, and trust in others; trustworthiness, honesty, and acting in good faith (in personal and business relationships); philosophical proofs; and political protection and suzerainty.[72] This latter aspect is illustrated by Polybius (*Hist.* 20.9), who writes about the Aetolians, who pledged themselves "to the faith of the Romans" (εἰς τὴν Ῥωμαίων πίστιν) expecting a pardon: "But with the Romans to commit oneself to the faith of a victor is equivalent to surrendering at discretion."[73] Teresa Morgan argues that *fides* is one aspect of imperial ideology that expresses the relationship between the Roman military and imperial rulers, and between imperial rulers and their subjects (See figure 4.1). One example of this ideology of mutual benefit is found in Julius Caesar (*Civil Wars* 3.64 [Peskett, LCL]), where an *aquilifer* (eagle-standard bearer) is mortally wounded in battle; seeking to deliver the *aquila* to allied troops, he says: "This eagle in my life I defended with great care for many years, and now, dying, I restore it to Caesar with the same loyalty (*eadem fide*)." Morgan notes that "his *fides* is not only his oath of allegiance, but also the trust that has been placed in him and the responsibility he has discharged. He dies knowing that Caesar and his commanders have relied on his loyalty as certainly as he has been loyal to them."[74]

Morgan also points to Roman coins that feature the legends *fides exercituum*, *fides cohortium*, or *fides praetorianorum*, which promote the mutual

Figure 4.1 A bronze as minted in Rome (73 CE). The obverse features the emperor Titus ("T CAESAR VESPASIAN IMP"); the reverse displays clasped hands with a caduceus and stalks of wheat. These signs of friendship, health, and sustenance proclaim the ruler's faithfulness ("FIDES PVBLICA") to basic elements of society and the public good. *(Source: Image from Wildwinds Coins, admin. Dane Kurth, https://www.wildwinds.com/coins/ric/titus/RIC_0571[vesp].jpg. Used with permission.)*

fidelity of the army and the emperors: they depend upon one another to act faithfully and in good faith to uphold each other.[75] She writes:

> The imagery of *fides* on coins is richly varied, and by no means all military: civil, religious, and economic images also appear, and images are variously combined for greater symbolic richness. The goddess Fides frequently appears either in person or represented by clasped right hands, the ubiquitous symbol of good faith.... [She] often carries ears of corn and/or a basket or plate of fruit. The corn (sometimes visibly wheat or barley) is usually taken to symbolize the emperor's control of the grain supply; hence his guarantee of food at reasonable prices, especially for the Roman poor. Outside Rome, the image might also stand more generally for prosperity, arising from peace in the empire.... All this imagery is combined in many ways, not least with military imagery and legends. The legend *fides exercituum* or *fides cohortium*, for instance, is often shown with corn ears of a cornucopia. The same legend, or clasped right hands, may be shown with corn ears and poppies or military standards or both. The cumulative effect (at least to a modern audience which has the benefit of seeing large numbers of coins together) is to emphasize the interdependence of all the benefits of *fides*. Peace, ensured by armies, together with strong government, brings prosperity, trade, fair prices, and satisfaction to all the subjects of the empire.[76]

When Matthew's Jesus praises the centurion's πίστις, then, it must be read in relation to imperial claims of *fides*, where emperors and soldiers pledge faithfulness to each other; and where rulers backed by military power demand faithfulness from provincial residents. Jesus's response, in fact, makes perfect sense when read alongside the centurion's claim to his place in the vast Roman military network (8:8–9). Like Caesar's *aquilifer* who died faithfully discharging his duty, Matthew's centurion proclaims his faithfulness as a loyal and dutiful soldier and Jesus acknowledges it. This articulation of *fides* by imperial agents proclaiming their honesty and trustworthiness is a common trope of imperial ideology, and Matthew's portrayal of Jesus and his work also draws upon the image of soldiers and others as truthful and reliable actors. He is calling disciples to trust in and follow him, and then shows he is worthy of their faith by healing, feeding, and teaching about God's reign. While positive character traits such as honesty and faithfulness are not exclusive to imperial claims of authority, a case can be made that Matthew is mimicking imperial claims here. Not only does Matthew's Jesus act in similar ways to Roman emperors by demanding acts of faith in him from his followers, he also shows his faithfulness toward them by providing food and healing, and backs up his demands with threats of divine punishment—"outer darkness, where there will be weeping and gnashing of teeth" (8:12; 22:13; 25:30)[77] backed by "twelve legions of angels" (26:52–55).

Related to faith/faithfulness is the concept of ἔλεος/*clementia* ("mercy, compassion, pity, concern for someone in need"), which was also claimed by imperial rulers as part of their ideological repertoire.[78] The first emperor, Augustus (*Res Gestae* 32), asserts that "a large number of other nations experienced the good faith of the Roman people during my principate who never before had had any interchange of embassies or of friendship with the Roman people,"[79] and portrays himself (*Res Gestae* 34) as honored by the Roman people "in recognition of my valor, my mercy [*clementiae*], my justice, and my piety." Augustus connects his humane and benevolent rule with military conquest and victory (*Res Gestae* 3, 26 [Shipley, LCL]): "Wars, both civil and foreign, I undertook throughout the world, on sea and land, and when victorious I spared all citizens who sued for pardon. The foreign nations which could with safety be pardoned I preferred to save rather than to destroy.... I extended the boundaries of all the provinces which were bordered by races not yet subject to our empire.... [These nations] I brought to a state of peace without waging on any tribe an unjust war [*bellum inuria*]." A similar claim is made by Seneca (*On Mercy* 1.1 [Basore, LCL]) on behalf of his pupil the Emperor Nero, for whom he writes an imagined soliloquy:

> Have I of all mortals found favor with Heaven and been chosen to serve on earth as vicar of the gods? I am the arbiter of life and death for the nations; it rests in my power what each man's lot and state shall be . . . without my favor and grace no part of the wide world can prosper; all those many thousands of swords which my peace restrains will be drawn at my nod; what nations shall be utterly destroyed, which banished, which shall receive the gift of liberty, which have it taken from them, what kings shall become slaves and whose heads shall be crowned with royal honour, what cities shall fall and which shall rise—this it is mine to decree. With all things thus at my disposal . . . I am sparing to the utmost of even the meanest blood; no man fails to find favor at my hands though he lack all else but the name of man. Sternness I keep hidden, but mercy [*clementia*] ever ready at hand.[80]

These incongruous claims of mercy/compassion and domination through military power are intertwined in an imperial ideology designed to justify Roman claims of power and control. In this ideology, mercy is the withholding of military power—but only if domination/submission to Roman power can be achieved by other means. These two aspects of imperial ideology—mercy mixed with threats of destruction—are also found in Jesus's actions and language in Matthew 8:11–13.

Although the term ἔλεος ("mercy") does not appear in Matthew 8:11–13, Jesus's actions toward the slave may be categorized as such. His work of healing here and throughout the gospel may be understood in the Biblical tradition of God's mercy (רחם / ἔλεος), which is deep and theologically significant for all Israel. On many occasions Matthew's Jesus is one who is asked for and displays mercy to others (Matt 5:7; 9:13, 27; 12:7; 15:22; 17:15; 18:33; 20:30f; 23:23).[81] On the basis of Biblical tradition, Jesus's healing of the centurion's slave is merciful insofar as it alleviates suffering. At the same time, in the context of Roman imperial ideology, Jesus's response to the problem of the slave's "terrible suffering" is an expression of Jesus's masculine virtue and authority: rather than remaining passive, Jesus acts to confront problems and threats to the established order; his action maintains hierarchical relationships between centurion and underlings, master and slave. Thus, Matthew mimics imperial ideology by portraying Jesus in a fashion typical of elite Roman males who seek to control the world.

The other strand of the imperial ideology of "mercy" is found in Jesus's condemnation of those who refuse his authority. Matthew connects Jesus's promise that the "heirs of the kingdom"—Israel's leaders—will be punished for resisting his rule (8:12) to a number of other passages (9:13, 27; 12:7; 15:22; 17:15; 20:30–31; and 23:23) where similar views are expressed. As in the claims of Roman emperors, those who do not submit to Jesus's authority and power will be destroyed. A number of these texts are eschatological in nature—and are the subject of chapter 5.

As with other facets of Matthew's scene, Jesus's act of mercy, words of judgment, and praise of the centurion's "faith" in 8:11–13 do not directly confront Roman military power. Instead, Matthew's Jesus mimics the language and ideology of the emperors, criticizing elite Jewish leaders who cooperate with and benefit from the structures of the Empire, and point toward a time when divine judgment and justice will be carried out against those leaders who do not accept his authority. At the same time, Jesus's sharing of divine mercy through acts of healing and inclusion are indicative of a difference between the Roman Empire and that of God. In this scene, the mercy of Matthew's Jesus is not predicated on the prior submission to his power and authority. The scene includes a centurion of opaque motives, a slave who is still under the dominion of the Empire, and others "from the east and from the west" who will come because of their faith and acknowledgment of God's power.

CONCLUSION

Matthew's portrayal of a deferential centurion in 8:5–13 evokes the vast Roman military network, which included legions, auxiliary cohorts, and the armies of allied rulers under Roman patronage and control. The discipline and hierarchical assumptions about military relationships were well known in the ancient world, as given voice by Tacitus (*History* 1.84): "It is by obeying, not by questioning, the orders of commanders that military power is kept together. And that army is the most courageous in the moment of peril, which is the most orderly before the peril comes."[82] When Jesus encounters a centurion who expresses these values, he does not challenge him directly concerning his involvement in military action and slavery but agrees to heal the soldier's slave who is suffering and afflicted. This is in keeping with Jesus's work to proclaim God's kingdom and manifest its presence by healing many people. The centurion prompts Jesus to respond positively to his request, however, by directly acknowledging Jesus's ability and authority. Jesus does so, although the centurion's motives remain unclear throughout the scene. Despite the fact that Matthew's account leaves unchallenged the structures of imperial power and domination represented by both the military and institution of slavery, Jesus's healing of the slave and verbal response to the centurion shows that there are times—if and when agents of the Empire are engaged—that imperial agents can be included in God's work and God's people.

NOTES

1. Polybius, *Histories*, transl. Evelyn S. Shuckburgh (London, New York: Macmillan, 1889; Reprint Bloomington, 1962).

2. Alfred John Church, William Jackson Brodribb, and Sara Bryant trans. (New York: Random House, 1873, 1942).

3. In Matthew 8:1–4 Jesus heals a man with leprosy; in 8:14–17 he heals Peter's mother-in-law from a fever—like the soldier's slave, "she got up and began to serve him" (8:14), returning to work and to her traditional role.

4. Polybius, *Histories*, 6.24, transl. Shuckburgh. The full quote appears at the beginning of this chapter.

5. The varying ways that centurions are characterized are categorized by Laurie Brink, *Soldiers in Luke-Acts*, *Soldiers in Luke-Acts: Engaging, Contradicting, and Transcending the Stereotypes* (Tübingen, DE: Mohr Siebeck, 2014), x, 60–86, discussed below.

6. Saddington, "Roman Military Personnel," 2413, argues that "as he was in Galilee, then under Antipas, he [the centurion] must have belonged to his army.... the Herods recruited many of their forces from the non-Jewish elements in the populations under their control." Saddington, 2411, notes the general practice throughout the period in question: "Client kings had their own armies, increasingly modelled on Roman lines," and, 2424, regarding Herod and his descendants, "The client kings were fully integrated into the Roman administrative apparatus." Haynes, *Blood of the Provinces*, 46, 117–118, points to this affiliation, noting the assimilation of some Herodian forces into Roman *auxilia* at Herod's death. Andrew Schoenfeld, "Sons of Israel in Caesar's Service: Jewish Soldiers in the Roman Military" (Shofar 24.3, 2006), 115–126, complicates the picture of identity by pointing out evidence for Jewish *milites*, centurions, and high ranking officers in the Roman legions throughout

this period. For further discussion, see Brink, *Soldiers*, 94; Marshak, *Herod the Great*, 190; and Raul González Salinero, "El servicio militar de los judíos en el ejército romano," *Aquila Legionis* 4 (Madrid 2003): 45–91.

7. Overman, *Church and Community in Crisis,* 117, recognizes how the Gospel's Christology is deeply embedded in imperial structures: "The centurion understands how authority works. He understands that both he and Jesus receive their power and authority from somewhere or someone. In the case of the centurion it is Caesar or the regional imperial lord or governor, and it seems he recognizes, in the case of Jesus it is God.... There is palpable irony in this conversation with the centurion. That someone so entrenched within the imperial power structure should understand so deeply, almost intrinsically, the nature of Jesus, how and why he does what he does, is certainly poignant.... The man is able to see something in the way Jesus acts, or is able to act, that others hitherto have been unable to see. There is something analogous in their lives that enables the centurion to make this connection with Jesus." Overman notes the possible after-effects of the Jewish-Roman War in 66–70 CE on Matthew and his audience, but is less interested in the imperial context, focusing instead on Matthew's relationship to other Jewish groups and their competing claims for legitimacy. In this he follows a similar approach to Saldarini, *Christian-Jewish Community,* 171, 196, who identifies the centurion as one of several Gentiles in the narrative that represent an effort towards Gentile inclusion in the Matthean community.

8. Davies and Allison, *Matthew*, 2:7–8, 17–32; Luz, *Matthew 8–20*, 8–9; Keener, *Matthew*, 263–264, couple questions of source and redactional history (comparing Matthew's scene to Luke 7:1–10 and John 4:46–54, as well as Mark 2:1–12; 5:22–23) with observations about Matthew's thematic and theological intent. Davies and Allison, *Matthew*, 2:19, offer a typical conclusion: "What is the significance of the centurion in Mt 8:5–13? He is first of all a Gentile. The man foreshadows (as did the magi) the successful evangelization of the nations (28:16–20) . . . [and is] a paradigm for the believer in so far as he exhibits true faith . . . This is why his faith is mentioned not once but twice (8:10, 13). See also discussion on Brink, *Soldiers in Luke–Acts,* and Jennings and Liew, "Mistaken Identities," below.

9. Scholars note that these three episodes comprise the first of several healing stories in Matthew 8–9: nine episodes with a total of ten healings, separated by blocks of teaching. See discussion by Luz, *Matthew 8–20*, 1–4; Davies and Allison, *Matthew*, 2:1–2 Keener, *Matthew*, 258.

10. Matthew uses the verb προσφέρω ("they brought to him") to describe the crowd's actions at 4:24 and 8:16; the leprous man and the centurion's approaching Jesus is therefore not unusual.

11. There are two examples of Jesus healing the παραλυτικός as referred to in Matt 4:24: this account and 9:1–8, which also takes place in Capernaum.

12. κύριος, BDAG, 3rd ed., 577–578 also includes the sense of ownership: "one who is in charge by virtue of possession," including slaves.

13. Matthew uses two words to describe the paralyzed man: παῖς (8:6, 13) and δοῦλος (8:9). The implications of this identification in relation to the man's status and relationship with the centurion will be discussed below.

14. Jesus' reference to the paralyzed man is simple: "I will come and heal him."

15. παῖς, παιδός, BDAG, 3rd ed., 750–751. The other occurrence of ὁ παῖς in this scene is Matt 8:13. The range of meaning of παῖς also explains certain features of John 4:46–54, which tells a version of the scene in which a royal official's son (ὁ υἱὸς) is sick, and Jesus heals him from afar. See also Matt 14:2, where Antipas' courtiers are called οἱ παῖδες. See also Jennings and Liew, "Mistaken Identities," 467–494, discussed below.

16. The verb used to describe this condition is σεληνιάζομαι ("moonstruck") also mentioned in Matt 4:24 in the list of diseases Jesus comes to heal. As in Matt 8:5–13, the boy's healing prompts Jesus to make further comments to his disciples about the "faithless (ἄπιστος) and perverse generation" and having "faith (πίστις) like a mustard seed."

17. This reading is strengthened by Luke 7:1–10, in which a series of Jewish elders vouch for the centurion's character, citing his love and generosity towards the people and synagogue. Matthew's scene, it must be emphasized, does not include such characterization at all.

18. I read "heirs of the kingdom" (8:12) as a reference to Israel's leaders—elite power-holders and their associates allied with Herod, Antipas, and the Romans. Jesus' criticism here is tied to his challenge of these leaders' authority in Matt 7:29 and anticipates the growing conflict in Matt 9:36; 12:14; 21:1–22:10; and 23:1–39. This reference should not be read as a blanket condemnation of Israel or Judaism.

19. θαυμάζω, BDAG, 3rd ed., 444–445. Emphasis mine.

20. Such advice on master-slave relationships was a trope in ancient literature (c.f. Xenophon, *Oeconomicus*), and could be offered by New Testament (Colossians 3:18–4:1 // Ephesians 5:21–6:9; 1 Peter 2:13–3:7, 1 Timothy 2:1–6:1; Titus 1:5–9 and 2:1–10) and later Christian writers (*Didache*; Polycarp, *Letter to the Philippians*). See David C. Verner, *The Household of God* (Chico, CA: Scholar's Press, 1983), 1, 17, 24; David Balch, *Let Wives Be Submissive: The Domestic Code in I Peter* (Atlanta, GA: Scholar's Press, 1981); Wayne Meeks, *The First Urban Christians* (New Haven, CT: Yale University Press, 1983), 75–77, 125–127.

21. See Wainwright, *Shall We Look for Another*, 47–48, who identifies "the story [as] being told not just as a healing but also as a call story parallel to that of the call of Matthew (8:14–15; 9:9)." The nature of her service is discussed by a number of scholars, who comment on the parallel scene in Mark 1:29–31. See Deborah Krause, "Simon Peter's Mother-in-Law—Disciple or Domestic Servant? Feminist Biblical Hermeneutics and the Interpretation of Mark 1:29–31," in *A Feminist Companion to Mark*, ed. Amy-Jill Levine, with Marianne Blickenstaff (Sheffield: Sheffield Academic Press, 2001), 37–53; Monika Fander, "Gospel of Mark," in *Feminist Biblical Interpretation*, ed. Luise Schottroff and Marie-Theres Wacker (Grand Rapids: Eerdmans, 2012), 629; Joanna Dewey, "The Gospel of Mark," in *Searching the Scriptures*, ed. Fiorenza (New York: Crossroads, 1997), 2.476–477; Elizabeth Struthers Malbon "Fallible Follower: Women and Men in the Gospel of Mark," *Semeia* 28 (1983): 29–48, esp. 34–35; and Corley, *Private Women Public Meals*, 87–88.

22. διακονέω, BDAG, 3rd ed., 229–230. The positive statements include Matthew 20:26 ("It will not be so among you; but whoever wishes to be great among you must

be your servant"); 20:28 ("the Son of Man came not to be served but to serve, and to give his life a ransom for many"); 23:11 ("The greatest among you will be your servant"); and 27:55 ("Many women were also there, looking on from a distance; they had followed Jesus from Galilee and had provided for him"). Matt 22:13 also represents another instance of eschatological banqueting wherein the servants (διάκονοι) help God to enforce inclusion/exclusion: "Then the king said to the servants, 'Bind him hand and foot, and throw him into the outer darkness, where there will be weeping and gnashing of teeth.'"

23. The strategy of Matt 24:1–51 will be discussed in the following chapter.

24. This centurion is one of two who appear in Matthew's gospel; the second is present at the crucifixion, death, and burial of Jesus (27:27–38, 54), and will be discussed in chapter 6.

25. Livy, *History of Rome* 1.52 (Foster, LCL), writes that in the earliest period of Roman history King Tarquin (sixth century BCE), "mingled Latins and Romans in the maniples, making one maniple of two and two of one, and over the maniples thus doubled he put centurions." Polybius, *Hist.* 6.24, describing the Republican era army, writes that: "From each of the classes except the youngest they elect ten centurions according to merit, and then they elect a second ten. All these are called centurions, and the first man elected has a seat in the military council.... Next, in conjunction with the centurions, they divide each class into ten companies . . . and assign to each company two centurions . . . When both centurions are on the spot, the first elected commands the right half of the maniple and the second the left, but if both are not present the one who is commands the whole."

26. Graham Webster, *The Roman Imperial Army of the First and Second centuries A.D.*, 3rd ed. (Norman, OK: University of Oklahoma Press), 112–114.

27. Webster, *Roman Imperial Army*, 112, 116.

28. Watson, *Roman Soldier*, 87.

29. Webster, *Roman Imperial Army*, 116. Grant, *Army of the Caesars*, 74, concurs: "Some centurions were commissioned direct from the legionary ranks. Others came —in mid-service or after retirement—from the praetorian guard.... Others again were brought straight in from civilian life, having been working, perhaps, in the administration of some Italian city."

30. Entry into the Equestrian Order was based on property qualifications, which a high-ranking centurion could achieve because of the difference in pay scales between centurions and common soldiers. This distinction began in the Republican period when, according to Polybius (*Histories* 6.39), the regular salary was 10 2/3 *ases* per day during active (seasonal) service; the centurion could expect to receive any additional monetary gift (*donatio*) at double that of the regular *milites* (see Livy, *History* 37.59.5; 39.5.17; 39.7.2; 40.59.3; 36.40.7; Strabo, *Geography* 11.14; Appian, *Civil Wars* 2.15.102). This remuneration was frequently provided by a commander after a Roman victory and was typically funded by looting the defeated enemy—although occasionally it came from a commander's own resources. During the Imperial period, the difference in pay scales for centurions was even greater. Grant, *Army of the Caesars*, 77, 303, notes that the base salary for the common legionary *milites* was 225 *denarii* per year (with 1 *denarius* equaling 4 *sestertii*, and 1 *sestertii* equaling 4 *ases*). He goes on to

point out, 73, that: "Augustus bestowed upon the centurions . . . [according to grades] within the centurionate . . . salaries . . . [which] varied enormously from about 3,750 up to 15,000 denarii per year. That is to say the lowest grade of centurion received nearly seventeen times as much as an ordinary legionary, and the highest grade was paid four times as much again." In addition to this, the tradition of *donatio* continued, both after a victory and on other varied occasions according to the emperor's prerogative.

31. D. Kennedy, "C. Velius Rufus," *Britannia* 14 (1983): 183–196. Velius' gravestone at Baalbek, Syria records his *cursus publicus*. Josephus, *JW* 7.13–15, describes the ceremony in the ruins of Jerusalem at which Velius received his awards from Titus.
32. Grant, *Army of the Caesars*, 74.
33. Grant, *Army of the Caesars*, 73.
34. Watson, *Roman Soldier*, 54–72.
35. Webster, *Roman Imperial Army*, 116.
36. Webster, *Roman Imperial Army*, 117; Grant, *Army of the Caesars*, 75.
37. Josephus, *JW* 1.290–294, 299–302; *Ant.* 17.198.
38. Marshak, *Herod the Great*, 188–189, refers to Josephus, *Ant.* 14.269, 439–447; 15.317, *JW* 1.217, 320–322 (where Herod reinforces Antony at Samosata). See also Josephus, *JW* 1. 327–330, 346.
39. Marshak, *Herod the Great*, 190, *emphasis* mine. Saddington, "Roman Military," 2411, may well agree with Marshak: "Client kings had their own armies, increasingly modelled on Roman lines," and, 2424, regarding Herod and his descendants, "The client kings were fully integrated into the Roman administrative apparatus." See also Haynes, *Blood of the Provinces*, 46, 117–118, on the integration of Herodian armies into Roman *auxilia* at Herod's death. Schoenfeld, "Sons of Israel," 115–126, and Salinero, "El servicio militar," 45–91, complicate the picture of identity by pointing out evidence for Jewish *milites*, centurions, and high ranking officers in the Roman legions throughout this period.
40. Saddington, "Roman Military," 2413.
41. Webster, *Roman Imperial Army*, 113.
42. προσκυνέω, BDAG, 3rd ed., 882: "to express in attitude or gesture one's complete dependence on or submission to a high authority figure, (fall down and) worship, do obeisance to, prostrate oneself before, do reverence to, welcome respectfully."
43. Brink, *Soldiers, x*, 60–86.
44. Brink, *Soldiers, x*, 60–68, 74–78, 82–84, 88.
45. Brink, *Soldiers*, 141.
46. Luke 7:4–5: "he is worthy (ἄξιος) . . . for he loves our people (ἀγαπᾷ γὰρ τὸ ἔθνος ἡμῶν), and it is he who built our synagogue for us."
47. Theodore Jennings and Tat-Siong Benny Liew, "Mistaken Identities but Model Faith: Rereading the Centurion, the Chap, and the Christ in Matthew 8:5–13," *JBL* 123/3 (Atlanta 2004): 467–494.
48. Jennings and Liew, "Mistaken Identities," 478.
49. Jennings and Liew, "Mistaken Identities," 472–473.
50. Jennings and Liew, "Mistaken Identities," 473–474. They cite a number of examples (Callimachus, *Epigrams*; Xenophon, *Anabasis*) pertaining to Greek armies

in the 3rd century BCE before turning to several from the Roman sources. These sources, although they describe the prohibition of pederastic relationships between older males and Roman freeborn youth (Polybius, *Hist.* 6.37; Valerius Maximus, *Sayings* 6.1; Plutarch, *Moralia* 202b–c; Quintilian, *Inst* 3.11), imply that such relationships were practiced and perhaps sought out by certain elite Roman males.

51. Jennings and Liew, "Mistaken Identities," 476.

52. Tacitus, *History* 3.33: "Forty thousand armed men burst in [to Cremona], along with a greater number of servants and attendants even more corrupt when it came to lust and cruelty. Neither respectability nor age prevented an intermingling of *stuprum* and slaughter. Aged men and women of advanced years, worthless as booty, were dragged off for sport; and when a mature maiden or someone [masc.] of outstanding beauty appeared, they would be pulled in various directions by the violent hands of those who were seizing them; ultimately they would lead into mutual slaughter the very men who had seized them." Jennings and Liew refer to Moore, LCL; I quote from Williams, *Roman Homosexuality*, 105, whose translation better highlights the uncomfortable phrase "*stupra caedibus caedes stupris*." Tacitus, *History* 4.14 (Moore and Jackson, LCL): "At the orders of Vitellius a levy of young Batavians was now being made. This burden, which is naturally grievous, was made the heavier by the greed and license of those in charge of the levy: they hunted out the old and the weak that they might get a price [bribe] for letting them off; again they dragged away children to satisfy their lust, choosing the handsomest—and the Batavian children are generally tall beyond their years." It should be noted while these examples do provide accounts of *stupra* (rape, sexual assault, illicit sexual activity) by soldiers against civilians and young provincials, Tacitus censures both incidents as abuses of power and transgressions of Roman *virtus* (discipline, self-control). While Jennings and Liew, 475, are correct that "it is no surprise that Roman soldiers are (discursively and/or factually) known for what they do to their captives," they could be clearer in delineating the differences between the experiences of people captured during the sacking of cities (*direpta*: which included *stupra*, looting, killing) with the *stuprum* experienced by captive people during the course of their enslavement, and the possible relationship between Matthew's centurion and his παῖς.

53. Jennings and Liew, "Mistaken Identities," 485.

54. D.B. Saddington, "The Centurion in Matthew 8:5–13: Consideration of the Proposal of Theodore W. Jennings, Jr. and Tat-Siong Benny Liew," *JBL* 125.1 (2006): 140–142, rejects Jennings and Liew's reading scenario on the basis of ethnicity, arguing that: "the centurion is portrayed [in their article] as a Roman.... However, the soldiers stationed in Judea in the first century C.E. were non-Roman auxiliaries, not legionaries. Moreover, the incident took place not in Judea but in Galilee, which at the time was a nominally independent kingdom of the Herodian Antipas.... All that can be definitely said is that the centurion in Matthew was a Gentile: his actual ethnicity cannot be determined." From my perspective, this is not a strong argument; rather, whether we imagine the centurion as representing a legionary, auxiliary, or allied Herodian royal army officer, he is part of the Roman imperial system in which the elite and powerful maintain control over non-elite populations to which Jesus, the παῖς, and Matthew's audience belong.

55. Shuckburgh translation; see quotation at the beginning of this chapter.
56. Julius Caesar, *Gallic Wars* 1.46.
57. Scaeva is mentioned by numerous authors: Julius Caesar, *Civil Wars* 3.53; Appian, *Civil Wars* 2.9; Suetonius, *Divine Julius* 68; Lucan, *Pharsalia* 6.119.
58. Julius Caesar, *Gallic Wars* 5.44.
59. Tacitus, *Ann.* 1.23–28.
60. Both writers tell how the captured woman, Chiomara, took her revenge: signaling to her tribesmen when the centurion was receiving the ransom payment, they killed him, and she took his head to her husband, a Galatian chieftain, to show that revenge had been served.
61. πίστις, BDAG, 3rd ed., 818–820. The first sense of the word—faithfulness, fidelity, commitment—may apply here to Jesus' evaluation of the centurion's relationships (with military personnel or his slave), but also to the soldier's belief that Jesus has power that can help his slave to be well.
62. Although the LXX makes use of different vocabulary than Matthew 8:6 does when describing the slave's "suffering in terrible distress" (δεινῶς βασανιζόμενος), it is noteworthy that the psalm (106 in the LXX) also refers in v.6 to those who "cried out to the LORD . . . and he delivered them from their distress (ἐκ τῶν ἀναγκῶν αὐτῶν ἐρρύσατο αὐτούς)." Similar language is used in verses 13, 19, and 28. This thematic connection to the entire scene in Matt 8:5–13 is also seen in Psalm 107:20: "he sent out his word and healed them, and delivered them from destruction."
63. Davies and Allison, *Matthew*, 2:27.
64. Davies and Allison, *Matthew*, 2:27. Jesus' language also echoes other scriptural texts that do include Gentiles (discussed below).
65. On the possible ethnic identity of the centurion, see n.6 above. Herod's armies, inherited by his sons, were composed of Galileans, Samaritans, Idumeans, Thracians, Germans, and Gauls (Josephus *JW* 1.290); see n. 37. For discussion on the possible religious affiliations of such a soldier, see Oliver Stoll, "The Religion of the Armies," in *A Companion to the Roman Army*, ed. Paul Erdkamp (Blackwell, 2007), 451–476; Isaac Haynes, "The Romanisation of Religion in the 'Auxilia' of the Roman Imperial Army from Augustus to Septimus Severus," *Britannia* 24 (1993): 141–157; Duncan Fishwick, "Dated Inscriptions and the 'Feriale Duranum,'" *Syria* 65.3/4 (1988): 349–361.
66. Faircloth, LCL: *his ego nec metas rerum nec tempora pono; imperium sine fine dedi*. This gift has heavenly elements; Jupiter also "will raise on high to the starry heaven" his son, the Roman progenitor Aeneas (1.259).
67. See also Isa 2:1–4; 25:1–10a; Micah 4:1–13; Zech 8:1–23. These and other texts widen the scope of Matthew's eschatological vision to include both Jews and Gentiles.
68. Davies and Allison, *Matthew*, 2:28.
69. cf. Overman, *Formative Judaism*, 1–4, "The factor within the locale and setting of Matthew's community which most profoundly influenced its development was the competition and conflict with so-called formative Judaism." Stanton, *Gospel for a New People*, 146–157, also addresses the possibility, concluding that such intra-Judaic competition has recently passed. See also Saldarini, *Matthew's Christian-Jewish Community*, 1–4, 7–9.

70. There are a number of different relationships between submission/faith and healing in Matthew: faith may lead to healing (8:1–4; twice in 9:18–26; 9:27–31); healing may be performed without faith (8:14–17; 9:2–8); healing may by performed although it is opposed (8:28–34).

71. Konradt, *Israel, Church, and the Gentiles*, 208–243, argues that the γενεά should be identified primarily as elite leaders who reject Jesus.

72. πίστις, Liddell and Scott, *Greek-English Lexicon*, 9th ed., 1408.

73. Paton, et al., LCL: παρὰ < δὲ > Ῥωμαίοις ἰσοδυναμεῖ τὸ τ' εἰς τὴν πίστιν αὐτὸν ἐγχειρίσαι καὶ τὸ τὴν ἐπιτροπὴν δοῦναι περὶ αὐτοῦ τῷ κρατοῦντι.

74. Teresa Morgan, *Roman Faith and Christian Faith: Pistis and Fides in the Early Roman Empire and Early Churches* (London: Oxford University Press, 2017), 78–79.

75. Morgan, *Roman Faith and Christian Faith*, 83. Colin Kraay, "Revolt and Subversion: The So-Called 'Military' Coinage of A.D. 69 Reexamined," *Numismatic Chronicle and Journal of the Royal Numismatic Society*, Sixth Series 12.42 (1952): 78–86, argues that coin types associated with the short reign of Vitellius in 68 CE were minted in an effort to influence the loyalty of Praetorian cohorts away from Galba. One such coin has the unusual feature of almost identical obverse and reverse sides: each presenting the clasped right hands (*dextras*) with the legends on each side reading FIDES EXERCITVVM and FIDES PRAETORIANORVM. Another such coin features the *dextras* and FIDES EXERCITVVM on the obverse, and a figure of Concordia holding a branch and cornucopia and CONCORDIA PRAETORIANORVM on the reverse. The *dextras* were common symbols of goodwill exchanged by formal delegations to proclaim *fides* and mutual support. See Tacitus, *Hist.* 1.54, where the city of Lingonum sent "clasped right hands, an emblem of friendship, as gifts to the legions" (*dona legionibus dextras hospitii insigne*); and 2.8, where one of Vespasian's centurions, Sisenna, was sent to Rome in 69 CE, "carrying clasped right hands, the symbol of friendship [*dextras concordiae insignia*], to the praetorians in the name of the army in Syria."

76. Morgan, *Roman Faith and Christian Faith*, 83–84.

77. See also Matt 13:42, 50, where there is a "furnace of fire, where there will be weeping and gnashing of teeth."

78. ἔλεος, BDAG, 3rd ed., 316.

79. The Latin reads: *Plúrimaeque aliae gentes exper(tae sunt p. R.) fidem me principe*. The Greek refers to: Ῥωμαίων πίστεως.

80. In a similar fashion, but with different vocabulary, Josephus (*JW* 5.332–335) praises the way in which Titus acts with φιλανθρώπως ("benevolence/love and concern for humanity") during the siege of Jerusalem in 70 CE, when in one quarter of the city he sought to spare the people: "he would not allow his troops to kill any persons caught or to fire the houses . . . and promised restoration of their property." When the Jewish fighters refuse to surrender, fighting resumes in the streets.

81. Two related words are found in Matthew, the verb ἐλεέω and the noun ἔλεος.

82. Transl. Alfred John Church, William Jackson Brodribb, and Sara Bryant (New York: Random House, 1873, 1942).

Chapter 5

Imagining the Destruction of Eagles
Divine Retribution on the Roman Empire (Matthew 24:27-31)

And then, while our troops still hung back, chiefly on account of the depth of the sea, the eagle-bearer [*aquilifer*] of the Tenth Legion, after a prayer to heaven to bless the legion by his act, cried: "Leap down, soldiers, unless you wish to betray your eagle [*aquila*] to the enemy; it shall be told that I at any rate did my duty to my country and my general." When he had said this with a loud voice, he cast himself forth from the ship, and began to bear the eagle against the enemy. Then our troops exhorted one another not to allow so dire a disgrace, and leapt down from the ship with one accord.

Julius Caesar, *Gallic War* 4.25[1]

As Titus advanced into enemy territory, his vanguard consisted of the contingents of the kings with the whole body of auxiliaries. Next to these were the pioneers and camp-measurers, then the officers' baggage-train; behind the troops protecting these came the commander in chief, escorted by the cavalry and other picked troops, and followed by the legionary cavalry. These were succeeded by the [siege] engines, and these by the tribunes and prefects of cohorts with a picked escort; after them and surrounding the eagle came the army standards preceded by their trumpeters, and behind them solid column six abreast.

Josephus, *Jewish War* 5.47–48[2]

INTRODUCTION

Just as previous chapters have argued that Matthew uses a variety of strategies for negotiating Roman military power (including avoidance when possible; non-violent resistance; and cooperation and mimicry), this chapter turns to another strategy of negotiation in which Matthew increases the stakes for all involved. Recalling the imperial context in which provincials often bear the brunt of Roman policies designed to control and dominate, Matthew 24:27–31 presents a vision of divine punishment which stands in marked contrast to the eschatological feast to which Jesus invites the centurion in 8:5–13. Here Matthew's Jesus is not simply a teacher with large crowds and a healer with a growing reputation: he is also ὁ υἱὸς τοῦ ἀνθρώπου ("the Son of Man"), an eschatological figure with roots in Hebrew scripture who will come at the end of the age to judge the nations and with heavenly military power destroy God's enemies—including the Roman Empire—forever.[3] In both cases, Matthew's eschatological landscape includes the righteous and excludes the unrighteous. However, while 8:10–12 depicts the inclusion of those like the centurion who acknowledge God's power and authority, the scene in 24:27–31 is one in which Roman military power, depicted as a complete entity, is judged and punished while those chosen by the Son of Man are gathered from the four corners of the earth.

While acknowledging connections to elements of prophetic discourse from Hebrew scripture, this chapter reads Matthew 24:27–31 as a private expression of dissent with the imperial order, in contrast to other more public strategies of negotiation discussed in previous chapters. Matthew here envisions revenge and divine punishment on "the eagles" (24:27) of Roman military power. This vision is, however, opaque to those in power, and only shared privately with Jesus's disciples (24:3) for the present time. At other points in the narrative, Matthew's strategies of negotiation (avoidance; non-violent resistance; cooperation and mimicry) have been designed to provide guidance for public behavior toward imperial agents by those who must bear the brunt of abusive imperial practices. In contrast to prior advice, the vision of 24:27–31 does not depend on the performance of certain behaviors for daily survival, but directs Matthew's audience to imagine and anticipate divine action that will one day overthrow and destroy the oppressors of God's people. The fierce urgency of these and other "off-stage" comments in Matthew 24–25 represent what Scott calls the "most elementary level" of the hidden transcript, in which revenge fantasies are enacted and elaborate curses are prayed as an expression "of the anger and reciprocal aggression denied by the presence of domination. . . . [in which] the frustration, tension, and control necessary in the public setting give way to unbridled retaliation in a safer setting, where the accounts of reciprocity are, symbolically at least, finally balanced."[4] Thus the purpose of such a vision, no less than other facets of Matthew's negotiation, is to assist those who suffer under imperial domination by giving voice to the deep yearning for change to the present networks of power.

THE DESTRUCTION OF EAGLES (MATT 24:27-31)

Anti-Imperial Eschatological Discourse

In Matthew's narrative, the occasion for Jesus's eschatological discourse (Matt 24–25) is prompted by his disciples, who marvel at the construction of the Temple complex and are stopped short by Jesus's response: "not one stone will be left here upon another; all will be thrown down" (24:2), commonly interpreted as a reference to the Jerusalem temple's destruction by Roman troops in 70 CE. The following discussion, in which Jesus talks about "the sign of [his] coming and of the end of the age" (24:3), includes warnings about false Messiahs (24:4–8, 23–26), persecutions (24:9-14), and the destruction of the Temple (24:15–22); admonitions to be ready for the Son of Man's return (24:32–44); parables about watchfulness (24:45–25:30); and a vision of the judgment of nations, where the unrighteous "will go away into eternal punishment, but the righteous into eternal life" (24:13–46). Within this discourse is a smaller unit, Matthew 24:27–31, which includes stark imagery of lightning in a darkened sky; a corpse surrounded by eagles; sun and moon eclipsed; stars falling; and planets shaken. Each of these heavenly portents is a prelude to the arrival of the Son of Man, who will appear to the consternation of all people on earth, except for "the elect" (τοὺς ἐκλεκτούς), who will be gathered and brought home (24:30–31). Matthew's scene depicts a *parousia* which heralds the end of the age: a military battle that overturns the present order of things—including Rome's empire—and replaces it with the Empire of God.[5] This will not be accomplished by any earthly power, but awaits divine intervention when the Son of Man returns "on the clouds of heaven with power and great glory" (24:31).

While a number of scholars make insightful commentary on Matthew 24–25 based on textual sources, these, insofar as they ignore Matthew's imperial context, are incomplete. Thus Davies and Allison assign portions to Mark 13 and other portions to Q (based on the parallel with Luke 17:23–24, 37),[6] arguing that Matthew 24–25 includes interpretation of prophetic texts (especially Daniel), and reflect on current events (perhaps including the destruction of the Temple in 70 CE) and eschatological statements traceable to the historical Jesus.[7] Reliance on textual sources alone, however, has led to conclusions about the setting and history of the Matthean community (including which elements of the discourse were interpreted by Matthew's audience as past/present/future events) that inadequately represent the pressures faced in the imperial setting. Reliance on textual history approaches has also led to minimizing the connection between the ἀετοί (24:28) and Roman military forces, including the conflation of identity between vultures and eagles.[8] In contrast, this chapter argues that the vehemence of Matthew's Jesus in

24:27–31 is not merely a religious vision based on specific traumatic historical events, but an expression of dissent against imperial military control in which the eschatological vision functions to call down judgment on God's enemies, and to caution his followers to remain faithful.

Following Carter's argument about the identity of the ἀετοί as "eagles" and not vultures (γύψ) in 24:28, the following sections contend that Matthew's eschatological vision includes the overthrow of the Roman Empire, which will be replaced with the Empire of God at the end of the age.[9] These "eschatological eagles" should be read in connection to occurrences of a Biblical cypher used by Matthew's Jesus as a self-referential depiction: ὁ υἱὸς τοῦ ἀνθρώπου ("the Son of Man"). These in turn may be linked to other military imagery: the "sign" or "ensign" (LXX: σημεῖον or Vulgate: *signum*) of the Son of Man; and angelic forces announced by a war-trumpet (σάλπιγξ) and sent (ἀποστέλλω) from heaven to rescue the followers of Jesus from the four corners of the earth. Each of these components of the scene strengthens the contention that Matthew 24:27–31 is yet another facet of the gospel's negotiation with Roman military power.

In this eschatological vision, Matthew mimics expressions of Roman military practice and power and coopts it by envisioning its overthrow by a stronger power. His strategy here is different than those discussed so far in this work, picturing Jesus—amidst a grisly scene of Roman corpses and mourning nations—as a military conqueror, "coming on the clouds of heaven with power and great glory" (24:30). Matthew's portrayal of Jesus as the eschatological Son of Man in 24:27–31 presents his audience with a figure whose agency is more potent and formidable than any Roman political and military power. Here the Son of Man appears like lightning (24:27) and sends out angels like soldiers (24:31); he will come at an unexpected time (24:39, 44) to judge the nations (25:31) while seated at the right hand of God (26:64). This vision is not a call to arms and revolt, however, but a private assertion in which Matthew's Jesus speaks off-stage to his disciples, affirming that their daily and outward compliance with Roman military domination will one day end in a defeat of the Roman military, and giving voice to their distress with a dream of divine justice and retribution.

Identifying Imperial Eagles

The first and most important element to establish is the identity of the birds in Matthew 24:28. These ἀετοί are commonly understood to be "vultures" that gather around a corpse (πτῶμα), and this is reflected in most English translations. Carter notes correctly that this "consensus reading has . . . some serious shortcomings"[10] because it is inaccurate: ἀετοί are not vultures but "eagles."[11] Allowing that there are occasions in which the identities of the ἀετός/*aquila* ("eagle") and γύψ/*vultur* ("vulture") are blurred, Carter points out that, "ancient writers generally do not equate eagles and vultures. . . . [and this equivalence] is not as pervasive as some argue."[12] Ancient writers such as Homer, *Iliad* 4.235; 11.162; 16.836; Aelianus *Hist. Anim.* 2.38; Virgil *Aeneid* 11.752–56; and Job 9:26 knew, for instance, that the two birds find food differently, with eagles generally hunting live prey, and vultures subsisting on carrion. While there is a corpse (πτῶμα) in Matthew 24:28, there is no mention of hunting or eating. This atypical association of eagles and a dead body has created confusion among many interpreters as to Matthew's meaning.[13]

Carter continues, arguing that the birds in question in Matthew 24:28 are indeed eagles, providing a detailed Biblical and historical context which links eagles to imperial nations that serve as agents of divine punishment and are in turn punished for their own transgressions.[14] The first aspect of this argument connects eagles with imperial power as agents of divine punishment. In Deuteronomy 28:47–68 eagles represent imperial nations, and Moses warns the children of Israel what will happen if they do not follow God's commands (28:49–51): "The LORD will bring a nation from far away, from the end of the earth, to swoop down on you like an eagle (LXX: ἀετός), a nation whose language you do not understand, a grim-faced nation showing no respect to the old or favor to the young. It shall consume the fruit of your livestock and the fruit of your ground until you are destroyed . . . until it has made you perish."[15] This judgment, referring to the Babylonian invasion of Israel and destruction of Jerusalem in 587 BCE, when followed by repentance (Deut 30:1–10), will lead to Israel's restoration—and divine judgment upon Babylon.[16]

A second example comes from Ezekiel 17, where the Biblical text uses the image of eagles to evoke imperial powers and divine judgment. In this passage two eagles arrive in the land of Israel:

> The word of the LORD came to me: O Son of Man, propound a riddle (LXX: παραβολή), and speak an allegory to the house of Israel. Say: Thus says the Lord GOD: A great eagle, with great wings and long pinions, full of talons, came to the Lebanon. He took the top of the cedar, broke off its topmost shoot . . . Then he took a seed from the land . . . It sprouted and became a vine spreading out. . . .
>
> There was another great eagle, with great wings and large talons. And behold! This vine stretched out its roots toward him; it shot out its branches toward him, so that he might water it. . . .
>
> Thus says the Lord GOD: I myself will take a sprig from the lofty top of a cedar . . . I myself will plant it on a high and lofty mountain. On the mountain height of Israel I will plant it, in order that it may produce boughs and bear fruit, and become a noble cedar. . . . All the trees of the field shall know that I am the

LORD. I bring low the high tree, I make high the low tree; I dry up the green tree and make the dry tree flourish. I the LORD have spoken; I will accomplish it.[17]

Carter points out that, just as in Deuteronomy 28, the eagles that invade and upset the land will have their way for a time, but ultimately will be judged by God, who is sovereign over both eagles (Babylon and Egypt), and who intervenes to frustrate their plans.[18] Ezekiel 17:1 (LXX) also introduces the phrase υἱὸς ἀνθρώπου ("Son of Man") as a figure who hears God's word and to whom God reveals future events, although it is not here one who executes punishment as in Matthew 24:27–31.

Furthermore, Carter shows how prophetic judgment can be merged with an eschatological vision. In a similar manner to Matthew 24:27–31, the writer of 4 Ezra 11–12 prophesies the destruction of Rome in the "last days." In this scene, an eagle with three heads represents the Roman Empire ruled by the father and two sons (Vespasian, Titus, and Domitian) of the Flavian dynasty:[19]

> I saw rising from the sea an eagle that had twelve feathered wings and three heads. I saw it spread its wings over the whole earth, and all the winds of heaven blew upon it, and the clouds were gathered around it. . . . He said to me, "This is the interpretation of this vision that you have seen: The eagle that you saw coming up from the sea is the fourth kingdom that appeared in a vision to your brother Daniel. . . .
>
> In its last days the Most High will raise up three kings, and they shall renew many things in it, and shall rule the earth and its inhabitants more oppressively than all who were before them. Therefore they are called the heads of the eagle, because it is they who shall sum up his wickedness and perform his last actions. . . .
>
> [T]he Messiah whom the Most High has kept until the end of days, who will arise from the offspring of David . . . will come and speak with them. He will denounce them for their ungodliness and for their wickedness, and will display before them their contemptuous dealings. For first he will bring them alive before his judgment seat, and when he has reproved them, then he will destroy them. But in mercy he will set free the remnant of my people, those who have been saved throughout my borders, and he will make them joyful until the end comes, the day of judgment, of which I spoke to you at the beginning.[20]

Like Matthew's eschatological vision in 24:27–31, in which eagles gather with corpses and the Son of Man causes the nations to mourn (24:28, 30), 4 Ezra condemns the Roman Empire for its oppressive rule, ungodliness, and wickedness. Like the Son of Man sitting on a throne to judge and separate the righteous from the unrighteous (Matt 25:31–32, 46), 4 Ezra looks forward to a day of divine judgment at which time a Messiah in the line of Davidic kings will appear to free God's people and save them. In both Matthew and 4 Ezra, the power of the Roman "eagles" is subject to divine judgment and destruction, and God's faithful are saved by divine intervention.

Carter thus demonstrates the context in which the ἀετοί of Matthew 24:28 should be read: Biblical "eagles" often represent imperial power, which may be used by God to punish Israel's sins and, in turn, may be punished by God for their own unrighteousness.[21] Ultimately this divine punishment is cosmic and eschatological. In the case of Matthew 24:27–31 it is the imperial power of Rome to which the gospel writer refers. Set in the Roman imperial context discussed throughout this work, Roman use of eagles as imperial and military imagery is widespread. The following sections demonstrate the ways in which Matthew negotiates this dimension of imperial system: mimicking and overturning its imagery by envisioning the eschatological judgment and destruction of Roman eagles when the Son of Man returns.

THE ESCHATOLOGICAL SON OF MAN

Much has been written about the identity of the Son of Man in relation to Matthew's Christology and characterization of Jesus, and a full discussion of this identity is beyond the scope of the present work.[22] The argument here is much narrower: remaining focused on the eschatological passage of Matthew 24:27–31, it contends that the Son of Man's purpose in this passage is to express Matthew's usually veiled resentment towards the indignities of Roman military control. Mimicking Roman ideology of domination and control through military superiority, Matthew's portrayal here of Jesus as the eschatological Son of Man builds on previous references to his eschatological roles (13:36–43; 16:13–28; 19:27–30).[23] Yet the portrayal of Jesus here in this scene in relation to the Roman military is noticeably and qualitatively different from that of the previous scenes concerning negotiation of the Roman military. No longer an infant fleeing soldiers in his mother's arms; no longer at risk from speaking prophetic truth to power; no longer forced to creatively resist compulsory labor by abusive military personnel; no longer compliantly acquiescing to requests for assistance while guessing about motives, Jesus is here an authoritative ruler who will return suddenly with glory and power, commanding angelic armies to gather his scattered people, and to judge and destroy Roman military power.

Matthew's Jesus refers to himself as "the Son of Man" (τοῦ υἱοῦ τοῦ ἀνθρώπου) throughout the gospel narrative, and these occurrences, as have been noted by a number of scholars, may be grouped into statements about the Son of Man's (1) everyday activity (cf. 8:20; 9:6; 11:19; 12:8); (2) suffering and death (17:9, 12, 22; 20:18; 26:45); and (3) eschatological identity (13:41; 16:27, 28; 19:28; 24:44; 25:31; 26:64).[24] Located in the final act of Matthew's narrative (chapters 21–27),[25] the long eschatological discourse in Matthew 24:3–25:36[26] builds on these previous eschatological Son of Man references. The chapters depict Jesus as pronouncing judgment upon his opponents and warning that suffering will occur for his followers before the "end of the age" (24:3) when Jesus returns as the "Son of Man" (24:27, 30, 37, 39, 44; 25:31). Jesus's discourse is not, however, a public declaration of war and revolt against the current order: it is spoken privately to his disciples (24:3), and remains a concealed expression of dissent, envisioning the destruction of Roman power (and their elite allies who control the Temple) only at some future date—when the Son of Man returns.[27]

In other Biblical texts, the Son of Man is envisioned as an eschatological figure coming in the clouds from heaven (Dan 7:13–14); judging and destroying foreign nations who oppress God's people (Dan 7:10–11, 26–27; 4 Ezra 11:38–46; 12:32–33); and gathering the remnant of God's scattered people (4 Ezra 12:34). In Matthew 24:27–31, the gospel writer uses similar imagery to portray Jesus as the eschatological Son of Man:

- He will return suddenly, like a flash of lightning (24:27).
- His return will be accompanied by heavenly portents (24:29).
- His sign will appear in heaven, causing all nations to mourn (24:30).[28]
- He will appear in clouds of heaven with power and glory (24:30).
- Announced by a trumpet call, he will send out angels to gather the elect (24:31).[29]

At the same time, the motifs Matthew uses here—lightning, heavenly signs and omens, command of angelic armies by war-standard and trumpet—mimic language and imagery used by the Romans to describe their authority and military power.

THE POWER OF LIGHTNING AND EAGLES

When the Son of Man appears like a flash of lightning (24:27), it is both a symbol of Biblical theophany and associated with Roman power. Throughout the Hebrew scripture, lightning is associated with the divine—it is a tool at God's disposal and a metaphor for God's actions. In Exod. 19:16, God appears on Mount Horeb with "thunder and lightning . . . and a blast of a trumpet so loud that all the people . . . trembled."[30] In 2 Sam. 22:14–15, King

Saul is thankful for the defeat of his enemies, because God "sent out arrows, and scattered them—lightning, and routed them." Likewise, God appears as a commanding general in Zechariah 9:14, "marching forth" to a sounding trumpet (LXX: σάλπιγξ) and appearing over the enemy "like lightning" (LXX: ἀστραπὴ).[31]

Among its eagles, Roman imperial imagery also featured lightning prominently. In the Roman army, many Roman legionary shields carried a lightning image in various configurations, often with wings; these are associated with Jupiter's power.[32] The Twelfth Legion, based in Syria and involved in the early stages of the Jewish-Roman War in 66 CE as well as the siege and destruction of Jerusalem in 70 CE (Josephus, *JW* 2.510–555; 5.10), was nicknamed *Fulminata*, "Lightning-hurler"—another reference to Jupiter's power.[33] Carter notes "the association of lightning (Latin *fulgar*) with the [Greek and Roman] gods, notably Zeus/Jupiter, and its role in portending the gods' (dis)favor in military and political successes or failures."[34]

Each legion in the Roman army carried an *aquila*, a marching standard depicting an eagle holding lightning in its claws. The *aquila* was a potent religious symbol, representing the power of Rome and the spirit of the legion, and cared for by assigned soldiers in a legionary shrine when the army was not on the march. There are multiple depictions of the *aquila* on coins and sculpture, including coins from 69 CE featuring Vespasian and an eagle perched on lightning bolts (see fig. 5.1) and the tombstone at Mainz

Figure 5.1 The obverse of this tetradrachm of Vespasian (69 CE) shows the emperor in profile, wearing a wreath that is likely associated with his recent victory in the civil war. The reverse features an eagle clasping lightning bolts in its talons; to the right is a palm branch, another symbol of victory. The design mimics a previous coin issued by Vespasian's immediate predecessor, Nero, and was minted in the East—perhaps in Antioch. (*Source: Image from Wildwinds Coins, admin. Dane Kurth. www.wildwinds.com/coins/ric/vespasian/RPC_1936.jpg. Used with permission.*)

of Cn. Musius, *aquilifer* (eagle-bearer) of the Fourteenth Legion, which shows his shield adorned with radiating lightning bolts and the legionary "eagle with its raised wings garlanded, perched on a thunderbolt, on top of an elongated square-sectioned plinth."[35] Josephus (*JW* 5.47–48, quoted at the beginning of this chapter) describes how the march of a Roman army on campaign included the eagle (ἀετός), surrounded by the other army standards (αἱ σημαῖαι) and led by trumpeters (αἱ σάλπικταὶ), all of whom preceded the main column of soldiers marching six abreast. Elsewhere, Josephus (*JW* 3.123) remarks on "the eagle (ἀετός), which in the Roman army precedes every legion, because it is the king and bravest of all the birds: it is regarded by them as the symbol of empire, and, whoever may be their adversaries, an omen of victory."[36]

Roman soldiers would go to great lengths to defend the *aquila*—even sacrificing their lives to defend the sacred symbol of their legion. Tacitus (*Hist.* 3.22) tells of Atilius Verus, a centurion of the first rank (*primipilus*) from Galba's Legio VII who sacrificed his life to save his *aquila*. In two accounts by Livy (*Hist.* 25.14; 33.23), the *aquila* served as a catalyst in battle: centurions took the eagle into dangerous situations among the enemy and challenged their soldiers to follow in order to fight for it. Similarly, Caesar's famous account of the first Roman military landing in Britain (*Gallic War* 4.25, quoted at the beginning of this chapter) shows a centurion using the symbol of the Roman eagle to call upon his hesitant soldiers' piety, courage, sense of duty, and patriotism when leading them ashore to conquer a new land.

When *aquilae* were lost in defeat, Romans would go to great lengths to recover them. The statue of Augustus from the villa of Livia *ad Gallina* at Prima Porta shows the recovery of eagles from the Parthians in 20 BCE.[37] Roman writers praise the efforts of Germanicus, whose army recovered three lost eagles following the Roman defeat in the German Teutoberg Forest (Varusschlacht) in 9 CE (Tacitus, *Ann.* 1.60; 2.25; Dio, *Hist.* 60.8).

All of these examples illustrate the widespread use and importance of lightning and eagle imagery in the Roman military context. When Matthew pictures the Son of Man appearing like a flash of lightning to overpower these same Roman eagles, he shows Jesus as eschatological victor. While rooted in Biblical imagery, Matthew's scene at the same time mimics Roman symbolism and predicts the overthrow of Roman military power, condemning those who have previously subjugated, dominated, and controlled God's people.

INTERPRETING HEAVENLY PORTENTS

The eagles and lightning are not alone, however; they are accompanied by other powerful symbols of the eschatological Son of Man's power. Matthew

24:28–30 describes a number of heavenly omens that will indicate that the Son of Man will soon return. The frightening signs of eclipsed sun and moon, falling stars, and shaken planets are, together, well-known eschatological signs. In the Hebrew Scriptures, the day of divine judgment includes all these portents (Isa 13:10; 34:4; Ezek 32:7–8; Joel 2:1–2, 10–11, 30–31), which are directed at foreign empires (Babylon and Egypt) and the people of Israel. To cite one example, Joel 2:1–2, 10 warns that: "the day of the Lord is coming, it is near—a day of darkness and gloom, a day of clouds and thick darkness! ... The sun and the moon are darkened, and the stars withdraw their shining."

As with eagles and lightning, there are also many instances in which Roman imperial ideology laid claim to and aligned its dominion with that of solar, lunar, and astral divinities. Examples from the Flavian dynasty, during which time Matthew was likely written, will illustrate this pervasive phenomenon. Suetonius (*Vesp.* 5.7) writes that eagles and a dream sent by Jupiter Optimus Maximus (the sun god) indicated Vespasian's rise to power. Vespasian's son Titus, conqueror of Jerusalem, is depicted on the back of an eagle in the upper arch of a monument (The Arch of Titus) erected after his death in 81 CE: ascending through to the heavens to join the gods, it is his apotheosis. Naomi Norman notes that another major relief on the Arch depicts "Titus in his triumphal chariot and accompanied by a crowd ... He wears the costume of the *triumphator* and holds in his left hand Jupiter's scepter crowned with an eagle and extends a palm branch in his right. ... The chariot, decorated with a frieze of baetyls on its rim and an eagle standing on a thunderbolt ... is guided by [the goddess] Roma."[38] Norman observes that identical portrayals of the emperor on this triumphal frieze and the apotheosis at the apex of the Arch "encourage us to read the panels together and to acknowledge that Titus's divinization is grounded in his triumph ... [and his] apotheosis is founded on his significant military achievements."[39]

In contrast to these claims of imperial rulers, Matthew's eschatological vision depicts the end of Roman rule. As Carter writes, "In extinguishing the sun and moon, and causing stars to fall from heaven (24:29), Jesus' coming ends all imperial claims about and identification with the cosmic order and ... deities that sanction Roman power."[40] Standing in opposition to the cosmological claims of Roman imperial power, Matthew draws on the traditions and imagery of Biblical prophets to envision a day in which Rome is judged and punished for its oppressions and God's people and creation are restored.

THE SIGNUM OF THE SON OF MAN

There is much scholarly debate over the meaning of the σημεῖον ("sign") of the Son of Man in Matthew 24:30. Luz notes three positions on the identity of the sign: (1) that of the ancient church (*Didache* 16.6; *Epistle of Barnabas* 12.4; *Odes of Solomon* 42:1–2), which looks for a cross in the sky; (2) following Biblical traditions of holy war, it refers to a flag or war-banner; and (3) with reference to Matt 12:39–40, the "sign" is the Son of Man himself.[41] The latter is Luz's position; I argue here for the second option.

In addition to those aspects of Matthew's construction of an anti-imperial eschatological discourse discussed above, the phrase τὸ σημεῖον τοῦ υἱοῦ τοῦ ἀνθρώπου ("the sign of the Son of Man") in 24:30 may be understood as another facet of Jesus's return as glorious military victor. No longer forced to flee and hide in Egypt (2:14), worry about forced service by soldiers on the road (5:41), or wonder about the motives of Roman personnel (8:10), Jesus's return "with power and great glory" will herald a new and triumphant reality for his followers. As the eschatological Son of Man, Matthew's Jesus will command angelic armies (discussed below), who marshal like Roman troops led by military standards and trumpet calls.

The term נס, which Jonathan Draper notes is translated as σημεῖον (LXX) or *signum* (Vulgate), is often translated into English as God's "banner," "sign," or "ensign," and is used throughout Scripture.[42] Draper refers to a number of instances in which σημεῖον indicates a variety of military purposes.[43] In Isaiah 11:10–12, "the totem is raised to gather Israel for a holy war against her enemies, in which the Lord will be the major actor . . . The ingathering of the dispersed tribes of Israel introduces [the idea that] the totem is raised not for a war of punishment against Israel, but for the gathering in of the lost tribes."[44] In Isaiah 13:2, 4, "the raising of the war totem is to signal that the Lord is mustering a host for war against Babylon because of its iniquity. . . . [and] broadens imperceptibly into a general punishment of the wicked on the Day of the Lord."[45] The נס/σημεῖον could also be a signal of judgment against Israel, as in Isaiah 5:25–26: "Therefore the anger of the LORD was kindled against his people, and he stretched out his hand against them and struck them; the mountains quaked, and their corpses were like refuse in the streets. For all this his anger has not turned away, and his hand is stretched out still. He will raise a signal for a nation far away, and whistle for a people at the ends of the earth; here they come, swiftly, speedily!"[46] Thus, the expectations surrounding the symbol σημεῖον are mixed:

> The totem is to be raised on a mountain or some other prominent place to announce the beginning of war, either by God or on his behalf. It is ambiguous, to the extent that the war is sometimes envisaged as *against* Israel and sometimes *on behalf of* Israel against her enemies. It always involves the ingathering of peoples: either the ingathering of nations for war against Israel—for victory or calamitous defeat—or the ingathering of the dispersed people of Israel and

Judah from the four winds or corners of the earth. The raising of the totem is often accompanied by the blowing of the [*shofar*].[47]

Carter notes that "seven LXX texts employ σημεῖον, to designate a military standard and to represent either Babylonian aggression (Ps 73:4 [LXX 74:4]) and judgment on Judah (Jer 6:1), or, more commonly . . . judgment on Israel's enemies (Isa 18:3), including imperial powers Babylon (Isa 13:1–2; Jer 28:12, 27 [LXX 51:12, 27]) and Assyria (Isa 11:11–12)."[48]

In addition to these Biblical traditions, Matthew would have also been familiar with the military practices of Roman legions and auxiliary forces. Besides the *aquila* (discussed above), Roman troops marched with a variety of banners. Each Century of soldiers possessed a *signum*, "typically a decorated spear with a crossbar and attached pendant straps, the shaft bearing a mixture of discs and crescents . . . and a conical butt."[49] These symbols indicated legion or auxiliary cohort affiliation and perhaps unit awards; exact meaning is difficult to determine.[50] The *signum* was carried by the *signifer*, an officer who received double pay and was second in command of the Century after the centurion.[51] Detachments of legionary or auxiliary soldiers marched with a *vexilla*, a square flag mounted on a spear and held by a crossbar; the cloth could be marked with the unit name and insignia, or name of the ruling emperor.[52] The single surviving example of a *vexillum* was found in Egypt, dated to the third century CE; it is made of linen painted with an image of personified Victory surmounting a globe.[53] Finally, legions possessed one or more *imagines* ("images") of the emperor and imperial family; these busts were also mounted for carrying, but typically kept in the base shrine (*sacellum*).[54] Throughout the army, the standards were used to communicate orders. Josephus (*JW* 3.106) notes that visual signals (σημεῖον) along with verbal orders given to Roman soldiers resulted in "perfect discipline" while marching and in battle. He also describes (*JW* 3.123) how, while on the march, a legion was led by the *aquila* surrounded by σημαία (Latin: *signum*) which were considered "sacred emblems" (ἱερός). They were accompanied by trumpeters (αἱ σάλπικται), discussed below.[55] All of the standards were integrated into the religious practices of the Roman army—revered and held sacred by means of public sacrifices, prayers, and oaths.[56]

With all of these associations widely attested everywhere the Roman army was present, it is not difficult to imagine how Matthew's "sign of the Son of Man" (24:30) could have been heard by his audience as military in nature. Like the standards that herald and represent the power of the Roman army, the σημεῖον/*signum* that accompanies the Son of Man will cause "all the tribes of the earth to mourn" as he appears with "power and great glory" (24:30)—and they are expected to submit to his power.

ANTICIPATING ANGELS WITH TRUMPETS

The final aspect of Matthew 24:27–31 that supports the argument that the eschatological vision of the text is a hidden transcript of revenge on the Roman army is the appearance of angels (ἄγγελοι, 24:31). Like the soldiers sent by Herod and Antipas in Matthew 2:16 and 14:10, the angels are "sent" (ἀποστέλλω) from heaven by the Son of Man who commands them like an imperially sanctioned ruler. The angels, pictured elsewhere as "twelve legions" (δώδεκα λεγιῶνας) standing ready to assist the Son of Man (26:53), go out to defeat Roman power and rescue God's people. These heavenly soldiers follow orders that are signaled "with a loud trumpet call" (μετὰ σάλπιγγος μεγάλης), in order to "gather the elect from the four winds, from one end of heaven to the other" (24:31). Their work stands in contrast to the actions of Roman-affiliated soldiers elsewhere in the gospel, who have killed the children of Bethlehem and John the Baptist (and soon, Jesus himself), force civilians to comply with demands for labor, and seek to uphold the imperial order by ordering healed slaves to work. Like the rest of Matthew's "off-stage" dissent, the angels will appear at a future date—when the Son of Man comes from heaven with power and glory (24:30).

Throughout Matthew's gospel, angels are portrayed as envoys and agents of God who deliver divine messages, offer assistance, and serve Jesus in a variety of ways. Angels warn Joseph and Mary to flee Herod's soldiers after Jesus's birth (1:20, 24; 2:13, 19); assist Jesus in his ordeal in the wilderness (4:6, 11); watch over the "little ones" of God's kingdom (18:10); show the women that Jesus's tomb is empty (28:2); and tell them that he has been raised (28:5). Besides the eschatological vision of 24:27–31, Matthew portrays angels as appearing at the end of the age as "reapers" (οἱ θερισταὶ) or agents of judgment who will collect "all causes of sin and all evildoers" in order to "throw them into the furnace of fire, where there will be weeping and gnashing of teeth" (13:40–42, 49–50). Angels accompany the Son of Man at his glorious return (16:27; 25:31, 41), when he will "repay" the chief priests and scribes (16:21) and judge all nations based on their treatment of those on the margins of imperial society (25:31–46). The actions of the angelic army in 24:31 cohere with Matthew's other accounts of future angelic punishment of the unrighteous. Within this context there is a good reason why their appearance with the Son of Man will cause "all the tribes of the earth to mourn" (24:30): the angels are sent to bring about divine vengeance and destruction.

Beyond the larger context of Matthew's eschatology, the "loud trumpet call" (σάλπιγξ μεγάλη) that signals the angelic forces to advance is another instance of Matthew's mimicking imperial military practice. In the LXX and New Testament the σάλπιγξ may refer to "a wide range of musical instruments," in the trumpet and horn family.[57] In the LXX, these instruments include the *shophar* (a horn or trumpet with military and worship associations),[58] *qeren* ("horn," likely a synonym to *shophar*),[59] and *hasoserot* (silver trumpets used by Levitical priests).[60] In the New Testament period, the σάλπιγξ may refer to several Roman instruments—all of which were used by the military—including the *cornu, buccina, tuba* ("C"-shaped curved metal trumpets of varying sizes), and *lituus* (a long, straight metal trumpet similar in shape to the later alpine-horn). All of these instruments "despite their raucous character, were used in various instrumental combinations. . . . [including] solemn funeral processions, civic ceremonies . . . and military triumphs. . . . The *tuba* (as the relief on Trajan's Column indicates) accompanied military marching and marked the strategic movements of troops in war . . . and with the *buccina* and *cornu* it was intended to create panic among the enemy."[61] Josephus (*JW* 3.124; 5.47–48), as noted above, describes how Roman forces on the march were led by their standards accompanied by trumpet players (σάλπικταὶ). Elsewhere in the New Testament, the trumpet call signals Jesus's return as a triumphant conqueror, when the righteous dead are raised, and angelic forces unleash destruction on the unrighteous (1 Thess 4:16; 1 Cor 15:50-58; Rev 1:10; 4:1; 8:7–10:7; 11:15).[62]

CONCLUSION

This chapter has argued that Matthew's scene in 24:27–31 makes use of both Biblical traditions and Roman military practices to provide an eschatological vision that opposes the networks of Roman imperial power and envisions their destruction. The elements of this vision include heavenly portents that indicate a day of divine judgment; a militarily triumphant "Son of Man" who returns from heaven in clouds with lightning, possessing power and glory, and leading an army of angelic soldiers following military standards and trumpets; defeated imperial eagles signifying the defeat of Roman troops; mourning nations; and people recovered from the far ends of creation. As Carter writes, "Jesus' return, consistently presented with imperial and military images, ends Rome's empire with its military, divine, and cosmic sanctions. God's empire is established with judgment on the nations and the cosmic deities who sanction them and with salvation for the elect in a new heaven and new earth."[63]

Matthew's eschatological vision in 24:27–31 reveals another facet to the ways in which Matthew constructs and negotiates Roman military power for his audience. It is a hidden transcript of dissent, resentment, and vengeance that makes use of Biblical imagery and features of contemporary Roman military practice. Matthew's Jesus provides for his disciples a scenario in which the scattered righteous are gathered together and the unrighteous Roman military is punished and destroyed as representative of the end of the Roman Empire. This vision must be kept quiet for the time being but will be manifest to the world when the Son of Man appears.

NOTES

1. Edwards, LCL. The aquilifer is from *Legio X Equestris*, raised by Julius Caesar for campaigns in Gaul and later discharged; a different legion, *X Fretensis*, fought at Jerusalem and was later stationed there.

2. Thackeray, LCL.

3. Matthew's Jesus teaches his disciples another aspect of the Son of Man's identity: he will suffer betrayal, crucifixion, and death before being raised (20:18–19; 26:2, 24, 45).

4. Scott, *Domination*, 37–38, 42.

5. Matthew uses the term παρουσία ("coming") in reference to Jesus/the Son of Man's return at 24:3, 27, 37, 39.

6. Davies and Allison, *Matthew*, 3:327. Luke 17:23–24 reads: "They will say to you, 'Look there!' or 'Look here!' Do not go; do not set off in pursuit. For as the lightning flashes and lights up the sky from one side to the other, so will the Son of Man be in his day." Luke 17:37: "Then they asked him, 'Where, Lord?' He said to them, 'Where the corpse is, there the eagles will gather' (ὅπου τὸ σῶμα, ἐκεῖ καὶ οἱ ἀετοὶ ἐπισυναχθήσονται)."

7. Davies and Allison, *Matthew*, 3:331–332.

8. Examples include Davies and Allison, *Matthew*, 3:356; Luz, *Matthew 21–28*, 199–200; Keener, *Matthew*, 583.

9. Warren Carter, "Are There Imperial Texts in the Class? Intertextual Eagles and Matthean Eschatology as 'Lights Out' Time for Imperial Rome (Matthew 24:27–31)," *JBL* 122/3 (2003): 467–487.

10. Carter, "Imperial Texts," 468.

11. ἀετός, Liddell and Scott, 9th ed., 29.

12. Carter, "Imperial Texts," 469, 469 n.12. cf. Luz, *Matthew 21–28*,199, who notes that Aristotle *Hist. Animals* 618b–619a, refers to an eagle that eats carrion like vultures. If the consensus reading is followed, there are nonetheless connections to Roman imperial ideology: vultures (γύψ/*vultures*) are said to have appeared as auguries to Romulus and Remus at the founding of Rome, and to Octavian when taking his first consulship (Livy, *Hist* 1.7; Plutarch, *Romulus* 9; Suetonius, *Augustus* 95). See Reeder, "Statue of Augustus from Prima Porta," 89–118, for a fuller treatment of birds, auguries, lightning, and imperial victory ideology.

13. Carter, "Imperial Texts," 470.

14. Carter, "Imperial Texts," 469–472.

15. Carter, "Imperial Texts," 473.

16. Carter, "Imperial Texts," 473.

17. Ezekiel 17:1–7, 22–24. I have followed the LXX in translating ὄνυξ as "talon" rather than the Hebrew נוֹצָה ("plumage") in 17:3, 7.

18. Carter, "Imperial Texts," 473–474.
19. Michael Stone, *Fourth Ezra,* Hermeneia, ed. Frank Moore Cross (Minneapolis, MN: Fortress, 1990), 363–366.
20. 4 Ezra 11:1–2; 12:10–11, 22–25, 32–34. See Carter, "Imperial Texts," 474.
21. In addition to these images of the eagles, Carter, "Imperial Eagles," 478, goes on to argue that "the verb 'gathered together' (συναχθήσονται) supports the claim that eschatological judgment on Rome is the focus of Matt 24:28 . . . by means of the prefix *sun,* the verb designates in part, solidarity with a group . . . mostly those who oppose him [Jesus] and seek his death (2:4; 12:30; 22:34, 41; 26:3, 57). This emphasis on participation and solidarity suggests that what happens to the corpse happens to the eagles."
22. See Luz, *Matthew 8–20,* 388–392; Davies and Allison, *Matthew,* 2:43–53; Jack Dean Kingsbury, "The Title 'Son of Man' in Matthew's Gospel," *CBQ* 37.2 (1975): 193–202; E. G. Jay, "Jesus the Son of Man," in *Son of Man, Son of God* (Montreal, Quebec: McGill-Queen's University Press, 1965).
23. Following Matt 24:17–31 there are other instances: 24:36–44; 25:31–46; 26:64.
24. Davies and Allison, *Matthew,* 2:43; Luz, *Matthew 8–20,* 388, notes how the "Son of Man sayings are not equally distributed . . . Between 16:13 and 17:22 they are somewhat clustered (six logia) . . . [and] an even stronger cluster at the end of the gospel between 24:27 and 26:64 (twelve logia)." These final twelve occurrences are also found in passages that refer to eschatological judgment as well as Jesus' death as fulfillment of scriptural prophecy. A full picture of the ways in which Matthew's Jesus refers to himself as "the Son of Man" includes references to his itinerant lifestyle (8:20); healing activity (9:6; 12:8); eschatological return (10:23; 12:32; 16:27–28); and identity (11:19; 12:40; 13:37, 41). These scattered occurrences begin to take on more focus in Matthew 16:13–28, when Jesus asks his disciples "Who do people say that the Son of Man is?" It is here the disciples state clearly what Matthew's readers have known since the beginning: that Jesus is the Messiah, the Son of God (1:1; 16:15).
25. Carter, *Matthew and the Margins,* 413, identifies these chapters as the "fifth narrative block . . . [which] brings Jesus into Jerusalem, the center of religious power and the place where he has predicted he will be crucified (16:21; 20:17–19).... a deadly conflict with the political and religious elite. Jesus' entry parodies Rome's military and political power and represents God's empire." Events in this final act include Jesus' arrival at Jerusalem, where he enters the city in triumph and exaltation (21:1–11); undertakes a public protest at the Temple (21:12–17); defends the authority of his teaching (21:23–27; 22:15–45); and tells parables against and denounces the elite leaders of Jerusalem (21:28–22:14; 23:1–36). Jesus' challenge to the Roman power structures in Jerusalem that lead to his crucifixion are discussed in the following chapter.
26. See Luz, *Matthew 21–28,* 178ff.
27. Luz, *Matthew 8–20,* 388, notes that "except for the final trial scene in 26:64, Jesus never speaks publicly of the coming Son of Man. Nor does he speak of the suffering and rising Son of Man except in the paradoxical sign of Jonah of 12:40. Thus only the sayings about his present activity, almost all of which occur in the first part of the gospel, are public."

28. The nature of the "sign" (σημεῖον) is discussed below.

29. Matthew repeats these motifs later in the eschatological discourse, writing that the Son of Man will appear suddenly when no one expects it (24:37, 39, 44); and return in glory with angels to sit on a throne, to gather all nations to judge them (25:31–32).

30. See also Exod 20:18.

31. An additional parallel is found in Matthew's narrative of Jesus' entry into Jerusalem (Matt 21:2–7), where he quotes Zech 9:9: God's king returns to Jerusalem "triumphant and victorious . . . humble and riding on a donkey, on a colt, the foal of a donkey."

32. Bishop and Coulston, *Roman Military Equipment*, 92, 94; Webster, *Roman Imperial Army*, 127.

33. Webster, *Roman Imperial Army*, 105.

34. Carter, "Imperial Texts," 481.

35. Bishop and Coulston, *Roman Military Equipment*, 113. Larry Kreitzer, *Striking New Images: Roman Imperial Coinage and the New Testament World*, JSNT Supplemental Series 134, ed. Stanley Porter (1996): 30–68, offers copious evidence of coinage bearing imagery of eagles, lightning, military insignia, and imperial portraiture to illustrate his argument about the imperial context of Matthew 24:28 and Luke 17:37.

36. Thackeray, LCL. Josephus, *JW* 3.70–107, gives another account of Roman army practices here, including temporary camps, marching order, and training.

37. Karl Gallinsky, *Augustan Culture: An Interpretive Introduction* (Princeton, NJ: Princeton University Press, 1996), 156, 158, notes that the peaceful settlement of the long-simmering dispute between Rome and Parthia "was portrayed as a tremendous triumph" by Augustus and the Roman government: "the representations on the armor's central panel proclaim the Roman domination over east and west. It is, of course, an Augustan domination, too: he himself fought the principal campaign against the Cantabrians in Spain in the 20s; he was in Syria when Phraates [the Parthian king] surrendered the standards; and the key provinces in the east and west were under his direct control."

38. Naomi J. Norman, "Imperial Triumph and Apotheosis: The Arch of Titus in Rome," in *Koine: Mediterranean Studies in Honor of R. Ross Holloway*, ed. Derek B. Counts and Anthony S. Tuck (London: Oxbow, 2009), 44.

39. Norman, "Imperial Triumph," 50.

40. Carter, "Imperial Texts," 485.

41. Luz, *Matthew, 21–28*, 201–202.

42. Jonathan Draper, "The Development of 'The Sign of the Son of Man' in the Jesus Tradition," *NTS* 39 (1993): 1–21.

43. Draper, "Sign of the Son of Man," 3, prefers the term "totem" rather than "banner" or "military standard" connoted by the Latin *signum*. For Draper, "totem" connotes the physical appearance of the נס, which first appears as a bronze serpent on a pole (Num 21:8–9; 2 Kings 18:4). I agree with his observation and add that the נס may have a similar appearance to the Egyptian *syrt*, military standards which could feature a semi-circular fan; squares of various colors (red, yellow, white) with hieroglyphs or

devices denoting units; or sphinxes, falcons, horses, and serpents, each on a long pole. See Paul Elliot, *Warfare in New Kingdom Egypt* (London: Fonthill, 2017), 32, 40–41, 78; Raymond Faulkner, "Egyptian Military Standards," *Journal of Egyptian Archaeology* 27 (Dec 1941): 12–18. Faulkner, 17, also writes, "Egyptians appear to have had 'divisional' standards, corresponding to the main divisions of the Egyptian army, which were named after the principal gods of the realm; at the battle of Kadesh under Ramesses II the divisions mentioned are those of Amun, Re, Ptah, and Seth . . . [The] standard of Amun which preceded King Ramesses II on the march . . . consisted of the ram's head of Amun crowned with the solar disk and erected on a tall pole mounted in a chariot driven by a single man; on the front of the pole, below the ram's head, appears a statuette of the king, who is thus placed under the protection of the god."

44. Jonathan Draper, "Sign of the Son of Man," 6.
45. Jonathan Draper, "Sign of the Son of Man," 7.
46. Jonathan Draper, "Sign of the Son of Man," 5.
47. Jonathan Draper, "Sign of the Son of Man," 11.
48. Carter, "Imperial Texts," 485.
49. Bishop and Coulston, *Roman Military Equipment,* 113; see also 114, Fig. 65.
50. Lee Ann Riccardi, "Military Standards, 'Imagines', and the Gold and Silver Imperial Portraits from Aventicum, Plitinoupolis, and the Marengo Treasure," *Atike Kunst* 45 (2002): 93.
51. Webster, *Roman Imperial Army,* 117, 118. Riccardi, "Military Standards," 95, also notes the duties of *signiferi* included protecting and keeping account records for the legionary pay chest. In this capacity, the *sacellum* functioned in a military base as a temple did in a city—with both religious and banking roles.
52. Bishop and Coulston, *Roman Military Equipment,* 114; M. Rostovtzeff, "Vexillum and Victory," *JRS* 32.1-2 (1942): 92, 96–97.
53. Michael Rostovtzeff, "Vexillum and Victory," 92–106, especially Plate IV. Rostovtzeff, 93, writes that another important example comes from Dura Europos, where a painting from the temple of Bel shows "a sacrifice to the Palmyrene triad and to the Fortunes of Palmyra and Dura performed by Julius Terentius, the tribune, commander of the *cohors XX Palmyrenorum,* in the presence of some of his non-commissioned officers and men. Between the tribune and the gods stand in frontal view the *vexillarius* of the cohort holding in his hands the heavy *vexillum* of the *cohors.*"
54. Riccardi, "Military Standards," 95–98.
55. Josephus, *JW* 3.124.
56. Webster, *Roman Imperial Army,* 133–139.
57. Ivor H. Jones, "Music and Musical Instruments," *ABD,* 4:938. See also σάλπιγξ, BDAG, 3rd ed., 911.
58. Jones, "Musical Instruments," 936, including: battle (Josh 6:4–20); signaling (1 Sam 13:3; Isa 18:3, 58:1); watchmen (Jer 6:1, 17).
59. Jones, "Musical Instruments," 937.
60. Jones, "Musical Instruments," 936–937. See Num 10:1 and 2 Chr 5:12.
61. Jones, "Musical Instruments," 938–939. Jones also notes that the Greeks themselves had a trumpet that was called a σάλπιγξ. Peter Krentz, "The *Salpinx* in Greek

Warfare," in *Hoplites: The Classical Battle Experience,* ed. Victor Davis Hanson (London and New York: Routledge, 1991), 111, describes the σάλπιγξ as "a narrow cylindrical tube leading to a bell (*kodon*). Both . . . were normally bronze . . . [and in] vase paintings the bell varies in shape from a ball to a bulb to a cone." Krentz, 114–117, describes how the σάλπιγξ was used from fourth to fifth century BCE hoplite warfare to call soldiers to arms, sound reveille, form the line of battle, call for silence (for public prayer or to hear a herald), to signal a charge or retreat.

62. Paul writes in 1 Corinthians 15:52, "in a moment, in the twinkling of an eye, at the last trumpet (ἐν τῇ ἐσχάτῃ σάλπιγγι). For the trumpet will sound (σαλπίσει), and the dead will be raised imperishable, and we will all be changed."

63. Carter, "Imperial Texts," 486.

Chapter 6

Enduring Imperial Power over Life and Death

Jesus in the Hands of the Roman Military (Matthew 26:1–28:20)

Proceeding thence to Jerusalem, he [Varus, the Roman governor of Syria] had only to show himself at the head of his troops to disperse the Jewish camps. Their occupants fled up country; but the Jews in the city received him and disclaimed all responsibility for the revolt, asserting that they themselves had never stirred, that the festival had compelled them to admit the crowd . . . Varus now detached part of his army to scour the country in search of the authors of the insurrection, many of whom were brought in. Those who appeared to be the less turbulent individuals he imprisoned; the most culpable, in number of about two thousand, he crucified.

Josephus, *Jewish War* 2.72–75[1]

When caught, they [the starving poor besieged in Jerusalem] were driven to resist . . . They were accordingly scourged and subjected to torture of every description, before being killed, and then crucified opposite the walls. Titus indeed . . . hope[d] that the spectacle might perhaps induce the Jews to surrender, for fear that continued resistance would involve them in a similar fate. The soldiers out of rage and hatred amused themselves by nailing their prisoners in different postures; and so great was their number, that space could not be found for the crosses nor crosses for the bodies.

Josephus, *Jewish War* 5.449–45[2]

INTRODUCTION

Matthew 26–28, the final act of the gospel's narrative, contains perhaps the most intense and personally impactful scenes for Matthew's Jesus, for it is here that agents of the Roman Empire (elite Jerusalem leaders, allied with the Roman governor and soldiers) conspire to silence him and extinguish his movement. The scenes in table 6.1 portray strategies of social control, which include covert tactics of seizure and rendition followed by predetermined judicial proceedings, incidental abuse and humiliation, and crucifixion. Jesus, for his part, is depicted as aware of the conspiracy against him, yet committed to the "fulfillment" of prophetic scriptural texts (cf. 26:54–56) and non-violent resistance (at his arrest in Gethsemane; refusal to answer Pilate), while anticipating his own return as the eschatological Son of Man.[3] For this reason, the narrative concludes with the failure of the conspiracy—as all the military powers summoned by the elite leaders of the Roman state cannot defeat the divine power at work in Jesus, through which he is resurrected, and granted "all authority in heaven and on earth . . . until the end of the age" (28:18, 20). This vision of God's yet-to-be-established future empire is good news for Jesus's disciples, who—although they have frequently misunderstood (16:21–23; 20:17–28) and failed Jesus (26:56, 69–75), or been overlooked and dismissed by imperial society (5:1–12; 26:6–13; 27:55–56; 28:1–10)—are now part of a kingdom/empire whose victory is not yet complete, but is growing closer as his return approaches.

Countless scholars have written about the scenes of Jesus's passion, death, and resurrection in Matthew 26–28. These passages are, along with similar accounts in Mark, Luke, and John, of central importance to New Testament interpretation. Mindful of the hazard of repeating what has already been written and cogently argued by others, the purpose in this chapter is to continue to focus on the central inquiry of this entire work: asking how Matthew constructs and negotiates Roman military power. For this reason, the sections below will not address each scene in Matthew 26–28, but instead focus on three aspects of the narrative in which Roman military personnel feature prominently, and several other occasions in which their presence appears to be assumed or implied by the narrative. This discussion will make explicit Matthew's portrayal of military presence and power as well as the narrative's concluding strategies for negotiating the threat of Roman military violence.

The first section focuses on the cooperation of elite Jerusalem leaders with Pontius Pilate the Roman governor who together use their position and authority (granted by the Emperor) to bribe Judas (26:1–5, 14–16); send armed retainers to arrest Jesus (26:47–56); put him on "trial" with a predetermined

Table 6.1 Matthew 26–28

I. 26:1–16		The Plot against Jesus is Set in Motion
	a. 26:1–5	Conspiracy of the Chief Priests and Elders
	b. 26:6–13	Anointing and Anger
	c. 26:14–16	Betrayal and Bribe
II. 26:17–30		The Passover Meal
	a. 26:17–19	Meal Preparations
	b. 26:20–25	Jesus Confronts Judas' Betrayal
	c. 26:26–30	Jesus Indicates his Coming Self-sacrifice
III. 26:31–56		Armed Retainers Arrest Jesus
	a. 26:31–35	Jesus Predicts Desertion . . . and Resurrection
	b. 26:36–46	Jesus Prays for Deliverance and Accepts his Fate
	c. 26:47–56	Soldiers of the Chief Priests and Elders Arrest Jesus
IV. 26:57–27:10		Jerusalem Leaders Take Control of Jesus
	a. 26:57–68	Caiaphas the High Priest Puts Jesus on Trial
	b. 26:69–75	Peter Denies Knowing Jesus
	c. 27:1–10	Judgment of Chief Priests and Elders
	i. 27:1–2	Transfer of Jesus to Roman Governor Pilate
	ii. 27:3–10	Refusal of Judas; Disposing of Returned Bribe Money
V. 27:11–31		Roman Authority Condemns Jesus to Death
	a. 27:11–19	Pilate Investigates Jesus
	b. 27:20–26	Calling for Crucifixion of Jesus
	c. 27:27–31	Roman Soldiers Abuse Jesus
VI. 27:32–61		Roman Military Forces Execute Jesus
	a. 27:32–38	Soldiers Crucify Jesus
	b. 27:39–44	Enemies of Jesus Verbally Shame Him
	c. 27:45–54	Death of Jesus and Eschatological Signs
	d. 27:55–61	Burial of Jesus
VII. 27:62–28:20		God's Answer to Imperial Power
	a. 27:62–66	Seeking to Discredit the Empire of Heaven
	b. 28:1–10	Resurrection and Victory of Jesus
	c. 28:11–15	Bribed Soldiers Lie About Jesus
	d. 28:16–20	Jesus' Authority in Heaven and Earth

outcome (26:57–69); transfer him to Roman custody (27:1–2); investigate Jesus's supposed claims to kingship and sentence him to death (27:11–26); wrap up loose ends (27:62–66); and cover their tracks (28:12–15).

The second section focuses on aspects of Matthew's narrative that occur alongside of the first: the work of soldiers who operate under the authority of the Roman Empire and follow the commands of its appointed leaders. This work includes holding Jesus for trial (27:2); preparing him (including abuse and humiliation) for execution (27:27–31, 32–38); crucifying him (27:45–54); watching over his tomb (27:65–66; 28:4), including receiving a bribe to lie about their dereliction of duty (28:12–15).

The third section turns attention to Matthew's portrayal of Jesus who is aware of the threats against his life yet maintains his purpose of non-violently confronting Roman imperial power until such time as he returns in eschatological victory. This is seen in Jesus's confrontation of Judas's betrayal (26:20–25); discussion and acceptance of his impending death (26:26–30, 31–35, 36–46); refusal to cooperate with the imposition of imperial judicial power (26:63–64; 27:11–12); resurrection appearance (28:1–10); and acceptance of divine authority to rule over earth and heaven (28:16–20).

These ways in which Matthew both characterizes and treats Roman military power in chapters 26–28 are an important element of the narrative and of critical importance in understanding the gospel's message about the ultimate failure of Roman imperial power.

JESUS IN THE HANDS OF ROMAN MILITARY PERSONNEL

Armed Retainers Arrest Jesus (Matt 26:47–56)

The first scene in which Roman-aligned military forces appear in Matthew 26–28 is at the arrest of Jesus, where Judas comes to Gethsemane along with "a large crowd with swords and clubs (ὄχλος πολὺς μετὰ μαχαιρῶν καὶ ξύλων) from the chief priests and the elders of the people" (26:47). Their purpose, according to the Matthean Jesus, is to "strike down/kill (πατάσσω) the shepherd, and the sheep of the flock will be scattered" (26:31).[4] Unlike John 18:3, where Judas brings "a detachment of soldiers together with police (τὴν σπεῖραν καὶ ... ὑπηρέτας) ... with lanterns and torches and weapons," Matthew does not state directly that the crowd that arrests Jesus is composed of soldiers/guards. This section demonstrates, however, that soldiers are present in the "large crowd with swords and clubs" (26:47) and that they may be identified with the ὑπηρέται (soldiers/guards) named at 26:58, who also may be the ἑστῶτες ("bystanders") gathered in the high priest's courtyard (26:73) and those who conduct Jesus into Pilate's custody (27:2). This contention is upheld with seven arguments.

The first of these arguments centers on the ways in which Matthew portrays the events surrounding Jesus's arrest in Gethsemane. Prior to sending the soldiers and armed crowd with Judas (27:47), the chief priests and elders have decided to seek Jesus's death (26:3–5). They have determined that his continued presence in and around the Temple—beginning with his act of prophetic protest (21:12–13; cf. 12:14) and continuing with his pointed critiques of their leadership (21:28–22:14; 23:1–39)—has increased the possibility of social unrest throughout the city. They are aware, however, of Jesus's popularity (21:8–16, 23–27, 46) and concerned that laying hands on him during the thronging Passover festival will cause θόρυβος ("clamor, unrest, turmoil, uproar") in which festival goers will flock to defend him (26:5).[5] Concern over public unrest is not unique to Matthew; Josephus (*JW* 5.244 [Thackeray, LCL]) confirms that Roman soldiers from the Fortress Antonia (attached to the Temple complex) were regularly on duty during festivals for security purposes, and "took up positions in arms around the porticoes to watch the people and repress any insurrectionary movement (μή τι νεωτερισθείη παρεφύλαττον)." Thus, following their evaluation that Jesus and his followers pose a serious threat to civic order and stability, the chief priests and elders decide they must isolate and neutralize him. Like Herod and Antipas earlier in the gospel, the leaders of Jerusalem will deploy military forces for just this purpose.

The leaders' response is, in fact, expected by Jesus, who warns his disciples that he will be left alone once they are scattered (Matt 26:31).[6] Matthew's depiction of Jesus relying on scriptural models to guide his choices can be found throughout the gospel (cf. 2:5; 4:4, 6–7, 10; 11:10; 21:13; 26:24, 31), and is one of the narrative's defining features in comparison to other gospels.[7] Here in 26:31 Matthew's Jesus draws from Zechariah 13:7–9, weaving a version of the prophetic words into the narrative and applying them to the events of Jesus's life.[8] In this case, as Luz notes, the quotation from Zech 13:7 implies that the shepherd (Jesus) will receive a fatal blow.[9] In this scene, Jesus accepts his fate as the fulfillment of prophetic writings at several points (26:31, 54, 56): it is the motivation for his willingness to suffer before his ultimate victory. The method by which the chief priests arrest Jesus and deliver him to the Roman governor is demonstrated below: it is not by *ad hoc* crowd of thugs and back-alley enforcers—but by soldiers sent on a nighttime mission for just this purpose.

The second argument for involvement of military figures in the arrest of Matthew's Jesus concerns a more precise definition of the "swords and clubs" carried by the crowd when they lay hands on Jesus and arrest him (Matt 26:47). The use of the sword (μάχαιρα) by soldiers as an emblematic weapon needs little discussion.[10] The use of the club or cudgel (ξύλον) as a military weapon, however, requires attention. Ancient writers identify the ξύλον (the common word for "wood," including it being shaped for a purpose; Latin: *clava*; *fustis*) as a weapon used by soldiers and others.[11] As illustrated in figure 6.1, the club by its nature was irregularly shaped, resembling the tree branch or trunk from which it was cut, perhaps with knobs from branches.

Josephus (*JW* 2.175–77) describes an occasion in which Pilate, expecting trouble from the residents of Jerusalem, "interspersed among the crowd a troop of his soldiers, armed but disguised in civilian dress, with orders not to use their swords (ξίφος), but to beat any rioters with cudgels (ξύλον)."[12] In a similar fashion (*JW* 2.326), Roman soldiers under Florus sought to disperse a crowd in Jerusalem with clubs and charging horses: "The cohorts making no response, the rebels started clamoring against Florus. This was the given signal for falling upon the Jews. In an instant the soldiers (οἱ στρατιῶται) were round them, striking out with their clubs (ξύλον), and on their taking flight the cavalry pursued and trampled them under their horses' feet."[13]

Clubs were also used by *paegniarii*, fighters armed with clubs and whips who were called upon to entertain the crowd without serious bloodshed between gladiatorial contests and were seen commonly at such events throughout the Roman Empire.[14] Moreover, Polybius (*Hist.* 6.37–39) reports an old form of military punishment called *fustuarium* or ξυλοκοτία, in which a soldier guilty of serious breaches of discipline was beaten to death: "The tribune takes a cudgel (ξύλον) and just touches the condemned man with it, after which all in the camp beat or stone him."[15] Thus the ξύλον was a weapon used by and associated with soldiers, and this possibility must also hold true of the armed crowd portrayed in Matthew 26:47.[16] When facing a crowd so armed, Matthew's Jesus and his disciples cannot resist such a display of force successfully (26:52), and it is for this reason that he chooses strategies other than armed violence by which to face imperial power in this scene.

The third argument regarding the presence of soldiers in Matthew 26:47–56 is that Matthew's Jesus responds to the crowd as if they hold military power and authority. When Jesus commands his disciple to put away a sword, saying "all who take the sword will die by the sword" (26:52), he is referring to the principle of non-violent resistance to Roman military might expressed earlier at Matt 5:38–41. This previous teaching counseled provincial farmers to stand up for themselves and creatively resist oppressive practices by turning another cheek when struck by social superiors; going a second mile when forced by Roman military personnel to carry burdens; and walking out

(a)   (b)

Figures 6.1a and 6.1b Similar to Figure 5.1, this tetradrachm from 69–70 CE features on the obverse the emperor Vespasian wearing a victory laurel; the reverse depicts an eagle and palm branch. In this case, the eagle stands on a club associated with both Herakles and military power. *(Source: Image from Wildwinds Coins, admin. Dane Kurth, https://www.wildwinds.com/coins/ric/vespasian/RPC_1961.jpg. Used with permission.)*

of court naked to protest exploitative economic practices. Jesus's strategy for negotiating this power is twofold. He has taught—and models here—verbal protest with non-violent resistance. He also uses prayer. Having earlier taught his followers to pray for God's empire (βασιλεία) to arrive; God's will to be done; and to be delivered (ῥύομαι) from evil doers (6:10, 13), here Matthew's Jesus models his own teaching. He prays earnestly for deliverance, yet accepts God's will (26:39, 42, 44), while noting that he could also "call upon" (παρακαλέω) God to send "more than twelve legions of angels" (26:53)—but chooses not to at the present time. Paradoxically, the reference to these "legions of angels" envisions a military response in keeping with the return of the eschatological Son of Man (13:37–43; 16:27–28; 24:3, 14, 27–31; 28:18–20), which begins with the neutralization of Roman soldiers at the death and resurrection of Jesus (27:54; 28:3–4), discussed below. Imitation of Roman military power coexists with an anticipation of its eventual defeat. For Matthew's Jesus, however, the timing of this response is not for him to decide but remains the prerogative God (24:36; 26:39, 42).

When the crowd lays hands on Jesus, he challenges their authority and purpose, asking rhetorically if he is deserving of suppression by military forces (26:55): "Have you come out with swords and clubs to arrest me as though I were an insurrectionist (λῃστής)?"[17] Although frequently translated as "robber," Matthew's use of λῃστής indicates a broader category ("robber, bandit, revolutionary, insurrectionist, guerilla") that often prompted a military response. Josephus (*JW* 2.253) relates how Felix, the Roman procurator of Judaea, conducted military operations to capture "Eleazar, the brigand chief (ἀρχιλῃστής), who for twenty years had ravaged the country, with many of his associates" and sent him to Rome for trial; Felix also captured many other λῃστοί "whom he crucified" and punished "the common people who were convicted of complicity with them."[18] For elite Romans, the identification of a person as λῃστής (Latin: *latro, -onis*) was another means of maintaining social control. Werner Riess describes how Roman jurists sought to define the *latro* as broadly undesirable: "it came to designate, from quite early on, not only highwaymen and bandits, but also guerilla fighters, political opponents, usurpers, and barbarians,"[19] as well as temple robbers, grave robbers, kidnappers, and cattle rustlers (who were viewed as a subcategory of *latrones*).[20] In the Roman legal system, the *latro* was guilty of *vis armata* (the use of armed force), *dolus malus* (criminal intent), and the creation of gangs. The punishment for *latrocinium* (banditry) was akin to that of murder (*homicidium*): execution by *furca* (a machine designed to break the neck), crucifixion, or being thrown to beasts in the arena.[21] Riess concludes that "the broad classification of certain malefactors as *latrones* reflects the attitudes of the ruling elites, and this practice likewise betrays some of the elite's strategies to maintain its own position of power ... [They] stigmatized ... [and] marginalized [all those] who, for whatever reason, resisted the monopoly on power, government, and societal standards fixed by the Roman elite."[22] Thus Matthew's Jesus is correct that, from the chief priests' and elders' perspective, he is a ληστής: he opposes their claims of authority in the streets of Jerusalem and disrupts their control of the Temple (21:1–17). As discussed below, this is also the view of the Roman governor who orders Jesus crucified beside two λησταὶ and under the written charge that he is a rebellious and illegitimate "King of the Jews" (27:37–38).

Despite his awareness of the military forces aligning against him (26:2) and the direct threat of those laying hands on him in Gethsemane (26:50), Matthew's Jesus refuses to participate in escalating a spiral of violence. When one of his disciples pulls out a sword and injures the slave of the high priest (26:51), Jesus commands that disciple: "Return your sword to its place!" (Ἀπόστρεψόν τὴν μάχαιράν σου εἰς τὸν τόπον αὐτῆς), and directs him (and the rest of his followers) not to respond in kind: "all who take the sword will die by the sword" (26:52). These statements, when coupled with Jesus's question to the armed crowd about his treatment, reveal that he is a different kind of ληστής than they are used to—and Jesus's refusal to use (non-eschatological) military means to accomplish his goals is a hallmark of his strategy throughout Matthew's narrative. Thus this scene shows that Jesus remains committed to his principles of non-violent resistance (5:38–41) and vision of eschatological judgment and punishment (24:27–31) through which he believes "the scriptures of the prophets will be fulfilled" (26:56).

The fourth argument is the identity of those present when Jesus is brought by the armed crowd to the high priest, scribes, and elders for interrogation (26:57). Matthew writes that after Jesus is taken inside the high priest's house (26:59–68), Peter followed and "sat with the guards (ὑπηρέτης) in order to see how this would end" (26:58). In comparison to other scenes in the gospel in which soldiers (στρατιῶται) are clearly identified (8:9; 27:27, 65; 28:12),[23] the identity of Matthew's ὑπηρέται as soldiers/guards requires some explanation. The term ὑπηρέτης (verbal form: ὑπηρετέω) covers a wide semantic range that identifies a number of actions and types of people who serve, assist, follow orders, and obey.[24] While Davies and Allison refer to the ὑπηρέται in 26:58 as "servants," a preferable option in this context is to emphasize the strong associations of the term with military personnel to describe the people surrounding Peter.[25] In Josephus, ὑπηρέται include Hyrcanus, the father of Herod, who "assisted" (ὑπηρετέω) or joined in military action with Pompey in his campaigns (*Ant.* 14.60). They also identify Herod's "guards" (also called τῶν βασιλικῶν), who as military figures put prisoners to death (*Ant.* 14.99; 15.287, 289), including the protestors who removed golden eagle statues from the Temple (*JW* 1.665). The term also names the "lieutenants" of Menaham, a Jewish rebel leader, who were captured and killed in a military conflict in Jerusalem (*JW* 2.448). And the term identifies Roman officials like the procurator Florus (*JW* 2.352), who provoked public protests in 66 CE by misappropriating funds from the Temple, and then ordered soldiers under his command to massacre and crucify civilians in Jerusalem (*JW* 2.293–308).[26] Besides 26:58, Matthew also refers to ὑπηρέται as guards in 5:25, where Jesus warns that legal problems should be settled quickly out of court, "or your accuser may hand you over to the judge, and the judge to the guard (ὑπηρέτης), and you will be thrown into prison."[27] These examples illustrate the contention that although ὑπηρέται may refer to many types of people under orders in a hierarchical system, it does in appropriate contexts refer to military agents, and thus it is correct to interpret Matthew's ὑπηρέται in 26:58 as soldiers/guards attached to the high priest's household—a view which informs the rest of the reading of Matthew 26:47–27:2 presented here.

This argument about the identity of the soldiers/guards in the high priest's courtyard leads to a fifth argument concerning Matthew's Peter in 26:69–75 who follows Jesus's captors "at a distance . . . [and then] sat with the guards (ὑπηρέται) in order to see how this would end" (26:58). Many commentators have speculated on the reasons for Peter's passionate denial of Jesus in 26:69–75 when two female slaves (παιδίσκη) attached to the high priest's household and other "bystanders" (οἱ ἑστῶτες) question Peter as to his affiliation and Galilean origin. Writing on 26:69, for instance, Davies and Allison observe: "Surely Peter's cowardice is enhanced by his accuser's status: she is only a female slave."[28] Likewise, Luz on 26:69 argues that in comparison to Jesus before the Council, "Peter's situation is relatively harmless. He whose life thus far no one has threatened is called to account not by the high priest but by an anonymous woman, merely a slave."[29]

In my view such readings underplay the identity and possible relationships of the characters in Matthew's courtyard scene. Matthew clearly identifies Peter and the two female slaves (26:69, 71), but is less explicit about "the ones who were there" (τοῖς ἐκεῖ, 26:71), naming them "the bystanders" (οἱ ἑστῶτες) in 26:73 and focusing on Peter's statement "he denied it before all of them" (ὁ δὲ ἠρνήσατο ἔμπροσθεν πάντων) in 26:70. Rather than downplaying the identity of those in the courtyard, the presence of ὑπηρέται at 26:58 indicates that any reading of Peter's denial must incorporate the presence of these armed soldiers/guards—who are likely waiting in the courtyard for further orders to escort Jesus as a prisoner to Pilate (27:2) once his interrogation by the Council is over.

The dynamics of power in this scene dictate that Matthew's Peter is rightfully afraid of the armed soldiers/guards, who could easily lay hands on him as they have on Jesus in the previous scene (26:50, 57). Matthew shows the necessity of Peter's negotiation with military forces: when confronted with the possibility of his own arrest, interrogation, torture, and death, Peter seeks to preserve his own life in a perilous and threatening situation. These dangers that Peter faces are among the risks of family censure; trials before synagogue councils, governors, and kings; scourging; execution; and public humiliation (carrying crosses to crucifixion) that Matthew's Jesus has said will be ever-present for all who follow him (10:16–23, 32–39; 16:21–28).

Further, when the two female slaves are understood as having affiliations with the high priest's household (including the soldiers/guards), their questions can be seen in a new light. Regardless of the possible relationships we can imagine these women having or not having with the soldiers/guards,[30] Matthew's portrayal of them here shows them also negotiating with Roman-affiliated military power. The women's decision to challenge and unmask Peter rather than risk concealing his identity speaks to their interest in preserving themselves and their place in the household both in the moment (surrounded, like Peter, by soldiers/guards; or perhaps asked, like the Magi b to gather information for their master) and longer-term (assuming the ongoing association of both slaves and guards with the household). These dynamics of power are more evident when attention is paid to the identity of the soldiers/guards in the courtyard in Matthew 26:69–75.

The sixth argument for the involvement of soldiers/guards throughout Matthew's portrayal of Jesus's arrest (26:47–56) and interrogation (26:57–27:2) is located toward the end of these scenes. Although the gospel merely implies (rather than stating directly), careful readers should be sure to note the presence of soldiers here as well. After Jesus defies the high priest Caiaphas with a declaration of eschatological judgment (26:64) and the assembled Council declares Jesus guilty, Matthew (26:67–68) depicts their vehemence toward him: "Then they spat in his face and struck him; and some slapped him, saying, 'Prophesy to us, you Anointed One! Who is it that struck you?'" In Matthew's portrayal, it appears that the subjects of the verbs in this verse are the members of the Council who have just condemned Jesus guilty and deserving death (26:66). This is the traditional reading, exemplified by Luz, who writes that "the previously mentioned Council members . . . show Jesus their contempt and their brutal scorn."[31] It is possible, however, that here Matthew again implies (rather than stating directly) the presence of soldiers, some of whom are likely to be present in the room to continue guarding Jesus, their prisoner, and thus nearby to participate in striking Jesus (26:67).[32] If this is so, the actions of the ὑπηρέται can be read in conspicuous parallel to Matthew 27:30, where—following Pilate's verdict and condemnation of Jesus to death—Roman soldiers "spat on him, and took the reed and struck him on the head."[33] As anticipated from prior scenes in which Jesus has prepared himself for this fate, he continues to follow the strategy of submitting to this ugly mistreatment while awaiting deliverance and vindication by God.

The seventh and final way in which Matthew implies the presence of soldiers/guards is related to the sixth—and can be viewed as a practical matter.

Matthew writes (27:2) that, "They bound him, led him away, and handed him over to Pilate the governor." Again, the subject points toward the chief priest and members of the Council. But rather than envisioning these elite power holders taking hold of Jesus (now bruised and covered in spittle) themselves, it is more fitting to understand that this work was done by the ὑπηρέται, who have arrested Jesus in Gethsemane, led him to the high priest's house, and brought him to the Council for interrogation (while some of their number await further orders in the courtyard). Viewed in this way, Matthew depicts the Jerusalem leaders acting consistently with other elite actors who command soldiers to enforce claims of authority over people and territory. Thus—until God's definitive eschatological act to overturn this authority—Jesus must submit to Caiaphas and the Council who use military force to uphold imperial authority in similar ways as Herod (2:16), Antipas (14:10), Roman officials and soldiers practicing *angaria* (5:41), and the centurion (8:9)—as well as Pilate the Roman governor, whose role is discussed in the following section.

These seven factors render visible the presence of soldiers throughout the opening scenes of Matthew 26–28, in which Jesus is arrested and brought for interrogation before the Jerusalem Council. The reasons for Matthew's indirect treatment of these soldiers/guards and their work are twofold. First, the cultural experience of Matthew and his audience in the Roman Empire dictates familiarity with pervasive military presence; the ways in which elite actors asserted life-and-death power over marginalized provincial λῃσταί was common knowledge and could be left understated. Second, Matthew's indirect treatment creates room for negotiation: Matthew alludes to and assumes the ever-present and inescapable military power of Rome and its allied local leaders, while also focusing on the ways that Jesus anticipates (26:1–2), faces (26:52–56, 63–64), and is subjected to such power. While he will ultimately overcome (28:1–20) such power, that is not in view in this section. The ways in which Matthew's Jesus interacts with and negotiates expressions of imperial authority and military dominance are similar to ways in which he has done so earlier in the gospel: he seeks guidance for his actions through scriptural paradigms (26:1–2, 24, 31, 56) and prayer (26:36–44); he refuses to violently resist the armed might of the soldiers who come to lay hands on him (26:51–54); he anticipates his own victorious return as the eschatological Son of Man (26:64) and God's ultimate defeat of Roman military power (24:27–31; 28:18–20).

The Roman Governor and his Soldiers Kill Jesus (Matt 27:26–54)

The second place in which Roman-aligned military forces appear in Matthew 26–28 begins at 27:1–2 when Pilate, the Roman governor, receives the prisoner Jesus from soldiers accompanying a delegation of chief priests and elders. As will soon be evident, Pilate is not alone, but works in cooperation with Roman military personnel—including a centurion (ἑκατόνταρχος, *centurio*) and cohort (σπεῖρα, *cohors*) of roughly 500 soldiers—who are ready to follow his commands immediately.[34]

In the company of Jesus's accusers, the chief priests and elders, Pilate conducts his own interrogation (27:11–26).[35] After a memorable scene in which he manipulates a chanting crowd to beg for Jesus's death, Pilate performs a public hand washing to show his (supposed) lack of culpability (27:15–24). Finally, Pilate renders his verdict, which Matthew describes indirectly: "So . . . after flogging Jesus, he handed him over to be crucified" (27:26). Matthew's language in 27:26 points to Pilate as the one conducting these actions,[36] and brings into focus the conflict between God's empire, represented by Jesus, and that of Rome, represented by the governor. At the same time, however, this construction should be understood as authorial convention that assigns to the leader the actions of all those who work or serve under him.[37] Thus, Pilate's soldiers, rather than Pilate himself, scourge, mock, and abuse Jesus (27:26–31a); escort him to Golgotha (27:31b–32); crucify him and watch over his death (27:33–38); and—upon witnessing eschatological portents—declare that he is God's Son (27:54).

Matthew's depiction of Pilate and the soldiers he commands is more explicit than the portrayal of the soldiers/guards discussed in the previous section—and this clarity serves a specific narrative purpose. For, if Matthew's Jesus will one day overthrow Roman military domination (24:27–31; 28:18–20), he will first directly face its terrible power—the power of condemnation, torture, humiliation, and death. The comments below highlight the ways in which Matthew realistically constructs Pilate and his soldiers: they are agents of the imperial system who use their deadly power to eliminate a perceived threat, all the while embodying its values of hegemonic masculinity—until they are undone by divine power. Matthew's Jesus, for now, is unable to defend himself against Roman domination and control over his life and death. At the same time, Matthew's narrative demonstrates clearly that Jesus's suffering and death are not the final word: Roman military power is limited by divine power revealed through eschatological signs, angelic appearance, and Jesus's resurrection—and will ultimately be defeated when Jesus returns as the eschatological Son of Man.

Pilate

"Pilate, the governor" (Πιλᾶτος ὁ ἡγεμών), named in Matt 27:2, 13, 17, 22, 24, 58, 62, 65, is the highest ranking Roman official in the gospel, and thus represents the most direct encounter between Matthew's Jesus and the seat of Roman imperial power. The fact that Jesus is also called ὁ ἡγεμών (2:6;

27:11) underscores the opposition between these two agents who represent empires in conflict with one another.

Matthew depicts Pilate's authority and administration in ways that are typical for a Roman governor (ἡγεμών, 27:2, 11): he sits on a judgment seat (βῆμα, 27:19) in his official residence (πραιτώριον/*praetorium*, 27:27); he hears accusations against and pronounces judgments on provincial lawbreakers (27:11–14, 26); he and his personnel are responsible for holding prisoners until their release or condemnation (27:15–17, 24, 26); they also dispose of bodies of the executed (27:57–58, 65). Matthew portrays Pilate in a similar fashion to Herod (2:1–18) and Antipas (14:1–12); like these Roman client rulers, the Roman governor works closely with local elites (the chief priests and elders) and relies on their advice and support to maintain public order (27:2, 12, 20, 57–58, 62–66). In cooperation with them, Pilate directs his soldiers to kill Jesus (27:27) because he represents a threat to imperial order and control over the territory of Judaea and its people. Thus, each element of Matthew's portrayal of Pilate comports with the role and duties of a Roman provincial governor, including his overlapping political, judicial, and military responsibilities.[38]

Matthew's portrayal of Pilate as an effective politician and military commander broadly conforms to that of other sources.[39] Appointed by the Emperor Tiberius, Pontius Pilate held the post of *praefectus* (governor) over Judaea for eleven years, from 26 to 37 CE.[40] Several coin types minted in Judaea and an inscription from the theater in Caesarea attest to his presence there during this time.[41] Josephus records two incidents that reveal Pilate's direct command of Roman military forces. In the first, Pilate sought to introduce army standards with images of the emperor (τὰς Καίσαρος εἰκόνας αἳ σημαῖαι) into Jerusalem (*JW* 2.169).[42] When large-scale non-violent protests broke out against his action, Pilate—sitting on his official seat (βῆμα) in Caesarea—threatened the delegation appealing to him with a ring of soldiers holding drawn swords (*JW* 2.170–72). This threat proved ineffective, however, when the delegation laid down and exposed their necks, daring him to give the order to kill them; Pilate "overcome with amazement" (ὑπερθαυμάζω) and unwilling to commit his troops to mass slaughter reversed his decision (*JW* 2.169–74).

In the second incident, Pilate used Temple funds for an aqueduct project in Jerusalem and was also met with protests. Anticipating resistance, the governor stationed disguised soldiers among the crowd who gathered to protest his decision, ordering the troops to disperse the crowd with clubs—a supposedly less-lethal weapon which, in the hands of Pilate's soldiers, nonetheless caused injury and deaths from the ensuing stampede to avoid them (*JW* 2.175–77).[43]

The deployment of soldiers under his command was an important aspect of any Roman governor's administration and rule, and these incidents reveal

Pilate's application of imperial authority and military power in various and creative ways. Although Josephus does not portray Pilate as infallible (in Caesarea he underestimated the resolve of Jewish commitment to their ancestral laws), the fact that he acted with decisiveness should come as no surprise. A similar sense of purpose can be seen in Matthew's depiction of Pilate in the events surrounding Jesus's death.

For many New Testament interpreters, especially those who do not take into consideration Matthew's Roman imperial context, Pilate is an enigma: his character and actions have been evaluated in a variety of ways. Carter categorizes five ways in which Pilate has been understood over time by readers: (1) as a villainous tyrant; (2) as weak, easily swayed by the chief priests, and without conviction;[44] (3) as a typical Roman official who cared little for Jewish sensitivities;[45] (4) as a (later) Christian convert; and (5) as a saint.[46] Many of these readings of Pilate stretch back centuries;[47] each of them reflects some aspect of the way that Matthew depicts his interaction with Jesus (27:11, 14), the chief priests and elders (27:12–13), his wife (27:19), and the crowd (27:15–18, 20–23). From the perspective advocated here, which foregrounds the structures, networks of power, and elite alliances of the Roman Empire, Carter is surely correct when he writes of Matthew's scenes that "it is most unlikely . . . Pilate will resist the decision of the local leaders to kill Jesus. . . . A system administered by the Roman governor and his allies, the local elite, means a stacked deck against a low-status provincial like Jesus."[48] If Matthew is well-aware of the ways in which Roman power is held and wielded in his context, it remains to be seen how he depicts the application of this power in taking the life of Jesus, and how this construction serves to help Matthew negotiate Roman military power.

Matthew's Pilate begins his interrogation of Jesus with a question that goes directly to the heart of the case against the prisoner: will Jesus respond to accusations of being a king unsanctioned by Rome, and thus guilty of opposition to imperial claims of power (27:11)? Attentive readers will notice that the governor's inquiry echoes the questions of Herod (another ruler authorized personally by the emperor) about the identity of the "king of the Jews" (2:1–6).[49] Pilate is "greatly amazed" (θαυμάζω . . . λίαν) when Jesus refuses to acknowledge or respond to these charges—remaining silent despite the numerous allegations leveled by his accusers, the chief priests and elders (27:12–14). Jesus's response of silence toward Pilate is not surprising when read together with other instances in which Matthew portrays him negotiating directly with the threat of violence from Roman military power: he has run (in his parents' arms) from Herod's soldiers (2:14–15); he counsels his followers to respond non-violently when coerced by Roman soldiers and officials (5:38–41); he acquiesces to a centurion's request (8:7, 13); and he refuses to fight the armed crowd in Gethsemane (26:51–56).

Jesus's silent response is also consistent with his status in the gospel as a non-elite member of provincial society whose hidden transcript of dissent is only occasionally revealed to those in power.[50] Silence is a form of public compliance which is, according to Scott, one of several possible avenues of disguised resistance to domination; it is ambiguous enough to be interpreted as acquiescence, but hides in plain sight as an act of dignity, creating space for dissenting imagination and ideologies of revenge and overturning the status quo.[51]

Matthew interrupts Pilate's interrogation of Jesus with a brief interlude that serves to heighten narrative tension: Pilate's (unnamed) wife sends him word that he should "have nothing to do with that righteous (δίκαιος) man" because she has "suffered a great deal because of a dream about him [Jesus]" (27:19). Scholars have discussed this interlude in relation to Matthew's portrayal of dreams (ὄναρ, 1:20; 2:12, 13, 19, 22) and other Gentile women (1:1–17; 12:42; 15:22–28); like her husband, Pilate's (unnamed) wife has been viewed in a variety of ways, from sympathetic advocate to oppositional challenger of Jesus.[52] In the view advocated here, the position of Pilate's wife as an elite woman in Roman imperial society is important. While not holding any official position in the imperial political or military hierarchies, she nonetheless possesses a degree of autonomy, access, and agency in relation to these structures that allows her to act and seek to influence events.[53] Her position is analogous to that of Antipas's wife Herodias and her daughter (14:6–11), and her elite status ensures that she shares in and benefits from the networks of imperial power. Likewise, she has a vested interest in supporting Roman claims of power and seeking to maintain her own and her husband Pilate's position in it. At the same time, her message to Pilate is not directly threatening like the message of Herodias to Antipas, which demanded John's head on a platter (14:8). Regardless of one's view about the intentions of Pilate's (unnamed) wife toward Jesus,[54] Matthew's portrayal of her in a brief narrative interlude underscores the multiple interlocking systems and personal interests which are aligned against Jesus now that he is directly under the control of Roman imperial power.

After hearing (but not clearly responding to) his wife's request, Pilate returns to consideration of the accusations brought by his allies, the chief priests and elders (27:12), and to Jesus's non-response. The governor is ready to demonstrate his authority and political acumen through a masterful display of showmanship in which he "orchestrates" the crowd to demand Jesus's death (27:21–25).[55] This accomplished, Pilate turns Jesus over to his soldiers for torture and execution (27:26).

At this point in Matthew's narrative, Jesus's fate is apparently sealed, and the inexorable grip of Roman military power—which began at Jesus's birth with the slaughter of the infants of Bethlehem (2:16) and continued throughout his ministry (20:18-19), as exemplified by the killing of John the Baptist (14:9–10)—has now closed around him, seemingly triumphant. However, as Carter argues, Matthew's portrayal of the scene "does not join in the celebration; rather, it exposes the self-serving workings of Roman justice administered by and for the elite. . . . It rips away the masks. It shows the self-serving nature of Roman administration that masquerades behind claims of benefiting the people and responding to their demands. . . . Matthew's narrative, then, is not deceived."[56]

Matthew's Jesus, for his part, is aware of the scope of Roman power and the manner of suffering he must undergo to defeat it (20:19; 23:29–39; 26:2).[57] His unwillingness to answer the accusations against him is a refusal to participate in the public transcript of compliance and acquiescence to the Roman ideology of control.[58] It is a further expression of Jesus's teaching on justice, making peace, and creative non-violent resistance when faced with judges, trials, guards, and soldiers (5:25, 38–41). In the hands of Pilate, his soldiers, and the chief priests and elders, Jesus shows his followers that he will, indeed, "be mocked and scourged and crucified" (Matt 20:18–19; also 16:21; 17:23). Jesus's willingness to undergo suffering to defeat the military power of Rome and its allies is a direct result of his prayer in Gethsemane where he prays for his Father's will to be done (26:39–44).[59] His victory, Matthew tells his readers, will not come in the present with drawn swords (26:52–54), but by a demonstration of divine power that mimics imperial expressions even as it ends human empires in a final battle that ushers in a new era at the end of the age (24:27–31; 28:1–4; 28:18–20).

Pilate's Soldiers

Following Pilate's condemnation of Jesus, the next stage of Jesus's direct encounter with Roman military personnel begins: Pilate hands him over to Roman soldiers who torture and mock him (27:27–30); escort him to his execution (27:31–32); crucify him and stand watch over his dying (27:33–38); and finally exclaim that he is "God's Son" (27:54). Each of these actions reveals Matthew's portrait of soldiers who enforce the Empire's claims of privilege and control over provincial subjects. In the case of one like Jesus, who dares to speak up and step out of line, this enforcement is deadly.

The scenes in which Pilate's soldiers interact directly with Jesus are found in 27:27–31 (Roman Soldiers Abuse Jesus); 27:32–38 (Soldiers Crucify Jesus); and 27:45–54 (Death of Jesus and Eschatological Signs). While there are several elements that Matthew brings together in the larger narrative of 27:11–61, the focus here remains on Matthew's portrayal of the Roman soldiers who escort Jesus to Golgotha; crucify him; watch over his dying; and respond to the eschatological signs that accompany his death. Matthew portrays these soldiers acting in typical ways; their final responses, however, are surprising—and offer a significant moment in Matthew's ongoing negotiation with the Empire.

From the outset of their interaction with Jesus, Matthew characterizes "the governor's soldiers" (οἱ στρατιῶται τοῦ ἡγεμόνος, 27:27) by their actions, which include a series of cruel punishments designed to inflict pain and humiliation and result in the public spectacle of their prisoner's death.[60] The first of these occurs immediately in conjunction with Jesus's death sentence: Pilate has him "scourged" or "flogged" (φραγελλόω) with, as the transliterated Latin verb implies, a *flagellum*—a whip composed of several tails and frequently tipped with metal or bone.[61] In Roman practice, scourging/flogging often preceded crucifixion.[62] Josephus (*JW* 2.306) records how, just before the outbreak of the Jewish-Roman War, the Governor Florus ordered his soldiers to arrest a large number of protestors who were "brought before Florus, who had them first scourged and then crucified (οὓς μάστιξιν προαικισάμενος ἀνεσταύρωσεν)."[63] Likewise (*JW* 5.449), during the siege of Jerusalem in 70 CE, when soldiers of Titus captured the starving poor trying to escape, they scourged (μαστιγόω), tortured to death (προβασανίζω), and crucified (ἀναστα υρόω) them outside the walls to terrorize those left inside the city.[64] In another case (*JW* 6.300–305), Jesus son of Ananias, "a rude peasant," walked through the streets of Jerusalem prophesying its downfall; he was arrested and beaten by the elite leaders of the city who then brought him to the Roman governor Albinus (62–64 CE), who ordered him "flayed to the bone with scourges" (μάστιξι μέχρι ὀστέων ξαινόμενος) before declaring him insane and letting him go. Thus, Matthew shows that the first action of Pilate's soldiers toward Jesus is standard practice toward condemned enemies of the Roman state. The soldiers on duty at the governor's interrogation follow orders to cruelly scourge their prisoner, likely leaving Jesus with deep lacerations, heavily bleeding, and in a weakened state.

Once Pilate's soldiers (who may be pictured as guarding Jesus and providing security and crowd control around Pilate's βῆμα) finish the bloody task of scourging, they take Jesus into the *praetorium* (πραιτώριον, another Latin transliteration), where they "gathered the entire cohort (ὅλος σπεῖρα) around him" (27:27) for cruel sport and derision.[65] Matthew's specific vocabulary here evokes the scope of the scene: the ὅλος σπεῖρα includes almost 500 armed men—six centuries of highly trained soldiers under the command of six capable centurions.[66] Even if readers may imagine some number of soldiers remaining on duty with Pilate to dismiss the crowd or while he attended to other matters, and some stationed elsewhere in the Temple complex or around the city, Matthew's picture of a solitary bloodied prisoner surrounded by overwhelming military numbers is an effective way to communicate the soldiers' palpable menace and Jesus's vulnerability.

Knowing that this prisoner's life is completely in their hands, the soldiers—in ironic humor based on the crime for which he has been convicted—conduct a mock ceremony which "honors" Jesus as the "King of the Jews" (27:29).[67] The soldiers strip him naked; they place a scarlet/red cloak (χλαμύς κόκκινος), which likely belonged to a soldier, on his shoulders;[68] they force a "crown" of twisted thorns on his head, and a reed (κάλαμος)—a symbol of kingship—into his trembling hand (27:28–29).[69] From the Roman perspective, the authority to rule could only be granted by the Emperor, and was intertwined with Roman military support: Herod was granted the title "King" after appearing before the Roman Senate, and received military forces to take the throne; his sons were refused this title, but still granted the right to rule as Ethnarch and Tetrarchs, with continuing responsibilities to support Roman military campaigns when called upon.[70] Matthew's depiction clearly shows the soldiers' attitude toward Jesus as an unsanctioned king. They seek to humiliate him by spitting (ἐμπτύω) on him (like the soldiers and Council in 26:67) and hitting him on the head with the reed; finally, they "knelt before him and mocked him (ἐμπαίζω)" (27:29). Luz notes that the same verb for mocking/ridiculing is repeated at 27:41, when Jesus's enemies taunt him at Golgotha; and previously at 20:19, where he has warned his disciples that the Son of Man will be "mocked and scourged and crucified; and on the third day he will be raised."[71] When the soldiers decide they have had their sport, they replace the "kingly" regalia with Jesus's own clothes and lead him away (ἀπάγω) to be crucified (27:31).

This march from the Praetorium to the crucifixion site is not a simple one for Jesus. Matthew's readers may imagine him led along by the soldiers, weakened from scourging and beating, and soon unable to continue. Somewhere along the route, the soldiers must find Jesus help to carry his cross; they compel (ἀγγαρεύω) a man named Simon to assist them (27:32).[72] While Jesus's previous journey through the streets of Jerusalem consisted of triumphant symbolism, joyful disciples, and supportive crowds (21:1–17), this one consists of a bloody condemned prisoner and a man impressed into service, accompanied by two other men condemned as insurrectionists (δύο λῃσταί, 27:38), ushered along by a detachment of soldiers following their centurion's commands.

Arriving at "a place called Golgotha" (27:33), the soldiers offer Jesus a drink of "wine . . . mixed with gall" (27:34), which he refuses. As he has told his disciples at 26:29, he will not drink wine again "until that day when I drink it new with you in my Father's kingdom" (ἕως τῆς ἡμέρας ἐκείνης ὅταν αὐτὸ πίνω μεθ' ὑμῶν καινὸν ἐν τῇ βασιλείᾳ τοῦ πατρός μου).[73] Just as he has refused to answer the Roman governor, Matthew's Jesus again refuses to participate in the machinery of imperial (in)justice: without words, he takes what small initiative he can by refusing the drink.

Enduring Imperial Power over Life and Death

Most likely because of widespread cultural knowledge of Roman practices, Matthew does not provide details of Jesus's actual crucifixion—skipping over the necessary actions of the soldiers (laying the prisoner out; nailing wrists and feet; binding arms and torso; raising the cross and securing it). Instead, Matthew notes that, "when they had crucified him, they divided his clothes among themselves by casting lots; then they sat down there and kept watch over him" (27:35-36). Matthew's language here is influenced by Psalms 22 and 69, and, for those who know these Psalms of lament, reveals a message of hope insofar as suffering and lament are followed by vindication and restoration: "For dominion belongs to the LORD, and he rules over the nations" (Ps 22:28).[74] Matthew may also be mimicking the conventions of other Roman writers such as Josephus (quoted above), Livy (*Hist.* 22.33; 33.36), and Appian (*Civil War* 1.120) who believe that crucifixion is reserved for slaves and enemies of the state; thus, while they readily report numbers of crucified to show the deserved fate of those who threaten the Roman order, the mechanics of such a torment are not worthy of comment.[75]

Matthew does include two details, the first of which is chronologically out of place (likely taking place before the soldiers sit down to keep watch) but intended to be the focus of the scene. The soldiers hang a sign above Jesus's head that declares the Empire's verdict: "This is Jesus, the King of the Jews" (οὗτός ἐστιν Ἰησοῦς ὁ βασιλεὺς τῶν Ἰουδαίων). They also crucify two insurrectionists (δύο λῃσταί) on either side of him (27:38), associating him with those who resist the Empire's assertion of power over the lives of its subjects. At this juncture, this power over life—and death—is on full display for all to see.[76]

The soldiers are still sitting on Golgotha keeping watch in typical fashion some hours later, when Jesus cries out to God (27:46), then moans again and dies (27:50). It is "at that moment" that Matthew's narrative viewpoint widens to include the entirety of Jerusalem, wherein the curtain inside the Temple is ripped in two (27:51a); there is an earthquake (27:51b); and the dead are raised (ἐγείρω) from their tombs (27:52). Each of these signs is associated with eschatological fulfillment that Matthew's Jesus has spoken of throughout the gospel (cf. 16:27-28; 19:28-30; 24:27-31).[77] Davies and Allison note the narrative significance of the three signs in Matt 27:51-52:

> The veil [τὸ καταπέτασμα τοῦ ναοῦ] is the outer veil [separating the sanctuary from the forecourt] and its rending foreshadows or symbolizes the destruction of the temple in AD 70. . . . similar portents announcing the doom of the temple are recorded by both Josephus (*JW* 6.288-309) and the Talmud (*b. Yoma* 39b; *y. Yoma* 6.43c). . . . If [this] . . . rending of the veil anticipates or inaugurates the end of the temple, it thereby vindicates Jesus' prophecy against the place (24:2). . . . Eschatological earthquakes . . . which ancients typically viewed not

as whims of nature but responses to human sinfulness—are sometimes linked with the advent of God or a supernatural being, with judgment, with the deaths of great persons, and with tragedy in general. . . . For "the Holy Ones" [who are resurrected] (cf. LXX Zech 14:4–5) as a designation . . . of saints in an eschatological context see LXX Isa 4.3; Dan 7:18 . . . We should here think of pious Jews from ancient times . . . the primary purpose of which is testimony to Jesus in and around Jerusalem.[78]

Each of these signs of eschatological fulfillment also points toward the final scenes in which Roman-appointed guards are overcome and defeated, and Jesus himself is raised and is given "all authority in heaven and on earth" (28:2–3, 18). The signs also justify Jesus's earlier contention: that he *could* call upon divine power (26:53) if that were that the best way to bring about his Father's desire (26:39–44) and fulfill the writings of scripture (26:53).[79]

When the signs appear at the moment of Jesus's death, Matthew emphasizes the soldiers' and centurion's response: they "were extremely afraid (φοβέω σφόδρα) and said, 'Truly this man was God's Son'" (27:54).[80] There is much discussion over the character of the soldiers' response, with scholarly consensus pointing toward a "confession" of faith in which the soldiers recognize Jesus's identity and acknowledge it. Davies and Allison represent this view well, arguing that "the confession . . . represents a fundamental reformation of opinion. Weight is also added to the confession by the status of the high rank of the Roman centurion, who reminds us of the believing centurion in 8:5–12."[81] In contradiction to this view, Sim argues that the soldiers' and centurion's "acknowledgement of Jesus as the Son of God is intended as a cry of defeat in the face of divine power. . . . Matthew uses the narrative of Jesus' death in 27:51–54 as a proleptic judgment scene (cf. Matt 25:31–46). The soldiers at the scene of the crucifixion represent the wicked on the day of judgment . . . as the torturers and murderers of the Messiah, they are Gentiles of the worst type."[82] From the perspective argued here, Sim's position is in alignment with Matthew's ongoing negotiation with and critique of Roman military power. In characterizing the soldiers as φοβέω σφόδρα, Matthew shows these soldiers failing to act as soldiers ought to. Rather than displaying the Roman ideals of *virtus* and *imperium*, which would lead to courageous, firm, and heroic responses to the eschatological signs, the soldiers and their centurion are overwhelmed and defeated.[83]

This crushing fear is critical to understanding the soldiers' and centurion's statement about Jesus's identity. Throughout the gospel, Matthew depicts a number of occasions in which characters exhibit fear, expressed in the verb φοβέω and ταράσσω (and their related cognates). These occasions are frequently provoked by competing claims of power between Rome and its elite Judaean allies on the one hand, and the Empire of God on the other. Thus, God's angel counsels Joseph not to be afraid (μὴ φοβέω) to wed the pregnant Mary, "for the child conceived in her is from the Holy Spirit" (1:20). Jesus's disciples are afraid (ταράσσω φόβος) of the divine power present in Jesus upon seeing him walking on the water (14:26–27), and when hearing God's voice at his mountain-top transfiguration (17:7): in both cases, Jesus commands them "you must not be afraid" (μὴ φοβεῖσθε). These appeals to overcome fear are connected with the performance of masculinity embodied in such traits as courage, dignity, firmness, control, and self-discipline. Jesus warns his followers "you must not fear (μὴ φοβεῖσθε) those who kill the body but cannot kill the soul" (10:28); rather, they are to fear (φοβέω) God who judges human behavior (10:28) yet values them "more than many sparrows" (10:31). Thus, Jesus indicates that while his followers may be persecuted they should also look forward to vindication through resurrection. Similarly, the women at the tomb are also encouraged to perform their role with masculine courage: although they "were filled with fear and great joy" (28:8) upon being told of Jesus's resurrection, they are commanded, by God's angel and by Jesus himself, not to be afraid (μὴ φοβεῖσθε, 28:5, 10). The women's ability and willingness to follow these commands (they "ran to tell the disciples," 28:8) stands in contrast to the fear and immobility of the soldiers (28:3), discussed below. Matthew's audience, then, has no need to fear—because through Jesus and his followers (which include them) God is addressing the assertion of Roman power over the lives of God's people.

In contrast to his followers, those who oppose Jesus and his proclamation of God's kingdom have reason to be afraid. Upon learning of Jesus's birth from the Magi, Herod "and all Jerusalem with him" are frightened (ταράσσω, 2:3) at news of an unsanctioned rival king. The chief priests and elders, when challenging Jesus's authority, are afraid (φοβέω) of Jesus's association with the legacy of John the Baptist (21:23–27), and of Jesus's popularity with the crowds in Jerusalem (21:46).[84] Finally, Matthew draws a clear narrative connection between the soldiers' fear of the eschatological signs they witness on Golgotha (27:54) and the fear (φοβέω) of the soldiers guarding Jesus's tomb, who "shook and became like dead men" when witnessing another manifestation of divine power (28:3, discussed below).

The problem with the soldiers' fear is all the more pronounced when comparing Matthew's portrayal with that of other Roman writers who praise and glorify soldiers who display hegemonic masculinity by performing its values of valor, resolution, domination, and courage. Julius Caesar (*Civil Wars* 1.46), for instance, praises his *primus pilus*, Quintus Fulginus, for *eximiam virtutem* ("exceptional valor"): Fulginus died while leading a detachment *antesignanos* (ahead of the standards) in a failed attempt to capture a hill outside Ilerda, Spain. Tacitus (*Ann.* 15.11) praises Tarquitius Crescens, a centurion who chose to remain alone defending a tower against the Parthians while the rest of his unit fled; and (*Hist.* 3.22) Atilius Verus, another *primus pilus* centurion from the Seventh Legion, who died while saving the legion's *aquila*. Josephus (*JW* 6.81–91) also tells of a personal acquaintance, the centurion Julianus, who died bravely during the siege of Jerusalem in 70 CE:

> Seeing the Romans beginning to give way and offering but a sorry resistance, [Julianus] sprang forward—he had been standing beside Titus on Antonia—and single-handed drove back the Jews, already victorious, to the corner of the inner temple. The multitude fled in crowds before him, regarding such strength (ἰσχύς) and courage (τόλμα) as superhuman; while he . . . slew all whom he overtook, and no spectacle that met the eye of Caesar was more wonderful than that, nor more terrifying to his foes . . . [When Julianus' hobnailed boots slipped on the stone pavement, he fell but continued fighting.] A cry of concern for the hero went up from the Romans in Antonia, while the Jews crowding round him struck at him from all sides . . . many a time he tried to rise but was thrown back by the number of his assailants . . . At length, when all his other limbs were hacked and no comrade ventured to his aid, he succumbed. Caesar was deeply moved at the fall of so valiant a soldier . . . while those who might have [helped him] . . . were withheld by terror (κατάπληξις). Thus Julianus, after a hard struggle with death . . . [left] behind him the highest reputation, not only with the Romans and Caesar, but even with his enemies.[85]

All of these illustrate the contention of Graeme Ward who argues for the importance of the effect of such performances on participants and audience: "In addition to the soldier who inflicted the violence and the victim who suffered it, the reactions of nearby observers—Roman and foreign—were crucial to how such acts were later interpreted and judged. This was especially true in instances when Roman soldiers appeared to have succumbed to fear (*timor*) and become panic stricken (*pavidi*)."[86] Ward notes that in the Republican period, Roman military punishments for "desertion, lying under oath, cowardice witnessed in battle, and disobedience . . . were punishable by death—by collective stoning and cudgeling (*fustuarium*) or by scourging and beheading in a formal ceremony in front of the entire legion. . . . Ancient authors who record these ceremonies seem most interested in describing the emotions and opinions among spectators who watched the punishment rather than in representing the suffering of the victims."[87] While it is not clear that all such military punishments continued into the first century CE, Roman attitudes toward masculine behavior were based on continuing appeals to courage, domination, and control—the values of *virtus* and *imperium*.[88] Thus, Matthew's depiction of the φοβέω σφόδρα of soldiers and their centurion at Golgotha shows them in violation of every value they are trained and expected to uphold: they are unmanned and paralyzed with fear by the divine power shown at Jesus's death. Matthew underscores the soldiers' failure with the presence of several women followers of Jesus who show more courage than either the soldiers or Jesus's male disciples: the women are present at the crucifixion, and continue to show their loyalty to Jesus at his death, burial, and in the days that follow (27:55–56, 61: 28:1–10).[89]

In these scenes Matthew shows imperial military claims at the full extent of their power, taking control of Jesus's life and bringing about his suffering, humiliation, and death. This military power is embodied by the Roman governor Pilate and his soldiers. However, at the end of this display of power—at the very moment when Jesus dies at their hands—the gospel audience witnesses divine power as eschatological portents appear in Jerusalem. The soldiers, Rome's front-line agents of imperial domination and control, are filled with terror, unmanned, and undone. Matthew's audience sees the soldiers' performance of imperial hegemony slip and the mask of Roman military invulnerability crack. Their position is no longer unassailable, but relativized as readers witness the beginning of God's defeat of Roman military power. The next steps of this divine campaign are discussed in the following section.

The Defeat of Roman Military Power (Matt 27:62–28:20)

The third place in chapters 26–28 where Matthew depicts Roman military power is 27:62–28:20, which fall under Part VII (God's Answer to Imperial Power) of the outline above. It is here, in four scenes, that Matthew's negotiation with the Roman Empire reaches its conclusion:

a. 27:62–66 Seeking to Discredit the Empire of Heaven
b. 28:1–10 Resurrection and Victory of Jesus
c. 28:11–15 Bribed Soldiers Lie About Jesus
d. 28:16–20 Jesus's Authority in Heaven and Earth

The expected actions of imperial agents (Pilate, elite Jerusalem allies, soldiers) who oppose and seek to silence Jesus are well-established by this point in the narrative. Appearances of a heavenly messenger and the resurrected Jesus at his tomb, however, signal that imperial claims over Jesus's life and death have been negated by divine power—and that such claims are also relativized for Matthew's audience. This section addresses Matthew's depiction of Roman soldiers in three places: (1) their cooperation with the chief priests and Pharisees, who seek to fully discredit Jesus's followers and his work by sealing and guarding the tomb (27:62–66); (2) their defeat by divine power in the form of a heavenly angel (28:1–4); and (3) their agreement to accept a bribe from the chief priests and elders and to lie about their failure to secure the tomb (28:11–15). The argument that follows contends first, that whereas the soldiers/guards (ὑπηρέται) who arrest and guard Jesus in Matt 26 are under the control of the chief priest, the soldiers assigned to guard Jesus's tomb are under the command of the Roman governor[90]—and that their place in this chain of command is an important aspect of Matthew's negotiation with Roman military power. In addition, the way in which Matthew depicts these soldiers (following orders, conducting official security, defeated by an agent of the heavenly army, and compared to women followers of Jesus) signals the imminent defeat of Roman military power.

At the outset, it is important to recognize that the soldiers who appear in Matthew 27:62–66 and 28:1–4, 12–15 are under the direct command of the Roman governor. This relationship is seen at three points in the gospel narrative. First, Matthew's language recognizes that the soldiers in these scenes are Pilate's to command, rather than soldiers/guards (ὑπηρέται) who report to the high priest and Council (26:58) (discussed above). At Matt 27:65, 66; and 28:11 these soldiers are called a κουστωδία (Latin: *custodia*), a "group of soldiers doing guard duty" or "a guard composed of soldiers."[91] While it is true that this noun is a functional description that may not directly point to the identity of the soldiers, it should be noted as another example of Matthew's use of a transliterated Latin loanword. In these scenes κουστωδία joins φραγελλόω (*flágello*) and πραιτώριον (*Praetorium*) from Matt 27:26–27 to give a distinctly Roman identity to these soldiers.

Second, as a Roman unit, the soldiers are commanded by Pilate (27:64; 28:14) throughout the final scenes in which they appear. The need for these soldiers arises when Matthew pictures the chief priests and Pharisees "gathered before Pilate" (27:62) to present him with a formal request to secure Jesus's tomb.[92] Previously the Jerusalem leaders brought Jesus as an accused prisoner to Pilate (27:1–2); here Matthew presents them again as working cooperatively with the Roman governor to mitigate a perceived danger to public order in the city (27:64). Once Pilate hears their request to secure the tomb (27:64), he orders his soldiers to go with the Jerusalem leaders to help them "make it as secure as you know how" (27:65). As he did previously, Pilate is again willing to deploy Roman military forces to support his allies in their shared goal of eliminating the threat posed by Jesus and his followers. Pilate's role as commander of soldiers has been discussed in the previous section, including the ways in which his soldiers follow his commands to scourge and execute Jesus (27:26–37); it is in this same capacity that he acts when sending his soldiers with the chief priests and Pharisees at 27:65–66.

The final reason that the soldiers in these scenes should be identified as Roman is found in their final appearance, when "some of the *custodia*" report to the chief priests about events at the tomb (28:11). Upon hearing this report, the Jerusalem leaders seek to quash the news by offering the soldiers a large bribe to lie about what happened (28:12). Matthew identifies the soldiers here as στρατιῶται (28:12), mirroring the language at 27:27, where they are introduced as οἱ στρατιῶται τοῦ ἡγεμόνος ("the governor's soldiers").[93] The chief priests also appeal to the soldiers by reminding them of their duty and direct responsibility to the governor: "If this comes to the governor's ears, we will satisfy him and keep you out of trouble" (28:14). Taken together, these three reasons—identified by a Latin word; commanded by Pilate; and called στρατιῶται—support the contention that the guards at Jesus's tomb are Roman soldiers.

The identification of the guards at the tomb as Roman soldiers under the command of Pilate connects Matthew's final scenes under consideration here with this chapter's overall argument: that in chapters 26–28 Matthew is showing his audience the failure of Roman military domination. This power, although it has used all the tools of life and death at its disposal, cannot defeat the divine power at work in Jesus.

Under orders from the Roman governor, the soldiers have assisted the elite leaders of Jerusalem in making Jesus's tomb "as secure as you know how" (ἀ σφαλίσασθε ὡς οἴδατε, 27:65) by placing an official mark (σφραγίσαντες) on the stone to seal it (27:66),[94] and remaining on duty, guarding it until dawn on the first day of the week (28:1). At this moment, "suddenly there was a great earthquake (σεισμὸς . . . μέγας), for an angel of the Lord (ἄγγελος κυρίου), descending from heaven, came and rolled back the stone and sat on it" (28:2). Matthew's depiction of this action connects events at the tomb with the earlier scene on Golgotha, where eschatological signs at the death of Jesus lead to the reversal and downfall of the soldiers and centurion deployed there. The events at Jesus's death include an earthquake (ἡ γῆ ἐσείσθη, "the earth shook") and the resurrection of the sacred dead, who appear in Jerusalem (27:51–52), causing the soldiers and centurion to be extremely afraid (φοβέω σφόδρα) and exclaim worriedly that Jesus is God's Son (27:54). At the tomb, soldiers from this same cohort that had tortured and executed Jesus are petrified by the earthquake and transfixed by the angel's appearance: "For fear (φόβος) of him the guards shook (ἐσείσθησαν) and became like dead men" (28:4)[95] in the very place that Jesus receives new life. The implications of this fear for the soldiers include personal shame; accusations of cowardice; and possible punishment if their paralysis is judged by the governor as dereliction of duty.[96] Matthew's depiction of these soldiers failing to live up to the ideals of *virtus* and *imperium* does not, however, overturn such values. Rather, Matthew's negotiation here involves showing how divine power associated with Jesus overpowers and outperforms agents of the Roman Empire—so as to replace their dominion with that of God.

In addition to the soldiers' own failure, there are three other aspects of Matthew's presentation that emphasize the inadequacy of Roman claims of militarily-based and -enforced domination. These narrative features come in the form of characters that represent God's Empire: the angel, the women at the tomb, and the resurrected Jesus himself. Each of these characters contributes to defining Jesus's victory as an initial eschatological victory inaugurated by his resurrection. The interaction of these characters with the immobilized soldiers also points toward the imminent downfall of Roman military power.

First, Matthew depicts "an angel of the Lord" (ἄγγελος κυρίου) who causes an earthquake (σεισμὸς) by descending from heaven, rolling back the stone door of Jesus's tomb (breaking the official seal the soldiers have placed), and sitting down on top of it (28:2).[97] The angel's affiliation with "the Lord" (ὁ κύριος)—a reference to God—stands in opposition to that of the chief priests and soldiers, who appeal to Pilate as κύριος (27:63).[98] The angel's ability is portrayed in terms reminiscent of Jesus at his transfiguration (17:2) and eschatological return (24:27): with a "face . . . like lightning and clothing white as snow" (28:3), the angel is filled with heavenly power.[99] Just as the soldiers are members of the cohort under Pilate's command, this angel seems perhaps to be one of the "twelve legions of angels" that Jesus could call upon (27:53), who is now sent by God.

The angel's appearance is shocking to the soldiers stationed at the tomb, and Matthew connects the angel's arrival and actions with their failure to fulfill their duty: "For fear (φόβος) of him the guards shook and became like dead men (ἐσείσθησαν οἱ τηροῦντες καὶ ἐγενήθησαν ὡς νεκροί)" (28:4). Like the angels who will appear to punish the unrighteous on the day of judgment (13:37–43, 49; 16:27; 24:31, 36; 25:31), this angel also overpowers the soldiers who are members of the cohort that has scourged, mocked, spit upon, beaten, and crucified Jesus (27:26–36). Matthew's depiction thus connects the angel who appears at the tomb with those who will one day come with divine power to judge and punish the unrighteous (24:31); this judgment is prefigured at the tomb with the abject fear and death-like state of the soldiers.

Second, Matthew's portrayal of the women who had traveled from Galilee with Jesus (27:55) stands in sharp contrast to the fate of the soldiers. These women, unlike the male disciples, have not run or scattered (26:56) or denied Jesus (26:69–75) but have remained close to Jesus throughout the events depicted in Matthew 26–28. As a group, the women have stood at the crucifixion and observed the eschatological events that accompanied his death (27:55–56); two of them, "Mary Magdalene and Mary the mother of James and Joseph" have watched his burial (27:61);[100] and now at sunrise go "to see the tomb" (θεωρῆσαι τὸν τάφον, 28:1).[101] The effect of such positive characterization leading up to the final scenes in Matthew's narrative sets the stage for the failure of the soldiers at the tomb.

Janice Capel Anderson argues that the category of gender influences Matthew's characterization of the women in these scenes negatively:

"Although the women play an important part in the narrative, gender seems to prevent their identification as [full] disciples. They are an auxiliary group . . . not strangers or outsiders, but neither are they among the inner circle of disciples."[102] For this reason, "the exemplary behavior of women [is portrayed] as more of an achievement and heightens contrasts with male characters. . . . [The] women at Bethany, cross, and tomb are contained within a model that assumes male gender as a requirement for becoming a disciple."[103] The degree to which Capel Anderson's argument about Matthew's patriarchal assumptions is true underscores my contention about Matthew's portrayal of the soldiers' failure in these scenes. The soldiers are not only overcome by the appearance of a messenger with heavenly power, but outperformed in manly courage and faithfulness by the women who follow Jesus.

Although Mary and Mary, like the soldiers, are afraid at the appearance of the angel, their affiliation with Jesus and therefore God's work provides room for a command to reassure and steady them: "You must not be afraid" (μὴ φοβεῖσθε ὑμεῖς, 28:5), and an invitation to view the empty tomb (28:6). In contrast to Mark 16:5 and Luke 24:3, Matthew does not indicate that the women enter the tomb—but their courage is displayed by not running from the earthquake or the angel, seated as he is among the bodies of the corpse-like soldiers. This courage is doubly evident, given the recent actions of the soldiers against Jesus, and the general caution that provincial women had to use in the presence of Roman soldiers.[104] Standing attentively at Jesus's tomb, the two women are entrusted by God's messenger with news for the rest of the disciples: "he has been raised, as he said" (28:6). In contrast to the soldiers' later report of failure and dereliction of duty (28:11), the women hurry immediately to proclaim the good news, leaving "the tomb quickly with fear and great joy" (28:8). The importance of this mission is emphasized once the women leave the tomb by the appearance of the resurrected Jesus who greets them and repeats the angel's message (28:8–10).

Mary Magdalene and the "other" Mary's role as participants in and agents of God's Empire is confirmed when they approach Jesus, take hold of (κρατέω) his feet and worship him (28:9). In this they mirror the devotion of another (unnamed) woman who anointed Jesus for burial (26:6–13). They also act in precisely the opposite way to the chief priests, elders, and their soldiers who take hold of (κρατέω) Jesus to arrest and harm him (21:46; 26:4, 48, 50, 57).[105] Matthew's portrayal of the two women's joy and devotion stands in sharp relief to the response of the soldiers at the tomb, who are forced to lie about their experience, pretend that they fell asleep on duty, and then worry about punishment if their commander, the governor, finds out.[106] Likewise, the women's acts of recognition and worship are models for Matthew's community—who must perform their own acts of courage in relation to the ever-present threat of Roman military violence while seeking to maintain faithful discipleship to Jesus while proclaiming and participating in God's heavenly kingdom.

Third, Matthew's portrayal of Jesus in 28:9–10, 16–20 reveals that God has worked through him—by resurrection and displays of divine power—to overpower Roman military personnel and anticipate the ultimate defeat of Roman military power when he will appear as the Son of Man to deliver eschatological judgment (24:27–31; 25:31–33). Although a Roman governor and his elite provincial allies have condemned him to death, and Roman soldiers have tortured and executed him, and guarded his tomb, Jesus "has been raised (ἠγέρθη), just as he said" (28:6). The passive voice of ἐγείρω underscores the divine action. Like the earlier resurrection of the "holy ones" at Jesus's death (27:52), Jesus's resurrection is an eschatological event that reveals divine power. Coupled with other portents—earthquakes (24:7; 27:54; 28:2); occluded sun and moon (24:29; 27:45); and angelic appearances that immobilize (28:4) and will destroy (13:37–42; 24:28) God's enemies—Jesus's resurrection appearance anticipates the final victory of eschatological fulfillment.[107] When Jesus appears to Mary and Mary, he accepts their worship (προσκυνέω) as an exalted, royal, and transcendent figure (28:9),[108] whose status places him in opposition to the claims of "the rulers of the Gentiles [who] lord it over them, and their great ones [who] are tyrants over them" (20:25).

The final words of Matthew's Jesus claim imperial power: "All authority (ἐξουσία) in heaven and on earth has been given to me" (28:18). This language and the concepts of divine rulership that are associated with it have deep biblical roots (cf. Ps 110; Isa 9:6–7; 32:1), and previously have been used by Matthew to describe Jesus, his work, and his teaching (7:29; 9:8; 10:1; 21:23–24, 27). Jesus's claims of authority may also be read as mimicking, opposing, and overturning the claims of Roman imperial power. These claims have been discussed in chapter 1 under the heading of Imperial Ideology, and include such expressions as the imagery on the Arch of Titus which celebrates his conquest of Jerusalem and apotheosis;[109] and Virgil's *Aeneid* (1.279), which claims divine sanction for the Roman Empire, when Jupiter declares: "For these I set no bounds in space or time; but have given empire without end."[110]

Throughout the gospel, Matthew has negotiated the reality of Roman military power by representing capricious rulers such as Herod and Antipas; unjust and abusive application of force such as the *angaria*; ambiguously motivated imperial agents such as the centurion in Capernaum; and imperial elites and their retainers such as Pilate and his soldiers, and the Jerusalem chief priests and elders and their soldiers/guards. The threats of these agents will soon, in the words of Matthew's Jesus, be rendered powerless when he returns as the eschatological Son of Man. Until that day, Matthew's audience can have hope and confidence because this same divine power has been revealed in signs at Jesus's death and through his resurrection. Now, Jesus's final commission to his followers imitates imperial assertions: they are to go to "all nations," claiming them through baptism for God's Empire (28:19) and "teaching them to obey" all Jesus's commands (28:20). This commission is itself Matthew's final negotiation with Roman military power: his depiction of Jesus's return as victorious ruler and Jesus's followers as (non-violent) conquerors of all nations envisions the yet future replacement Rome's unjust rule with the just and righteous rule of God, and reassures Matthew's audience that their work will continue with Jesus's presence and guidance, until their Lord returns in eschatological judgment at the "end of the age" (28:20).

CONCLUSION

This chapter has argued that Matthew's portrayal of Jesus's arrest, suffering, death, and resurrection serves to frame an important message for Matthew's audience about the ultimate failure of Roman military power. It has shown how, in Matthew 26–28, elite leaders in Jerusalem work together with the Roman governor to arrest, sentence to death, and execute Jesus. Their purpose is to end his perceived threat to their claims of domination and control. This work involves two groups of soldiers who use the application of violence and cruelty to enforce the death sentence against Jesus. However, although these soldiers succeed at killing Jesus, they expose themselves to shame and failure. This failure—indicated by their terrified response to the divine actions in a series of eschatological events—prefigures an ultimate divine judgment upon them and all those who participate in upholding Roman military power at Jesus's eschatological return as the Son of Man. Finally, Matthew emphasizes the soldiers' failure by contrasting their paralysis with the power of the angel, the courage of the women, and the authority of Jesus himself.

For these reasons, Matthew's narrative concludes with a hopeful vision. The divine power at work in Jesus, and through which he is resurrected, also grants him "all authority in heaven and on earth . . . until the end of the age" (28:18, 20) until such time as Roman military power is ultimately defeated. Matthew's vision of the soon-to-be-fulfilled Empire of God imitates the claims and assertions of the Roman Empire—and yet is good news for Jesus's disciples, whose ongoing negotiation with the Roman Empire is now assisted by the concurrent reality of God's victorious, though not-yet-established, empire.

NOTES

1. Thackeray, LCL.
2. Thackeray, LCL.
3. Matthew's "fulfillment" passages (signaled by the verb πληρόω, often in the aorist subjunctive as in 26:54) are found throughout the gospel (1:22; 2:15, 17, 23; 3:15; 4:14; 5:17; 8:17; 12:17; 13:14, 35; 21:4; 26:54, 56; 27:9). Matthew uses this construction to connect his narrative to previous texts from the Hebrew Bible and demonstrate to his audience that Jesus' identity and work are a continuation of Israel's story. I do not intend to suggest here or elsewhere that these Biblical texts refer only to Jesus, but instead that Matthew uses such texts to sustain and exemplify his claims about Jesus identity as God's agent.
4. πατάσσω, BDAG, 3rd ed., 786. Jesus is quoting Zech 13.7 and intent on allowing the prophetic words to be fulfilled, while also pointing to his ultimate victory.
5. θόρυβος, BDAG, 3rd ed., 458.
6. The NRSV gives the impression that Jesus uses a military term, "deserters" to describe the disciples' flight. This verb, σκανδαλίζω, BDAG, 3rd ed., 926, more typically has the sense of "cause to fall away, to repel, to give offence." As a noun, σκάνδαλον, it refers to traps of various kinds, including verbal/rhetorical and those used for animals in hunting. See LXX Josh 23:13; 1 Kings 18:21.
7. Luz, *Matthew 21–28*, 387–388; Davies and Allison, *Matthew*, 3:484–485.
8. Davies and Allison, *Matthew*, 3:119, referring to C.H. Dodd, *According to the Scriptures* (London, UK: Nisbet & Co., 1962), 64, 67: "Zechariah 9–14, which 'has the character of an apocalypse,' was 'one of the scriptures which from a very early time were adduced in illustration of the Gospel facts.' Matthew presumably viewed the whole section as largely messianic and thus about Jesus and so was free to mine it for prophetic ore."
9. Luz, *Matthew 21–28*, 388.
10. μάχαιρα, BDAG, 3rd ed., 622, is used consistently by Matthew at 10:34; 26:47, 51, 52, 55. Another term, ρομφαία, is used less frequently: by Luke at 2:35, and interchangeably with μάχαιρα throughout Revelation (1:16; 2:12, 16; 6:4, 8; 13:10, 14; 19:15, 21).
11. ξύλον, BDAG, 3rd ed., 665. See Herodotus, *Hist.* 2.63; 4.180; Polybius, *Hist.* 6.37; Tacitus, *Ann.* 13.57; *Ger.* 45; Pliny, *Nat. Hist.* 7.57; Virgil, *Aen.* 7.730, 511; 10.308.
12. Thackeray, LCL.
13. Thackeray, LCL.
14. Ben Hubbard, *Gladiator: Fighting for Life, Glory, and Freedom* (New York: Metro Books, 2015), 141, 182–183.
15. Paton and Walbank, LCL. On the occasion of group infraction (such as cowardice in battle), Polybius (*Hist.* 6.39) also reports that a tenth of the guilty soldiers were punished (*decimatio*) in a similar way, and the rest forced to live outside the camp. It is unclear if these practices continued into the Imperial period of Roman

history. However, Tacitus (*Ann.* 13.35–36 [Jackson, LCL]) relates the efforts of the Roman general Corbulo in 58 CE to enforce a new standard of discipline on the supposedly lax legions of Syria: he ordered his soldiers to camp in tents during winter, resulting in desertions and punishment: "contrary to the rule in other armies, mercy did not attend first and second offenses, but the man who had left the standards made immediate atonement with his life." Then, when auxiliary soldiers under the command of the Paccius Orficius engaged in battle contrary to orders, Corbulo reprimanded the officers and shamed the soldiers by having them camp outside the ramparts for a lengthy period of time (*Ann.* 13.36).

16. It should be noted that this reason alone does not justify my contention, as non-soldiers such as Jesus' disciple (26:51) might also wield a sword or club. It does, however, serve to expand the basis for the argument. One additional example of a ξύλον is the famous club of Herakles (Latin: *Hercules*), frequently pictured in sculpture and iconography for centuries throughout the Greek and Roman world. Plutarch, *Lycurgus* 30, writes: Ἡρακλέα μυθολογοῦσι δέρμα καὶ ξύλον ἔχοντα τὴν οἰκυομένην ἐπιπορεύεσθαι. Herakles was worshipped throughout the Roman period by men and women and was popular with soldiers. The *ara maximus*, a sacred site dedicated to Herakles was located in Rome from earliest times; other altars, shrines, and dedications are widespread. See Celia Schultz, "Modern Prejudice and Ancient Praxis: Female Worship of Hercules at Rome," *Zeitschrift für Papyrologie und Epigraphik* 133 (2000): 291–297; Harriet Flower, "Lots of Small Shrines: Compita and Sacella," in *Religion at the Roman Street Corner* (Princeton, NJ: Princeton University Press, 2017), 137–144.

17. λῃστής, BDAG, 3rd ed., 594, refers also to Josephus, *JW* 2.253; 4.504; *Ant.* 14.159ff. See Richard Horsley, *Bandits, Prophets, and Messiahs: Popular Movements in the Time of Jesus* (Harrisburg, PA: Trinity Press, 1999), 48–87, and "Ancient Jewish Banditry and the Revolt against Rome, A.D. 66–70," *CBQ* 43 (1981): 410–411, who writes about the spread of λῃσταί prior to 66 CE: "Jewish banditry, which became epidemic under the last few procurators before the Revolt, was a significant, perhaps the most significant, identifiable social form taken by nascent Jewish rebellion against the Romans as well as their sacerdotal aristocracy."

18. Thackeray, LCL.

19. Werner Riess, "The Roman Bandit (*Latro*) as Criminal and Outsider," in *Social Relations in the Roman World,* ed. Michael Peachin, 693–714 (New York: Oxford University Press, 2011), 694.

20. Riess, "Roman Bandit," 696.

21. Riess, "Roman Bandit," 695–696.

22. Riess, "Roman Bandit," 696. Scott, *Domination,* 55, concurs: "rebels or revolutionaries are labelled bandits, criminals, hooligans in a way that attempts to divert attention from their political claims. Religious practices that meet with disapproval might similarly be termed heresy, satanism, or witchcraft."

23. cf. Matt 27:27: "the soldiers of the governor" (οἱ στρατιῶται τοῦ ἡγεμόνος). See discussion below.

24. ὑπηρετέω, ὑπηρέτης, BDAG, 3rd ed., 1035.

25. Davies and Allison, *Matthew*, 3:523. ὑπηρετέω, ὑπηρέτης, TDNT, 8:530–544: "The military world offers good examples. Hdt. 5.111, 4; Thuc. 3.17.3 call the carriers of shields or weapons ὑπηρέτης because they have always to be ready to obey the one they are assisting. The meaning is the same when the immediate aides of a commander are called his ὑπηρέται e.g., Plato, *Euthyphr.* 14a; Xenophon, *Cyrop.* 6.2, 13." Luz, *Matthew 21–28*, 424, does not address the term in his comments on 27:58. Carter, *Matthew and the Margins,* 516, identifies the "guards" but focuses instead on the location at Caiaphas' house and the foreshadowing of Peter's denial in 26:69–75.

26. ὑπηρέται also may be used as a general title for non-military "servants" of elite Romans, who may yet fulfill quasi-military roles, such as delivering written commands directly from the emperor to a provincial governor (*JW* 2.203), or being armed and ordered to work directly with legionaries to collect tribute from a province (*JW* 2.41). On one occasion, Josephus (*JW* 2.321) calls each Jewish priest a "servant of God" (ὑπηρέτης τοῦ θεοῦ): these go out, led by the high priest, to humbly beg a restless crowd in Jerusalem not to rebel and provoke the Romans to military reprisal. These sorts of roles are also seen in the few occurrences of ὑπηρέτης in the LXX: Prov 14:35 (the king's servants); Dan 4:46 (the king's servants throw Daniel's friends into a fiery furnace and stoke it). The proverb in Isa 32:5 reflects the more general sense of the term.

27. ὑπηρέται are also found elsewhere in the New Testament, including Mark 14: 54, 65, where Peter warms himself at a fire with the guards, and the guards slap or strike (ῥάπισμα) Jesus; John 7:32, 45, 46; 18:3, 12, 18, 22; and 19:6, where guards act as temple police, work beside a Roman cohort to arrest Jesus, strike Jesus, and shout "crucify him!" and Jesus declares his "followers would be fighting" (18:36) if his kingdom was of this world; and Acts 5:22, 26, where temple police report to the high priest and then arrest Peter and the other apostles.

28. Davies and Allison, *Matthew,* 3:545.

29. Luz, *Matthew 21–28*, 455.

30. As demonstrated in Chapter 1, these may have included a range of relationships from simple negotiation of work in the presence of soldiers (Were they serving food and drink to those just returned from the mission to Gethsemane?) to more personal relationships (Were they daughters, sisters or wives of the soldiers?) including complex matters of social status (Were they enslaved or free? If enslaved, who may have owned them? Were they forced to work as prostitutes or would association with the high priests' household preclude this, based on Deut 23:17–18?).

31. Luz, *Matthew 21–28*, 448. See also Carter, *Matthew and Margins*, 519, who writes, "the Sanhedrin mocks and humiliates him," and Davies and Allison, *Matthew*, 3:535, who also suggest that Matthew's redaction may have served to emphasize scriptural allusions to such texts as Jer 26:8–11 and Isa 50:6.

32. Luz, *Matthew 21–28*, 447, notices some ways in which Matthew uses his Markan source, referring to Matthew's redaction of Jesus' blindfold in Mark 14:65; however, Luz overlooks the presence of ὑπηρέται in this same verse, where Mark writes (14:65): "Some began to spit on him, to blindfold him, and to strike him, saying to him, 'Prophesy!' The guards also took him over and beat him."

33. Matthew's verb choices are varied and serve to heighten the impact of his opponents' abuse. At 26:31 Jesus has told his disciples he will be struck down (πατάσσω). In the high priest's house, he is struck with fists (κολαφίζω), slapped (ῥαπίζω), and then asked "who hit you? (παίω)" (26:67). At 27:30, the Roman soldiers strike (τύπτω) Jesus' head with a reed. At both 26:67 and 27:30, Jesus' opponents spit (ἐμπτύω) upon him.

34. The role of the centurion is discussed in chapter 4. On the identity and role of legionary and auxiliary cohorts in the Roman military system, see chapter 1 and further discussion below.

35. Carter, *Matthew and Margins*, 522, calls attention to Matt 27:3 ("When Judas, his betrayer, saw that Jesus was condemned . . .") and notes that "Judas's conclusion that Jesus is condemned is interesting in that it agrees with Jesus' prediction in 20:17-19, yet it precedes Pilate's decision. It attests that Jesus' death is inevitable because of the elite's alliance. It is in the interests of both to kill Jesus."

36. The active verbs in Matt 27:26 point to Pilate as the one who acts: "when he had scourged Jesus, he handed him over" (τὸν δὲ Ἰησοῦν φραγελλώσας παρέδωκεν ἵνα σταυρωθῇ). Φραγελλώσας is an aorist, active, nominative, masculine participle from the verb φραγελλόω. Παρέδωκεν is an aorist, active, third person singular verb from παραδίδωμι.

37. This convention began at least as early as Herodotus (*Hist.*, 1.26 [Goodley LCL]): "After the death of Alyattes Croesus his son came to the throne, being then thirty-five years of age. The first Greeks whom he attacked were the Ephesians. These, being besieged by him, dedicated their city to Artemis." An example more contemporaneous to Matthew is Josephus' (*JW* 1.204 [Thackeray, LCL]) description of Herod, who upon appointment to the governorship of Galilee, "found . . . Ezekias, a brigand-chief, at the head of a large horde, was ravaging land on the Syrian frontier, he caught him and put him and many of the brigands to death (συλλαβὼν ἀποκτείνει καὶ πολλοὺς τῶν λῃστῶν)." In a similar way as Matthew, Josephus uses an aorist, active nominative third person singular participle (συλλαβὼν) and a present indicative, third person verb (ἀποκτείνει) to describe Herod's actions: the work, however, was done by soldiers under Herod's command.

38. Colin Wells, "Roman Empire," *ABD* 5:805, describes the role of provincial governors in the Roman Empire, who were directly appointed (and removed) by the emperor.

39. *Contra* Davies and Allison, *Matthew*, 3:438, 552, 554–555, who do not foreground the networks of imperial power in their analysis, thereby concluding that Matthew's depiction of the Roman governor is simply of a Gentile whose role fulfills prophecy about the Messiah's suffering: Pilate "gives cowardly heed to the hostile Jewish leaders and the crowd they have agitated" and his role is secondary to that of "the guilt of the chief priests and elders, who manipulate Pilate and stir up the crowd against the Messiah." Due to their emphasis on religious and theological aspects of the text, Davies and Allison, *Matthew*, 3:579, affirm that Pilate is "the official representative of Caesar" who commands Roman military forces to suppress dissent throughout his appointed region, but argue that he "does not take charge" of Jesus' trial and is guilty of ineffective leadership.

40. For historical summaries of Pilate and his career, see Daniel Schwartz, "Pontius Pilate," *ABD* 5: 395–401; Saddington, "Roman Military Personnel," 2426; Davies and Allison, *Matthew*, 3:554–555.

41. Helen Bond, "The Coins of Pontius Pilate: Part of an Attempt to Provoke the People or to Integrate Them into the Empire?" *Journal for the Study of Judaism in the Persian, Hellenistic, and Roman Period* 27.3 (1996): 241–262; Jerry Vardaman, "A New Inscription Which Mentions Pilate as 'Prefect'," *JBL* 81.1 (1962): 70–71: this inscription identifies him as "PRAEFECUS IUDAEAE."

42. Perhaps *imagines* (busts of the emperor and imperial family used in military expressions of the imperial cult); see chapter 5.

43. On the clubs/cudgels used by soldiers, see previous section. A third event in which Pilate's command of soldiers is not explicitly stated, but may be surmised, is Luke 13:1–3: the governor is said to be responsible for the deaths of Galileans, "whose blood Pilate mingled with their sacrifices."

44. This is the view of Davies and Allison, *Matthew*, 3:554, 583, who argue that "Pilate does not take charge . . . [his] title is ironic: the governor leaves the governing to others." Likewise, 3:593: "the governor does not govern."

45. See Luz, *Matthew 21–28*, 465, who concludes from a survey of historical sources that Pilate "was certainly not the fanatical enemy of the Jews who allegedly conducted his evil administration in Palestine as the henchman of the temporarily powerful praetorian prefect, Sejanus. He was an energetic but somewhat ruthless governor who was not sensitive to the particular religious and cultural situation of his province." This view is challenged by Brian McGing, "Pontius Pilate and the Sources," *CBQ* 53.3 (1991): 416–438, who argues for Pilate's ability to astutely negotiate changing circumstances throughout his tenure as governor.

46. Carter, *Pontius Pilate*, 3–11.

47. Carter's categories apply to understandings of Pilate informed by the four canonical gospels, plus historical sources. Not every category applies equally to Matthew; the focus here remains on reading Matthew's depiction of Pilate in its appropriate imperial context.

48. Carter, *Pontius Pilate*, 82.

49. The language is the same: ὁ βασιλεὺς τῶν Ἰουδαίων. For discussion of traditions of popular (unsanctioned) kingship in late Second Temple Jewish society, see Horsley, *Bandits, Prophets, and Messiahs*, 88–135.

50. cf. 26:63–64, where Jesus speaks only after keeping silent before the high priest. See Chapter 4 for my comment on how Jesus was "amazed" (θαυμάζω) at the centurion asking for his slave to be healed (Matt 8:5–13).

51. Scott, *Domination*, 8, 55–57, 66–68, 198–200.

52. Dorothy Jean Weaver, "'Wherever This Good News is Proclaimed': Women and God in the Gospel of Matthew," *Interpretation* 64.4 (2010): 390–401: "Pilate's wife . . . stands straight and tall in contrast to her husband (27:1–2, 11–26, 62–66). She, like her counterparts Joseph and the wise men, has a 'dream' concerning Jesus . . . to which she pays heed . . . pleading for the life of 'that innocent man' (27:19c)." Davies and Allison, *Matthew*, 3:587–588; and Nadja Troi-Boeck, "Non-Jewish Women as Precursors of Universalism," *Lectio Difficilor* (http://www.lectio.unibe

.ch, 2014), 6, also view her request as an unsuccessful attempt to intervene on Jesus' behalf. Jean K. Moore, "Matthew's Decolonial Desire (Matthew 12:42; 27:19). A Postcolonial Feminist Reading of the Two Royal Women," *Lectio Difficilor* (http://www.lectio.unibe.ch, 2013), 13, argues that "colonial females are often figures of cause and conscience, by which they subvert the empire in their critique of the way in which it is being governed.... In this regard, Pilate's wife's role may not be limited to declaring Jesus' righteousness. Rather ... [her] action can be better understood as Matthew's act of appropriation" in which her heaven-sent dream and call for action is a critique of Pilate's use of imperial power. Luz, *Matthew 21–28*, 492, connects her dream-influenced warning with Pilate's hand washing: listening to her advice, he seeks to disassociate himself from Jesus. Carter, *Pilate,* 93–94, argues that "her dream seems to have revealed Jesus being faithful to God's saving purposes, and that is clearly bad news for Rome and Pilate! Pilate should have nothing to do with this dangerous threat.... [and her] statement, then, must function as encouragement to Pilate to remove Jesus quickly."

53. Dorothy Jean Weaver, "'Thus You Will Know Them by Their Fruits': The Roman Characters of the Gospel of Matthew," in *The Gospel of Matthew in its Roman Imperial Context,* 107–127, ed. John Riches and David Sim (London and New York: T&T Clark, 2005), 114: "Matthew's narrative offers no clues that as the wife of the Roman governor she is a woman of considerable authority. Her appeal to her husband ... is one that could presumably be taken only by a person of such authority."

54. Some questions that influence interpretation: Does Pilate's wife seek Jesus' release or swift death? How might either option benefit her and/or her husband's position? Or is her goal to simply warn her husband about the ramifications of entanglement in this local matter? Is her dream sent from God? If so, does God intend to provide for Jesus' safety? If not, what is the purpose? Is Matthew's model for Pilate's wife Herodias? If so, what sort of "trouble" does Jesus represent for her? Does she wish him dead, and seek to work through non-traditional avenues of power as Herodias does at the feast to help Antipas execute John?

55. Carter, *Pontius Pilate*, 96–97, writes that Pilate's "handwashing and declaration of innocence acknowledge what he and his allies have accomplished in this scene. They have successfully identified a threat to their power, decided on Jesus' execution, and manipulated the crowd not only into not supporting Jesus but also into actively (almost riotously) advocating that he be executed ... Such is the extent to which the crowd has 'owned' the elite's agenda."

56. Carter, *Pontius Pilate*, 97–98.

57. This Roman power includes alliance with the Jerusalem elite, as Matthew's Jesus pronounces in 23:29–39: "Woe to you, scribes and Pharisees, hypocrites! For you build the tombs of the prophets and decorate the graves of the righteous, and you say, 'If we had lived in the days of our ancestors, we would not have taken part with them in shedding the blood of the prophets.' Thus, you testify against yourselves that you are descendants of those who murdered the prophets. Fill up, then, the measure of your ancestors. You snakes, you brood of vipers! How can you escape being sentenced to hell? Therefore, I send you prophets, sages, and scribes, some of whom you will kill and crucify, and some you will flog in your synagogues and pursue from

town to town, so that upon you may come all the righteous blood shed on earth . . . Jerusalem, Jerusalem, the city that kills the prophets and stones those who are sent to it! How often have I desired to gather your children together as a hen gathers her brood under her wings, and you were not willing! See, your house is left to you, desolate. For I tell you, you will not see me again until you say, 'Blessed is the one who comes in the name of the Lord.'"

58. Scott, *Domination*, 8, 55–57, 66–68, 198–200.

59. See below, n.79.

60. Unlike the centurion in Capernaum (8:5–13), Jesus does not speak to these soldiers in the final scenes of the Gospel, directing his few words to reject Pilate's accusation (27:11); cry out to God (27:46); the women at the tomb (28:9–10); to his disciples (28:18–20).

61. φραγελλόω, BDAG, 3rd ed., 1064: "a punishment inflicted on slaves and provincials after a sentence of death had been pronounced on them." Apuleius, *Metamorphoses* 8.30, describes the use of bone tips.

62. Gerald O'Collins, "Crucifixion," *ABD* 1:1208. See Philo (*Flaccus* 72 [Colson, LCL]), who describes how the Jews of Alexandria, during civil unrest allowed by Flaccus, the governor, "were arrested, scourged (μαστιγόω), tortured and after all these outrages, which were all their bodies could make room for, the final punishment kept in reserve was the cross."

63. Thackeray, LCL.

64. See full quote at the beginning of this chapter. Josephus uses the Greek verb μαστιγόω (noun: μάστιξ), rather than φραγελλόω, which is transliterated from Latin. Matthew uses μαστιγόω at 10:17; 20:19; and 23:34 in reference to flogging by synagogue authorities; it is only at 27:27, when the flogging is done by Romans, that he uses the Latinized verb.

65. There has been some effort made to identify the type of cohort (legionary vs. auxiliary) these soldiers were from, based on known positions and troop deployments at the time. The intention here is not to repeat these discussions, nor quest for historical detail, but rather to argue that Matthew portrays these soldiers (whether legionary or auxiliary) as upholding the Roman Empire's priorities— through the torture, public humiliation, and execution of one who ran afoul of the powerful elite. For discussion, see Saddington, "Roman Military Personnel," 2413–2414, who points first to "five cohorts and one *ala* (a total of 3,000 men) of Sebastenians (i.e., Samaritans) and Caesareans in Judaea" who supported Roman governance at the death of Herod, and argues that "the soldiers at the Cross, then, could have been drawn from any auxiliary regiment transferred into Judaea after the fall of Archelaus, or have been members of more 'local' units drafted from such areas as Samaria, Caesarea or Syria. Whatever the ethnic composition of the regiment involved, to the Jews it was of course 'Roman': thus Josephus called the unit stationed in the Antonia near the Temple during Passover ἡ Ῥωμαϊκός σπεῖρα." See also, Haynes, *Blood of the Provinces,* 46, 5–53, 117–118, who describes the incorporation of Herod's royal army into Roman auxiliary forces after his death in 6 CE, mentioning especially the Sebastenians and their effectiveness in service to both Herod and Rome. This contrasts with Brown, *Death of Messiah*, 874, who

misleadingly asserts that "these are not first-class imperial legionaries, but auxiliary troops from the Syro-Palestinian region"; although he is correct that "many . . . could very well have been anti-Jewish." Brown, *Death of Messiah*, 874–876, also provides descriptions of other public figures who were mocked, including Herod Agrippa II, who was insulted by the people of Alexandria by dressing a man named Karabas in false-regalia (Philo, *In Flaccum* 6); and Herod Agrippa I, when citizens, indulging in schadenfreude at his death, dressed in festal garlands and perfume (Josephus, *Ant.* 19.9).

66. For the legions, Webster, *Roman Imperial Army*, 109, writes: "The smallest unit in the legion was the century, which may originally have been a hundred men but by the time of Polybius contained eighty. It was divided into ten sections of eight men each (*contubernia*) sharing a tent and a mule in the field and a pair of rooms in permanent barracks; it seems likely that this was also a mess unit.... The century was, however, the basic unit of the imperial legion. Six centuries made up a cohort (480 men) and ten cohorts the legion." For auxiliary cohorts, George Cheeseman, *The Auxilia of the Roman Imperial Army* (Oxford, UK: Clarendon Press, 1914), 27–28, writes that the "*cohors miliaria* was divided into ten centuries . . . [and the] *cohors quingenaria* into six . . . The question to be decided is whether these centuries contained 80 or 100 men each. . . . the lower is probably to be preferred.... [And,] therefore, it seems safer to assume establishments of 480 and 800 men for *cohortes quingenariae* and *miliariae* respectively."

67. Luz, *Matthew 21–28*, 514: "The soldiers strip Jesus and give him imitations of the three insignia of a Near Eastern client king . . . the royal purple robe . . . the golden laurel-berry crown, and . . . golden scepter."

68. χλαμύς, BDAG, 3rd ed., 1085: "a military cloak, *mantle* worn by Roman soldiers." See Appian, *Civil War*, 2.90; Josephus, *Ant.* 5.33; 2 Macc 12:35. Bishop and Coulston, *Military Equipment*, 111, note that "there were two types of over garment habitually worn by soldiers under the early Principate and these were the *sagum* and *paenula*. The *sagum* was a draped cloak, fastened at the wearer's right shoulder by a brooch, whilst the *paenula* was a cape which the soldier put on over his head." In shape, the much earlier Greek χλαμύς and *sagum* are similarly rectangular; Bishop and Coulston, *Military Equipment*, 111, however, report that, "tombstones of the 1st century AD show rather more men wearing the *paenula* than the *sagum*. In either case, Matthew's intent is to show the soldiers' impromptu 'ceremony' to shame Jesus using items at hand."

69. James Strange, "Tiberias," *ABD* 6:547, notes "the earliest extant coins [from the mint at Tiberias] show a reed and an inscription in Greek, 'Of Herod the Tetrarch.' The reverse displays the name Tiberias written in Greek letters within a wreath." These coins, from the reign of Antipas, are dated to 20 CE. See also, Morten Hørning Jensen, *Herod Antipas in Galilee: The Literary and Archaeological Sources on the Reign of Herod Antipas and its Socio-Economic Impact on Galilee.* (Tübingen, DE: Mohr Siebeck, 2006), 204. For a contrary view, see W. Wirgin, "A Note on the 'Reed' of Tiberias," *Israel Exploration Journal* 18.4 (1968): 248–249.

70. Josephus, *JW* 1.283–285, 290–294, 301–302, 346 (on Herod); *JW* 2.93–100; *Ant.* 17.317–323 (on his sons). Josephus (*Ant.* 17.355; 18.1–6) also reports how

Herod's son Archelaus was removed from power in 6 CE by the Emperor Augustus, who appointed governors to rule Judaea directly from that point forward.

71. Luz, *Matthew 21–28*, 515.

72. This is the second place in Matthew's narrative where the verb ἀγγαρεύω (5:41) is used. The parallel text of Mark 15:21 (likely Matthew's source) underscores what has been argued in chapter 3: the soldiers "compelled a passerby, Simon of Cyrene, who was coming in from the country (ἀγγαρεύουσιν παράγοντά τινα Σίμωνα Κυρηναῖον ἐρχόμενον ἀπ' ἀγροῦ)." Another parallel in Luke 23:26 emphasizes the demanding nature of the soldiers' actions: "they seized Simon . . . laid the cross on him, to carry it behind Jesus (ἐπιλαβόμενοι Σίμωνά . . . ἐπέθηκαν αὐτῷ τὸν σταυρὸν φέρειν ὄπισθεν τοῦ Ἰησοῦ)."

73. Luz, *Matthew 21–28*, 530, notes Matthew's editorial changes to Mark 15:23, in which Jesus is offered "intoxicating wine flavored with myrrh, probably to deaden the pain. However, Matthew is thinking of Ps 68:22 LXX, the same verse whose second half will appear in v.48. Like the petitioner of Psalm 68 LXX, Jesus is also tormented and ridiculed by his enemies. In order to fulfill Ps 68:22 LXX, he must taste the bitter drink, which he rejects in Mark 15:23."

74. Matthew's Jesus alludes to this in several places: cf. 16:21; 17:12, 22–23; 26:31–32.

75. One exception to this is Josephus' description of those crucified at the siege of Jerusalem (*JW* 5.449–451, see above); his purpose, however, is similar to that of other writers—to show the fate of those who resist Roman claims of power and authority.

76. Matthew 27:39–44 shows a series of people continuing to ridicule and disdain Jesus, heaping derision upon his already shameful death. These include people passing by (27:39–40); the chief priests and scribes (27:41–43); and the insurrectionists crucified alongside him (27:43). The opprobrium from the chief priests and scribes is not surprising, given their prior conspiracy to kill Jesus (26:3–4). Matthew's portrayal of the insurrections highlights the difference between Jesus' approach and theirs. Like Barabbas the "notorious prisoner" (27:16), who Mark 15:7 and Luke 23:19 name as guilty of civil uprising and strife (στάσις), Matthew shows that while Jesus may be crucified alongside of two λῃσταί, he is not to be identified with them.

77. The currency of such thought is demonstrated in 2 Maccabees 7, which gives an account of resistance by faithful Jews against the Hellenistic tyrant Antiochus. When threatened with torture and death, each of seven brothers appeals to their belief in resurrection while refusing to comply with the king's demands. This belief views resurrection as an eschatological event (7:14, 16–17); a vindication for resistance (7:9, 11, 22–23); and provides the initiative to overthrow tyranny. It is typified by the speech of the youngest brother, who is the last to be executed (2 Macc 7:30–38): "I will not obey the king's command, but I obey the command of the law that was given to our ancestors through Moses. But you, who have contrived all sorts of evil against the Hebrews, will certainly not escape the hands of God.... You have not yet escaped the judgment of the almighty, all-seeing God . . . [but] you will receive just punishment for your arrogance. I, like my brothers, give up body and life for the laws of our ancestors, appealing to God to show mercy soon to our nation and by trials and

plagues to make you confess that he alone is God, and through me and my brothers to bring to an end the wrath of the Almighty that has justly fallen on our whole nation."

78. Davies and Allison, *Matthew*, 3:630–633. On the curtain, they note, 3:631–632, "According to Josephus (*JW* 5.512–514), a Babylonian curtain, embroidered with blue, scarlet, linen thread, and purple hung before the main entrance of the sanctuary, at the back of the vestibule, and 'worked into the tapestry was the whole vista of the heavens.' If this is the curtain of v.51a the picture is of the heavens splitting, something which occurs in the [Hebrew Bible] and came to be a common item of eschatological expectation." They also notice how Matthew's Jesus has warned of such earthquakes in 24:7, and list, 341 n.86, similar earthquakes in Biblical tradition: Joel 2:10; Hag 2:6; Zech 14:5; 1 Enoch 1:6–7; 102:2; 4 Ezra 5:8; 6:13–16; 9:3; and 2 Bar 27:7.

79. Davies and Allison, *Matthew*, 3:497, note the parallel between Jesus' prayer in Gethsemane (26:39–44) and the prayer he taught his disciples (6:9–13): "Your will be done (γενηθήτω τὸ θέλημά σου)." In both cases, Matthew's views of divine will are rooted in traditions of theological hegemony in which divine power overwhelms all who encounter it (cf. Isa 6:1–5; Matt 17:5–6)—including here even the Father's Beloved Son (Matt 3:17; 17:5), who submits to suffering and death in order to attain eschatological victory. Luz, *Matthew 21–28*, 398–409, provides a history of interpretation that reveals various attempts to wrestle with Matthew's portrayal here.

80. Translation of the phrase: ἀληθῶς θεοῦ υἱὸς ἦν οὗτος, which is based on the centurion's so-called "confession" in Mark 15:39, has prompted scholarly discussion over interpretation of υἱὸς θεοῦ, and whether the anarthrous phrase should be translated as "a" or "the" Son of God. Carter, *Matthew and the Margins*, 537, notes that "this is the same title (in anarthrous form, lacking a definite article) that the disciples use to confess Jesus' identity in 14:33." For contrasting views on Mark, see Tae Hun Kim, "The Anarthrous υἱὸς θεοῦ In Mark 15.39 and the Roman Imperial Cult," *Biblica* 79 (1998): 221–241 and Earl Johnson, Jr., "Mark 15,39 and the So-Called Confession of the Roman Centurion," *Biblica* 81.3 (2000): 406–413. For the purposes of this chapter, the results of this discussion ("a" vs. "the") are immaterial: the focus here is on Matthew's presentation of the soldiers' response to divine power and its threat to their imperial claims of power over life and death.

81. Davies and Allison, *Matthew*, 3:635. See also Luz, *Matthew 21–28*, 569, who concurs. See Chapter 4 for comment on the ambiguity of Jesus' response to the centurion in Matt 8:5–12.

82. Sim, *Christian Judaism*, 226. See also Sim, "The 'Confession' of the Soldiers in Matthew 27:54," *Heythrop Journal* 34.4 (1993): 401–424; Carter, *Matthew and Margins*, 537.

83. On *virtus* (virtue, honor, manliness) and *imperium* (domination, control, rule) as values of Roman hegemonic masculinity, see Williams, *Homosexuality*, 133. Although see Tacitus, *Ann.* 13.35–36.

84. Similarly, Antipas is aware of Jesus' popularity with the same crowds who supported John, whom Antipas had executed (Matt 14:1–13).

85. Thackeray, LCL.

86. Graeme Ward, "The Roman Battlefield: Individual Exploits in Warfare of the Roman Republic," in *The Topography of Violence in the Greco-Roman World*, ed. Werner Riess and Garrett Fagan (Ann Arbor, MI: University of Michigan Press, 2016), 301.

87. Ward, "Roman Battlefield," 304.

88. See n.83.

89. Janice Capel Anderson, "Matthew: Gender and Reading," in *A Feminist Companion to Matthew*, ed. Amy-Jill Levine (Cleveland, OH: Pilgrim Press, 2004), 40–44; Amy-Jill Levine, "Matthew," in *The Women's Bible Commentary*, ed. Carol Newsome and Sharon Ringe (Louisville, KY: Westminster/John Knox, 1992), 262; Weaver, "Women in Matthew," 399–400.

90. Support for this contention is found in Davies and Allison, *Matthew*, 3:655; Brown, *Death*, 1297; and Luz, *Matthew 21–28*, 588. These soldiers are not necessarily identical to those who crucified Jesus, although Matthew wants readers to see how both are under the command of the Roman governor.

91. κουστωδία, BDAG, 3rd ed., 563. The word appears at only these three places in the NT.

92. Luz, *Matthew 21–28*, 588, points out that the Pharisees, who have thus far been absent in Matthew 26–28, reappear—likely for the narrative purpose of connecting them to the initial threats against Jesus (12:14) and his response (12:38–42).

93. In 28:4 the soldiers are identified as οἱ τηροῦντες, a substantive participle (present, active, nominative, masculine, plural) from the verb τηρέω: they are "the ones guarding" or "the guards."

94. σφραγίζω, BDAG, 3rd ed., 980.

95. Matthew's vocabulary is not identical, but similar between the two scenes. At 27:51, "the earth shook" (ἡ γῆ ἐσείσθη); at 28:4, "the ones guarding him shook" (ἐσείσθησαν οἱ τηροῦντες). In both cases Matthew uses the aorist, passive, indicative verb σείω, "to cause to be in a state of commotion" including shaking, agitating, or mental anguish (BDAG, 3rd ed., 918).

96. Polybius, *Hist.* 6.37–39; Tacitus, *Ann.* 13.55–56; Ward, "Roman Battlefield," 304. See notes 15 and 86.

97. I read the γὰρ in 28:2 as causative (γὰρ, BDAG, 3rd ed., 189); see Luz, *Matthew 21–28*, 595–596: Matthew "has the angel descend from heaven, shake the earth, and open the tomb. He creates a powerful sign, unmistakable for all, including the guards, that God is at work here."

98. An ἄγγελος κυρίου first appears in Matt 1:20–24, speaking to Joseph about Jesus' birth, and 2:13–20, warning Joseph about Herod's threat to the family. Granted that κύριος, BDAG, 3rd ed., 576–578, has a range of meaning that includes personal honorifics ("sir, master, lord") and divine identity ("the Lord"), Matthew's usage here subtly indicates the one to whom each party looks for authority: to Rome or to God. The angel, as an agent of God who works to support Jesus, may also be compared to "the governor's soldiers" (οἱ στρατιῶται τοῦ ἡγεμόνος, Matt 27:27), who torture and kill him.

99. Davies and Allison, *Matthew*, 3:666: "The description of the angel's garment draws upon the theophany of Dan 7:9..., and Dan 10:6 could be the source of

the description of the angel's countenance (LXX: τὸ πρόσωπον αὐτοῦ ὡσεὶ ὅρασις ἀστραπῆς)." Lightning imagery in relation to the Son of Man and Roman military power at Matt 24:27 is discussed in chapter 5.

100. At 27:61 and 28:1 Matthew calls them "Mary Magdalene and the other Mary," referring to his previous identification of the second Mary ("the mother of James and Joseph") in 27:56. Some scholars, based on Matt 13:55–56 ("the mother of James and Joseph and Simon and Judas . . . and all of his sisters"), identify the second Mary at the tomb as Jesus' mother; Davies and Allison, *Matthew*, 3:638, note that it is "odd that Jesus' mother would be identified by something other than her relationship with her son Jesus; Luz, *Matthew 21–28*, 574, goes further, arguing that "she was certainly not the mother of Jesus."

101. Kathleen Corley, *Maranatha: Women's Funerary Rituals and Christian Origins* (Minneapolis, MN: Fortress Press, 2010), 44–56, argues that purpose of this visit, according to ancient behavioral paradigms, may have been to care for the family dead, to weep, to sing laments, and to undertake personal mourning. Corley, 50, refers to Matt 11:16–17, in which public mourning practices are described. See also Thomas Longstaff, "What Are Those Women Doing at the Tomb of Jesus," *A Feminist Companion to Matthew*, ed. Amy-Jill Levine and Marianne Blickenstaff (Cleveland, OH: Pilgrim Press, 2001), 199, who writes, with reference to Corley, that "it was likely customary in early Judaism for loved ones (family and friends) to watch (i.e. to visit, פקד) the tomb until the third day after the death in order to confirm that a premature burial had not taken place.... Matthew portrays them as coming to visit the tomb to confirm the death of Jesus." Carter, *Matthew and Margins*, 544ff., argues that just as the women have witnessed Jesus' crucifixion (27:55–56) and burial (27:61), they have now come to "see" (θεωρέω) the resurrection (28:1), and do so in a variety of ways (28:6, 7, 10, 17).

102. Capel Anderson, "Gender and Reading," 43–44.

103. Capel Anderson, "Gender and Reading," 44–45.

104. See chapter 3 on strategies women might use to negotiate Roman military presence.

105. Carter, *Matthew and Margins*, 547.

106. Carolyn Osiek, "The Women at the Tomb," *A Feminist Companion to Matthew*, ed. Amy-Jill Levine and Marianne Blickenstaff (Cleveland, OH: Pilgrim Press, 2001), 208, notes "the contrasting reaction" of the soldiers, who "accepted bribes to falsify what they witnessed," and the women, who "received the angelic message . . . including the promise to see Jesus himself in Galilee."

107. See also Davies and Allison, *Matthew* 3.632–634, 664–665.

108. προσκυνέω, BDAG, 3rd ed., 882.

109. Claridge, *Rome*, 121–123. The triumphal parades in Rome and elsewhere associated with this triumphal arch are described by Josephus, *JW* 7.96–97, 116–157.

110. Fairclough, LCL.

Conclusion

> When they saw him, they worshiped him; but some doubted. And Jesus came and said to them, "All authority in heaven and on earth has been given to me. Go therefore and make disciples of all nations, baptizing them in the name of the Father and of the Son and of the Holy Spirit, and teaching them to obey everything that I have commanded you. And remember, I am with you always, to the end of the age."
>
> —Matthew 28:17–20

This work has argued that the gospel of Matthew constructs and negotiates Roman military power in a variety of ways. This construction is seen in a number of scenes throughout the narrative, including Herod ordering soldiers to kill infants in Bethlehem (2:1–23); Antipas ordering the death of John the Baptist in prison (14:1–12); Roman soldiers who abuse the inconvenient and resented practice of ἀγγαρήιον/*angaria* (5:41); a centurion in Capernaum who approaches Jesus to ask for his slave to be healed (8:5–13); an eschatological vision of Roman eagles who are destroyed when the Son of Man returns (24:27–31); and in the arrest, trials, torture, execution, death, burial, and resurrection of Jesus (26:1–28:20)—in which the Roman governor, assisted by elite Jerusalem allies and soldiers lay hands on Jesus, seek to silence him and end his perceived threat to their rule. In each of these scenes, Matthew portrays the potential threats and dangers of Roman military violence and demonstrates for his audience strategies for coping with this facet of everyday life in Roman-ruled Syria and surrounding regions. These strategies include avoidance, cooperation, acquiescence, private dreams of revenge, appeals to scripture, prayer, and worshipful devotion to Jesus, whose resurrection anticipates the full establishment of God's Empire, and through whom Roman military power will one day be judged.

In contrast to other approaches to reading Matthew, this work has argued for the importance of an empire-critical view that foregrounds Roman military power, emphasizing the integral part that organized military personnel played in the ever-present networks of social power with which Matthew's audience coped and negotiated on a daily basis. While I have not attempted to address every aspect of Matthew's presentation and negotiation with his Roman imperial context, the chapters included here have highlighted the ways in which Matthew's use of military figures and imagery characterize and depict aspects of his narrative world in particular (and realistic) ways. The argumentation offered here underscores the importance of acknowledgment of the Roman imperial context for New Testament interpretation—not as background, but foreground—and emphasizes the ongoing need for Biblical interpreters to recognize how Biblical writers and their communities interacted with, created spaces within, and found spaces to survive and thrive in places like Antioch throughout Roman imperial society. Throughout the previous chapters I have shown a number of ways in which Roman military power permeated the society in which Matthew was written, and the discussion presented here will serve as a needed contribution to future studies on the ways in which Matthew and his audience interacted with such power. It should be noted that my thesis does not depend on the correctness of any single interpretation offered here, but presents an aggregate view of Matthew as a complex whole, responding to and coping with Roman military power in a variety of ways.

Thus, a next step will be to further integrate readings of Matthew's portrayal of the Roman imperial context: while other aspects of the imperial system (political, economic, and ideological networks) have been frequently cited by those paying attention to Matthew's context, the presence of military has not been. Integrating the role of imperial military power in future discussions will influence readings of the texts cited here as well as others that may be primarily about other topics, but which contain some overlap with military power. Examples of such texts include parables found in Matthew 18:23–35 and 22:1–14, which feature kings who are not only wealthy, with treasuries of coin at their disposal (economic networks), and interested in affirming their role as ruler (political networks), but who are also willing to punish disobedient subjects using military forces. In a similar way, an understanding of the ways in which imperial power may be resisted (opaquely and off-stage) calls for a re-evaluation of Matthew's eschatological texts. While it is true that such texts are deeply integrated with Matthew's Christology and his presentation of Jesus as one who "fulfills" a certain reading of Hebrew scripture, it is also true that Jesus's eschatological teachings (in sayings, parables, and prophetic declarations) are, in part, expressions of resistance to imperial power. In such texts Matthew's Jesus counters imperial claims while also mimicking military ideology, and his eschatology looks forward to a future in which such claims are overturned by divine judgment and replaced by the Kingdom/Empire of Heaven. Thus, though the full implications require further exploration, there are a number of additional Matthean texts that evince a similarly complex negotiation of imperial systems and structures as has been presented here.

When considering broader work on New Testament and early Christian communities, this work indicates the need for further nuance in ongoing discussions. It should be clear that Matthew's views and presentation of the Roman military differ from other texts such as Luke-Acts (which has a generally more positive portrayal of Roman political and military figures) or Paul, who anticipates the return of Jesus as an eschatological heavenly figure (1 Thess 4:13–18; 1 Cor 15:20–26), but also calls for obedience to Roman governance, because: "those authorities that exist have been instituted by God . . . [and] authority does not bear the sword in vain" (Rom 13:1–14). It is noteworthy that Luke, like Matthew, writes in the decades following the Jewish-Roman War in 66–70 CE, yet Luke's presentation on Roman authority and military power has more affinity to that of Paul who writes prior to the war. Beyond understanding the ways each author suggests negotiating Roman military power, noting these differences may offer insight into the localized context in which each author wrote, and the circumstances of their communities. I have contended here that a lack of attention to Roman military presence results in the misinterpretation of Matthew's context and narrative. Likewise, a more detailed understanding of deployment, structures, and history of Roman military forces will result in refinement and further precision in New Testament interpretation and the situation(s) of early Christianity as a whole, and can only benefit future discussions.

This work points beyond the New Testament period as well by adding to the framework for a history of interpretation of Matthew in the second century CE and beyond. Ignatius indicates that Matthew was read in Antioch during this time—a time in which residents saw the division of Syria into three new Roman provinces (Syria, Syria Coele, Syria Palaestina); the Bar Kokhba revolt (132–135 CE); the further expansion of Roman territory into Parthian lands under Trajan (116–117 CE), and subsequent withdrawal from that same territory under Trajan's successor Hadrian. It is possible to draw lines of continuity between these events and those detailed here: Roman desire for military expansion and pacification of conquered peoples continued as it had in the previous century. These events may indicate possibilities for ways in which Matthew's narrative was read by a new audience in new (but similar) circumstances. As Christian communities continued to seek a place in Antioch and the territory of Roman Syria, they continued to negotiate the presence of the Roman military, including such events as the buildup of military forces, subsequent victory celebrations, and the acclamation of Hadrian by Roman troops in Antioch in 117 CE.[1] The discussion presented here of Roman military presence in the previous century (and Matthew's negotiation with it) offers lines of continuity through which to more fully understand the development of Antiochene Christianity in the post-New Testament period.

Finally, this work has highlighted and foregrounded the Roman imperial context of Matthew's gospel, and some of the ways in which the narrative constructs and negotiates Roman military power. From this perspective, the gospel of Matthew represents an uncommon account: a non-elite perspective on Roman imperial expansion and rule, the often-tumultuous integration of new territories and peoples into the Empire, and the ways in which non-elite provincials could find ways to resist, adapt to, and survive such experiences while envisioning a different future in which God's priorities took precedence, rather than those of Rome. It is my hope that I have contributed to Matthean studies in such a way that encourages others to take into account the ongoing presence of and regular interaction with Roman soldiers that Matthew's audience took for granted but is often overlooked today. In so doing, our understanding of both history and the gospel are improved.

NOTE

1. *Historia Augusta*, Life of Hadrian 6.

Bibliography

Alföldy, Geza. "Eine Bauinschrift aus dem Colosseum." *Zeitschrift für Papyrologie und Epigraphik* 109 (1995): 195–226.

Alston, Richard. *Soldier and Society in Roman Egypt*. New York: Routledge, 1995.

Anderson, Janice Capel. "The Dancing Daughter." In *Mark and Method: New Approaches in Biblical Studies,* edited by Janice Capel Anderson and Stephen D. Moore (pp. 111–143). Minneapolis, MN: Fortress, 2008.

———. "Matthew: Gender and Reading." In *A Feminist Companion to Matthew,* edited by Amy-Jill Levine and Marianne Blickenstaff (pp. 25–51). Cleveland, OH: Pilgrim Press, 2004.

Andrade, Nathanael. "Ambiguity, Violence, and Community in the Cities of Judaea and Syria." *Historia: Zeitschrift fur Alte Geschichte*, 59, no. 3 (2010): 342–370.

———. *Syrian Identity in the Greco-Roman World*. Cambridge: Cambridge University Press, 2013.

Appian. *Civil Wars*. Translated by Horace White. 2 vols. LCL. Cambridge: Harvard University Press, 1913.

———. *Roman History*. Translated by Horace White. 4 vols. LCL. Cambridge, MA: Harvard University Press, 1913.

Apuleius. *Metamorphoses*. vol. 1: Books 1–6. Edited and translated by J. Arthur Hanson. LCL. Cambridge, MA: Harvard University Press, 1996.

Aristotle, *Politics*. Translated by H. Rackham. LCL. Cambridge, MA: Harvard University Press, 1932.

Attansio, Donato, Matthias Bruno and Walter Prochaska. "The Docimian Marble of the Ludovisi and Capitoline Gauls and Other Replicas of the Pergamene Dedications." *AJA* 115, no. 4 (2011): 575–587.

Augustine. *Confessions*. Edited and translated by Carolyn J.-B. Hammond. LCL. Cambridge, MA: Harvard University Press, 2014.

Augustus. *Res Gestae Divi Augusti*. Translated by Fredrick W. Shipley. LCL. Cambridge: Harvard University Press, 1924.

Avi-Yonah, Michael. "The Development of the Roman Road System in Palestine." *Israel Exploration Journal* 1, no. 1 (1950–51): 54–60.

Bach, Alice. "Calling the Shots: Directing Salome's Dance of Death." *Semeia* 74 (1996): 103–124.

Balch, David. *Let Wives Be Submissive: The Domestic Code in I Peter*. Atlanta, GA: Scholar's Press, 1981.

Bang, Peter Fibiger. "Trade and Empire: In Search of Organizing Concepts for the Roman Economy." *Past and Present* 195 (2007): 3–54.

Bauer, Walter, William Arndt, F. Wilbur Gingrich and Frederick W. Danker. *A Greek-English Lexicon of the New Testament and Other Early Christian Literature*, 3rd edition. Chicago, IL: University of Chicago Press, 2000.

Beckmann, Martin. "Trajan's Column and Mars Ultor." *Journal of Roman Studies* 106 (2016):124–146.

Bhabha, Homi. *The Location of Culture*. New York and London: Routledge, 1994.

———. "Signs Taken for Wonders: Questions of Ambivalence and Authority under a Tree Outside Delhi, May 1817." *Critical Inquiry* 12, no. 1 (1985): 144–165.

Bijovsky, Gabriela. "The Coins from Khirbat Burnaṭ (Southwest)." *'Atiqot* 69 (2012): 147–155.

Bilde, Per. "The Causes of the Jewish War According to Josephus." *Journal for the Study of Judaism in the Persian, Hellenistic, and Roman Period* 10, no. 2 (1979): 179–202.

Birley, Eric. "The Religion of the Roman Army: 1895–1977." *ANRW* II (1978): 1506–1541.

———. "Veterans of the Roman Army in Britain and Elsewhere." *Ancient Society* 13/14 (1982/1983): 265–276.

Bishop, M. C. and J. C. N. Coulston. *Roman Military Equipment: From the Punic Wars to the Fall of Rome*, 2nd editon. Havertown, PA: Oxbow Books, 2016.

Black, E. W. *Cursus Publicus: The Infrastructure of Government in Roman Britain*. Oxford, UK: Hadrian Books, 1995.

Boer, Roland and Christina Petterson. *Time of Troubles: A New Economic Framework for Early Christianity*. Minneapolis, MN: Fortress, 2017.

Bond, Helen. "The Coins of Pontius Pilate: Part of an Attempt to Provoke the People or to Integrate Them into the Empire?" *Journal for the Study of Judaism in the Persian, Hellenistic, and Roman Period* 27, no. 3 (1996): 241–262.

Bosworth, A. B. "Vespasian and the Slave Trade." *Classical Quarterly* 52, no. 1 (2002): 350–357.

Bowersock, G. W. "Syria Under Vespasian." *JRS* 63 (1973): 133–140.

Brink, Laurie. *Soldiers in Luke-Acts: Engaging, Contradicting, and Transcending the Stereotypes*. Wissenschaftliche Untersuchungen Zum Neuen Testament 2, 326. Tübingen: Mohr Siebeck, 2014.

Broadhead, Will. "Colonization, Land Distribution, and Veteran Settlement." In *A Companion to the Roman Army*, edited by Paul Erdkamp (pp. 148–63). Hoboken, NJ: Wiley-Blackwell, 2007.

Broux, Yanne. "Trade Networks among the Army Camps of the Eastern Desert of Roman Egypt." In *Sinews of Empire: Networks in the Roman Near East and*

Beyond, edited by Håkon Fiane Teigen and Eivind Heldaas Seland (chapter 9). Oxford: Oxbow Books, 2017.

Brown, Raymond. *The Birth of the Messiah: A Commentary on the Infancy Narratives in the Gospels of Matthew and Luke*. New York: Doubleday, 1999.

———. *The Death of Messiah: A Commentary on the Passion Narratives in the Four Gospels*. 2 vols. New York: Doubleday, 1994.

Brown, Raymond E., and John P. Meier. *Antioch and Rome: New Testament Cradles of Catholic Christianity*. New York: Paulist Press, 1982.

Butcher, Kevin. *Roman Syria and the Near East*. Los Angeles: J. Paul Getty Museum, 2003.

Butler, Judith. *Gender Trouble: Feminism and the Subversion of Identity*. New York: Routledge, 1990.

Caesar, Julius. *Civil Wars*. Translated by A. G. Peskett. LCL. Cambridge: Harvard University Press, 1914.

———. *The Gallic War*. Translated by H. J. Edwards. LCL. Cambridge: Harvard University Press, 1917.

Campbell, Brian. "Who were the 'Viri Militares'?" *JRS* 65 (1975): 11–31.

Carrigan, Tim, Bob Connell, and John Lee, "Toward a New Sociology of Masculinity." In *The Making of Masculinities: The New Men's Studies,* edited by Harry Brod (pp. 63–100). Boston, MA: Allen & Unwin, 1987.

Carter, Warren. "Are There Imperial Texts in the Class? Intertextual Eagles and Matthean Eschatology as 'Lights Out' Time for Imperial Rome (Matthew 24:27-31)." *JBL* 122/3 (2003): 467–487.

———. "Empire Studies and Biblical Interpretation." *Oxford Encyclopedia of Biblical Interpretation*. Oxford Biblical Studies Online. http://www.oxfordbiblicalstudies.com.ezproxy.tcu.edu/article/opr/t373/e15.

———. "Matthew: Empire, Synagogues, and Horizontal Violence." In *Matthew and Mark I: Comparative Readings: Understanding the Earliest Gospels in their First-Century Settings,* edited by Eve-Marie Becker and Anders Runesson (pp. 285–308). Tübingen: Mohr Siebeck, 2011.

———. *Matthew and Empire: Initial Explorations*. Valley Forge, PA: Trinity Press International, 2001.

———. *Matthew and the Margins: A Sociopolitical and Religious Reading*. Maryknoll, NY: Orbis Books, 2000.

———. "Paying the Tax to Rome as Subversive Praxis: Matthew 17:24-27." *JSNT* 76 (1999): , 3–31.

———. *Pontius Pilate: Portraits of the Roman Governor*. Collegeville, MN: Liturgical Press, 2003.

Cheeseman, George. *The Auxilia of the Roman Imperial Army*. Oxford, UK: Clarendon Press, 1914.

Christianson, John. "The Centurion in History and Literature: A Context for Reading in the Gospels." MA Research Portfolio. Springfield, MO: Missouri State University, 2010.

Cicero. *In Pisonem*. Translated by N. H. Watts. LCL. Cambridge, MA: Harvard University Press, 1931.

———. *Tusculan Disputations*. Translated by J. E. King. LCL. Cambridge, MA: Harvard University Press, 1927.

Claridge, Amanda. *Rome: An Oxford Archaeological Guide*. New York: Oxford University Press, 2010.

Clunn, Tony. *The Quest for the Lost Roman Legions: Discovering the Varus Battlefield*. New York: Savas Beatie, 2005.

Cody, Jane. "Conquerors and Conquered on Flavian Coins." In *Flavian Rome: Culture, Image, Text*, edited by A. J. Boyle and W. J. Dominik (pp. 103–24). Leiden: Brill, 2003.

Coleman, Kathleen. "Entertaining Rome." In *Ancient Rome: The Archaeology of the Eternal City*, edited by Jon Coulston and Hazel Dodge (pp. 210–58). Oxford: Oxbow Books, 2011.

Colwell, Ernest C. "A Definite Rule for the Use of the Article in the Greek New Testament." *JBL* 52 (1933): 12–21.

Connell, R. W. *Masculinities*. Berkeley, CA: University of California Press, 1995.

Conway, Colleen. *Behold the Man: Jesus and Greco-Roman Masculinity*. New York and London: Oxford University Press, 2008.

Corley, Kathleen. *Maranatha: Women's Funerary Rituals and Christian Origins*. Minneapolis, MN: Fortress Press, 2010.

———. *Private Women, Public Meals: Social Conflict in the Synoptic Tradition*. Peabody, MA: Hendrickson, 1993.

Coulston, Jonathan. "Trajan's Column." In *The Oxford Classical Dictionary* (4th edition), edited by Simon Hornblower and Antony Spawforth. Oxford University Press, 2012.

Crook, Zeba. "Honor, Shame, and Social Status Revisited." *JBL* 128, no. 3 (2009): 591–611.

Curchin, Leonard. *The Local Magistrates of Roman Spain*. Toronto, ON: University of Toronto Press, 1990.

Cyprian, *Epistles*. Translated by Robert Ernest Wallis. In *Ante-Nicene Fathers* (vol. 5), edited by Alexander Roberts, James Donaldson, and A. Cleveland Coxe. Buffalo, NY: Christian Literature Publishing Company, 1886. Revised and edited by Kevin Knight. http://www.newadvent.org/fathers/050655.htm

Dąbrowa, Edward. "The Date of the Census of Quirinius and the Chronology of the Governors of the Province of Syria." *Zeitschrift für Papyrologie und Epigraphik* 178 (2011): 137–142.

———. "Military Colonisation in the Near East and Mesopotamia under the Severi." *Acta Classica* 55 (2012): 31–42.

Dani, Maziel Barreto. "This Land is 'Our' Land: Recolonization in Matthew's Gospel." PhD diss., Brite Divinity School, Texas Christian University, 2019.

Davies, Penelope. "The Politics of Perpetuation: Trajan's Column and the Art of Commemoration." *American Journal of Archaeology* 101, no. 1 (1997): 41–65.

Davies, R. W. "The Daily Life of the Roman Soldier." *ANRW* 2, no. 1 (1975): 508–533.

Davies, William D. and Dale Allison. *A Critical and Exegetical Commentary on the Gospel according to Saint Matthew*. 3 vols. Edinburgh: Bloomsbury T&T Clark, 1988–1997.

Dewey, Joanna. "The Gospel of Mark." In *Searching the Scriptures* (Vol. 2), edited by Elisabeth Schussler Fiorenza and Shelly Matthews (pp. 470–509). New York: Crossroads, 1997.

Dio Cassius. *Roman History*. Translated by Earnest Cary and Herbert Foster. 5 vols. LCL. Cambridge, MA: Harvard University Press, 1914.

Dodd, C. H. *According to the Scriptures*. London: Nisbet & Co., 1962.

Draper, Jonathan. "The Development of 'The Sign of the Son of Man' in the Jesus Tradition." *NTS* 39 (1993): 1–21.

Dube, Musa. *Postcolonial Feminist Interpretation of the Bible*. St. Louis: Chalice Press, 2000.

Duthoy, R. "The 'Augustales.'" *ANRW* 2, no. 16 (1978): 1254–1309.

Dyson, Stephen L. "Native Revolt Patterns in the Roman Empire." *ANRW* 2, no. 3 (1975): 138–175.

Elliot, Paul. *Warfare in New Kingdom Egypt*. London: Fonthill, 2017.

Elliot, Simon. *Empire State: How the Roman Military Built an Empire*. Oxford: Oxbow Books, 2017.

Erdkamp, Paul. "The Corn Supply of the Roman Armies During the Principate (27 BC–235 AD)." In *The Roman Army and the Economy*, edited by Paul Erdkamp (pp. 47–69). Amsterdam: J.C. Gieben, 2002.

Eyben, Emiel. *Restless Youth in Ancient Rome*. London: Routledge, 1993.

Fagan, Garrett. "Violence in Roman Social Relations." In *Social Relations in the Roman World*, edited by Michael Peachin (pp. 467–495). Oxford: Oxford University Press, 2011.

Fander, Monika. "Gospel of Mark: Women as True Disciples of Jesus." In *Feminist Biblical Interpretation*, edited by Luise Schottroff and Marie-Theres Wacker (pp. 626–644). Grand Rapids: Eerdmans, 2012.

Fanon, Frantz. *Black Skins/White Masks*. Translated by Charles Lam Markmann. New York: Grove Press, 1967.

———. *The Wretched of the Earth*. Translated by Richard Philcox. New York: Grove Press, 2004.

Faulkner, Raymond. "Egyptian Military Standards." *Journal of Egyptian Archaeology* 27 (1941): 12–18.

Fishwick, Duncan. "Dated Inscriptions and the 'Feriale Duranum.'" *Syria* 65, no. 3/4 (1988): 349–361.

Flemming, Rebecca. "Quae Corpore Quaestum Facit: The Sexual Economy of Female Prostitution in the Roman Empire," *JRS* 89 (1999): 38–61.

Flower, Harriet. *The Dancing Lares and the Serpent in the Garden: Religion at the Roman Street Corner*. Princeton, NJ: Princeton University Press, 2017.

France, R.T. *Matthew: Evangelist and Teacher*. Exeter: Paternoster Press, 1995.

Freedman, David Noel, Gary Heriod, David Graf, and John David Pleins, eds. *Anchor Bible Dictionary*. 6 vols. New York: Doubleday, 1992.

French, D. H., and J. R. Summerly. "Four Latin Inscriptions from Satala." *Anatolian Studies* 37 (1987): 17–22.

Freyne, Sean. "Bandits in Galilee: A Contribution to the Study of Social Conditions in First-Century Palestine." In *The Social World of Formative Christianity: Essays in Tribute to Howard Clark Kee,* edited by Jacob Nuesner, Ernest S. Frerichs, Peder Borgen, and Richard Horsley (pp. 50–68). Philadelphia: Fortress, 1988.

Friesen, Steven. "Poverty in Pauline Studies: Beyond the So-called New Consensus." *JSNT* 26, no. 3 (2004): 323–361.

Fuhrmann, Christopher. *Policing the Roman Empire: Soldiers, Administration, and the Public Order.* Oxford: Oxford University Press, 2014.

Gallinsky, Karl. *Augustan Culture: An Interpretive Introduction.* Princeton, NJ: Princeton University Press, 1996.

Gardner, Andrew. "Thinking about Roman Imperialism: Postcolonialism, Globalisation and Beyond?" *Britannia* 44 (2013): 1–25.

Gillman, Florence Morgan. *Herodias: At Home in That Fox's Den.* Collegeville, MN: Liturgical Press, 1989.

Given, Michael. *The Archaeology of the Colonized.* New York: Routledge, 2004.

Glancy, Jennifer. *Slavery in Early Christianity.* Minneapolis, MN: Fortress, 2006.

———. "Unveiling Masculinity: The Construction of Gender in Mark 6:17–29." *Biblical Interpretation* 2, no. 1 (1994): 34–50.

Goodman, Martin. "Coinage and Identity: The Jewish Evidence." In *Coinage and Identity in the Roman Provinces,* edited by Christopher Howgego, Volker Heuchert, and Andrew Burnett (pp. 163–167). Oxford, UK: Oxford University Press, 2005.

———. "Nerva, the Fiscus Judaicus and Jewish Identity." *JRS* 79 (1989): 40–44.

Grant, Michael. *The Army of the Caesars.* New York: Scribner's Sons, 1974.

Hagner, Donald. "The *sitz im leben* of the Gospel of Matthew." in 1996.

Hanson, K. C. "Jesus and the Social Bandits." In *The Social Setting of Jesus and the Gospels,* edited by Wolfgang Stegemann, Bruce J. Malina, and Gerd Theissen (pp. 283–300). Minneapolis: Fortress, 2002.

Hanson, K. C., and Douglas Oakman. *Palestine in the Time of Jesus: Social Structures and Social Conflicts.* Minneapolis, MN: Fortress, 1998.

Harner, Philip B. "Qualitative Anarthrous Predicate Nouns: Mark 15:39 and John 1:1." *JBL* 92, no. 1 (1973): 75–87.

Harrill, J. Albert. *Slaves in the New Testament: Literary, Moral and Social Dimensions.* Minneapolis, MN: Fortress Press, 2006.

Harrington, Daniel. *The Gospel of Matthew.* Sacra Pagina 1. Collegeville, MN: The Liturgical Press, 1991.

Haverfield, Francis. "The Romanization of Roman Britain." *Proceedings of the British Academy* (1905–1906): 185–217.

Haynes, Ian. *Blood of the Provinces: The Roman Auxilia and the Making of Provincial Society from Augustus to the Severans.* New York: Oxford University Press, 2016.

———. "The Romanisation of Religion in the 'Auxilia' of the Roman Imperial Army from Augustus to Septimus Severus." *Britannia* 24 (1993): 141–157.

Helgeland, J. "Roman Army Religion." *ANRW* 2.16.2 (1978): 1470–1505.

Herodotus. *Histories.* Translated by A.D. Goodley. 4 vols. LCL. Cambridge, MA: Harvard University Press, 1920–1925.

———. *Histories.* Translated by Andrea Purvis. In *The Landmark Herodotus: The Histories,* edited by Robert Strassler. New York: Pantheon, 2007.

Hirt, Alfred Michael. *Imperial Mines and Quarries in the Roman World: Organizational Aspects 27 BC–AD 235*. Oxford, UK: Oxford University Press, 2010.
Hobbs, T. R. "Soldiers in the Gospels: a Neglected Agent." In *Social Scientific Models for Interpreting the Bible: Essays by the Context Group in Honor of Bruce J. Malina*, edited by Bruce J. Malina and John J. Pilch (pp. 328–348). Leiden and Boston: Brill, 2001.
Horsley, Richard. "Ancient Jewish Banditry and the Revolt against Rome, A.D. 66–70." *CBQ* 43 (1981): 409–432.
———. "Bandits, Messiahs, and Longshoremen: Popular Unrest in Galilee in the Time of Jesus." In *SBL 1988 Seminar Papers* 27, edited by David J. Lull (pp. 183–199). Atlanta, GA: Scholars Press, 1988.
———. *Bandits, Prophets, and Messiahs: Popular Messianic Movements in the Time of Jesus*. Harrisburg, PA: Trinity Press, 1999.
———. *Galilee: History, Politics, People*. Valley Forge, PA: Trinity Press International, 1995.
———. *The Liberation of Christmas: The Infancy Narratives in Social Context*. Eugene, OR: Wipf and Stock, 2006.
Horsley, Richard, ed. *In the Shadow of Empire: Reclaiming the Bible as a History of Faithful Resistance*. Louisville: Westminster John Knox, 2008.
Hubbard, Ben. *Gladiator: Fighting for Life, Glory, and Freedom*. New York: Metro Books, 2015.
Husselman, Elinor. "The Granaries of Karanis." *Transactions and Proceedings of the American Philological Association* 83 (1952): 56–73.
Inscriptions grecques et latines de la Syrie. vol. 5. Translated by R. K. Sherk. Edited by L. Jalabert, R. Mouterde, et al. Paris: Institut Français du Proche-Orient, 1998.
Isaac, Benjamin. *The Limits of Empire: The Roman Army in the East*. New York: Oxford University Press, 1990.
Iverson, Kelly R. "A Centurion's 'Confession': A Performance-Critical Analysis of Mark 15:39." *JBL* 130, no. 2 (2011): 329–350.
Jay, E. G. *Son of Man, Son of God*. Montreal, QC: McGill-Queen's University Press, 1965.
Jennings, Theodore W. and Tat-Siong Benny Liew. "Mistaken Identities but Model Faith: Rereading the Centurion, the Chap, and the Christ in Matthew 8:5-13." *JBL* 123, no. 3 (2004): 467–494.
Jensen, Morten Hørning. *Herod Antipas in Galilee: The Literary and Archaeological Sources on the Reign of Herod Antipas and its Socio-Economic Impact on Galilee*. Tübingen: Mohr Siebeck, 2006.
Johnson, Earl S. "Mark 15, 39 and the So-Called Confession of the Roman Centurion." *Biblica* 81, no. 3 (2000): 406–413.
Josephus. Translated by H. St. J. Thackeray, et al. 10 vols. LCL. Cambridge: Harvard University Press, 1926–1965.
Juvenal. *Satires*. Edited and translated by Susanna Morton Braund. LCL. Cambridge, MA: Harvard University Press, 2004.
Kaden, David. "Flavius Josephus and the 'Gentes Devictae' in Roman Imperial Discourse: Hybridity, Mimicry, and Irony in the Agrippa II Speech (Judean War

2.345–402)." *Journal for the Study of Judaism in the Persian, Hellenistic, and Roman Period* 42, no. 4/5 (2011): 481–507.

Karris, Robert J. "Luke 23:47 and the Lucan View of Jesus' Death." *JBL* 105, no. 1: (1986): 65–74.

Kaufman, David. "Horrea Romana: Roman Storehouses." *The Classical Weekly* 23, no. 7 (1929): 49–54.

Keener, Craig. *A Commentary on the Gospel of Matthew*. Grand Rapids, MI: Eerdmans, 1999.

Kehne, Peter. "War- and Peacetime Logistics: Supplying Imperial Armies in East and West." In *A Companion to the Roman Army*, edited by Paul Erdkamp (pp. 232–238). Hoboken, NJ: Wiley-Blackwell, 2007.

Kehoe, Dennis. "Contract Labor." In *The Cambridge Companion to the Roman Economy*, edited by Walter Scheidel (pp. 114–130). Cambridge: University of Cambridge Press, 2012.

Kennedy, David. "C. Velius Rufus." *Britannia* 14 (1983): 183–196.

———. "Legio VI Ferrata: The Annexation and Early Garrison of Arabia." *Harvard Studies in Classical Philology* 84 (1980): 283–309.

Kennedy, David, editor. *The Roman Army in the East*. JRA Supplementary Series 18. Ann Arbor, MI: Journal of Roman Archaeology, 1996.

Keppie, Lawrence. "The Changing Face of the Roman Legions (49 BC–AD 69)." *Papers of the British School at Rome* 65 (1997): 89–102.

Kessler, David and Peter Temin. "The Organization of the Grain Trade in the Early Roman Empire." *Economic History Review* 60, no. 2 (2007): 313–332.

Kim, Tae Hun. "The Anathrous ὁ σῖτος in Mark 15, 39 and the Roman Imperial Cult." *Biblica* 79 (1998): 221–241.

Kingsbury, Jack Dean. *Matthew: Structure, Christology, Kingdom*. Minneapolis: Fortress, 1975.

———. *Matthew as Story*. Minneapolis, MN: Fortress, 1988.

———. "The Title 'Son of Man' in Matthew's Gospel." *CBQ* 37, no. 2 (1975): 193–202.

Kissel, Theodor. "Road-Building as Munus Publicum." In *The Roman Army and the Economy*, edited by Paul Erdkamp (pp. 127–160). Amsterdam: J.C. Gieben, 2002.

Kittel, Gerhard, and Gerhard Friedrich. *Theological Dictionary of the New Testament*. 10 vols. Translated and edited by Geoffrey Bromiley. Grand Rapids: Eerdmans, 1972.

Kolb, Anne. "Transport and Communication in the Roman State: The *Cursus Publicus*." In *Travel and Geography in the Roman Empire*, edited by Colin Adams and Ray Laurence (pp. 95–105). New York: Routledge, 2001.

Konradt, Matthias. *Israel, Church and the Gentiles in the Gospel of Matthew*. Waco, TX: Baylor/Mohr Siebeck, 2014.

Koon, Kelsey. "Granaries and the Grain Supply of Roman Frontier Forts: Case Studies in Local Grain Production from Haurra (Jordan), Vindolanda (Britain), and Vindonissa (Switzerland)." MA Thesis, University of Victoria. ProQuest Publishing, 2012.

Kraay, Colin. "Revolt and Subversion: The So-Called 'Military' Coinage of A.D. 69 Reexamined." *Numismatic Chronicle and Journal of the Royal Numismatic Society*, Sixth Series 12, no. 42 (1952): 78–86.

Kraemer, Ross. "Implicating Herodias and Her Daughter in the Death of John the Baptizer: A (Christian) Theological Strategy?" *JBL* 125, no. 2 (2006): 321–349.

Krause, Deborah. "Simon Peter's Mother-in-Law—Disciple or Domestic Servant? Feminist Biblical Hermeneutics and the Interpretation of Mark 1:29–31." In *A Feminist Companion to Mark*, edited by Amy-Jill Levine and Marianne Blickenstaff (pp. 37–53). Sheffield: Sheffield Academic Press, 2001.

Kreitzer, Larry. *Striking New Images: Roman Imperial Coinage and the New Testament World*, JSNT Supplemental Series 134. Edited by Stanley Porter. Sheffield, UK: Sheffield Academic Press, 1996.

Krentz, Peter. "The *Salpinx* in Greek Warfare." In *Hoplites: The Classical Battle Experience*, edited by Victor David Hanson (pp. 110–120). London and New York: Routledge, 1991.

Kyrychenko, Alexander. *The Roman Army and the Expansion of the Gospel: The Role of the Centurion in Luke–Acts*. Boston: De Gruyter, 2014.

Lenski, Gerhard. *Power and Privilege: A Theory of Social Stratification*. Chapel Hill, NC: University of North Carolina Press, 1966, 1984.

Levick, Barbara. "Domitian and the Provinces." *Latomus* 41, no. 1 (1982): 50–73.

Levine, Amy-Jill. "Matthew." In *The Women's Bible Commentary*, edited by Carol Newsome and Sharon Ringe (pp. 252–262). Louisville, KY: Westminster/John Knox, 1992.

Lewis, Naphatali. "Domitian's Order on Requisitioned Transport and Lodgings." *Revue international des droits de l'antiquite* 15 (1968): 135–142.

Liddle, Henry, and Robert Scott. *A Greek-English Lexicon*, 9th edition. Oxford, UK: Clarendon Press, 1977.

Lintott, Andrew. *Violence in Republican Rome*. Oxford: Oxford University Press, 1999.

Livy. *History of Rome*. Translated by B.O. Foster. 2 vols. LCL. Cambridge: Harvard University Press, 1919.

Llewelyn, S. R. *New Documents Illustrating Early Christianity*. vol. 7. Marrickville, NSW: Southwood Press, 1994.

Longenecker, Bruce. "Peace, Prosperity, and Propaganda: Advertisement and Reality in the Early Roman Empire." In *Introduction to Empire in the New Testament*, edited by Adam Winn (pp. 15–45). Atlanta: SBL Press, 2016.

———. *Remember the Poor: Paul, Poverty, and the Greco-Roman World*. Grand Rapids: Eerdmans, 2010.

Longstaff, Thomas. "What are Those Women Doing at the Tomb of Jesus." In *A Feminist Companion to Matthew*, edited by Amy-Jill Levine and Marianne Blickenstaff (pp. 196–204). Cleveland, OH: Pilgrim Press, 2004.

Loomba, Ania. *Colonialism / Postcolonialism*, 2nd edition. New York: Routledge, 2005.

Lopez, Davina. *Apostle to the Conquered: Reimagining Paul's Mission*. Minneapolis, MN: Fortress, 2008.

Luttwak, Edward N. *The Grand Strategy of the Roman Empire: From the First Century A.D. to the Third.* Baltimore, MD: Johns Hopkins University Press, 1976.

Luz, Ulrich. *Matthew 1–7: A Commentary.* Hermeneia. Minneapolis, MN: Augsburg Fortress, 2007.

———. *Matthew 8–20: A Commentary.* Hermeneia. Minneapolis, MN: Augsburg Fortress, 2001.

———. *Matthew 21–28: A Commentary.* Hermeneia. Minneapolis, MN: Augsburg Fortress, 2005.

———. *Theology of the Gospel of Matthew.* Cambridge: Cambridge University Press, 1995.

MacDonald, Margaret. *Early Christian Women and Pagan Opinion.* Cambridge, UK: Cambridge University Press, 1996.

MacKenzie, Donald C. "Pay Differentials in the Early Empire." *The Classical World* 76, no. 5 (1983): 267–273.

MacMullen, Ramsey. *Enemies of the Roman Order: Treason, Unrest, and Alienation in the Empire.* Cambridge: Harvard University Press, 1966.

Madden, John. "Slavery in the Roman Empire Numbers and Origins." *Classics Ireland* 3 (Dublin: Classical Association of Ireland, 1996), 109–128.

Magness, Jodi. "Some Observations on the Flavian Victory Monuments of Rome." In *KOINE: Mediterranean Studies in Honor of R. Ross Holloway*, edited by Derek Counts and Anthony Tuck (pp. 35–40). Oxbow Books, 2009.

Mandell, Sara. "Who Paid the Temple Tax When the Jews Were under Roman Rule?" *Harvard Theological Review* 77, no. 2 (1984): 223–232.

Mann, J.C. "The Organization of Frumentarii." *Zeitschrift für Papyrologie und Epigraphik* 74 (1988): 149–150.

Mann, Michael. *Sources of Social Power: A History of Power from the Beginning to AD 1760*, 2nd edition. Cambridge, UK: Cambridge University Press, 2012.

Marshak, Adam Kolman. *The Many Faces of Herod the Great.* Grand Rapids, MI: Eerdmans, 2015.

Mayor, Adrienne. *The Poison King.* Princeton, NJ: Princeton University Press, 2011.

McGing, Brian. "Pontius Pilate and the Sources." *CBQ* 53, no. 3 (1991): 416–438.

McGinn, Thomas. "Roman Prostitutes and Marginalization." In *Social Relations in the Roman World*, edited by Michael Peachin (pp. 643–669). Oxford, Oxford University Press, 2011.

McLaren, James. *Power and Politics in Palestine: The Jews and the Governing of their Land 100 BC–AD 70.* JSNT Supplement Series 63. Sheffield, UK: University of Sheffield Press, 1991.

Meeks, Wayne. *The First Urban Christians.* New Haven, CT: Yale University Press, 1983.

Memmi, Albert. *The Colonizer and the Colonized.* Boston, MA: Beacon Press, 1967.

Millar, Fergus. *The Roman Near East: 31 BC–AD 337.* Cambridge: Harvard University Press, 1993.

Miller, Robert. *Born Divine: The Births of Jesus and Other Sons of God.* Salem, OR: Polebridge, 2003.

Mitchell, Stephen. "Requisitioned Transport in the Roman Empire: A New Inscription from Pisidia." *JRS* 66 (1976): 106–131.
Moore, Jean K. "Matthew's Decolonial Desire (Matthew 12:42; 27:19). A Postcolonial Feminist Reading of the Two Royal Women." *Lectio Difficilor* 2013. http://www.lectio.unibe.ch/13_1/moore_jean_k_matthews_decolonial_desire.html.
Morgan, Teresa. *Roman Faith and Christian Faith: Pistis and Fides in the Early Roman Empire and Early Churches.* London: Oxford University Press, 2017.
Mowery, Robert. "Subtle Differences: The Matthean 'Son of God' References." *Novum Testamentum* 32, no. 3 (1990): 193–200.
Noreña, Carlos. "Coins and Communication." In *The Oxford Handbook of Social Relations in the Roman World,* edited by Michael Peachin (pp. 248–268). New York: Oxford University Press, 2011.
———. "Medium and Message in Vespasian's Templum Pacis." *Memoirs of the American Academy in Rome* 48 (2003): 25–43.
Norman, Naomi. "Imperial Triumph and Apotheosis: The Arch of Titus in Rome." In *Koine: Mediterranean Studies in Honor of R. Ross Holloway,* edited by Derek Counts and Anthony Tuck (pp. 41–53). Oxford, UK: Oxbow, 2009.
Orientis Graeci Inscriptiones Selectae. Edited by Wilhelm Dittenberger. 2 vols. Leipzig: Hirzel, 1903–1905.
Oleson, John. "Landscape and Cityscape in the Hisma: The Resources of Ancient Al-Humayma." In *Studies in the History and Archaeology of Jordan VI.* London: Routledge, 1997.
Oleson, John, M. B. Reeves, G. S. Baker, E. de Bruijn, Y. Gerber, M. Nikolic, and A. N. Sherwoodet. Preliminary Report on Excavations at Al-Humayma, Ancient Hawara, 2004 and 2005. Amman, Jordan: Department of Antiquities of Jordan, 2008.
Osiek, Carolyn. "The Women at the Tomb: What are They Doing There?" In *A Feminist Companion to Matthew,* edited by Amy-Jill Levine and Marianne Blickenstaff (pp. 205–220). Cleveland, OH: Pilgrim Press, 2004.
Osiek, Carolyn, and Margaret MacDonald. *A Woman's Place.* Minneapolis, MN: Fortress Press, 2006.
Overman, J. Andrew. *Church and Community in Crisis: The Gospel According to Matthew.* Valley Forge, PA: Trinity Press International, 1996.
———. *Matthew's Gospel and Formative Judaism: The Social World of the Matthean Community.* Minneapolis, MN: Fortress, 1990.
Phang, Sara Elise. *The Marriage of Roman Soldiers (13 B.C–A.D. 235): Law and Family in the Imperial Army.* Boston, MA: Leiden, 2001.
Philo, *Flaccus.* Translated by F. H. Colson. vol. 9. LCL. Cambridge: Harvard University Press, 1941.
Pliny. *Natural History.* Translated by H. Rackham, W. H. S. Jones, and D. Eichholz. 10 vols. LCL. Cambridge: Harvard University Press, 1938–1963.
Plutarch. *Lives.* Translated by Bernadotte Perrin. 11 vols. LCL. Cambridge, MA: Harvard University Press, 1914–1926.
———. "The Virtuous Deeds of Women." In *Moralia.* Translated by Frank Cole Battitt. LCL. 1931.

Pollard, Nigel. *Soldiers, Cities, and Civilians in Roman Syria.* Ann Arbor, MI: University of Michigan Press, 2000.
Polybius. *Histories.* Translated by W. R. Patton. Revised by F. W. Walbank, Christian Habicht. 6 vols. LCL. Cambridge: Harvard University Press, 2010–2012.
———. *Histories.* Translated by Evelyn S. Shuckburgh. London, New York: Macmillan, 1889; Reprint Bloomington 1962.
Potter, David. "Introduction." In *Life, Death, and Entertainment in the Roman Empire*, edited by David Potter and David Mattingly (pp. 1–16). Ann Arbor, MI: University of Michigan Press, 1999.
Rajak, Tessa. "Friends, Romans, Subjects: Agrippa II's Speech in Josephus' Jewish War." In *Images of Empire*, edited by Loveday Alexander (pp. 122–134). JSOT Supplement Series 122. Sheffield, UK: JSOT Press, 1991.
Rankov, N. B. "Frumentarii, the Castra Peregrina and the Provincial Official." *Zeitschrift für Papyrologie und Epigraphik* (1990): 176–182.
Reeder, Jane Clark. "The Statue of Augustus from Prima Porta, the Underground Complex, and the Omen of the *Gallina Alba*." *American Journal of Philology* 118, no. 1 (1997): 89–118.
Riccardi, Lee Ann. "Military Standards, 'Imagines,' and the Gold and Silver Imperial Portraits from Aventicum, Plitinoupolis, and the Marengo Treasure." *Atike Kunst* 45 (2002): 86–100.
Richardson, Peter. *Herod: King of the Jews and Friend of the Romans.* Minneapolis, MN: Fortress, 1996.
Riches, John and David Sim, editors. *The Gospel of Matthew in its Roman Imperial Context.* The Library of New Testament Studies. London: Bloomsbury T&T Clark, 2005.
Riess, Werner. "The Roman Bandit (*Latro*) as Criminal and Outsider." In *Social Relations in the Roman World*, edited by Michael Peachin (pp. 693–714). New York: Oxford University Press, 2011.
Riess, Werner and Garrett Fagan, editors. *The Topography of Violence in the Greco-Roman World.* Ann Arbor, MI: University of Michigan Press, 2016.
Rives, James. "Religion in the Roman Empire." In *Experiencing Rome: Culture, Identity and Power in the Roman Empire*, edited by Janet Huskinson (pp. 245–276). New York: Routledge, 2009.
Rostovtzeff, M. "Vexillum and Victory," *JRS* 32, no. 1–2 (1942): 92–106.
Roth, Jonathan. *The Logistics of the Roman Army at War (264 BC–AD 235).* Leiden, Boston: Brill, 2012.
Runesson, Anders. "Rethinking Early Jewish—Christian Relations: Matthean Community History as Pharisaic Intragroup Conflict." *JBL* 127, no. 1 (2008): 95–132.
Saddington, D. B. "The Centurion of Matthew 8:5-13: Consideration of the Proposal of Theodore W. Jennings, Jr., and Tat-Siong Benny Liew." *JBL* 125, no. 1 (2006): 140–142.
———. "Roman Military and Administrative Personnel in the New Testament" *ANRW* 2.26.3 (1996): 2409–2435.
Said, Eduard. *Culture and Imperialism.* New York: Vintage Books, 1993.

———. *Orientalism.* New York: Vintage Books, 1994.
Saldarini, Anthony. *Matthew's Christian-Jewish Community.* Chicago, IL: University of Chicago Press, 1994.
———. *Pharisees, Scribes, and Sadducees in Palestinian Society: A Sociological Approach.* Grand Rapids, MI: Eerdman's, 2001.
Salinero, Raul González. "El servicio militar de los judíos en el ejército romano." *Aquila Legionis* 4 (2003): 45–91.
Scheidel, Walter and Steven Friesen. "The Size of the Economy and the Distribution of Income in the Roman Empire." *JRS* 99 (2009): 61–91.
Schoenfeld, Andrew. "Sons of Israel in Caesar's Service: Jewish Soldiers in the Roman Military." *Shofar* 24, no. 3 (2006): 115–126.
Schultz, Celia. "Modern Prejudice and Ancient Praxis: Female Worship of Hercules at Rome." *Zeitschrift für Papyrologie und Epigraphik* 133 (2000): 291–297.
Scott, James C. *Domination and the Arts of Resistance: Hidden Transcripts.* New Haven, CT: Yale University Press, 1990.
Sear, David. *Roman Coins and Their Values II: The Accession of Nerva to the Overthrow of the Severan Dynasty AD 96–AD 235.* London: Spink Books, 2002.
Shaw, Brent D. "Rebels and Outsiders." In *The Cambridge Ancient History, Second Edition, vol. XI: The High Empire, A.D. 70–192*, edited by Alan K. Bowman, Peter Garnsey, and Dominic Rathbone (pp. 361–403). Cambridge: Cambridge Univ. Press, 2000.
———. *Spartacus and the Slave Wars: A Brief History with Documents.* Boston & New York: Bedford/St. Martins, 2001.
Shelton, Jo-Ann. *As the Romans Did: A Sourcebook in Roman Social History*, 2nd edition. New York: Oxford University Press, 1998.
Sim, David. "The 'Confession' of the Soldiers in Matthew 27:54." *Heythrop Journal* 34, no. 4 (1993): 401–424.
———. *The Gospel of Matthew and Christian Judaism: The History and Social Setting of the Matthean Community.* Edinburgh: T & T Clark, 1998.
———. "Matthew: The Current State of Research." In *Mark and Matthew I: Comparative Readings: Understanding the Earliest Gospels in their First-Century Setting*, edited by Eve-Marie Becker and Anders Runesson (pp. 33–51). Wissenschaftliche Untersuchungen Zum Neuen Testament 271. Tübingen: Mohr Siebeck, 2011.
———. "Matthew's Anti-Paulinism: A Neglected Feature of Matthean Studies." *HTS Teologiese Studies / Theological Studies* 58, no. 2 (2002): 767–783.
———. "Matthew and Ignatius of Antioch." In *Matthew and His Christian Contemporaries*, edited by David Sim and Boris Repschinski (pp. 139–154). The Library of New Testament Studies 333. London: Bloomsbury T&T Clark, 2008.
———. "Matthew and the Pauline Corpus: A Preliminary Intertextual Study." *JSNT* 31 (2009): 401–422.
Sinnigen, William G. "The Origins of the 'Frumentarii.'" In *Memoirs of the American Academy in Rome* 27 (pp. 211–224). Ann Arbor, MI: University of Michigan Press for the American Academy in Rome, 1962.
Smith, Mark. "Of Jesus and Quirinius." *CBQ* 62, no. 2 (2000): 278–293.

Smith, R. R. R. "The Imperial Reliefs from the Sebasteion at Aphrodisias." *JRS* 77 (1987): 88–138.

Southern, Pat. *The Roman Army: A Social and Institutional History.* Santa Barbara, CA: ABC-Clio, 2006.

Speidel, Michael. "The Pay of the Auxilia." *JRS* 63 (1973): 141–147.

———. "The Roman Army Under the Procurators: The Italian and Augustan Cohort in the Acts of the Apostles." *Ancient Society* 13/14 (1982/3): 233–240.

Sperber, Dan. "Angaria in Rabbinic Literature." *L'Antiquite Classique* 38, no. 1 (1969): 164–168.

Staccioli, Romolo Augusto. *Roads of the Romans.* Los Angeles: J. Paul Getty Trust, 2003.

Stanton, Graham. *A Gospel for a New People: Studies in Matthew.* Louisville, KY: Westminster John Knox, 1992.

———. "The Origin and Purpose of Matthew's Gospel: Matthean Scholarship from 1945–1980." *ANRW* 2.23.3 (1985): 1890–1951.

Stoll, Oliver. "The Religions of the Armies." In *A Companion to the Roman Army*, edited by Paul Erdkamp (pp. 451–476). Hoboken, NJ: Blackwell, 2007.

Stone, Michael. *Fourth Ezra.* Hermeneia. Minneapolis, MN: Fortress, 1990.

Streeter, B.H. *The Four Gospels.* London: MacMillan, 1930.

Strong, D.E. "The Administration of the Public Building in Rome During the Late Republic and Early Empire." *Bulletin of the Institute of Classical Studies* 15 (1968): 97–109.

Struthers Malbon, Elizabeth. "Fallible Follower: Women and Men in the Gospel of Mark." *Semeia* 28 (1983): 29–48.

Suetonius. *Lives of the Caesars.* Translated by J.C. Rolfe. 2 vols. LCL. 1914, 1951.

Tacitus. *Agricola.* Translated by M. Hutton and revised by R. M. Ogilvie. LCL. Cambridge, MA: Harvard University Press, 1970.

———. *The Histories.* Translated by Alfred John Church, William Jackson Brodribb, and Sara Bryant. New York: Random House, 1873, 1942.

———. *The Histories and the Annals.* Translated by Clifford H. Moore and John Jackson. 4 vols. LCL. Cambridge: Harvard University Press, 1937.

Taraporewalla, Rashna. "The Templum Pacis: Construction of Memory Under Vespasian." *Acta Classica* 53 (2010): 145–163.

Temin, Peter. *The Roman Market Economy.* Princeton, NJ: Princeton University Press, 2013.

Thompson, L. A. "Domitian and the Jewish Tax." *Historia: Zeitschrift für Alte Geschichte* 31, no. 3 (1982): 329–342.

Troi-Boeck, Nadja. "Non-Jewish Women as Precursors of Universalism." *Lectio Difficilor* 2014. http://www.lectio.unibe.ch/14_2/troi_boeck_nadja_non_jewish_women_as_precursors_of_universalism.html.

Valerius Maximus. *Memorable Doings and Sayings.* Edited and Translated by D.R. Shackleton Bailey. 2 vols. LCL. Cambridge: Harvard University Press, 2000.

Vardaman, Jerry. "A New Inscription Which Mentions Pilate as 'Prefect.'" *JBL* 81, no. 1 (1962): 70–71.

"The Varus Battle." Varusschlacht im Osnabrücker Land Museum und Park, Kalkriese. http://www.kalkriese-varusschlacht.de/en/the-varus-battle/the-romans.

Verner, David C. *The Household of God*. Chico, CA: Scholar's Press, 1983.

Virgil. *Aeneid*. Translated by A. S. Kline, 2002. http://www.poetryintranslation.com/PITBR/Latin/VirgilAeneidVI.htm#anchor_Toc2242942.

———. *Eclogues. Georgics. Aeneid: Books 1-6* and *Aeneid: Books 7-12*. Translated by H. Rushton Fairclough. Revised by G. P. Goold. 2 vols. LCL. Cambridge, MA: Harvard University Press, 1916.

Vörös, Győző. "Machaerus: The Golgotha of Saint John the Baptist." *Revue Biblique*, 119, no. 2 (2012): 232–270.

Wainwright, Elaine. *Shall We Look for Another? A Feminist Rereading of the Matthean Jesus*. Maryknoll, NY: Orbis, 1998.

Ward, Graeme. "The Roman Battlefield: Individual Exploits in Warfare of the Roman Republic." In *The Topography of Violence in the Greco-Roman World*, edited by Werner Riess and Garrett Fagan (pp. 299–324). Ann Arbor, MI: University of Michigan Press, 2016.

Watson, G.R. *The Roman Soldier*. Ithaca, NY: Cornell University Press, 1985.

Weaver, Dorothy. "'Thus You Will Know Them by Their Fruits': The Roman Characters of the Gospel of Matthew." In *The Gospel of Matthew in its Roman Imperial Context*, edited by John Riches and David Sim (pp. 107–127). London and New York: T&T Clark, 2005.

———. "'Wherever This Good News is Proclaimed': Women and God in the Gospel of Matthew," *Interpretation* 64, no. 4 (2010): 390–401.

Webster, Graham. *The Roman Imperial Army of the First and Second Centuries A.D.*, 3rd edition. Norman, OK: University of Oklahoma Press, 1985.

Webster, Jane. "Creolizing the Roman Provinces." *AJA* 105, no. 2 (2001): 209–225.

Wesch-Klein, Gabriele. "Recruits and Veterans." In *A Companion to the Roman Army*, edited by Paul Erdkamp (pp. 435–450). Hoboken, NJ: Blackwell, 2007.

Wheeler, E. L. "The Laxity of the Roman Legions." In *The Roman Army in the East*, edited by David Kennedy, JRA Supplement 18 (pp. 229–276). Ann Arbor, MI: Journal of Roman Archaeology, 1996.

Wildwinds Coins. Administered by Dane Kurth. http://www.wildwinds.com.

Williams, Craig. *Roman Homosexuality*. New York: Oxford University Press, 1999.

Wink, Walter. "Beyond Just War and Pacifism: Jesus' Nonviolent Way." *Review and Expositor* 89 (1992): 197–214.

———. *Engaging the Powers*. Minneapolis, MN: Fortress Press, 1992.

Wirgin, W. "A Note on the 'Reed' of Tiberias" *Israel Exploration Journal* 18, no. 4 (1968): 248–249.

Woolf, Greg. "Imperialism, Empire and the Integration of the Roman Economy." *World Archaeology* 23, no. 3 (1992): 283–293.

Yarbro Collins, Adela. *Mark: A Commentary*. Hermeneia. Minneapolis, MN: Augsburg Fortress, 2007.

Zanker, Paul. *The Power of Images in the Age of Augustus*. Translated by Alan Shapiro. Ann Arbor, MI: University of Michigan Press, 1990.

Ziolkowski, Adam. "*Urbs direpta*, or How the Romans Sacked Cities." In *War and Society in the Roman World,* edited by John Rich and Graham Shipley (pp. 69–91). New York: Routledge, 1993.

Zitterkopf, Ronald, and Steven Sidebotham. "Stations and Towers on the Quseir-Nile Road." *The Journal of Egyptian Archaeology* 75 (1989): 155–189.

Index

Aeneid, 5, 45–46, 200
Ἀγγαρήιον/*Angaria*, 30–32, 99, 101ff., 178, 183, 190
angel/divine messenger, 75, 79, 164, 166–67, 179, 184, 193, 195, 197, 198
Antioch, 3, 4, 15, 17, 21, 22, 29, 33, 36, 42, 47, 77, 216, 218
Antipas. *See* Herod Antipas
Apamea, 19, 30
Ara Pacis (Altar of Peace), 5, 45, 46
Archelaus, 70, 83, 89
Arch of Titus, 2, 5, 47, 163, 200
Augustus, Caesar (Octavian), 32, 45, 66, 70, 83, 88, 89, 103, 139, 143, 162

Bar Kochba Revolt, 217
Beroea, 19
Boudicca, 42, 89, 115–16
Britain, 29, 41–42, 89, 103–4, 115–16, 153, 162

Calgacus, 18, 35
chief priests, elders, and scribes, 69, 77, 78, 82, 86, 166, 176–77, 180–84, 186, 187, 196, 199
children of Bethlehem, 64, 75–77, 84, 86, 166, 215

Chiomara, 42–43, 138n60
client ruler, 64, 67, 70–71, 78, 82–83, 86, 185
Coinage, 47
Commagene, 50, 71
crucifixion, 173, 175, 179, 181, 182, 184, 189–91
cursus publicus, 103–9, 113

Domitian. *See* Flavian rulers, Domitian
donkey, 13, 31–32, 105–7
Dura Europos, 19, 21, 40, 52, 59, 76, 171n53

Egypt, 17, 40, 76, 104, 158, 165
Emmaus, 21
empire critical approaches, 4–7, 69
Empire of God. *See* Kingdom/Empire of God
enslaved people, 104, 113, 117, 128–30; trafficked boys, 44; women, 38–41, 181–82
Epiphania, 30, 105, 109
eschatological fulfillment, 63, 131, 132, 138–40, 144, 154, 159, 160, 176, 180, 182–84, 188, 191–92
eschatological signs, 197, 198, 200

Flavian Amphitheater (Colosseum), 46
Flavian rulers, 2, 46–48, 158, 163;
    Domitian, 30–31, 47, 54, 105, 158;
    Titus, 17, 46, 101, 133, 153, 158,
    163, 173; Vespasian, 17, 30, 44, 46,
    57, 105, 158, 161, 163

Galilee, 72
Gethsemane, 176, 180, 188
grain storage (*horrea*), 27–28, 55–56
grain supply, 18, 24–29
guard (ὑπηρέτης), 180–83, 196

Hauarra, 19, 28
heavenly portents, 70, 162–63
Herod, 64–78, 82, 86, 89, 134, 177, 183,
    185, 186, 190, 193, 215
Herod Antipas, 64, 66, 78–86, 134, 177,
    183, 185, 215
Herodias, 75, 80, 86, 187
Herodias' daughter, 75, 80, 86, 187
Herodium, 88
hidden transcript of resistance, 3, 77,
    111–13, 154, 166, 167, 187
homosexual relationships, 43–44
honor and shame, 115

imperial ideology, 45–48, 112, 128,
    130, 132, 139–44, 159, 188
insurrectionist, 1, 179, 190–91

Jerusalem, 22, 65, 101, 107, 173,
    191; destruction of, 133, 157, 161;
    Fortress Antonia, 22, 51, 177, 194;
    temple of, 22, 46, 77, 91, 176, 180,
    181, 185, 191–92
Jesus: Davidic Messiah, 67;
    eschatological Son of Man, 66, 102,
    154, 156, 158–60, 174, 179, 183,
    184, 200–201; King of the Jews, 65,
    70, 74; resurrection, 79, 184, 192,
    193, 195, 197, 200–201; worship of,
    135, 199–200
Jewish-Roman War, 2, 14, 15, 21, 29,
    77, 101, 161, 173, 189, 194, 217

John the Baptist, 64, 78, 79, 83–84, 86,
    127, 166, 193, 215
John the Baptist, Disciples of, 82, 84–86
Joseph and Mary, 64, 74–77, 86, 193
Judea, 83, 89
Julius Caesar, 66, 153

Kingdom/Empire of God, 44, 77, 78,
    100, 114, 117, 127, 131, 139–40,
    156, 167, 174, 179, 184, 192ff., 197,
    198, 199, 200–1

Luke-Acts, 217

Magi, 64, 65, 67, 71, 73, 75, 77, 79, 86,
    193
mansiones, 103, 113
Marcus Antonius, 66, 70, 88, 89
marriage. *See* Roman soldiers, marriage
Mary Magdalene, 198–200
masculinity, hegemonic, 35–36, 42, 184,
    193–95, 199
masculinity, Roman, 115, 137, 192

Nero, 44, 143
networks of social power, 5, 14, 45, 216
non-violent resistance, 100, 101, 109–
    12, 174, 176, 178, 180, 185, 188

pacification, 3, 16, 20, 43
Parthia, 50, 133, 162, 194, 217
Pilate, Pontius. *See* Roman governors,
    Pontius Pilate
Pilate's soldiers, 188ff.
Pilate's wife, 81, 186, 187
Pompey, eastern campaigns of, 15
Poverty Scales, 23–24, 50
proprietary theory of state, 23
provincial farmers, 105, 108, 109, 178,
    218
provincial rule, 15–16

Raphanaea, 19, 51
requisitioning, 13, 99, 105
Res Gestae Divi Augusti, 45, 139, 143

resistance, acts of, 20, 22, 50
road construction, 32–35
Roman eagle (*aquila*), 72, 141, 153, 154, 160–62, 194, 215
Roman governors: Britain (*Agricola*, 29); Judea (Florus, 22, 177–78, 181, 189; Pontius Pilate, 22, 177, 183ff.; Ventidius Cumanus, 23); Syria (Marcus Ulpius Traianus, 17–18, 33, 50, 51, 56; Varus, 173)
Roman soldiers: auxiliary units, 18–19, 23, 33, 36, 38, 45; *ala Sebastenorum*, 18, 19; *cohors I Sebastenorum*, 18, 19, 22, 171n53; *cohors XX Palmyrenorum*, 21; billeting (*hospitium*), 116; bravery, 137, 192; centurions, 31, 43, 103, 106–7, 116, 125, 126, 132–40, 137–38, 165, 183, 184, 189, 192, 215; deployment, 14, 17, 36; *diripio* (sacking cities), 42; food supply, 24, 27–28; *frumentarii*, 73–74; Herodian royal forces, 18, 22, 126, 134; legions (*Leg III Gallica*, 34, 51, 52; *Leg IIII Scythia*, 34, 51; *Leg VI Ferrata*, 50, 51, 91; *Leg X Equistris*, 153; *Leg X Fretensis*, 17, 51; *Leg XII Fulminata*, 51, 161; *Leg XV Apollinaris*, 37; *Leg XVI Flavia*, 51; *Leg XXI*, 104); marriage (*conubio*), 35–38; musical instruments, 167; road building, 33; threat and use of violence, 14, 20–22, 64, 65, 76, 77, 79, 85, 86, 107, 137–38, 184, 189, 194, 215; training, 20; veterans, 33, 89, 116
Rufus, C. Velius, 133

Sagalassus inscription, 103, 109
Samosata, 19
Seleucid, 15
sexual assault/violence, 115–17, 138
signum (military standard), 20, 164, 185
Simon of Cyrene, 109
Simon Peter, 85, 180–82
Simon Peter's mother-in-law, 127, 130–31
slaves. *See* enslaved people
synagogue, 67, 68
Syria, 2, 14, 15, 33, 105, 113, 127, 217

taxation: grain and produce, 24–29; Jewish Temple Tax, 25; prostitution, 39; tolls/toll collection, 40, 76
Templum Pacis (Temple of Peace), 46
theodicy, 65–66
Titus. *See* Flavian Rulers, Titus
Traianus, Marcus Ulpius. *See* Roman Governors, Syria
Trajan's Column, 167
Triumph, 2, 47, 61, 108
trumpet call, 165–67

Vespasian. *See* Flavian Rulers, Vespasian

women: cultural expectations for, 114–17; forced into prostitution, 38–41; married to soldiers, 35–38; non-elite, 114; at risk of sexual assault, 41–43, 115–16; at Tomb of Jesus, 193, 195, 198–200
wooden club (ξύλον), 177–78, 185

Zeugma, 19, 21, 25, 51, 76

Biblical References

Exod 1–2	75	Dan 7:10–11	160
Exod 1:22	65	Dan 7:26–7	160
Exod 19:16	160	Joel 2:1–2, 10	163
Exod 21:24	101	Mic 5:2	90
Lev 14:1–20	128	Zech 9:9	107
Lev 18:16	80	Zech 9:14	160
Lev 20:21	80	Zech 13:7–9	177
Lev 24:20	101		
Lev 26:37	101	4 Ezra 11–12	158, 160
Deut 19:21	101	3 Macc 6:19	101
Deut 28:47–68	157		
Deut 30:1–10	157	Matt	
Josh 7:13 (LXX)	101	1:1–17	70
Josh 23:9 (LXX)	101	1:18–25	70
2 Sam 22:14–15	160	1:1–25	67
Esth 2:4, 9	81	2:1–8	3, 6, 186
Ps 22	191	2:1–23	63, 64, 65, 67, 70, 75, 77, 86, 90
Ps 69	191		
Ps 73:4	165	2:1–18	6, 185
Ps 107	131, 138–39	2:1	70
Isa 5:25–6	164	2:2	64
Isa 9:1–2	85	2:4	69
Isa 11:10–12	164, 165	2:7	73
Isa 13:2, 4	164, 165	2:7–8	64
Isa 25:1–10a	131, 139	2:11	74
Jer 31:15	65, 77	2:12	64, 74
Jer 32:1–5	87	2:13	64
Ezek 17	157–8	2:16	64, 74, 76, 78, 84, 166
Ezek 37–39	139		

2:19	76	26:8	199
3:15	9	26:47	23
2:22	64	26:51–56	1, 3
3:1–12	84	26:51	58
3:5	85	26:52	180
4:12	78	26:53	179
4:17	117	26:55	8, 23
5:1–12	44	26:56	180, 183
5:21–38	100–101	26:57–58	85
5:38–42	6, 101, 110, 114, 178, 180	26:69–75	58, 85, 181
		26:64	3
5:38–39	110	26:67	182, 190
5:40	11, 114	27:1–2	23
5:41	99, 109, 110, 117, 130	27:11–44	23
		27:11–26	184ff.
5:43–48	110	27:19	81, 187
8:5–13	6	27:27–31	188
8:17	9	27:30	182
8:28–34	56	27:32–38	188
11:2–6	78	27:32	109, 115, 190
11:7–15	85	27:37–38	8, 180
11:29–30	51	27:45–54	188, 197
14:1–12	6, 63, 75, 78, 79, 82, 83, 85, 86, 185	27:51–52	191, 197
		27:62–66	195, 196–98
14:4	78, 80, 84	27:64	79
14:5	85	28:1–4	195, 198
14:6	80, 82	28:1–10	7
14:7	82	28:1–20	183
14:10	82, 166	28:2–4	3, 7
14:11	81	28:6–7	79
14:13–21	85	28:11–15	7, 195–96
14:13	78	28:16–17	7
14:34–36	85	28:18–20	3, 7, 184
17:24–27	9, 53	Mark 6:17	80
18:21–35	58	Mark 6:22, 28	87
21:1–17	180, 190	Mark 15:21	109
21:1–7	107	Luke 2:1–7	53
21:31–32	41	Luke 7:1–10	135–6
24:27–31	6, 180	Luke 17:23–4	155
24:29–30	3	Acts 2:7–11	52
24:45–51	58	Acts 11:19–30	52
25:14–30	58	Acts 21:27–39	53
26:1–28:20	6, 23, 174ff.	Rom 13:1–14	217
26:3–4	78	Rom 15:1–3	81
26:6–13	199	1 Cor 15:20–26	217

1 Cor 15:50–58	167	Jas 4:7	101
1 Thess 4:16	167	1 Pet 5:9	101
1 Thess 4:13–18	217	Rev 1:10	167
Gal 1:10	81	Rev 4:1	167
Eph 6:13	101	Rev 8:7–10:7	167

About the Author

John E. Christianson earned his PhD in Biblical Interpretation at Brite Divinity School, Texas Christian University. He has had a lifelong interest in both the New Testament and the Roman military. This is his first book.

www.ingramcontent.com/pod-product-compliance
Lightning Source LLC
Chambersburg PA
CBHW061711300426
44115CB00014B/2636